ORGA
NIZE!

ORGANIZING

FOR

SOCIAL CHANGE

A MANUAL FOR ACTIVISTS IN THE 1990s

KIM BOBO   **JACKIE KENDALL**   **STEVE MAX**

MIDWEST ACADEMY

Seven Locks Press
Santa Ana, CA
Minneapolis, MN
Washington, DC

Library of Congress Cataloging in Publication Data
  Bobo, Kimberley A.
  Organizing for Social Change: a manual for activists in the '90s/Kim Bobo, Jackie Kendall, and
Steve Max.
        p.   cm.
  Includes index.
  ISBN 0-929765-41-9 $19.95
      1. Direct action—Handbooks, manuals, etc. I. Kendall, Jackie. II. Max, Steve. III. Title.
  JC328.3.B63 1991
  322.4′3′068—dc20

                                                                                    90-47467
                                                                                    CIP

Manufactured in the United States of America
Cover design by Kirschner ■ Caroff Design, Inc., New York, NY

*Seven Locks Press is a formerly Washington-based book publisher of non-fiction works on social,
political, and cultural issues. It takes its name from a series of lift locks on the Chesapeake and Ohio
Canal. Seven Locks Press relocated to California in 1994.*

For more information, write or call:
  Seven Locks Press
  P.O. Box 25689
  Santa Ana, CA 92799
  800-354-5348

Let me give you a word on the philosophy of reform. The whole history of the progress of human liberty shows that all concessions yet made to her august claims have been born of earnest struggle. The conflict has been exciting, agitating, all absorbing, and for the time being putting all other tumults to silence. It must do this or it does nothing. If there is no struggle there is no progress. Those who profess to favor freedom, and yet depreciate agitation, are men who want crops without plowing up the ground. They want rain without thunder and lightning. They want the ocean without the awful roar of its many waters. This struggle may be a moral one; or it may be a physical one; or it may be both moral and physical; but it must be a struggle. Power concedes nothing without a demand. It never did and it never will. Find out just what people will submit to, and you have found the exact amount of injustice and wrong which will be imposed upon them; and these will continue until they are resisted with either words or blows, or with both. The limits of tyrants are prescribed by the endurance of those whom they oppress.

—Frederick Douglas
Letter to an abolitionist associate, 1849

Contents

Preface

Inspired by years of organizing in the student, labor, women's, and civil rights movements, and funded by a back pay award in an unfair labor practice suit, Heather Booth founded the Midwest Academy in 1973. With Steve Max, the Academy's first trainer and current training director, Heather developed a curriculum to pass on the lessons learned in these movements, provide organizers with a political and economic context, and teach the skills necessary for effective organizing.

The Academy was founded on three principles. For people to organize effectively for social, economic, and political justice, they must:

1. Win real improvements in their lives
2. Get a sense of their own power
3. Alter the relations of power

The Academy's program was premised on building a network across many different kinds of organizations where activists could share their experiences, develop relationships, and shape a vision not bound by the limitations of any one form of organizing.

In its early days, the Midwest Academy trained many of the leaders of the women's movement. At the Academy women found a place where they could be reinforced as organizers. As word of the training spread, many experienced and would-be organizers came, bringing a diversity to each session that has allowed activists from all parts of the country to benefit from each others' experience.

Together with a small group of organizers, Heather founded the Citizen Labor Energy Coalition in 1977 and participated with others in founding Citizen Action in 1979, passing the Academy's directorship to Karen Thomas. Karen directed the Academy from 1977 to 1982. In addition to the regular training sessions held in Chicago, Karen began conducting sessions throughout the country to help develop Citizen

Action, a national organization of 3 million members in 32 states.

Today, the Academy continues to provide training to Citizen Action as well as to numerous other organizations, including a joint project with the United States Student Association. The networking function of the Academy continues with the biennial Midwest Academy/Citizen Action Conference over a three-day weekend. These organizers analyze past work, develop strategies for the year ahead, and celebrate their victories.

The common thread connecting all of the Academy's work is the value placed on developing individuals so that they can work together toward a more just society. It is inspiring to watch a low-income mother, working on school issues in rural Virginia, share her experiences and expertise with an environmental researcher from Washington, D.C. and a housing organizer from Chicago; or to hear a New York student deep in conversation with a senior citizen from New Orleans and a trade unionist from Indiana.

In working together with the people we organize, honesty and caring are essential. How can we hope to build a better society if we cannot get along with our colleagues? How can we build coalitions that endure if our personal style alienates coalition partners? How can we even run a meeting if our need for control and efficiency overrides common decency?

It is also essential that the vision of what we work for be broad enough to make the small victories significant. As people participate in our organizations and gain power, self-confidence, and dignity, they must also share a common vision of a country and world in which they would like to live.

Whenever there are changes for the better, it is fundamentally because people have taken charge of their own lives, transforming society as well as themselves. Whether one's vision is an eight-hour workday, the right to vote, or the chance to have clean air and water for our children, it will be achieved only when people organize and take the future into their own hands.

Although much progress has been made, there is a great deal more to be done. Voter participation is at its lowest in the United States, indicating a lack of trust in the political process. Money and private special interests still dominate the way laws are made. Yet in the midst of this, we see where people have organized and won. The Academy has been a part of many of these efforts, training and building organizations and networks, learning and passing knowledge on to others.

It has been my privilege to direct the Midwest Academy since 1982. Under the leadership of Heather Booth and Steve Max, and with Kim Bobo, and adjunct trainers Paul Booth, George Buntin, Ron Charity, Tom Corrigan, Joan Flanagan, Bob Heineman, Barry Greever, and Karen Thomas, we have conducted hundreds of training sessions. We have had the distinct pleasure of working with some of the best organizers in the country. So many have come through the Academy and gone on to organize and direct today's major progressive institutions. All of them have contributed something of themselves to make the Midwest Academy one of the best progressive activist training centers in the United States.

As you read this book, keep in mind that the "steps," the "lists," and the "charts" are tools to help us do a better job. Coupled with a shared progressive vision and values that foster community, these tools help us develop the strategic framework for successful citizens' organizations and active participation in a democracy. Use the manual well, and organize.

—Jackie Kendall
Executive Director

Acknowledgements

This manual is not an original work. It is built upon the culture and experience of social change in the United States that has been spurred by organizing. Many of the concepts, principles, and charts were first developed by Heather Booth, the Midwest Academy's founder and first executive director.

We are also indebted to Steve Askin, whose computer addition to the Research Chapter is extraordinary. Thanks go to the many people who commented on all or parts of the manual and helped strengthen it: Jean Allison, Ira Arlook, Heather Booth, Harry Boyt, Robert Brandon, Stephen Coats, Rochelle Davis, Mark Dyen, Joan Flanagan, Jerry Kendall, Paul Lawrence, Joy Marshall, Judy Maslen, Kim Max, Lynn Max, Donna Parson, Jamie Pullen, Allan St. John, Barbara Samson, Marilyn Sneiderman, Charles Vestal, David West, and Marc Wetherhorn.

Regina Botterill, Joy Marshall, Amy Neill, Shelby Pera, Trelinda Pitchford, Kim Simmons, and Arlette Slachmuylder helped track down bibliographical information and permissions and assisted in modem communication. The Anita L. Mishler Education Fund provided financial support for writing the manual.

It was a pleasure to work with the staff of Seven Locks Press. Wynne Cougill and Roberta Shepherd's meticulous editing greatly improved the book's readability. The enthusiasm of our past and present publishers, James Morris and Jim Riordan, encouraged us throughout its writing.

Finally, we would like to express our appreciation to all the fine community organizers and activists we have worked with over the years, particularly our training session participants and the staff of Citizen Action. We've learned organizing from those with whom we've worked.

PART I
Direct Action Organizing

1

Dedication

Dedication

Majority Strategy

We Americans have an unbroken history of organizing for social, economic and political justice. The generation following the men and women who had been inspired by the words of Tom Paine, and who had fought alongside George Washington, made up abolitionist and feminist organizations that worked to extend the liberties of the American Revolution to the whole population. Often, those two movements were intertwined and mutually supportive. Feminist leaders such as Lucretia Mott, Elizabeth Cady Stanton, Lucy Stone, and Susan B. Anthony, and abolitionist leaders like Frederick Douglass, Sojourner Truth, Harriet Tubman, William Lloyd Garrison, James Birney, and Sarah and Angelina Grimke now occupy separate chapters of the history books, but in life they knew each other, worked together, and shared the same platforms, debates, and sense of mission.

After the Civil War, the veterans of Gettysburg and newly arrived immigrants worked as long as sixteen hours a day in the country's factories, mines, and mills. Hundreds of thousands of them joined the 1886 nationwide strike for the eight-hour workday. As their movement rose and faced fierce opposition, Eugene Victor Debs was already organizing and would eventually assume the leadership of growing national trade union and socialist movements. In the Western states the seeds of populism, which influenced Debs, were being sown. Turn of the century populism,

Introduction

socialism, and trade unionism shared a common language of economic democracy and the movements often connected.

Many of the generation that had organized with Debs lived to see the success of the Congress of Industrial Organizations in the 1930s. The CIO strengthened the New Deal of Franklin Roosevelt and helped to ensure the passage of legislation for the right to organize, the minimum wage, social security, unemployment compensation and the eight-hour workday. The stalwarts of the 1930s generation taught and inspired civil rights workers in the 1950s as well as activists of the movements of the 1960s, and are now part of the senior citizens' movement. Many of those who first joined the movements for peace and social justice during the turbulent sixties went on to become the leaders of the movements of the next three decades, and are now mobilizing women, environmentalists, people of color, labor, citizen action activists, industrial, social, and agricultural workers, citizens with disabilities, and people struggling for peace, disarmament, social and economic justice, education, health, family issues and the revitalization of the electoral system.

As the 1980s unfolded, a powerful grassroots right wing movement emerged. Cloaking itself in the legitimacy of religion and the flag while carrying out the political program of the multi-national corporations, this movement challenged us for the loyalty of middle America. At the same time, many of the progressive forces fragmented, and some moved away from majority themes to issues that addressed the needs of more limited constituencies, again posing the old problem of how to defend particular interests while fighting collectively for common goals.

Today, it is clear that the right wing economic policies have failed. "Getting government off our backs" and "freeing business to do its job" merely intensify the loss of our industries and farms, and their replacement with new low-wage jobs. While the Right destroys environmental protection, a tide of toxic chemicals, nuclear waste, pesticides, sewage, and garbage ruins the quality of life in communities across the country. Deregulation of the airlines leads to higher fares, worse service, and unsafe flights. Deregulated banks collapse in huge numbers and require massive bailouts with public money. Unbridled unregulated greed on Wall Street brings on an orgy of speculation. Our leading corporations are allowed to become truly transnational; and while they flood our markets with foreign products, there is no requirement that they put back into this economy what they take out. Poverty goes unabated. Homelessness, hunger, and inequality rise. Drugs and crime reach epidemic levels and there are indications that the government itself has cooperated with international drug dealers to promote its foreign policy, and even to finance unofficial wars.

But the 1990s can be a citizens' decade. The rapidly unfolding events in Eastern Europe herald an end to both the cold war and to the conservative mentality, which saw every social issue as inspired by a communist conspiracy. This, combined with the Right's inability to solve America's economic problems, creates the possibility of a new political debate. Many issues are still polarized along traditional liberal-conservative lines, but in areas such as the environment and family policy, a realignment appears to be taking place that transcends the political categories established during the New Deal and the cold war.

Although the failures of the Right are compounded daily, there is still not a single progressive movement that can win the confidence and loyalty of the majority of the people. Yet, the numbers of people striving for a better life are clearly growing. Where citizen organizations focus on unifying issues and build a majority base, they win. In state after state, coalitions of progressive organizations have already been built. They are supported by millions of individual members and are preparing to move to the center of the political stage.

While much of our language remains the language of protest, citizen organizing now goes beyond that. Many organizations strive to enlarge the participation of ordinary people in public life with a problem solving politics that has citizens at the core. In one city, organized communities stopped waiting for the board of education to figure out how to save the schools, and wrote their own comprehensive plan that the board adopted. Elsewhere, a statewide citizen coalition isn't merely protesting high taxes, but has drafted its own legislation for tax reform. A coalition of national organizations, no longer content with the options offered by "experts," is meeting to formulate a plan for public financing of elections. These are only examples of an approach to citizen organizing that is blossoming across the country, in which people are providing new alternatives, not just choosing between old ones, and are taking on themselves civic responsibilities previously left to government.

This book is dedicated to all who are committed to this effort, to all who will take control of their own lives and destiny, and who will make history in our time.

Majority Strategy

This is a handbook on the fundamentals of direct action organizing. Direct action implies a majority strategy. Much of its power derives from the fear haunting all elected officials, that they will be defeated at the polls by angry citizens, or a corporation's fear that it will face massive consumer pressure. This means that direct action works best with issues that a majority of the population would support, or at least not actively oppose. Nonetheless, most of this book's guidelines for thinking and acting strategically, and its recommendations on organizing skills are also useful for working on other, less popular, justice issues. We focus on direct action because we believe it is the best method for building local activist-based membership organizations as well as larger state and national coalitions.

Direct action is not the only form, nor the only "correct" form, of organizing. Electoral, union, service, public interest, advocacy, educational, and legal organizing all play a role in advancing progressive goals. The principles of direct action, which are described in Chapter 2, have applications in many other kinds of organizing, particularly electoral campaigns, advocacy, and union organizing.

We have no illusions that community-based organizations alone are sufficient to win lasting social change, no matter how strong or numerous they become. However, citizen organizations and electoral coalitions, statewide or national, need community-based strength and vitality at their roots if they are truly to represent their base and be able to win victories.

This book will use broadly applicable examples from different types of direct action organizations and issues. Readers who don't see their particular type of organization or issue mentioned should not assume that our approach does not apply to them. The sections on strategy, including criteria for choosing issues and mapping issue campaigns, can be directly applied to the widest range of constituencies, issues, and organizations from the local to the national level.

We treat issue organizing and elections as part of a single process. Although many organizations do not endorse candidates, an election is nonetheless part of the political environment in which an issue campaign takes place.

From this manual you will learn a systematic approach to the techniques of organizing, of building and using power, and of creating lasting institutions that are both self defense organizations and avenues for citizen participation in public life. You can treat this volume like a cook book, and go directly to the chapter that has the recipe for whatever you are doing at the moment. We urge you not to do this, though, because you will miss the two underlying themes of the book: First, all aspects of organizing are related, making an organization the sum total of what it actually does, not of what you intended it to be at the start, and second, the real goals of organizing go beyond the immediate issues; they are to build the unity and power of all who want control over their own lives.

2

The personal is political: Organizing is overwhelmingly about personal relationships. It is about changing the world and changing how individuals act together. The relationships organizers develop are their most important resource and most important talent. To form good relationships, it is essential that an organizer like people. A good organizer is motivated by strong feelings of love and caring. This should not be forgotten, because a good organizer is motivated as well by strong feelings of outrage and anger at how people are treated. Forming relationships with people is based on trust and respect. It is based on doing what you commit to do, and being honest and straightforward in order to advance the members' individual goals through building an organization. In doing this, it is central to understand people's perspectives and above all, self-interest.

Self-interest is one of the most important and misunderstood concepts in direct action organizing. Basically, what it comes down to is this: Unless you really are a member of the clergy, in whom people have voluntarily placed the authority to tell them what they morally ought to do, then preaching at them is not the best way to motivate them. What motivates people is their self-interest, not as the organizer interprets it, but as they actually express it to those who listen carefully.

Self-interest is sometimes thought of in the most narrow sense: people want more "stuff," and will organize to get it (often to get it away from someone else). But self-interest is actually

The Fundamentals of Direct Action Organizing

a much broader concept. People will fight to end their own oppression when they recognize it, and when there is a clear solution. People are also motivated across generational lines to do things that will help their children or grandchildren. Self-interest, then, applies to what makes people feel good, as well as to what materially benefits them. Helping others, being active in the community, being useful, doing something important, or doing what is morally right, are all forms of self-interest motivation. Self-interest can be very long range, as in working for peace or the environment.

More broadly still, many people feel a need to take on the responsibilities of citizenship and to play a role in shaping public affairs. People want interaction with the larger community and often enjoy working collectively for the common good. Self-interest generalized is often class interest or community interest.

The point here is not to make a list of all the forms of self-interest, and particularly not to imply that all of them apply to everyone. As an organizer, you can assume *nothing* about a person's self-interest that isn't actually expressed to you by that person. One of the worst mistakes an organizer can make is to say, "This is an issue about which everyone *must* care." It is risky enough to act on what the polls tell you people care about. It is one thing to say to a pollster that you care, and something else altogether to be willing to do anything about it.

Listening is an essential way for an organizer to learn what people's self-interest truly is. One-on-one interviews are an excellent way to get to know the values and concerns that motivate people. Listening can also be done by door-to-door canvassers, reporting back to the organizing staff, and it can be done at larger community meetings. Although there are risks, shortcuts can be tried such as calling people to a meeting or event, and seeing who responds. However you do it, organizing begins with finding out what people want as individuals, and then helping them find collective ways of getting it.

All organizing is based on relationships and self-interest, broadly defined. With this foundation, we can now proceed to the three basic principles that underlie direct action organizing.

The Three Principles of Direct Action

These three principles will be referred to throughout the manual. Understanding them will help you to use direct action.

Win Real, Immediate, Concrete Improvements in People's Lives

Whether the improvement is better health care, lower auto insurance rates, street lighting, or police protection, an organization attempts to win it for large numbers of people. This is different from helping individuals with their problems, which is the role of service agencies. It is also different from educating people about an issue or making a statement, although in the course of winning, those things may be accomplished as well.

Even when the problem being addressed is very large or long term-crime, unemployment or world hunger, for example-it must be broken down into short-term, attainable goals, called issues. Having small short-term issue goals not only strengthens the organization but it also builds in a reality principle. The problem with just educating people or working for very long-term goals is that there is rarely a way to measure progress, to determine if the organization is succeeding or failing, or even if it is relevant at all.

Give People a Sense of Their Own Power

Direct action organizations mobilize the power that people have. In doing so, they teach the value of united action through real-life examples, and build the self confidence of both the organization and the individuals in it. Direct action organizations avoid shortcuts that don't build people's power, such as bringing in a lawyer to handle the problem, asking a friendly politician to take care of it, or turning it over to a government agency.

Giving people a sense of their own power is as much a part of the organizing goal as is solving the problem. A local issue, such as getting abandoned houses repaired, illustrates this point. There are many ways in which the houses could get repaired. An outside organization could come in and fix them for the people. That would be a social service approach. Community members could take house repair classes and then repair the houses themselves. That would be a self-help approach. An outside organization could intercede for the community with the officials responsible. That would be an advocacy approach. Another outside group could propose legislation mandating the repair of all houses. That would be a public interest approach.

Finally, the community members themselves could organize, and with the strength of their numbers, pressure the politicians and officials responsible for abandoned houses. This method leads to the community developing the power and ability to hold city officials accountable to them. Community members feel that there is a victory and it is their victory. This motivates them to try

to solve other problems. When people who were not previously involved hear about the victory, and more important, see the houses repaired, they will join the group. Larger numbers mean more power, and more power means that bigger issues can be won. Eventually the organization becomes a force in the area. This power can be used again and again.

The question of the importance of direct service work, such as feeding the homeless or caring for the aged, comes up repeatedly when direct action organizing is discussed. Often the point of a campaign is to win just such programs. In general, we do not recommend combining service delivery with direct action in the same organization. Funding for the service often must come from sources that are opposed to or targets of the direct action. In such cases, funding is threatened and may really be lost. Often in such organizations a split develops between those who see the service aspect and those who see the more political aspect as being most important. Both are needed.

Alter the Relations of Power

Building a strong, lasting, and staffed organization alters the relations of power. Once such an organization exists, people on the "other side" must always consider the organization when making decisions. When the organization is strong enough, it will have to be consulted about decisions that affect its members. The organization further strives to alter power relations by passing laws and regulations that give it power and by putting into public office its own people or close allies, although many groups (e.g., ones to which contributions are tax deductible) are prevented by law from endorsing candidates. Winning on issues is never enough. The organization itself must be built up so that it can take on larger issues and play a political role.

Community and citizen organizations are democratic institutions; their very existence helps to make the whole system work better and opens avenues for ongoing participation. Without such democratic institutions, our concept of politics would be limited to voting every few years, a necessary but often uninspiring activity.

Building an organization is *not* a natural byproduct of good programs. Groups cannot assume that the organization will grow "naturally" if they just win on issues. While necessary for building the organization, winning on issues and involving people are not sufficient. Concrete plans must be made and steps taken to assure that the organization grows (e.g., money is raised and members are recruited).

How a Direct Action Organizing Issue Campaign Works

In organizing, the word campaign has many meanings. An *issue campaign* is waged to win a victory on an issue. It is different from an election campaign, which might happen to be fought on issues. It is also different from an education campaign to raise public awareness, a fund raising campaign to support a cause, or a service delivery campaign such as providing the homeless with shelter. An issue campaign ends in a specific victory. People get something they didn't have before. Someone with power agrees to do something that she or he previously refused to do. Implied in the word campaign is a series of connected events over a period of time, each of which builds the strength of the organization and brings it closer to victory. Few organizations are strong enough to win a major demand just by asking.

When used in organizing, the word "issue" has a special meaning. An issue is a specific solution to a general problem. For example, passing a law requiring sewage treatment is one solution to the problem of water pollution. An issue campaign has a beginning, a middle, and an end. It is seldom a one-shot event, nor is it simply a series of events linked by a common theme. It is a method of building power and building organization.

The Use of Power in an Issue Campaign

Power generally consists of having a lot of money or a lot of people. Citizen organizations tend to have people, not money. Thus, our ability to win depends on our being able to do with people, what the other side is able to do with money. For citizen organizations, power usually takes one of three forms:

You Can Deprive the Other Side of Something It Wants. **Examples:** A public official is directly or indirectly deprived of votes. A corporate executive is deprived of a promotion because you cost the company money when you forced a regulatory agency to come into the picture. A landlord is deprived of rent because of a rent strike. A city department head is deprived of a job when you show him or her to be incompetent. Conflict of interest is exposed, and corrupt people are deprived of the ability to do business as usual.

You Can Give the Other Side Something It Wants. **Examples:** Senior citizens sign pledges to use a hospital that accepts Medicare assignment. Your organization's endorsement counts with key groups of voters. Your voter registration work creates a base of support for specific issues or candidates.

Your Organization Can Elect Someone Who Supports Your Issues.

Often, having power means that your organization finds a way to stand on someone's foot until you are paid (by being given what you want) to go away. This isn't a shakedown, nor do we enjoy treating people in such a fashion. The targets of these tactics are people who have shown a serious disregard for our well being, or worse, are doing us actual harm.

Of course, a real-life issue campaign doesn't start out with high-pressure activities. It starts out with reasonable people asking nicely for things to which they feel entitled. Efforts are made to persuade on the merits and the facts, as well as on the morality of the issue. It is after people are refused things for which they shouldn't even have had to ask in the first place, that power must be applied.

A Tactical Guide to Power

While consulting with many groups over the years, we on the Midwest Academy staff have often heard organizers make shaky assumptions about the power of their own organizations. "We have people power." "We have consumer power." "The Law is on our side." Such assumptions are made on the basis of strategic principles that are true in general, but that may not hold up when applied tactically in a particular situation. Here are some brief guidelines for measuring the power that you actually have.

Political/Legislative Power: Getting Something Passed by an Elected Body

Most groups, with the exception of statewide citizen organizations and national organizations, often don't try to introduce legislation, as a lobbying organization would. Instead, they usually pressure administrators or regulators to do what is needed. How administrators or bureaucrats respond to you depends in large part on how they perceive your ability to bypass them and take your case directly to an elected body, as well as on their estimation of your ability to influence the outcome of elections, either directly or indirectly.

What matters:

- *Primarily:* Voters, especially those who care strongly enough about an issue to vote for candidates on the basis of their position on that issue.
- *Secondarily:* Money that can influence votes. Media that can influence votes.
- *Timing:* Most effective prior to an election.
- *Key Questions to Ask:*
  Regarding the whole legislative body
  - Is the decision made in committee or by the leadership or on the floor?
  - If the decision is made by leadership, how strong are you in their districts, are they seeking to run for higher office, and will they someday need votes in areas where you are strong?
  - If the decision is made by committee, the whole city council or legislature, you need half plus one of the voting members. Count up how many are firmly with you and how many will never support you. Look at who is left. Are there enough for a majority? Where do they come from? Can you influence them?

  Regarding a single elected official
  - How close was the last election?
  - Is this seat usually contested?

- What is the number of supporters you have in the district?
- Are there organizations that might cooperate?
- Who can you get to lobby the elected official from among:
  -Key contributors
  -Leaders of primary voting blocks
  -Religious and opinion leaders
  -Party leadership

Consumer Power: The Ability to Conduct a Boycott

What matters:

- *Primarily:* Cutting profits or demonstrating ability to cut profits by changing consumer purchasing.
- *Secondarily:* Media coverage that could influence purchasing.
- *Timing:* Most effective during times of stress for the company, such as during a merger, a strike, or tight financial times.
- *Key Questions to Ask:*
  - What is the company's profit margin?
  - Is it a local, regional, national, or international market?
  - Who, or what, really owns it?
  - Can you really hurt profits?

Legal/Regulatory Power: The Ability to Win in Court or in a Regulatory Process

What matters:

- *Primarily:* Clear laws or tight regulations.
- *Secondarily:* Money for lawyers or volunteer lawyers, or the ability to get a public agency to carry the case for you. Media to make it a political issue.
- *Timing:* Must be prepared to carry on for several years. Sometimes you are doing this to delay and actually want the process to last many years.
- *Key Questions to Ask:*
  - Are laws or regulations clearly on your side?
  - Have similar cases been won elsewhere?
  - What are the politics of the judges or regulators who will hear the case? Who appointed them?
  - What are the extra costs, e.g., fees for experts, or duplicating thousand-page transcripts? Who pays?

Strike/Disruptive Power

What matters:

- *Primarily:* Cutting profits or income by stopping a company or agency from functioning.
- *Timing:* Most effective during times of stress for a company or agency, such as during a merger, boycott, or tight financial times.
- *Key Questions to Ask*:
    - What are the company's profit margins?
    - Can you make a significant dent by stopping work (strikes) or disrupting work or customers (usually by civil disobedience)?
    - How costly will it be to replace you or get rid of you?
    - Do you have a strike fund sufficient to outlast the company by one day?
    - Do you have people willing to get arrested and money to bail them out?

The Stages of an Issue Campaign

Issue campaigns have a beginning, a middle and an end. Campaigns last for various lengths of time. A direct action organization can, by choosing its issue, influence the length of its campaigns. Frequently, new organizations want short campaigns and thus sometimes choose relatively "fixed fights" for their first issue. They ask for information they know they are entitled to, or ask for something to be done that would probably be done anyway, but at a later date. The purpose of the fight is to have a visible win. These quick victories build up the members' confidence in their ability to accomplish things and gain public recognition for the new organization. Later, longer campaigns, say of six months' duration, help to build a committee structure and give the organization's leadership experience. Issue campaigns may be timed either to coincide with elections or to avoid them.

Both long and short issue campaigns go through a series of steps, although shorter campaigns involve fewer tactics than described below.

Choose the Issue

The people who have the problem agree on a solution and how to get it. They may decide to define (or "cut" in organizing terms) the issue narrowly: "Make our landlord give us back our rent deposits when we move out." Or, they may define it more broadly: "Make the city council pass a law requiring the return of rent deposits."

Develop Your Issue Strategy

Next, communications are opened with the person who has the power to give the group what it wants. Requests are made and arguments are presented. At this point, problems are sometimes resolved and the organization's requests are met. When they are not resolved, however, the person with the power becomes the "target" of an issue campaign. The target (sometimes called the decision maker) is always the person who has the power to give you what you want. (If no one has such power, then you haven't cut the issue correctly.)

A target is always a person. It is never an institution such as the government, the corporation, the bank, the legislature, the board, or the agency. Break it down. Even the most powerful institutions are made up of people. Having already addressed the institution itself through the official channels, the campaign now moves outside that framework to focus pressure on one or more individuals who make up the institution and have the power to give you what you want. These people are actually the institution's weak point. As individuals, they have goals, aspirations, and interests that don't coincide completely with those of the institution. For example, it may be the institutional position of the state insurance commission to support the insurance companies, but the commissioner may hope to run for governor someday, and thus want to establish some appearance of independence. Your members can sometimes see themselves as being stronger than an individual politician, but they all know that "You can't fight City Hall."

Announce the Campaign

Frequently a media event announces the start of the campaign. A study may be released, or people may simply tell of their experiences and their efforts to correct the problem. If the campaign is to be a coalition effort, then most of the coalition's member organizations need to be on board before the announcement, and be present at the event. (A coalition is an organization of organizations. The Coalition for Interspecies Relationships does not become a true coalition because one member owns a hamster and another a turtle. Even if the members *were* hamsters and turtles, it would still not be a true coalition. Only if it is made up of organizations of hamsters and turtles, or organizations of their owners, is it a real coalition.)

Begin Outreach Activities

Because every campaign is an opportunity to reach new people, you now start outreach activities. In a statewide or national campaign, other organizations may be enlisted. When the organization has a local focus, individuals and local groups are brought in. Often a petition drive is used both to find supporters and to build a group of active volunteers who circulate the petition. Speakers may be sent out to meetings of such groups as senior clubs, unions, churches, or PTAs. The kickoff of each of these activities can be a press event in itself, at least in smaller cities.

The outreach drive builds toward a large turnout event such as a public hearing sponsored by the organization. The event establishes legitimacy and brings in more allies and volunteers. It is also fun and a media event.

Stage Direct Encounters with Targets

Now the organization is ready for direct encounters with the people who have the power to give it what it wants. Large face-to-face meetings (sometimes called "actions") are set up with the target. At this stage, the organization carefully considers what power it has over the target. It usually has more power over elected officials than over appointed ones, and it usually has more power over anyone in government than in private corporations.

Although several months may have passed, it is still early in the campaign, and the group is probably too weak to challenge its main target directly. Attention thus shifts to "secondary targets." These are people over whom the organization has more power than it has over the main target, and who have more power over the main target than does the organization. For example, the mayor might be the main target and the local ward leader the secondary target.

Because the organization's members are a large percentage of the voters in the ward leader's district but only a small percentage of the voters in a city-wide election, the organization usually has more power over the locally elected official than over the one elected city-wide. And because the local official helps to get the mayor elected, she has more influence at city hall than does the group. The organization therefore puts pressure on the ward leader to get her to pressure the mayor to meet the group's demands. (The terminology of organizing is often confusing on this point. The "secondary target" is not the same thing as the second target, the person to whom you would go second when you are done seeing the person to whom you went first. A better term for secondary target might be "indirect target." That is, a person to whom you go to put pressure on someone else indirectly.)

Plan for Building the Organization

A series of meetings with secondary targets builds support for the issue. Each meeting is an opportunity to recruit new supporters, train spokespersons, and try for media coverage. They are also fun. To demonstrate power, an elected official might be shown more signatures on petitions than the number of votes by which she won in the last election. The director of a local housing authority might be told that he is in violation of HUD regulations or local building codes, and that outside agencies will be called in to investigate if he doesn't make repairs. At this stage real power is shown, not just good arguments and facts. (Not every event needs to be a direct confrontation. A parade, picnic or even a party to celebrate a victory can also build the group, and become a show of numbers. Invite allied elected officials to join you.)

But the main reason for holding such events is often to develop the strength of the organization. Every planning session should thus include a discussion of how to use the event to build the group. Often people become so focused on what they will say to the target that organization building is forgotten. Planning to build the organization must be specific. How many new people will be recruited, where, how and by whom? Must the event be held after six o'clock so that working people can come? Must it be before three so that mothers of school age children can come? How will new people be integrated into the group? How will all the members be told what happened? Perhaps a telephone tree should be activated or an evening leaflet distribution planned. In general, each event should be larger than the last one. If this isn't happening, then you are not building the organization.

Another measure of organizational strength is the experience level of its leaders and members. A local organization that can hold two events at the same time is quite well developed. Plan leadership training into each event. This means practice beforehand and evaluate afterward.

In the course of the issue campaign an election may occur. This offers the organization a fine opportunity to build more strength. (The events described so far have probably taken four to five months to unfold.) During the election season, the organization may do some combination of the following:

- Hold a candidates' night and ask candidates to take a position on the organization's issue. This can be done even if the winner of the election can't really give the group what it wants. Candidates can take *symbolic* positions supporting all sorts of things, and an angle for real support can usually be found as well. Members can also attend candidates' nights sponsored by other groups, and raise the issue there.
- Allied candidates can be asked to campaign on the issue and mention it in their literature (if it is cut broadly enough to really win votes).

- The organization can register voters as a show of strength in specific areas.
- Some organizations, depending on their IRS tax status, can make endorsements and campaign for or against candidates. Others can't (see Chapter 24).

Win or Regroup

After a series of successful build-up events, the organization takes on its main target. Sometimes this is done in an action or confrontation, and sometimes in a negotiation. Often a victory is won or a compromise is reached. If not, the organization must be prepared to escalate its tactics. This may mean large demonstrations and picketing, a return to other secondary targets, or the selection of a new main target. Sometimes the issues have to be broadened to attract still more supporters and the campaign taken to a new level. The refusal of a locality to control toxic dumping leads, for example, to a broader fight for statewide legislation or enforcement. At other times, the organization may decide that it has reached the limit of its strength and that it will have to lower its demand and accept less.

At each of these stages, the organization is being strengthened internally in addition to power being built. The leadership is growing and gaining experience, skill and media recognition. The membership is growing. Other organizations are moving into closer alliance. Money is being raised. The staff is becoming experienced in organizing and electoral tactics.

3

In direct action organizing, there is a difference between an issue and a problem. A *problem* is a broad area of concern. For example, health care, war, hunger, pollution, racism, and unemployment are all problems. An *issue* is a solution or partial solution to a problem. Passing pollution controls or national health insurance are examples of issues.

Because direct action organizing is about winning issues, the first step is to analyze the problem and decide what kind of solution to work toward. Some people have the luxury of choosing the problems on which they work. For others, the problem chooses them and can't be avoided, no matter how long or difficult the effort; drugs, an oil spill, or racial discrimination are examples of such problems. In both cases, however, organizations and individuals still make choices about how to cut the issue, that is, how to define the solution to the problem.

There are many approaches to solving any problem and the implications of each must be thought through carefully. It isn't enough to ask which is the most far reaching solution (or for that matter, which is the most serious problem).

The organizational implications of any approach must be carefully thought through as well. To put it another way, think organizationally. Ask: What impact will taking up this issue have on our organization? What will happen to the organization if we ignore the issue? Don't just think about problems and solutions.

The difference between thinking organizationally and thinking in terms of issues

Checklist for Choosing an Issue

Choosing an Issue

is a major factor in organizational development. It is also a major cause of internal friction between members who come at things from these two different directions. In general, new members are attracted to an organization because of the issues, and are not particularly conscious of the structure and mechanics of organizing. There was one volunteer in a neighborhood organization, who after three months of faithfully coming twice a week to the office to make phone calls, looked up and asked, "What did you say the name of this group was?" The question was probably asked of her by someone being called, but it was nonetheless the first step toward thinking organizationally.

Members who think only about issues are often frustrated by the amount of time and effort that goes into organizational maintenance. Occasionally you will hear leaders accused of being "empire builders." While that may be the case, more often they are organization builders being criticized by someone who hasn't yet learned to value organization. It is to win victory after victory, protect victories already won from being taken away, and to build political power so that winning becomes easier. In the long run, of course, building an organization and winning issues are two interdependent sides of the same process.

It is still necessary, however, to consider the impact of the issue on the organization separately from the social value of the issue itself. For any given organization at a particular stage in its development, some issues will be better for organizational development and more winnable on their own terms than others. The following checklist is an aid to evaluating issues. We recommend that before a group starts to choose an issue, the members be asked, "What are the criteria for a good issue"? List what people say on a blackboard or large sheet of paper and try to develop a mutually agreed upon list similar to this one. It will make the choice of an issue much easier, and it will be a sounder choice as well.

Checklist for Choosing an Issue

A good issue is one that matches most of these criteria. The issue should:

1. Result in a Real Improvement in People's Lives

If you can see and feel the improvement, then you can be sure that it has actually been won. Say, for example, that a transit rider organization won a commitment for more frequent equipment inspections. Perhaps over a period of years, this led to improved service, but perhaps not. Riders could not tell. On the other hand, when the group asked for and got printed train schedules, there was a tangible victory. By making real improvement an explicit criterion, the organization must seek a broad consensus on what an improvement really is.

2. Give People a Sense of Their Own Power

People should come away from the campaign feeling that the victory was won by them, not by experts or lawyers. This builds both the confidence to take on larger issues and loyalty to the organization.

3. Alter the Relations of Power

Building a strong, ongoing staffed organization creates a new center of power that changes the way the other side makes decisions.

4. Be Worthwhile

Members should feel that they are fighting for something about which they feel good, and which merits the effort.

5. Be Winnable

The problem must not be so large or the solution so remote that the organization is overwhelmed. The members must be able to see from the start that there is a good chance of winning, or at least that there is a good strategy for winning. Ask who else has won on an issue and how, and then call on people with experience and ask for advice.

It is also necessary to figure out how much money your campaign will cost the other side and how much are they likely to spend to defeat you. Also, what will the non-monetary costs be to the other side which will make them want to hold out against you? This gives you an idea of how hard they will work to defeat you, and how much money they are likely to spend.

6. Be Widely Felt

Many people must feel that this is a real problem and must agree with the solution. It is not enough that a few people feel strongly about it.

7. Be Deeply Felt

People must not only agree, but feel strongly enough to do something about it. It is not enough that many people agree about the issue but don't feel strongly.

8. Be Easy to Understand

It is preferable that you don't have to convince people that the problem exists, that your solution is good, and that they want to help solve it. Sometimes this is necessary, however, particularly with those environmental issues where the source of the problem is not obvious, or the problem can't be seen or smelled. In general, a good issue should not require a lengthy and difficult explanation. "Look at all those dead fish floating in the water. That didn't happen before the chemical plant opened," should suffice.

9. Have a Clear Target

The target is the person who can give you what you want. A more difficult campaign usually requires several clear targets. This allows the campaign to have a longer time to build up strength, even if some of the targets refuse your demands in the early months. If you can't figure out who the target is, either you don't have a good issue, or you may be addressing a problem, not an issue.

10. Have a Clear Time Frame that Works for You

An issue campaign has a beginning, a middle, and an end. You should have an idea of the approximate dates on which those points will fall.

Some time frame factors are internal, that is, set by your organization. Some are external, set by someone else. The timetable for an election campaign is almost totally external. The timetable for a campaign to win a stop sign in your community is almost totally internal.

Does the time of major effort in your campaign fall at a particularly difficult part of the year, such as mid-August or Christmas week? The spring and fall are best for most groups in most places.

Even if your organization does not have specific electoral goals, you want the time frame to fit the electoral calendar. You usually have more power just before an election than just after one. Consider how the issue's timetable can be merged into the electoral timetable.

11. Be Non-Divisive

Avoid issues that divide your present constituency. Don't pit neighbor against neighbor, old against young, Black against White. Don't be content to get the traffic or the drug pusher off your block and onto the next block. (This is not just being "liberal"; both will soon be back on your doorstep.)

Look down the road several years. Who will you eventually need to bring into your organization? Will this issue help or hinder you in reaching them?

12. Build Leadership

The campaign should have many roles that people can play. Issues campaigns that meet most of the other criteria also build leadership if they are planned to do so. In a coalition organization, building leadership has a different meaning than in a neighborhood group, because the people who represent organizations in the coalition already are leaders. They don't need or want you to develop them. Often, however, they do need to learn to work with each other, to use direct action, and to merge electoral and issue campaigns where appropriate.

13. Set Your Organization Up for the Next Campaign

A campaign requiring employers to provide health insurance leads to new campaigns on other health or employee benefits issues. On the other hand, a campaign to make the city catch stray dogs generally leads only to catching more stray dogs. People who have problems paying for health care are likely to have other related problems in common. People whose link to each other is a dislike of stray dogs may not have a common second issue. In addition to thinking about future issue directions, consider the skills the group will develop in the campaign and the contacts it will make for the next one.

14. Have a Pocketbook Angle

Issues that get people money or save people money are usually widely and deeply felt.

15. Raise Money

This means having some idea of how you will obtain funding sources for your campaign.

16. Be Consistent with Your Values and Vision

The issues we choose to work on must reflect our values and our vision for an improved society.

Checklist for Choosing an Issue

A good issue is one that matches most of these criteria. Use this checklist to compare issues or develop your own criteria and chart for choosing an issue.

Issue 1	Issue 2	Issue 3	Will the Issue
			1) Result in a Real Improvement in People's Lives
			2) Give People a Sense of Their Own Power
			3) Alter the Relations of Power
			4) Be Worthwhile
			5) Be Winnable
			6) Be Widely Felt
			7) Be Deeply Felt
			8) Be Easy to Understand
			9) Have a Clear Target
			10) Have a Clear Time Frame that Works for You
			11) Be Non-Divisive
			12) Build Leadership
			13) Set Your Organization Up for the Next Campaign
			14) Have a Pocketbook Angle
			15) Raise Money
			16) Be Consistent with Your Values and Vision

Midwest Academy, 225 West Ohio, Suite 250, Chicago, Illinois 60610

**Citizens demand the cleanup of hazardous waste—
a good organizing issue**

4

The strategy chart is an extremely useful tool for campaign planning. It lends itself both to overall campaign strategy and to the planning of specific events such as a public hearing or an accountability session with an elected official. The chart is valuable as the focal point of a group planning process because it poses the necessary questions in a logical order and moves people through the planning process step by step.

In your campaign planning meetings, you should always display the chart prominently on a blackboard or large sheet of paper in the front of the room. Have the following resources on hand to complement the chart:

1. A large map of the area, city or state in which the campaign will take place. There are often critical relationships among issues, groups, neighborhoods, geography, and political districts that can only become apparent when you look at a map.
2. Overlays for the map to show political districts (or use separate district maps).
3. Election returns for relevant races for the last several years. Knowing voting patterns and totals in primaries and general elections is important to understanding the strength of allies and opponents, even if your organization is not involved in electoral work.
4. The Yellow Pages to identify potential constituent and opponent organizations.
5. A list of your own board members and, if you are a coalition, your affiliates by address.

Strategy Chart

Goals

Organizational Considerations

Constituents, Allies, and Opponents

Targets

Tactics

Notes on Tactics

Using the Chart

Timelines

Sample Strategy Chart

Developing a Strategy

6. Someone who knows the major institutions in the area, major employers, banks, corporations public buildings, etc.

Next, we outline the information to be filled in and the questions to be considered for each of the five columns of the chart, which is displayed on the next page. Planning and completing the chart in sufficient detail can take several hours.

There are five major strategy elements to consider. Each has a column to fill in on the chart.

1. Long-Term, Intermediate, and Short-Term Goals
2. Organizational Considerations
3. Constituents, Allies, and Opponents
4. Targets (who can give you what you want)
5. Tactics

At first glance it appears that the chart is a series of lists. What we are unable to show on paper, but what becomes clear when you actually use the chart in planning, is that it is more like a computer spreadsheet. Whenever you change anything in one column, corresponding changes need to be made in the others. For example, adding another goal may require finding a different type of constituent group that would employ another tactic against a new target.

To help illustrate the use of the chart, we will cite, among other examples, a hypothetical campaign to win tax reform on the state level.

Let's say that you are the organizer in charge of the campaign. Like many other states, yours has been hit by a major budget crunch. The governor, a middle-of-the-road Democrat, has announced that social services will have to be cut, aid to school districts must be cut, and many public employees laid off. He has also announced a package of regressive sales and excise tax increases. In addition to these, communities will be hit with higher property taxes to fund the schools unless they slash school budgets.

Your organization, the State Citizens Alliance, is a coalition. It includes many unions, senior citizen groups, environmentalists, community organizations, low-income organizations, women's organizations, and organizations of people of color. In addition, the organization has an individual membership of 46,000 people recruited by your professional door-to-door canvass. It has a fine track record, having won many statewide legislative battles.

Your organization supports increasing taxes, but you want it done in a progressive way, which puts the burden on the rich and the large corporations. You have obtained the assistance of a public interest organization to draft your own tax proposal—the Citizens' Fair Tax Plan—so your technical presentation will be as good as any the Governor can produce. You are now ready to plan how to get your proposal passed.

Midwest Academy Strategy Chart

After choosing your issue, fill in this chart as a guide
to developing strategy. Be specific. List all the possibilities.

Goals	Organizational Considerations	Constituents, Allies, and Opponents	Targets	Tactics
1. List the long-term objectives of your campaign.	1. List the resources that your organization brings to the campaign. Include: money, number of staff, facilities, reputation, canvass, etc.	1. Who cares about this issue enough to join in or help the organization?	1. Primary Targets A target is always a person. It is never an institution or elected body.	1. For each target, list the tactics that each constituent group can best use to make its power felt.
2. State the intermediate goals for this issue campaign. What constitutes victory?	What is the budget, including in-kind contributions, for this campaign?	• Whose problem is it? • What do they gain if they win?	• Who has the power to give you what you want? • What power do you have over them?	Tactics must be: • In context • Flexible and creative • Directed at a specific target • Make sense to the membership • Be backed up by a specific form of power.
How will the campaign:	2. List the specific ways in which you want your organization to be stengthened by this campaign. Fill in numbers for each:	• What risks are they taking? • What power do they have over the target? • Into what groups are they organized?	2. Secondary Targets	
• Win concrete improvements in people's lives? • Give people a sense of their own power? • Alter the relations of power?	• Expand leadership group. • Increase experience of existing leadership. • Build membership base. • Expand into new constituencies. • Raise more money.	2. Who are your opponents?	• Who has power over the people with the power to give you what you want? • What power do you have over them?	Tactics include:
3. What short-term or partial victories can you win as steps toward your long-term goal?	3. List internal problems that have to be considered if the campaign is to succeed.	• What will your victory cost them? • What will they do/spend to oppose you? • How strong are they?		• Media events • Actions for information and demands • Public hearings • Strikes • Voter registration and voter education • Law suits • Accountability sessions • Elections • Negotiations

Midwest Academy
225 West Ohio, Suite 250
Chicago, Illinois 60610

Column 1: Goals

Long-Term Goals

These are the goals that you eventually hope to win, and toward which the current campaign is a step. Using our example, your long-term goal might be to have the state budget well funded to provide the services that the people of the state require, and to obtain this funding through a progressive tax system based on the ability to pay.

The legislation you are now sponsoring won't accomplish all of that; it will only close the budget gap in the short run. Many regressive taxes will still be on the books and the schools will still have problems, but it is a good step.

Intermediate Goals

These are the goals that you hope to win in this campaign. In this case, it is the passage of the Citizens' Fair Tax Plan.

A housing group might state its goal as fair housing, and an environmental organization, to end toxic dumping. But these goals are so general that they only restate the problem. Another too-general campaign goal is "to educate people," because there is rarely a way to know when this has been accomplished. Intermediate goals must be specific, such as state mortgage guarantees for low-income home buyers or mandatory jail sentences for toxic dumpers.

Test the goals—are they specific steps toward your long-term goals? Do they meet the three major criteria for choosing an issue? Do they: 1) Win real improvements in people's lives? 2) Give people a sense of their own power? 3) Alter the relations of power? What does it mean to win? How will you know when you have?

Short-Term Goals

Short-term goals are steps toward your intermediate goals. They are necessary for two reasons. First, few groups are strong enough to win a major campaign without a period of building power. The support of individual officials must be won and often, power gathered at local levels of government. Second, just to sustain your organization in a long campaign, people must see small victories along the way.

Short-term goals for the Citizens' Fair Tax

Sample Goals Column

1. Long-Term Goals
- State budget well funded by a progressive tax system.
- Full funding of schools by the state.

2. Intermediate Goals
- Pass the Citizens Fair Tax Plan.
- Win support of key legislative leaders from the 5th, 7th & 14th districts, or develop an anti-Fair Tax records for future races.

3. Short-Term Goals
- Public support from local officials.
- Line up influential sponsors in House and Senate by April.
- 25 co-sponsors by June 1.

Plan campaign might be to obtain the endorsement of city council members or county commissioners around the state, and to move from there to asking members of the legislature to say that they agree in principle to the idea of progressive taxation before your bill comes out. Or, you might launch a campaign for 25 co-sponsors from carefully targeted districts.

For a local community organization working on a neighborhood issue, the short-term goal might be just to get a meeting with the city council member. When people see that the organization can do that much, they will be ready for the next step, perhaps a meeting with the mayor. (If someone gets up at your first meeting and says, "Oh the mayor is a friend of mine, I can get you a meeting any time," don't accept. The point is that the group must feel that it collectively won the meeting because of its strength. If the meeting comes about because of one person's personal relationship, the stature of that individual is built up, but the group isn't strengthened.)

Sometimes, before you can even decide on the intermediate goals, more information about a problem is needed. Then, short-term goals might consist of making an agency either compile or release information. For example: citizen organization, concerned about crime against seniors, had to make the police

Sample Organizational Considerations Column

1. Resources to Put In

- Salaries and expenses for six months = $45,000. On hand = $10,000. To raise = $35,000.
- Staff
  Mary—Lead Organizer Full time
  Fred—Organizer Half time
  Sam—Support Staff 1 day a week
  Liz—College Intern 1 day a week
  Kate—Supervisor 4 hrs. a week
  (Cash value of staff time = $40,000)
- Canvass offices (3). Approx. 15 canvassers hitting 9,000 doors a month for three months (cash value if people were hired to do this = $95,000).
- 7 board members on the tax committee. Each represents an affiliate organization.
- Committee chair. Very active. Good spokesperson.
- Lobbyist from allied union.
- Tax expert contributed to us by Citizens for Tax Neatness.
- Office space and phones for all staff (cash value = $700).
- 1 Xerox that works. 1 that sort of works. 2 computers.
  (cash value for use = $200)
- Good relations with press.
  Abner Berry at the *Sentinel* and
  Al Ferman at the *Herald*.

2. What We Want to Get Out of It

- Make back all expenses ($45,000) through contributions from affiliates and campaign fundraising.
- 4 new affiliates. Most likely choices are Carver City Taxpayers Against Waste, Newton Teachers Local 310, Association of Child Service Providers, Gotham City Save Our Schools Committee.
- Build a base in the 5th, 7th, and 14th districts. Promote George, Frieda, and Kim as respective spokespersons.
- Develop 15 active volunteers.
- Develop ways to activate 15,000 canvass members in key districts.

3. Problems to Solve

- Rivalry between teachers' unions may erupt. —Meet with them. Ask them to keep turf fight out of it.
- Uptown Seniors don't like Downtown Seniors.
  —Hold separate meetings in each community.
- Fred says that Mary whistles through her nose all day, and he can't work in the same office with her.
  —Seek treatment for Fred since no one else ever hears Mary do this.

department keep crime statistics by age just to prove that the problem existed.

And sometimes, short-term goals will be electoral. A specific person must be removed or more forceful leadership elected.

While listing goals, consider what the cost to someone will be if you win it. Who will pay? What is it worth to someone to defeat you? Knowing this helps you to get a sense of how much money is likely to be spent on defeating you. It also gives you some better idea of who will end up as allies or opponents.

When you are finished listing your goals, have the group put them more or less in the order in which they will have to be achieved.

Column 2: Organizational Considerations

This column is essentially an organizational expense and income statement. You list what resources you have to put into the campaign (expenses), what organizational gains you want to come out of the campaign (income), and internal problems that have to be solved.

Start with resources. This is essentially your campaign budget. Consider these to be expenses or better yet, investments. Be very specific, particularly about staff time and money. List names. Make sure that the people working on your campaign are in the room when you talk about how much of their time is going into the campaign. "Full time," for example, means that a person has no other responsibilities. Don't be one of those groups where the organizer works "full time" on each of five campaigns at once.

List the amount of money you are putting into the campaign and the amount that needs to be raised. Then put a fair market cash value on the in-kind contributions you are making, including staff time. Unless you do this, your allies, affiliates and members will never have any idea of the size of your real contribution, and neither will you.

In the second part of the column list everything that the organization wants to get out of the campaign, in addition to winning the issue. Consider this income and plan to make a profit, both in organizational gains and real dollars.

The last part of this column lists internal problems that will have to be considered or solved in the course of the campaign. Here, "internal" implies both within your organization (e.g., staff relationships) and problems within constituent or allied organizations.

Column 3: Constituents, Allies and Opponents

Constituents and Allies

This column is where you answer the questions, who cares about this issue, what do they stand to win or lose, what power do they have, and how are they organized? A constituency is a group of people, hopefully already organized, who you can contact and bring into the campaign. In filling out this column, be expansive, even far fetched. The idea is to come up with a long list of potential allies. During the campaign you may not get to all of them, but you can come back to the list later if events bog down and you need additional support.

When you start drawing up the list for the Citizens' Fair Tax Plan campaign, the first groups that come to mind are public employee organizations that face layoffs and taxpayer organizations. Some taxpayer groups will be very Right-wing, but some could join you. Clearly, organizations that get services or funding from the state will also be interested;

Sample Constituents, Allies, and Opponents Column

1. Constituents and Allies

- State Teachers Union: 7,000 members
  Local 210 Gotham City
  Local 113 Newton
  Local 69 Butler
  Local 666 Spuyten Duyvil
- State Teachers Association: 12,000 members
  List locals
- State Public Employees Union: 14,000 members
  List locals
- State Labor Federation: 40,000 members
  List active local and labor councils.
- Association of Day Care Centers: 1,200 members
- State Senior Council: 3,000 members
  Clubs in
  Parker (5th District)
  Gotham
  Newton (7th District)
  Salem
  Winchester (14th District)
  Westchester
- Council of Home Health Care Providers
- Newton Council of Civic Associations
- State Alliance of PTAs
- Taxpayers Union: 2,000 members

2. Opponents

- Chamber of Commerce
- Bankers Association
- Insurance Industry Council
- Johnson Corp.
- Taxpayers Association of Hatemail
- etc., etc.

---

examples include seniors and day care providers.

The problem is that in the face of a general sentiment in the state that favors budget cuts over tax hikes of any kind, this list is too short. Additional allies will be homeowners and parents, but to bring them in, the goals of the campaign will have to be expanded to include property tax relief and school funding. (This is an example of how the chart is like a computer spreadsheet. When you change one column, you will have to change others.) The next question is how are home owners and parents organized? The canvassers can reach some of them, and others will contact you after the media start to carry the story, but look for existing groups.

Even if you are organizing for an individual membership organization rather than a coalition, it is still useful to think of people as part of groups. For example, say that you are working on a public transportation issue and decide that senior citizens are a possible constituency. You could list seniors on the chart, or you could be more specific and say, "Seniors who ride the #1 and #2 buses." It would be much better, however, to look in the Yellow Pages to see what senior centers are served by those lines. Don't overlook churches that might have senior clubs. Mark them on a map. Put them on the chart by name. Go and visit them.

Then, look for constituencies that are less than obvious. On the tax issue, realtors or real estate associations might join with you because value is added to the houses they sell if taxes are lower and there is a good school system.

Think of each constituent group as the hub of a wheel. Then look at the spokes. Who cares about these people? Who does business with them? Who provides services to them? Who lends them money? Who borrows their money (banks, insurance companies)? For whom do they vote? If they had more money to spend, where would they spend it? Who would get it (local merchants or Swiss banks)? What organizations or churches do they belong to? Looking at your possible constituents in this way, it is easy to see that the self-interest of one group affects the self-interest of many others.

While it is necessary to think about potential areas of conflict between the groups, remember that people don't all have to love each other, agree on tactics, or even sit in the same room in order to support the same issue. In fact, sometimes the issue brings them together. This was the case in the classic campaign against the Chicago Crosstown Expressway. The proposed expressway route ran through different ethnic communities. One White group came with signs saying, "Black roads, white lines united against the Crosstown."

Break down your list according to whether the constituency is organized or unorganized. That is, homeowners in the Lincoln Park area, as opposed to homeowner associations in the Lincoln Park area. Then rank each group according to the power they bring to the campaign. Consider the following:

- How many of them are there? / How many members do they have?
- Did they work or vote for the incumbent office holder?
- Do they make campaign contributions?
- Will they give money to your campaign?
- Do they bring special credibility? (Clergy)
- Do they have special appeal? (Children)
- Are they part of a larger organized network? (Veterans)
- Do they have a reputation for being tough? (Unions)
- Do they have special skills? (Lawyers)
- Are they considered particularly newsworthy? (Penguins)

Last, examine the weakness of each constituency. Look at their reputation, past history, and the enemies that you might inherit by linking up with them.

Opponents

List all the groups, individuals and institutions that stand to lose or be very upset if you win. What will your victory cost them? Try to evaluate how actively each will oppose you, and what they will do or spend to defeat you. In a few cases you may find ways to neutralize them, but even if there is nothing you can do, it is best to have some idea of what to expect as the campaign unfolds. List the power of each opponent. How does the strength of your constituents stack up against the strength of your opponents in the eyes of the people who can give you what you want?

Column 4: Targets

Primary Targets

The person with the power to give you what you want is often referred to as the "target" of the campaign. This does not necessarily imply that the person is evil. It simply means that by virtue of having the power to give you what you want, that person is the focus of the campaign.

The target is always a person. "Personalize the target" is a fundamental rule of organizing. Even if the power to give you what you want is actually held by an institution such as a city council, a board of directors, the legislature, the police department, or the Environmental Protection Agency, personalize it. Find out the name of the person who can make the decision, or at least strongly influence it. Make that person the target. Not only does this help to narrow the focus of the campaign, but it makes your members feel that winning is possible. A campaign to change a person's mind is much more believable than one to change the policy of a big institution. In addition, individual decision makers have human responses such as fairness, guilt, fear, ambition, vanity or loyalty. These do not exist in institutions or formal bodies as a whole. Such responses can only come into play if you personalize the target.

When filling out this column, list all the possible people who can give you what you want. It helps if there is more than one of them because where power is divided, there are usually more weak spots and openings. Also, multiple targets provide an opportunity to sustain the campaign over a longer time. This allows you to build strength. In many types of campaigns, time is on your side if you can hold out. This is particularly true if you are trying to stop expensive things from being built, or large sums of money from being spent. A long campaign may also help you to keep the issue alive until an election intervenes or a court decision comes down. List the reasons that each target has to oppose you as well as to agree with you. List your power over each target. Go back to the constituency list and consider how to match the power of each constituency against the vulnerabilities of the target.

Secondary Targets

A secondary target is a person who has more power over the primary target than you do. But, you have more power over this person than you have over the primary target.

> ## Sample Targets Column
>
> ### 1. Primary Targets
> - Governor Winthrop
> - House Tax Committee Chair
>   Rep. Bacon (5th District)
> - Senate Committee Chair
>   Rep. Lax
> - Committee members, to be determined
> - Other legislators, to be determined
>
> ### 2. Secondary Targets
> - G. Groggy—Union County Dem. Chairman—includes 14th Dist.
> - R. Waterdown—Kent County Dem. Chairman—includes 7th Dist.
> - Selected campaign contributors to individuals listed above
> - County Commissioners in the counties containing target districts.

Tenants in public housing who wanted their buildings painted provide an example. The tenants made several members of the city housing authority their primary targets. When the tenants discovered that old lead paint was peeling off the walls, they made the head of the health department a secondary target. She didn't care about the tenants' dispute with the housing authority, but lead was a health hazard that had to be corrected. She told the housing authority that the walls had to be scraped and repainted.

When you list secondary targets, write down what power you have over them, and what power they have over the primary target.

In the Fair Tax campaign, the targets are determined by an analysis of the legislature. Clearly the governor will be a target, as will the heads of key committees. Once the legislation is introduced, and a head count taken of committee members and the legislature as a whole, specific districts can be targeted as well. Secondary targets for this campaign might include officials such as county chairs of the Democratic and Republican parties, lower-level elected officials, and campaign contributors.

Don't feel obliged to have a secondary target if you have power over the primary one.

Sample Tactics Column

(listed more or less in the order in which they might actually be used)

- Media hits. Feature unjust tax distribution between homeowners and EXXON refinery.
- More media hits. Spotlight education cuts. Kids come with symbols of cut programs, e.g., sports equipment, musical instruments.
- Do same day in four cities with teacher organizations and PTAs.
- Make this an issue in the next gubernatorial primary.
- Start postcard campaign for fair taxes. "Dear Gov. When my income goes over $100,000, I will happily pay higher taxes if you enact them now."
- Media hit in capital to release detailed Fair Tax Plan. Sponsors and co-sponsors on hand.
- Canvassers start petition drive in targeted districts.
- Media hits in targeted districts to announce formation of district Fair Tax committees to put legislature on the spot. Show petitions.
- Delegation meetings to get position of targeted legislators.
- Local hearings. Either sponsors hold them officially or we hold them. Aim for high turnout.
- Additional delegation meetings in target districts. Service providers, seniors, clients of programs are included.
- Save our schools. Rallies and picnics. Fund raiser.
- TV debate between our leader and legislative opponents.
- Tax bill burning day when tax bills are sent out.
- Accountability sessions in targeted districts, particularly the 5th, 7th, and 14th districts.
- Mass lobby day in capital when bill comes up for vote. Governor invited to speak for the bill. Empty chair if he doesn't. Invite potential opponents.

Column 5: Tactics

Tactics are steps in carrying out your overall plan. They are the specific things that the people in column 3 can do to the people in column 4 to put pressure on them. When you list tactics, put down who will do what, and to whom. Tactics should be fun. They should be within the experience of your members, but outside the experience of your targets.

Every tactic has an element of power behind it. None should be purely symbolic. Different tactics require different levels of organizational strength and sophistication to use. For that reason, some work better at the beginning of a campaign and some can only be used later after a certain level of strength is reached.

Notes on Tactics

Media Events

Media events are designed to get press and TV coverage, and little more. As stand-alone events, they are usually used at the start of the campaign to dramatize the issue and announce that the organization is working on it. Later in the campaign, the media will be used in conjunction with other tactics. A media event might consist of releasing information or a study, demanding information, having victims tell their story, or making demands on the target. For the Fair Tax Campaign, an opening media event might be held in front of property owned by a large corporation. The percentage of income paid in taxes by the corporation could be contrasted to that paid by nearby homeowners who would bring big enlargements of their tax bills to display to the press.

The press usually responds well to something funny or dramatic. A Citizen Action organization, for example, wanted to dramatize that the rising cost of auto insurance was forcing people to choose between paying for their homes or their cars. The group built a home into a car with the toilet in the trunk. The press loved it.

If the media event features groups such as low-income people, the homeless, the unemployed, or striking workers, be sure that they are presented with dignity and as whole people asking for the same rights that others enjoy. They are not objects of pity; nor are they looking for a handout.

Actions

Actions are a particularly useful tactic for local organizations, especially toward the start of a campaign. In an action, a group of people confront a target and make specific demands. They expect to get an answer on the spot. Organizations usually start with procedural demands such as asking for an appointment with someone or that a hearing be held. They also might ask for the release of information, the publication of rules, or time on the agenda. Later when the group is stronger, actions might be used to win some of its main demands.

Actions often involve the media, but they are not media events. That is to say, they have power behind them which goes beyond media coverage, and they are not simply held in an attempt to publicize a situation. The organization's real power may be the number of participants or the size of the constituency they represent, their ability to embarrass the target, or their ability to cause the target political harm if the target is a public official, or financial harm if it is a business.

Public Hearings

You might demand that the target hold an official public hearing, but often organizations have their own hearings with a panel of community leaders and allied political leaders who listen to testimony from your constituency. Often a report is issued. The hearing serves to educate, get publicity, and establish your organization as a leading force on the issue.

Accountability Sessions

Accountability sessions are large meetings with elected officials. They are sponsored by you and held on your turf. Several hundred people come to tell the official what they want done. The official is asked to agree to the demands on the spot.

Elections

Depending on what type of organization you are, you may actually endorse candidates. Even if you don't, October is a good time to negotiate with an incumbent candidate if the election is to be held in November, because the candidate is more vulnerable then.

Negotiations

Issue campaigns usually end in some form of negotiation. You must have shown considerable power to get the other side to agree to talk. If your target offers to negotiate too easily or too soon, watch out! It may be a device to make the other side look reasonable without any serious concessions being made. (But don't automatically assume that every offer is some kind of trick. There are groups that snatch defeat out of the jaws of victory because they can never believe that they actually won.)

The next chapter explores some of these and other tactics in greater detail.

Using the Chart

The strategy chart can be used to plan organizational development as well as issue campaigns. The starting point in the chart is determined by the type of planning you are doing. For example, to plan an issue campaign, start from left to right. To plan the startup of a new organization, say a new senior citizen group, begin at the lower half of the Organizational Considerations column and work out what the organizing model will be. For example, is it an organization of senior clubs? Then skip to the Constituents column and list all the existing clubs that could potentially join the coalition. Next, go back to the Goals column and decide what issues would appeal to the largest number of clubs. From there go to the Targets and then to the Tactics columns.

One reason that the chart works in so many ways is that an organization is literally the product of what it does. Once you are clear on what you want it to be, you can work backwards toward doing something that will shape the group in the desired direction. An example of a strategy chart that shows all five of the columns presented earlier appears at the end of this chapter.

The two questions most frequently asked about the strategy chart:

Question: In which column do I put an activity such as getting more publicity for my organization? Is that a Goal, an Organizational Consideration or a Tactic?

Answer: Nothing goes in the Goals column unless you intend to win it from someone. Tactics are always done by someone to someone, so a media event aimed at a target goes under tactics. Getting publicity in general is an Organizational Consideration.

Question: Exactly what is the relationship between the columns of the chart?

Answer: Tactics are what people in the Constituency column do to the people in the Targets column to make them give the organization the things in the Goals column so as to build the organization as outlined in the Organizational Considerations column.

Time Lines

To finish off the planning process, make time lines for the campaign. Include all the major campaign events and deadlines for preparing the publicity for each. Be sure to include the key dates in the electoral process. Even if you are not involved with candidates, note such information as when voter registration starts and ends, when nominating petitions start circulating, when petitions must be filed for major party candidates and independents, when candidate fundraising reports must be filed (you may want to look at them) and of course, all election dates. Also note when appropriate legislative bodies are in session, when members of congress and the legislature are home for recess, and when major civil, religious and school holidays occur.

Supporters of Nebraska Citizen Action and the Sustainable Energy for Economic Development (SEED) Campaign protest a Lincoln Electric Service proposal to invest in an out-of-state coal plant instead of developing Nebraska's extensive wind power resources.

Sample Midwest Academy Strategy Chart for "Fair Tax Campaign"

Goals

1. Long-Term Goals
- State budget well funded by a progressive tax system.
- Full funding of schools by the state.

2. Intermediate Goals
- Pass the Citizens Fair Tax Plan.
- Win support of key legislative leaders from the 5th, 7th & 14th districts or develop an anti-Fair Tax record for future races.

3. Short-Term Goals
- Public support from local officials.
- Line up influential sponsors in House and Senate by April.
- 25 co-sponsors by June 1.

Organizational Considerations

1. Resources to Put In
- Staff
  - Mary—Lead Organizer Full time
  - Fred—Organizer Half time
  - Sam—Support Staff 1 day a week
  - Liz—College Intern 1 day a week
  - Kate—Supervisor 4 hrs. a week
  (Cash value of staff time = $40,000)
- Canvass offices (3). Approx. 15 canvassers hitting 9,000 doors a month for three months (cash value if people were hired to do this = $95,000).
- 7 board members on the tax committee. Each represents an affiliate organization.
- Committee chair. Very active. Good spokesperson.
- Lobbyist from allied union.
- Tax expert contributed to us by Citizens for Tax Neatness.
- Office space and phones for all staff.
- 1 Xerox that works. 1 that sort of works.
- 2 computers.
- Good relations with press. Abner Berry at the *Sentinel* and Al Ferman at the *Herald*.

2. What We Want to Get Out of It
- Make back all expenses for six months = $45,000. On hand = $10,000. To raise = $35,000.
- Make back all expenses ($45,000) through contributions from affiliates and campaign fundraising:
  - 4 new affiliates. Most likely choices are Carver City Taxpayers Against Waste, Newton Teachers Local 310, Association of Child Service Providers, Gotham City Save Our Schools Committee.
- Build a base in the 5th, 7th, and 14th districts. Promote George, Frieda, and Kim as respective spokespersons.
- Develop 15 active volunteers.
- Develop ways to activate 15,000 canvass members in key districts.

3. Problems to Solve
- Rivalry between teachers' unions may erupt.
  —Meet with them. Ask them to keep turf fight out of it.
- Uptown Seniors don't like Downtown Seniors.
  —Hold separate meetings in each community.
- Fred says that Mary whistles through her nose all day, and he can't work in the same office with her.
  —Seek treatment for Fred since no one else ever hears Mary do this.

Constituents, Allies, and Opponents

1. Constituents and Allies
- State Teachers Union: 7,000 members
  - Local 210 Gotham City
  - Local 113 Newton
  - Local 69 Butler
  - Local 666 Spuyten Duyvil
- State Teachers Association: 12,000 members
  List locals
- State Public Employees Union: 14,000 members
  List locals
- State Labor Federation: 40,000 members
  List active local and labor councils.
- Association of Day Care Centers: 1,200 members
- State Senior Council: 3,000 members. Clubs in Parker (5th District) Gotham Newton (7th District) Salem Winchester (14th District) Westchester
- Council of Home Health Care Providers
- Newton Council of Civic Associations
- State Alliance of PTAs
- Taxpayers Union: 2,000 members

2. Opponents
- Chamber of Commerce
- Bankers Association
- Insurance Industry Council
- Johnson Corp.
- Rep. Bird (14th District)
- Taxpayers Association of Hatemail
- etc., etc.

Targets

1. Primary Targets
- Governor Winthrop
- House Tax Committee Chair
- Rep. Bacon (14th District)
- Senate Committee Chair
- Rep. Lax
- Committee members, to be determined
- Other legislators, to be determined

2. Secondary Targets
- G. Groggy—Union County Dem. Chairman—includes 14th Dist.
- R. Waterdown—Kent County Dem. Chairman—includes 7th Dist.
- Selected campaign contributors to individuals listed above
- County Commissioners in the counties containing target districts.

Tactics

- (listed more or less in the order in which they might actually be used)
- Media hits. Feature unjust tax distribution between homeowners and EXXON refinery.
- More media hits. Spotlight education cuts. Kids come with symbols of cut programs, e.g., sports equipment, musical instruments.
- Do same day in four cities with teacher organizations and PTAs.
- Make this a major issue in the next gubernatorial primary.
- Start postcard campaign for fair taxes. "Dear Gov. When my income goes over $100,000, I will happily pay higher taxes if you enact them now."
- Media hit in capital to release detailed Fair Tax Plan. Sponsors and co-sponsors on hand.
- Canvassers start petition drive in targeted districts.
- Media hits in targeted districts to announce formation of district Fair Tax committees to put legislature on the spot. Show petitions.
- Delegation meetings to get position of targeted legislators.
- Local hearings. Either sponsors hold them officially or we hold them. Aim for high turnout.
- Additional delegation meetings in target districts. Service providers, seniors, clients of programs are included.
- Save our schools. Rallies and picnics.
- Fund raiser.
- TV debate between our leader and legislative opponents.
- Tax bill burning day when tax bills are sent out.
- Accountability sessions in targeted districts, particularly the 5th, 7th, and 14th districts.
- Mass lobby day in capital when bill comes up for vote. Governor invited to speak for the bill. Empty chair if he doesn't. Invite potential opponents.

Midwest Academy Strategy Chart

Goals	Organizational Considerations	Constituents, Allies, and Opponents	Targets	Tactics

Midwest Academy, 225 West Ohio, Suite 250, Chicago, Illinois 60610

5

We are somewhat reluctant to present a guide to tactics for the same reason that we would not print biographies of characters in movies we have seen. The characters have no real existence outside of the plot of the movie. In the same vein, tactics have no meaningful existence outside the strategy of which they are a part. Standing alone, it is impossible to say that a given tactic is right or wrong, good or bad, clever or dumb. That's why tactics come at the end of the strategy chart.

All too often, organizations allow a tactic to take on a life of its own, independent of any strategic context. When this happens, a group will hear of a clever tactic that worked someplace else, and use it without considering why it worked the first time, or how their situation might be different. Take a case in point. Word arrived from a nearby state that because people had mailed band aids to their legislators, real progress was made on a bill to lower auto insurance rates. Mailing band aids became the new "in" tactic. All sorts of groups started doing it. No one realized that in the nearby state, the legislature was up for election, while their own state elections had been completed just before the band aid frenzy began. Tactics do not work just because they are smart or funny, although it helps. *The worst mistake an organizer can make is to act tactically instead of strategically.*

Criteria for Tactics

Considerations in Using Some Popular Tactics

Checklist for Tactics

Using the Strategy Chart to Plan a Tactic

A Guide to Tactics

Criteria for Tactics

Having placed a tactic in its strategic context, there are five basic criteria for a good tactic.

It is Focused on the Primary or Secondary Target of the Campaign. The tactic is not focused on someone else.

It Puts Power Behind a Specific Demand. The weakest tactic is one that is not aimed at anyone and makes no demand. A candlelight vigil that is held for the environment, but not connected to a specific issue, provides an example. (If a quarter of a million people show up, as they well might, that is a different story. A demand will be found soon enough.)

It Meets Your Organizational Goals as Well as Your Issue Goals. That is, it builds the organization as well as helping to win the issue. As far as we know, the Boston Tea Party dramatized the problem of taxation, but did not help to build an organization. No group took credit for it because it was illegal. Since then, many organizations have reenacted the tea party by dumping something appropriate into water. Usually the press is called and the group's name is prominently displayed, indicating that the use of this tactic has improved over the years, although it worked well enough the first time.

It Is Outside the Experience of the Target. An organization demanding postal service jobs for Hispanics xeroxed hundreds of job applications, and people in the community filled them out. The local postal service administrator was taken off guard and blundered by disqualifying the xeroxed forms, insisting that only original forms could be considered. This seemed so unfair and so prejudiced that he was forced to back down, thus handing the organization an easy first victory.

It Is Within the Experience of Your Own Members and They Are Comfortable with It. A citizen organization brought several hundred members to a meeting at a church, from which they were to march to the office of a state official. The members were not comfortable with the idea of the march and refused to leave the church. Had the organizers realized that the members were not used to marching, they might have arranged to have the state official meet with people at the church itself.

Considerations in Using Some Popular Tactics

Public Hearings

There are two kinds of public hearings, those which you sponsor and "official" ones held by public agencies.

Holding Your Own Public Hearing. The first victory in holding a public hearing lies in getting the public official to come. The virtue of this tactic is that it is very difficult for an official to refuse such an invitation. To do so would be an admission that the community's opinion doesn't count. To your own members, the appearance of an important decision maker at *their* event is a sign of growing power. Often, a group uses actions and other pressure tactics just to force someone to attend a hearing.

If an official does refuse to come, the hearing can be held anyway with a panel of prestigious allies listening to testimony. These might include members of the clergy, other elected officials, educators, heads of organizations, or people from special fields connected with the issue.

There are several advantages to holding your own hearing:

- It establishes your group as a force/authority on the issue.
- It is an opportunity to do outreach to other groups, individuals, or neighborhoods.
- It shows off your influential supporters or leaders. They can sit on the hearing panel or testify.
- It can showcase a candidate you are backing.
- It is a display of numbers.
- You control almost every aspect of it, which makes it a fine forum for your point of view.
- It is fun and not very hard to do.
- It is good training for your own leaders.
- It will probably get media coverage.

In planning your hearing, write and practice all testimony in advance. It need not be "expert" testimony, in fact, better that it not be. People telling their own story of how the issue affects them is just fine so long as each person represents a larger constituency.

Make the physical setting attractive both to participants and to the TV. A good job of decorating using banners or signs naming the organizations present is one way of showing strength. Always have more people than the room can comfortably hold. If you can't make the crowd bigger, make the room smaller by removing empty chairs or partitioning off part of it. As with most tactics, a really large turnout makes up for what is lacking in execution, so don't spend so much time writing testimony that you neglect recruitment.

Hearings, like any other meeting, should be over within two hours. The trick is to avoid having the hearing dribble away at the end. Save your strongest speaker until last, and end with a call to action and an announcement of the next step in the campaign.

Attending an Official Hearing. As a result of organizing activity during the 1970s, there was a great expansion of legally required citizen participation in government decision making processes. Often this has taken the form of an official public hearing. Where not required by law, groups often demand hearings as a way of opening the debate, delaying a decision, or creating an arena in which to show their strength.

Try to get the hearing held on your own turf at a time when your people can attend. Most official hearings are held downtown at 9 a.m. Fighting for neighborhood, evening hearings is often a good way to build the campaign. It is the type of demand that is hard for a public agency to refuse. If you win, however, you are obligated to produce a crowd.

When you are stuck with the morning time slot and downtown location, try to get on the agenda at the very opening of the hearing. That is when the media will come, and they will not stay long. Also, your people will get tired. Often you must register to speak weeks or months in advance. (This is particularly true for environmental hearings on big state or federal projects.)

Official hearings are boring. Do not plan on keeping a crowd at one for long. Consider having a picket line, press event, or demonstration outside until it is time for your spokesperson to testify. Technical hearings, say on utility load forecasting, are super boring. It is not often useful to bring large groups to them.

Use tactics that are humorous but that are also in good taste and make a political point. This is particularly important for gaining media coverage at an otherwise unnewsworthy event. A leader of a citizens' group, for example, appeared at a utility rate hearing dressed as King Com the Electric Gorilla (Commonwealth Edison). A public housing tenants' organization appeared in the city council chamber with mice that had been caught in their apartments.

Gimmicks like these are good for morale and press, but have little inherent power. They are no substitute for large numbers of people.

If the goal of appearing at the hearing is to get media coverage for your position, avoid appearing at a time when opposition groups will also be present. A confrontation between rival organizations will be covered, but the substance of your position is likely to get lost even more than usual. If you want television coverage, you will need to have something "visual" for the cameras.

The assumption here is that hearings are theater. Occasionally this is not true. Some legally mandated hearings can be used to build up a case for later court action or to win major delays. Some technical hearings really can modify the rulings of regulatory agencies. Someone on your team should know how to play it straight, which often requires expert technical and legal advice. If very technical testimony is required, try to find a public interest or advocacy group to provide it. And at any hearing, have printed copies of your testimony available for the media, the official record, and for general distribution.

Mass Demonstrations

Mass demonstrations are a good show of numbers, but they are also a lot of work. If you hold more than one during an issue campaign, each must be larger than the preceding one or you will appear to be losing support. This tactic works best when a single individual is the target. When aimed at a legislative body, it can lose focus and fail to apply pressure to individual members. Consequently, such demonstrations should be combined with direct lobbying.

The nice thing about a mass demonstration is that it is like money in the bank. Once you have produced a thousand people, or a million, you do not need to do it again for a long time. Your reputation will carry you. Location is critical. You want a place where passing street traffic will feed the event. It is cheating, however, to claim that everyone eating lunch on the mall at noon was part of your demonstration. Eventually, the truth will catch up with you. (Needless to say, what is actually considered large depends on where you live, and on how many people usually come to such things.)

Accountability Sessions

These are meetings that you hold with elected officials, and where you control the agenda. During the session people from your constituency present information and say why they expect the official to support a certain measure. Then, a panel of your leaders makes specific demands on the official. An immediate response is expected.

The success of this tactic is directly proportional to the numerical strength you can show in relation to the electoral weakness of the official. High numbers count, as do having speakers who represent large groups. Often, petitions or letters are presented to demonstrate even wider support.

The assumption, of course, is that the official is vulnerable and that many of your people either voted for him or her, or did not vote at all but will now. If all of your people always vote for the opposing party anyway, you will have much less leverage (see Chapter 8).

Petition Drives and Letter Writing Campaigns

By themselves, petitions and form letters (on which people sign their names to pre-printed letters) are not the most effective means for influencing elected leaders. Names collected on a petition that are simply mailed to a politician are basically useless. If letterwriting is to be used in isolation (not recommended), focus your energies on getting personal, hand-written letters, which are taken much more seriously.

On the other hand, these tactics can be very effective for collecting the names of supporters and potential new volunteers, building your organization, and, when used in combination with other tactics, for demonstrating your power. Letters, especially individual, hand-written letters, or petitions combined with actions, accountability sessions, or hearings are very valuable. If your organization has set up a meeting with an elected official, have several hundred letters start arriving a few days before the meeting. Petitions and letters in which people pledge to vote on the basis of a politician's stand on your issue are the strongest kind. Remember that many office holders actually answer letters, and thus will have the last word with your supporters. They may use it to explain why you are wrong.

Don't ever give your petitions away. Just display them and take them home. If you must, leave copies. You can use the same petitions on many occasions during a single campaign. Just keep adding names. Follow up on your signatures by mail or phone for fund-raising, recruitment, and turnout.

Everyone who signs a petition or writes a letter should be asked to volunteer on the spot. Letterwriters should be asked to contribute to postage expenses. Combine petition and letter writing drives with selling something such as buttons or T-shirts, and you can keep the petty cash box full.

Educational Meetings and Teach-Ins

An educational event should not be designed solely to inform people. It should also generate publicity and show strength. The measure of successful education is that it leads to action, and this should be built into the meeting. One speaker should present the organization's plans and tell the audience how it can become active. Everyone should leave the meeting with something specific to do.

You are under no moral obligation to represent the other side's position at an educational meeting. The only reason to hold a debate is if you think you can trounce an opposition spokesperson or win over his or her followers. And as with all events, whenever you get more than five people in a room, take a collection.

Civil Disobedience and Arrest

This tactic, like all tactics, should never be seen as an end in itself, but always as a way of moving forward a larger strategy. In the early part of this century, when the legendary Industrial Workers of the World (IWW or "Wobblies") packed the jails of the northwest during the free speech fights, they were not simply assuming a moral posture. Packing the jails in response to the arrest of their organizers really did create a crisis for many towns that had no place to put additional prisoners, and no budgets to cover all the extra food and guards. This tactic also brought publicity and built solidarity among the members, who might otherwise have been isolated and intimidated.

In the civil rights movement, civil disobedience often took the form of exercising legal rights that were recognized nationally but not locally. One part of the movement's strategy was to force the federal government to intervene and protect local activists.

When students protesting a tuition increase seized college buildings, the strategy was to force the governor either to increase funding or to risk violence by causing the arrest of students asking for no more than an affordable education. In part, the strategy worked because the governor had presidential ambitions and was very image conscious.

In the 1989 Pittston coal miners' strike, the miners sat on the road to stop the trucks from moving coal. They took over a breaker building to gain national media attention to the injustice of the use of scabs. Both acts of civil disobedience were part of a well-developed strategy to cut the company's profits and build national support for the miners' demands.

Civil disobedience works as part of a well thought out strategy. It is not an end in itself, as some romantics might suggest. In fact, in many organizing situations, civil disobedience frightens people and may hinder your ability to recruit members, and consequently your ability to win on an issue. You must carefully consider whether civil disobedience is an appropriate tactic for your group, given the situation and your constituency.

Civil disobedience can be effective when:

- Your constituency is comfortable with the tactic.
- Visible leadership roles are available for those who don't choose to participate directly in civil disobedience (many people can't because of family obligations).
- The tactic demonstrates power to the target. Civil disobedience shows your power by cutting into a company's profits or demonstrating the ability to do so (e.g., disrupting food service by sitting in at a Woolworth's counter). Civil disobedience shows power if large numbers of people participate or express support. Politicians realize that if people feel strongly enough about an issue to get arrested, they will feel strongly enough to vote against them on election day. Civil disobedience shows

power, for example, when physically handicapped people prevent workers from completing construction on an inaccessible building.

Legal Disruptive Tactics

With tactics such as strikes, picket lines, removing items from store shelves or withholding rent, the power actually lies in the implementation of the tactic itself. Such tactics are qualitatively different from those designed to imply an electoral threat by showing numbers. Picketing, when it succeeds in keeping people out of a place of business, goes beyond the symbolic to create financial loss. These forms of economic/consumer power, rather than political power, must be carefully focused on specific targets.

Boycotts

The popularity of the Montgomery bus boycott, the United Farm Workers' grape boycott, and Infact's boycott of Nestle make this one of the first tactics that many groups consider. In general, however, most national or international boycotts against products don't work. A careful analysis of the product and your ability to actually affect the company's profits is required. As corporations become more burdened by debt and operate closer to the brink, the requirements for a successful boycott may be lowered.

The requirements for a successful boycott are:

- A moral issue of national or international importance.
- A product that:
    —Everyone buys frequently.
    —Is easily identifiable by brand name.
    —Is non-essential, or even better, for

which there are competing brands or substitutes.

- A structure exists for getting information to a major portion of the market (beware of international markets).

It should be clear from the above that if someone suggests you boycott cement, there is a good chance that you are talking to a silly person.

Boycotts of local retail business are more manageable than are boycotts of products. Communities have successfully taken action, for example, against fast food franchises whose wrappers litter the streets.

A boycott, like a strike, is similar to a revolver with one bullet in the chamber. The threat of using it is more powerful than the weapon itself. But don't make the threat unless you are prepared to go through with it.

A Method for Planning Tactics

The strategy chart, discussed in Chapter 4, is as useful for planning individual tactics as it is for planning your overall campaign. To use it in this way, simply place the tactic (holding your own rally, for example) in the first column (Goals). The Organizational Considerations column becomes the budget and organizational goals for the event itself (organizational goals are always considered separately from issue goals). The Constituents column becomes the turnout plan for the event. The Targets column is used to identify the people with power at whom the event is aimed. Pay particular attention to secondary targets whom you may want to involve. The Tactics column then becomes a list of the things you will do at the event to show your own power, make the target uncomfortable, get media attention, and create an exciting activity.

Checklist for Tactics

All tactics must be considered within an overall strategy. Use this checklist to make sure that the tactics make sense given your strategy.

_____ Can you really do it? Do you have the needed people, time, and resources?

_____ Is it focused on either the primary or secondary target?

_____ Does it put real power behind a specific demand?

_____ Does it meet your organizational goals as well as your issue goals?

_____ Is it outside the experience of the target?

_____ Is it within the experience of your own members and are they comfortable with it?

_____ Do you have leaders experienced enough to do it?

_____ Will people enjoy working on it or participating in it?

_____ Will it play positively in the media?

Midwest Academy
225 West Ohio, Suite 250
Chicago, Illinois 60610

Using the Strategy Chart to Plan a Tactic
Newton Save Our Schools Rally

After using the strategy chart to plan an overall campaign, any tactic from the last column can become the basis of a new chart which is used to plan that particular tactic. The following chart demonstrates how this works.

Goals	Organizational Considerations	Constituents	Targets	Tactics
1. Long-Term Pass Fair Tax Plan.	1. Resources to Put In Budget = $300.00	Teachers organizations (200)*	1. Main Target Rep. Harry Hide	Hold rally outside Rep. Hide's office. Kids march up with symbols of discontinued school programs drawn on posters, e.g., basketball hoop, band instruments, theater masks, computers, microscopes. Each child calls to Hide through PA system to come down and save program. When he doesn't come, poster is thrown in big trash can labeled "Hide's Hope Chest."
2. Intermediate Force Rep. Hide to support the Fair Tax Plan.	$100.00 from coalition. Rest to be raised locally.	Black Issues Committee (50)	2. Secondary Targets	
	Fred: 3 weeks (half time first 2 weeks full time for 3rd week).	Fed. of Puerto Rican Home Town Associations (30)	School Board Members: Penny Black Allison Vandyke	
3. Short-Range Hold rally of 400 people.	Liz: 3 days	Kensington/Johnston Action Council (40)		Petitions taken up to Hide's office.
	Board member—Kim Max (lives in Newton)	CWA Local 72 (30)	Judge Thomas—strong school supporter	Collection taken.
	Newton office—2 phones	Newton Parents United (45)	Sarah Kendall—Hide contributor, big on education. Has millions $$$.	Speakers: Heads of major groups.
	2. What We Want to Get Out	Newton Real Estate Association (5)		Major push for press and TV.
	Closer relations with teachers organization and Newton PTAs.	Newton Civic Association (20)	Melvin Elvin—Rep. candidate for Supervisor. Wants ticket to win.	
	Build toward affiliation of Newton Black Issues Committee.	Individual parents and students (50)		Meet with all school board members. Ask them to attend the rally. Promise empty chairs on platform to those who don't show.
		Unorganized homeowners (40)		
		*These numbers are the turnout goals for each group.		

Midwest Academy
225 West Ohio, Suite 250
Chicago, Illinois 60610

6

Leaders lead people, but organizers organize organizations. Word play? Hardly! The role of an organizer is to build an organization that lasts.

An organizer who neglects the structure and rushes to organize people is like a taxi driver who picks up customers in his arms and carries them from place to place without the cab. Members love to have the organizer carry them because they are relieved of the burden of thinking about and maintaining an organization. Of course, most organizers do realize the importance of building a structure, but many make the equally serious error of thinking that the model, the architectural plan for the structure, is unimportant.

The Model Is a "What," Not a "How"

The concept of the model is often mistaken for the answer to the question, "How do we build whatever it is we are building"? But model isn't a "how" word, it is a "what" word. It is the answer to the question, "Exactly what are we building"? This is no small distinction. For any organization, there can be many ways to build successfully, but there is only one thing being built. Of course, what that thing is differs from group to group, and from time to time. We are not at all implying that there is only one correct kind of organization. Nonetheless, experience indicates that the range of successful possibilities is more limited than might be

The Model is a "What," Not a "How"

The Model is the Architecture of the Organization

The Model Must Be Clear and Consistent with Itself

Organizing Models:
The Underlying Structure of Organizations

imagined, particularly among groups that have survived more than ten years.

The Model Is the Architecture of the Organization

An organizational model or architectural plan is a conception of the essential skeleton of the organization. It is not necessarily the same as the organizational chart or by-laws, although they are related to the model. The organization's program, its formal leadership bodies, and its staffing pattern are all derived from its basic architecture.

The organizational model is put together from the following four elements:

The Function of the Organization

Is the function to win issues such as getting a stop sign put up, or saving the Great Lakes? Is it to pass legislation, to win elections, or to provide direct services? Is it to advocate, educate, or some combination of the above? Exactly what combination?

The Geographic Basis of the Organization

Is the organization based in a neighborhood, a housing development, or a political district such as a congressional district? Is it city-wide, county-wide, statewide, regional, or national? Obviously, the geography relates directly to the function.

The Basis of Membership

Do individual people join, or is it a coalition of organizations? If the members are individuals, are they organized into chapters or are they at-large? If it is a coalition, is it a formal coalition in which groups actually vote to join and put their names on the letterhead? If so, then those groups are the members. When a coalition is informal, and the officers or staff of other groups join its board as individuals, then the board is the membership. There are models in which a coalition builds an at-large base of individual members through its door-to-door canvassing. In yet another model, the staff is basically the membership. Once again, the point is not that any of these is better or worse than others, but simply that the basis of membership and the location of decision making power must be clear.

The Funding Base of the Organization

The funding base is included in the definition of the model because, more than any other single factor, it determines how the organization works and what it does. What percentage of the funds is actually raised by the members? How much comes from foundations or outside donors? Are there many foundations and donors which contribute, or only a few? Is there a field or phone canvass, and what percentage of the budget comes from it?

The Model Must Be Clear and Consistent with Itself

A model is clear when the board and the staff can see what it is that they are building. It is consistent with itself when all the pieces fit neatly into the basic concept and reinforce each other. None should appear to have been tacked on like tail fins on a Volkswagen Beetle. The best way to illustrate this point is with case histories that are actual composites of our own experience.

The Case of the Ambiguous Tenant Organization

A housing organization was unclear about the difference between providing services to tenants and organizing them. The staff thus did a little of both, considering them to be the same thing.

A man from a building to which an organizer had been assigned, came into the office. After being interviewed about his problem, he was advised to go to Legal Assistance and get a lawyer. The man said, "That's too much hassle," and he left. The organizer remarked, "See, that's why we can't ever get anything going in the building, nobody cares enough to do anything." The organizer didn't make the distinction between an individual problem requiring a lawyer, and a building-wide issue that could be addressed by organizing. More to the point, the organization as a whole made no such distinction because, in its underlying model, its function was neither clearly service nor clearly organizing. As long as it was "housing," they did it.

Had there been a clear *organizing* model, the staff member would not have made a referral. Instead, she would have gone back to the building with the man, talked to the other tenants, and seen who had the same problem. Even if the problem was an individual matter such as non-payment of rent, if many other people were also behind, the tenants might have tried to negotiate a payment plan in exchange for improved conditions. If legal action to improve building services was required, the action should have been brought by all the tenants, not one individual. If all else failed, then helping the man to get a lawyer would have been appropriate.

On the other hand, if the organization had a clear *service* model, not an organizing model, then the staff should have phoned Legal Assistance at once, explained the man's case, had the man talk about the case over the phone,

and made an appointment for him. Perhaps someone would even have driven him there.

Unfortunately, because the staff was unclear about what was being built, the man's request for help was handled inappropriately. The result was neither service nor organizing.

The Case of the Superfluous Office

A national disarmament organization, based on a model of individual membership in local chapters, had as its major function the passage of national legislation. This required building chapters to lobby in key congressional districts.

The organization decided to set up a regional office with organizing staff to service a major metropolitan area in which it had a very large membership. It thought that the members would be enthusiastic about the office, and would easily raise the money for it. As it turned out, the members never fully saw what purpose the office served, and didn't support it.

While far from a clear-cut situation, a basic problem emerged here because there really was no clear role for a regional office. The efforts of the chapters were focused on the congressional districts in which they were located. But because a region isn't a political district of any kind, there was no regional political target. Without a target, there was no regional program in which all the chapters could participate together. Without a program, the only role for regional staff was to help the individual chapters in their own congressional districts. Rightly or wrongly (probably wrongly), the chapters didn't feel that they needed "outside" help, and declined to raise the money to pay for it. Had a critical vote been coming up in the U.S. Senate, they would have given money for a statewide campaign office, but they couldn't see the logic of a regional office.

This is a very typical situation in which the model and the program do not coincide. In order for them to coincide, some meaningful program must exist at each geographic level of organizational structure, be it a neighborhood, district, city, region, county, or state. In direct action organizing, where the program is usually to win something, the structure can only exist at geographic levels where there is actually something to be won, and someone to win it from. For example, environmental groups from a number of areas could form a regional organization, the target of which was a regional office of the Environmental Protection Agency, but there was no regional target for the disarmament group.

The Case of the Statewide Coalition with Local Chapters

A statewide citizen organization had a formal coalition membership model. That is, organizations voted to join the coalition, and placed one of their officers on the coalition's board. Its function was to pass legislation and to elect (through a PAC) legislators who would support its program.

After a number of years, the board voted to set up several community chapters, which were to work on local neighborhood issues. On the surface, little appeared to have changed; however, a second organization with a different model had been created within the first.

Eventually, a number of problems with the dual structure became apparent. Because the chapters dealt with very local issues, they neither strengthened nor drew strength from the statewide campaigns. Had the chapter's turf conformed to legislative districts, and had the chapter members been organized to pressure their legislators for the organization's program, it might have been a better fit.

The local leaders, whom the organizers tried to involve, were naturally suspicious. They saw resources coming in, but had little interest in the statewide issues. They had been working on local issues all along, and didn't want to be diverted to someone else's agenda. Their attitude was to take what they could get from the state organization, but to keep their distance from it. The organizing staff was drawn into the local activity, which took them away from the statewide efforts. Much of the staff's work amounted to a subsidy to neighborhood groups, but when the coalition tried to raise funds for its community work, it found itself in competition with local organizations, and was resented for it.

The whole process threatened the existence of the statewide coalition, which lacked resources to carry out two levels of organization. In time, the original coalition could have drifted apart as a result of being understaffed. It might then have shifted from a legislative coalition to

being an agency that funded and serviced community groups. Launching the local chapters was a classic case of an activity that was at odds with the original model.

The Case of the Coalition That Started a Coalition

A statewide citizen organization had an informal coalition model. That is, leaders of other organizations sat on its board, but their groups did not formally vote to join the coalition. The coalition's function was passing legislation.

When funding became available for a state Family Leave Act campaign, a decision was made to set up a new coalition just for that issue. The hope was that groups not now a part of the state organization would join the campaign through this new structure. The money was channeled through the state organization, and some of its staff members were assigned to the new group, which was called the Family Coalition.

The first task of these staff people was to recruit some of the state organization's own board members to the board of the new Family Coalition. Next, they recruited additional Family Coalition board members from among the leaders of other organizations interested in the issue. The Family Coalition then held media events, published studies, and began lobbying in its own name. It was a big success. Although the state organization had started, raised funds for, and staffed the Family Coalition, it was listed on the letterhead as just another of 17 member groups. Before long, the board of the Family Coalition asked the organizers if they could apply for foundation grants independently, so that funds would no longer come through the state organization. They said they wanted to hire their own staff and go their own way.

When the state organization's leadership started the Family Coalition, they thought they were simply creating another program and another campaign. But, by not respecting the integrity of its model, the state organization had set up another coalition that could easily become a competitor. Their model could not accommodate a coalition within a coalition. An organizational model might be designed for that purpose. Indeed occasionally, one even comes across coalitions of coalitions. But here, no structural provision was made to tie the new coalition into the already existing one. Because the board created a free floating, self-governing program, not anchored into the underlying structure, a typical thing happened. The program took on a life of its own. It happens every time. Committees, locals, chapters, regions, temporary coalitions, and special programs all tend toward having an independent existence. Even field offices that are not closely supervised do this.

It is generally a bad idea to set up any structure that is not integral to your organizing model. The same principle applies to setting up organizations that you intend, some day, to absorb or merge into your own group. If such organizations have real people in them, they will develop their own identities, and will resist change. People who would readily have joined you had they been asked to do so in the first place, will become suspicious and hostile if, after setting up an independent group, you then suggest a merger. Not surprisingly, the fact that you raised the money for the independent group and staffed it only deepens their resentment.

The Case of the Inconsistent Board

A community-based organization referred to itself as an alliance of organizations and service agencies dealing with poor people. Its model was a very, very informal coalition.

As the group expanded, it added to the board individuals who were active in its programs, but who did not come from any organization. It also kept on the board people who had once represented organizations, but who were no longer connected with those groups. Everything went well enough until the organization received a very large grant. The board at once fell to fighting over how and where the money would be spent. In the process, board members from real organizations found themselves being out voted by people representing no one but themselves. They complained that they had joined an alliance of *organizations,* and now the rules were changed. The alliance didn't last a moment longer than the money did, then it self-destructed.

This organization was unclear about the basis of its membership, which is one aspect of the model. A group is either an organization of

individuals, or an organization of organizations. Trying to be both, a mixed model, can create problems in some kinds of organizations. Others, particularly service agencies, are well served by boards composed of people from allied groups, funders, and prominent individuals.

Mixed boards can work well until a crunch comes. Then, be the conflict over program, finances, or politics, different types of members are likely to question the legitimacy of decisions made by others. Structure matters most when the chips are down and the question is who has the votes.

Another difficulty in mixing individuals with group representatives on the board of a coalition is that they come with different viewpoints and are subject to different pressures. For example, an individual board member may have nothing to lose by attacking the mayor or taking on an unpopular issue, but an organizational board member may fear losing city funding or dividing the membership of the group he or she represents. Similarly, an organizational member may want the coalition to target someone with whom an individual board member happens to have an important business relationship. Of course, the same problems can and do occur on boards with either all individual or all organizational members, but they are less likely to get out of hand when all voting members have the same institutional relationship to the coalition.

Concluding Thoughts

Each of these cases has been presented to emphasize flaws in the conception of the model. In day-to-day organizing, such flaws may not be so obvious. Internal organizational problems can come disguised in the form of personality conflicts, feuding between member organizations, financial trouble, debates over philosophy, political rifts, and criticism of the director. It is the role of the organizer to look past the surface problems, no matter how serious, and determine if they have roots in a discordant model.

Model-related problems are present in every organization. Like the flu, they lurk about looking for a chance to strike. Unlike the flu, they are often disguised as something else. For example, staff members will complain that the director does not spend enough time with them, and therefore they don't understand what they are supposed to be *doing*. Frequently, what they are really saying is that they don't understand what they are supposed to be *building*. They sense that the model isn't clear, even though they may not say it that way. When the model isn't clear, no amount of time with a director can compensate for it.

An unclear model results in day-to-day organizing tasks becoming complicated policy matters instead of being part of a repeatable plan. If, for example, there is a clear individual membership chapter model, then it is *always* the elected leadership of the chapter who speak at the local press conference, and everyone knows it. But if the group has some individual members, some institutional members, some people with a real base in the community and others with none, a member of the clergy to whom everyone defers, a candidate for city council, and a college professor who really knows the issue, then who speaks at the press conference? The answer differs according to the day of the week, and no one is ever happy with it. No wonder the staff never seem to get enough direction, and the director never has enough time. When the model is not clear, very little else will be clear.

Board members will complain that there is not enough communication, and they no longer know what is going on in the organization. Often they are right, but sometimes it is a symptom of the program having moved away from the basic model so that leadership is less directly involved. This often occurs in a coalition where the program is supposed to be carried out through the affiliates, but the staff have gone off and started some other project involving different people, usually in response to a funding opportunity. Once that happens, increased communication will seldom bring the affiliates closer to a program that isn't theirs. People hear what they want to hear. No matter how much an organization communicates with affiliates or board members, if the communication isn't about something they are interested in, they won't hear it. Then they will complain that there isn't enough communication. The program must be brought back in line with the model—that is, with the way the organization was set up to operate.

Any given model affects the organization's program. It makes some types of campaigns easier to win, and some harder. It encourages the participation of some groups while discouraging others. It either enhances or diminishes the political power of the organization. It advances certain types of fund raising, and holds back others.

There are organizers who say that they have no model, want no model, and need no model. They are wrong. There is always a model! If you don't create it, it evolves on its own, often influenced by funding. It will always operate just as the force of gravity always operates, even upon those who believe that they have transcended it. Organizers, you have the choice: learn to understand and use the concept of model, or be blindly led by it.

7

An action is a tactic. In organizing, the word "action" has a special meaning for reasons that have been lost to history. While regular people might spring into action, be moved to action, or rent a video tape listed under "Action-Adventure," organizers "*do* an action." Worse still, we do it *on* someone. Don't blame the Midwest Academy, we didn't invent this language. We are merely reluctant to change it, so great is the burden of tradition.

As with other tactics, actions come at the end of the strategy chart. Actions are one of the things that the people listed in the constituency column do to the people listed in the target column. As explained in the chapter on strategy, an action involves a group of people confronting the individual who has the power to give them what they want, and making specific demands. They expect to have their demands met on the spot, and with proper planning, they do.

No other tactic does as much to win short- and medium-range demands, or to build the organization. In mere days, the use of actions can cut through months, and sometimes years, of bureaucratic red tape. More important is the impact on the participants. People come away with a heightened sense of their own power and dignity, while their opponents are made to appear smaller and more vulnerable. At the same time, relationships of power are clarified because problems that might have been attributed to misunderstanding or lack of communication are seen sharply for what they really are—the conflicting interests of public good against private greed. In the process,

Why Actions Work

When to Use Actions

Action Planning

Checklist for Planning an Action

Designing Actions

loyalty to the organization is built up because people see it actually working for them, and realize that their participation is essential to its success.

Why Actions Work

The principle of this tactic is deceptively simple and direct. You ask for something, and more often than not, you get it. It's like magic and you say, "Why didn't we do this months ago"? The answer is that it probably wouldn't have worked months ago because you hadn't built up your organized strength, nor had you made the necessary strategic calculations.

The real reason that actions work arises from a set of calculations about the relationship between your group and the target. It can best be described, from the target's point of view, as a cost-benefit analysis. The target, the person who can give you what you want, considers the damage you can cause, and then compares the cost of what you want to the benefit he or she gets from giving it to you.

The damage you can cause might be that pressure from your organization results in a loss of votes, or the target is fired because things got out of control, or the target's business loses customers, or an investigation is launched that discovers wrongdoing. When you are able to make anything like this happen, there is a clear and measurable benefit to the target in giving you what you want and getting rid of you.

What you want, however, also has a cost. It might be a financial cost like the expense of removing asbestos from a school, cleaning up a toxic dump, or providing child care. It might be a loss of campaign contributions from people who oppose your issue. It might cost credibility when giving in means admitting a mistake was made. The target usually comes out of this wishing that he or she had never done to you whatever it was that caused you to react in this way, but the target must also get something positive out of reaching an agreement with you. If you don't plan on giving anything, then don't use this tactic.

Your strategy should be to raise the level of damage you can cause to the target, so that the benefit of having you go away happy is greater than the cost of what you are asking for. The whole process is a bit like finding a way to stand on someone's foot until they pay you to leave.

When To Use Actions

Tactics are rated from weak to strong according to how much pressure they put on the target. Of course, the more pressure the tactic applies, the more powerful the organization using it must be.

An action is a low- to medium-power tactic. It has more power than a few hours of picketing a building, but less power than a strike or a boycott. It is most useful in the opening phases of a campaign, when you need to assemble a core group and get it moving quickly. An action can be done with fewer than fifteen people, but more is better. Successful actions are great organization builders because after the first one, the members will want to do more, and they will see the need to bring larger numbers of people. Actions are also fun.

Actions are a good measure of the organization's ability to turn out people and they test the ability of the leadership. This gives the members a criterion for judging leaders other than by how well they speak at meetings. In addition, publicity from actions will bring in some new recruits. The expectation should be that for a period of months, each action will be a little larger than the one preceding it, as you take on more important targets. Actions are used to build toward large turnout events of your own, such as public hearings or accountability sessions.

One of the reasons that actions work is that they take the organization outside established channels for getting things done, and move it to terrain where officials are less sure of how to handle the situation. It is always wise to make the effort of going through the proper channels first. Send letters, fill out forms, file formal complaints, and generally do whatever is necessary to establish that you tried the "normal" way first, and it didn't work. If this step is skipped, many members may feel that the action is not appropriate, or is the wrong way to go about it. Most people want to give the other person the benefit of the doubt.

The strategy chart is an excellent tool for planning a single action as well as a whole campaign. Just plug in the information that is relevant to this particular activity. Here are some considerations for each column of the chart.

Action Planning

Goals (Demands)

Success in formulating demands depends on understanding the power relationships involved. This means not only accurately assessing the strength of your forces, but also understanding the self-interest of the other side. Knowing what the cost of a citizen victory will be to the other side and who will have to pay it brings you to an estimation of the amount of opposition that your organization will receive. This, in turn, is the basis for deciding what demands you will make.

Every increase in the cost of the organization's demands must be matched by a corresponding increase in the organization's power.

Because the whole process is logical, there is an underlying assumption that the target is rational and will act in her self-interest. If the target is not a rational person or reacts to pressure by stonewalling, or if the citizens make it clear that their negative view of the target will never improve no matter what, then this tactic is short circuited and will probably not work. A short-circuited action can have some advantages, however. After dealing with a target over a period of time, you may learn what makes that person pop, that is, go berserk or do inappropriate things in public. Such a display of odd behavior can discredit a public official, but be sure that you have another target to move on to, and remember that officials are often trying to do the same thing to you.

Demands are ranked according to whether they are main demands or fallback demands. A fallback demand means asking for something that is useful, but less than you wanted. Often, procedural ("hold hearings on cleaning up the dump") and information ("release your study on dump site hazards") demands are used as fallbacks. Every action should have one main, or substantive ("clean up the dump"), demand and several fallbacks. It is part of the role of the spokesperson to decide when to switch from one to the other.

The information demand is the easiest to win, and is a good type of demand for your first action. In later actions, it would probably be a fallback. Your final fallback demand, if you got nothing else, should always be a commitment to another meeting. This gives you an opportunity to regroup and increase your strength.

Any agreement that is reached should include these specifics:

- When it will be done.
- How much will be done.
- Who will do it.
- What is the review process if it isn't done, or is done improperly.

In addition, longer-term changes can be won and included in the agreement. Some are administrative: "inspections must be done every six months forever." Others involve a structural reform that increases citizen power: "a permanent citizen oversight board will be established."

Organizational Considerations

An action, like every other event, should have its own budget and staff assigned to it. Because the recruitment is done by word of mouth and by phone, the biggest expense will usually be staff time.

In addition to victory on the issue, the action will strengthen the organization if you build that into the plan. Actions are most useful for leadership development. Speaking to the target or the press develops leadership skills, and the planning process teaches strategy as well. As a rule, speaking roles should be awarded to those who bring out the most people. The long-term result will be a leadership composed of people who actually have a base, rather than people who merely speak well. The ability to mobilize people, be it six friends or stewards from a union local, is the most important criterion for leadership in a citizens' organization.

As with other events, the organizer should have an idea of who potential leaders are, and build action roles around them. During the planning process, the group should set modest goals for the number of leaders it would like to see gain experience, as well as for the number of new people who ought to be recruited from the membership.

Constituency (Turnout)

The people who come to an action should be active members of your organization or coalition. Because the event needs to be tightly controlled and run, this is not the time to advertise. Participants should be representative of all of the different types of people who are affected by the problem and will benefit from the solution. If your organization is a coalition, the heads of member groups should be clearly visible at the action.

If yours is an individual membership organization, consider bringing people who are influential in the community, such as clergy, political supporters, or the heads of major civic organizations or unions. Always be sure to explain the nature of the action to them first. No one should be surprised by unusual tactics. People who are, sometimes start apologizing to the target, or criticizing the organization.

If you invite sympathetic office holders to join you, figure out a way that they will get recognition in the media because what elected officials want most is publicity. Discuss it with them in advance. If you don't, they often try to grab the spokesperson role (who should always be a leader of your own group) the moment a TV camera shows up.

The Target (Decision Maker)

The target is always a person who has the power to give you what you want. In real life, there are often several such people. In public housing, a building manager could order repairs, as could someone at the housing authority or a higher-up at the federal level. In this case, the choice of target is usually made according to what is most convenient for the group, and what location will favor the strongest turnout. People usually want to stay closer to home in their own neighborhood; as the group gains experience, it becomes an adventure to go to city hall, the capitol, or some agency's regional headquarters.

At any action, there should only be one target because for them, as for us, there is safety in numbers. The one exception is if at several previous actions, the targets all denied responsibility, and pointed to some other official. Then, getting them all in the same room can end buck passing.

In organizing there are two types of targets, "primary" and "secondary." The primary target, such as the mayor, can give you what you want, but you may not have enough power to challenge him or her directly. The secondary target is a person who can't deliver what you want, but who can pressure the main target better than you can, and over whom you have more power, such as the local ward leader or a council member. Actions are most often used against secondary targets to secure their help in pressuring the main target. "We have come to ask you to pick up the phone right now, and tell the Mayor that next November your party is going to have a revolt on its hands in this district, unless he sets up a meeting this week to hear our complaints." (The fallback demand in this case is, "Would you send a letter to the Mayor making this point, and send a copy to us?")

Tactics

There are two requirements for every action:

- It must be *fun*.
- It must demonstrate real *power*.

Tactics are designed to accomplish these two goals. Wait a minute! You said that an action is a tactic. Can a tactic have tactics? Can a flea have fleas? Yes, and not only that, but a tactic can have a strategy. An action is a tactic in a larger campaign, but a mini-strategy is needed to carry out each tactic. As a particular tactic becomes your goal for the day, the steps to carrying it out become the tactics for the day.

Tactics for use in actions fall into three categories:

Tactics Aimed at the Target and that Show Your Power. These include presenting petitions, letters, voter registration forms, and statements of support from important people in the community. Other power tactics include demonstrating the size of your organization by large turnout, or showing the media-worthy nature of the issue by using clever visual props. Controlling the agenda and setting the tone of the meeting demonstrate the internal strength of your group.

Tactics Aimed at Raising the Morale of Your Own Members. These include singing or chanting, standing rather than sitting, displaying signs or funny props and, when appropriate, displaying anger at the target.

Tactics Aimed at Getting Media Coverage. Understanding the self-interest of the media is important in getting coverage. Editors wants a short punchy event in which every-day people, who are like their own audience, do something visually interesting. In other words, you gotta have a gimmick. This doesn't always have to be funny. A dramatic way of showing the seriousness of the problem or the toll it is taking on its victims is very effective.

A song, chant, emotional speech, or an animal will get covered where someone just talking wouldn't. Challenging the target to actually "drink this cup of polluted water," will get covered, where just saying "I'll bet you don't drink the water at home," wouldn't.

Bringing a seven-foot thermometer showing the rising anger of the community as the action progresses will get covered, where saying "People are really hot about this," wouldn't. Because the media usually dislike mentioning the names of citizen organizations, be sure that yours is prominently displayed on a large sign with someone assigned to hold it where the camera can't avoid including it in the scene.

Tactics give you a small edge during the action, but gimmicks don't win it for you. You win because of your power, based on the size of your support. If you lose, it is because you either didn't have the power, or failed to show it. Perhaps your costume was lost on the way to the action, and when the spokesperson said, "It was so cold without any heat that the cat froze," you got up looking frozen, but not at all like a cat. The lost costume was not the reason you failed to win and get the heat turned on. Winning does not depend on your degree of resemblance to any particular species.

The tone of the action must be appropriate to your community and constituency. People in small towns are often much more polite to the target than are city dwellers. The key factor is that everyone must feel comfortable about what occurs.

Action Planning Reminders

Stay Within the Experience of Your Group. Don't confuse loudness, rudeness or vulgarity with power. Don't suggest that, as a sign of contempt, your spokesperson sit at the target's desk and eat the target's lunch, unless there is some purpose to it. (If your issue is about hunger and homelessness, you actually might make a point this way, if everyone will go along and understand why it is being done.) Never make your own people feel uncomfortable at an action.

Try to Get Outside the Experience of the Target. The fact that you have come in person and are no longer just sending letters is a good start. Losing control of a meeting is usually outside the target's experience, but so is seeing confident, articulate, and knowledgeable people who will not be intimidated. If the action occurs on your own turf all the better; your neighborhood is often outside the target's experience. Media that respond to you, not to the target, is also outside the target's experience, as is showing up with a group at the target's home. Publicizing that the law has not been followed, or that the job someone is paid to do is not being done, is often, but not always, outside the target's experience.

It Is Better to Make an Appointment to See the Target, Than to Hope for a Surprise Encounter. If you hope for a surprise encounter, the person may not be there and your group will feel dumb and get mad at you.

Case the Joint. Organizers should look over the building, and make a floor plan. Check the location of the target's office as well as elevators, stairs, bathrooms, pay telephones, and parking/transit facilities. Is it accessible for disabled members?

Hold a Dress Rehearsal for Participants. You play the role of the target. Keep the action short (about 20 minutes, sometimes less). Remember that an action is not a negotiation. Don't attempt to educate the target about why you are morally right (although you really are). Logic is rarely a substitute for power.

There Is Only One Spokesperson in an Action. That person may call on a small number of others to present specific information. Have the group decide beforehand on the one or two people authorized to make decisions during the action. Inform everyone of this. If your organization believes in decision making by

consensus, or that everyone has the right to say anything at any time, forget about doing actions until the members are willing to delegate responsibility during the action to one or two trusted leaders.

Ask People to Come to the Action Fifteen Minutes Early. Have a quick briefing meeting outside the building.

If Media Are Wanted (They Aren't Always), Send a Press Release a Week Ahead of Time. Include a "notice of photo opportunity" highlighting your gimmick ("Councilman Jones will be presented with a three-foot apple symbolizing his inability to resist the temptation of commercial development"). Phone all assignment editors (city desks, day books) the night before. Hold the action in the morning and at a place convenient to the media if you have a choice. Assign someone to speak with the press and provide a press release describing what you are doing and why.

Keep Your Demands Clear and Simple. Be ready with both main demands and fallback demands. Have a note taker write down the positive and negative responses. Try to get any agreement signed.

At the end, use the notes to summarize what has been agreed to. Hold a short debriefing outside after the action to fill in everyone who couldn't hear, take attendance, thank people, and announce the next event.

Checklist for Planning an Action

_____ Will your action be both fun and based on real power?

_____ Is everyone in your group comfortable with the plan? (Is it within the experience of your group?)

_____ Will the plan be outside the experience of the target? Are you going outside the "official channels?"

_____ Are your demands clear and simple?

_____ Do you have several fallback demands?

_____ Do you have an appointment?

_____ Have you scouted the building and made a floorplan? Do you know where to find:

      _____ Elevator and stairs
      _____ Bathrooms
      _____ Payphone
      _____ Parking or nearest transit stops
      _____ The target's office.

_____ Can the site accommodate disabled members?

_____ Has the group selected who will present information at the action? Are people prepared for their roles?

_____ Has the group selected its spokesperson for the action?

_____ Have you held a dress rehearsal for the spokesperson and the participants?

_____ Have you calculated how you will demonstrate your power? Do you plan to have symbols with you (letters, petitions)?

_____ Is there a good turnout plan for the action, including last-minute reminder phone calls?

_____ If you want the media, have they been notified? Have you:

      _____ Sent a release, including a notice of your photo opportunity and highlighting your gimmick, a week ahead of time?
      _____ Called the daybook a week ahead of time?
      _____ Called assignment editors the day before the action?
      _____ Prepared a release for distribution on the day of the action?
      _____ Assigned someone to talk with the media at the action itself? (Your spokesperson may be busy.)

_____ Have you selected someone to take notes during the action and write the confirmation letter for sending to the target?

_____ Do you know who will debrief the action with participants and where the debriefing will occur?

The Midwest Academy
225 West Ohio, Suite 250, Chicago, Illinois 60610

PART II
Organizing Skills

8

An accountability session is a tactic. On the strategy chart, it is listed in the last column with other tactics that are part of the overall plan.

An accountability session is a large community meeting at which an elected official, or sometimes a high-level public administrator (the target), is held accountable to the community. Because accountability sessions ultimately rely on political pressure, they are rarely used against corporate targets. They may, however, be used to force regulators to hold corporations accountable. At the session, very specific demands are made about such things as legislation, funding, code enforcement, or community services, and your organization(s) expects a positive response on the spot.

An accountability session is a high power tactic. It is usually used toward the end of an issue campaign after a great deal of strength has been built up. It requires the ability to turn out hundreds of people, and a sophisticated leadership that can run the meeting and put heat on the target.

An accountability session is not simply a community "speak out" or legislator's town meeting, although the community does speak out and the official is invited to speak briefly. It is a much more rehearsed and controlled event, but the real difference is that it is a big show of organizational power.

Power is always a relative term. An assessment of how much power your group has is the starting point for planning an accountability session. Begin with an analysis of

Holding Accountability Sessions

the target, the person who can give you what you want. (To avoid such modern literary ambiguities as "he/she" we will refer to the target as "she," although more often than not, it will be a man.) Ask such questions as: What is her political strength? How close was the last primary and general election? Was it a landslide or a cliff hanger? What is her ability to raise campaign money, and has she a big debt? Is she up for reelection in three weeks or three years? Is there an opponent in the wings, or is she considered unbeatable? Has she ambitions for higher office?

If the target is a non-elected official, the task of estimating power is harder. It is approached on two levels. First, what is the person's career self-interest? No official wants to be publicly embarrassed. All want to appear to have good relations with the community and to be keeping things under control. Some are taking bribes, or drugs, giving jobs to friends, or are generally incompetent. Such people don't want to draw attention to themselves, and have an interest in keeping everything nice and quiet.

Second, what are the person's political connections? All appointed public officials are ultimately answerable to some elected person, and part of their job is to protect that person from criticism. An accountability session can be used to embarrass the elected employer of the appointed official, or to hold the elected official responsible for the actions of a civil servant.

Third, What are the person's business and social connections? Where has she worked?

Where does her spouse work? Is she old money or new money? Knowing these things will often suggest secondary targets and additional pressure points.

Having established this background reading of the target's power and susceptibility to pressure, it is time to gauge the strength of your organization in relation to it. If you are a turf-based group, look at the political map and see how much of your territory is really in her district. If you are a coalition, you should know roughly how many of the individual members of the member organizations live in the district. (A look at the zip codes of member organizations' mailing lists will give you a rough idea of this.) Now ask how important are your members to her? Did they vote for her? Might they? If all of your people backed the other candidate or party and will probably do so again, then it won't mean a whole lot when you threaten not to vote for her. You will have to broaden your base. On the other hand, if you represent a strong body of support for her, which will appear to be going soft during the session, you are in a very good position. If some of her campaign contributors are in your group, all the better. Seat them in the front row. A potential opponent or two working the crowd is a nice touch as well.

Having asked "Do we have any power over this person?" and having decided that you do, test it out by sending an invitation. What is the response? Did a high-level staff person get back to you at once, or was it an assistant making a call after a few weeks? Did you get a firm commitment, or was it left a bit vague until closer to the date? Schedulers rarely say, "Well, if nothing more important comes up, she'll be there"; but you can tell it from the tone of voice. Later, when you start to frame your demands, return to this question of power and begin by asking, "Why did she accept the invitation in the first place? What is she afraid of?" All of this supposes that eventually you did get a commitment *in writing* that she would come. Don't start organizing such an event without one.

If you are refused the meeting, it is probably a good thing because it shows that you didn't have the power to win in the first place. A series of build-up tactics are now needed to increase your strength and visibility in order to get the official to come to the meeting. These might include press hits or letter writing drives. Move up to holding your own hearing, or doing actions against the main target or secondary targets, at which you ask for their presence at the accountability session.

Demands: The Heart of the Matter

The art of figuring out what you can ask for takes some practice. Demands relate to column one of the strategy chart. They are the short-term issue goals for this event. As with actions, you are setting up an equation in which you ask for something that has a monetary or political cost to the target. If the target gives it to you, she is rewarded with the valuable good will of the community or organization (at least until the next time). If she doesn't give it to you, the bad feeling and adverse publicity will cost her more than giving you what you wanted in the first place. If this last condition isn't true, you are unlikely to get what you want.

The specifics of the demands also determine in part who will come to the accountability session. A community group that was asking for greater police protection increased turnout by extending its demands to include an adjoining neighborhood. This allowed the group to make alliances with civic associations in that area. Of course, each time the stakes are raised, the cost of what you are asking for goes up as well, and so does the amount of power required to win it.

An added complication is that the more demands you have and the more diverse items they cover, the greater the danger of becoming whipsawed or divided. Once the group feels that it got part of what it wanted, it is harder to get people to keep up the pressure for the rest. Worse, the target can divide the community by offering more police protection in one place and a study of the need for it in the other place. The target may tell you that she will support one piece of legislation you are trying to win but not another, or even that she will work for one section of your bill but not all of it. While your active members may see through such ploys, others might not, and believe that they should take whatever they can get. Indeed, organizations often have to make some close judgment calls in such cases.

The goal of an accountability session is to win. When you win, the organization grows. People see results. If you don't win anything folks become discouraged, and consider it all to have been a waste of time. In the future they won't work as hard for the organization, give as much money, or be there for the next fight.

Because accountability sessions need to end with a win, there must be at least one demand that you are quite sure you will get. You don't have to call attention to the fact that this is the bottom line. You can even try to hide it among more ambitious proposals, but it has to be there. What this means, however, is that just as there is pressure on the target to settle with you, there is also some need for you to settle with her.

Demands fall into two broad categories, substantive and procedural. Substantive means actually getting something of substance, like five more patrol cars. Procedural involves such things as getting a bill out of committee, a public hearing, or a study. This distinction is a useful basis for analyzing your demands. Main demands are usually substantive, and fallback demands, which are made after a main demand is refused, are often procedural. Another approach to fallback demands is simply to ask for less. "Well, if you won't give us five patrol cars by May, how about three by August?" Or you can mix and match. "You can't authorize three by August either? Our members will find this disregard for their safety very disappointing. Will your City Council committee come to our community and hold an official hearing?" This fallback, a public hearing, is really a way to keep the issue alive and buy time to build up your campaign. To the target it says, "You shouldn't have to take all the heat alone, bring those other turkeys around for a roasting." You each gain something.

In general, you should have three or four of each type of demand. Each fallback is attached to a main demand, and is made by the same person making the main demand. Also, have a few escalation demands ready in case you get what you want too easily. If you did, it is a sign that you didn't ask for enough. Escalation demands should not be simply numerical increases in what you first asked for. "We are very happy that you agreed to five cars, how about nine?" That is too obvious and is considered very bad form.

These, then, are the factors that go into the demands equation. You will have to figure out how to solve the equation on a case-by-case basis. We wish there were a magic formula for it. If you hear of one, write to us at once.

Planning

The key to holding a successful accountability meeting is planning. Try to allow six to eight weeks to prepare.

Organize a Planning Committee. Your organization's key leaders should be on it.

Start with a Discussion of Organizational Considerations. This corresponds to the second column of the strategy chart. Decide on the resources going into the accountability session, as well as what non-issue related things your group wants to get out of it. For example, how many more members? How many new leaders? Expand into which new areas? Bring in which new affiliates? Spend how much money on this event? Raise how much money? Show a profit of how much?

Decide on Demands. Agree on what your demands will be. You should have a list of at least three, usually substantive, main demands, a list of escalation demands, and some fallback demands, which are usually procedural.

Propose Dates. Contact the target with as many dates as possible, so that she can't say, "I'd love to, but I can't then." For example, tell the target

that any time in the last two weeks of May is fine, although you would prefer a Tuesday evening-or whatever the case may be. If the date has been set by phone, confirm it with a letter and keep copies.

Make a Turnout, Press, and Publicity Plan. This corresponds to the Constituency column in the strategy chart. Ask who cares about this issue and how you can reach them. Are they organized in any way? Can we contact them through unions, churches, or civic associations? Who has mailing lists? Are there gathering points such as rush-hour bus stops or shopping malls? The main part of the plan consists of your own volunteers contacting your members individually. The press and publicity aspects deal with both advance publicity and getting the press to the meeting.

Develop an Agenda. Developing the agenda is very political. Plan the agenda to show your power by choosing the right people to speak. You will have to strike some balance among the people who are needed to show power, people who are allies (particularly other elected officials) wanting visibility, and general community members. The total time for this event, and most meetings, should be limited to two hours at the most. A sample agenda is presented in the next section.

Plan the Logistics and Spirit of the Event. These are essentially tactics that you use at the accountability session to show more power, and to make the group more cohesive. They relate to column five of the strategy chart, and include everything from decorating the hall with posters to presenting petitions, singing, or other dramatic representations of the issue.

Rehearse. People speaking or presenting demands should all rehearse or roleplay beforehand.

Hold the meeting. Whew!

Follow Up. If the meeting was a success but media were not present, publicize the results yourself. In some cases you may want to do this jointly with the target. It gives the target some credit while locking her into the agreement publicly. If there is not a public statement, then immediately after the meeting send a letter to the target restating what has been agreed to.

Thank Everyone and Celebrate. Send personal thank you notes to everyone who helped in the planning and implementation of the meeting. Be sure to thank the legislator for coming. The same letter should again confirm the agreement that was reached, and review implementation steps. Find a way to celebrate with the key people.

Evaluate. Call a meeting of the planning committee to review the original plan, and then evaluate how it was carried out. This is most valuable for building leadership. Pay particular attention to your turnout plan. Check attendance sheets (sign in sheets) from the event against lists of people who said they would come. Did individuals and other organizations produce the people they were committed to bring? Did people come off the street in response to leaflets, posters or advance media coverage?

Sample Agenda

An accountability session is a tightly controlled meeting, with a clear purpose and clear demands that are formally conveyed to the target. Below is a sample agenda.

Welcome and Purpose: 5-10 Minutes

The moderator welcomes everyone to the meeting with a brief talk about the importance of the issue and the goals for the evening. This sets the spirit of the meeting and starts applause. The audience is reminded not to ask the target questions. "Representative Smith has two years to tell us what she thinks, but we have only two hours to tell her what we think, so please don't ask her questions or bring up other subjects. She has a few minutes on the agenda to say what is on her mind after she responds to our requests."

Opening Prayer or Song: 5 Minutes

In many community meetings, a local priest, minister, or rabbi leads an opening prayer, or else there is a patriotic observance. In other communities, a song about the issue is

appropriate. It's nice to have some sort of "opening." The decision on how to open should reflect the community's customs, not the organizer's biases.

Community Residents Speak: 45-60 Minutes

Community residents or coalition members speak about why they want the target to respond in a certain fashion. The presentations are pre-arranged, but they can be interspersed with a few spontaneous remarks from the floor. The speakers should represent major organizations or institutions in the community that have political clout.

The purpose of their talks is less to persuade by logic, and more to show numbers and strength. Be sure that people stress numbers-how many folks they represent either organizationally or by category. "Those of us who rent our homes make up half of the voters in this district. We are 14,000 voters, and we want rent control." It is always good to have people speak who are known contributors to the legislator's campaign, if they're supporters of your position. A time limit of 2 minutes a person should be set.

Collection: 5 Minutes

Pass the hat to raise money to win the campaign. After an officer of the organization makes a pitch, have a local musician entertain the group during the collection. This is a good opportunity for the leadership to caucus and tie up any loose ends. This item is always placed on the agenda before the main event (making the demands on the target) because if it is done after the main event, many people will get up and leave.

What We Expect of the Target: 15-20 Minutes

This is when the demands are made, but since "demands" is organizer talk and not an everyday word, call it something else such as, "Our organization's questions to Senator Smith." A panel of three or four people make the demands which, of course, have been decided upon and written out in advance. Everyone on the panel should have a script showing the order of the questions, and which fallback and escalator demands go with which question. Each panel member is assigned one or two main demands with their fallbacks. The target should be asked to respond to each demand before the next one is made. Generally, you are asking for "yes" or "no" responses, but allow the person some flexibility in answering the questions.

Some groups make a scoreboard for the responses with "yes," "no," and "waffle" categories. Others hand a scorecard to all meeting participants. Because fallback or escalator questions will be based upon the initial responses, the whole list of questions is not distributed or posted.

Summary Statement: 5 Minutes

The moderator should summarize the outcome of the meeting and express the group's pleasure or disappointment with the commitments. If things have not gone well, the moderator should nonetheless avoid the temptation to say, "We are livid with rage." In most halls "livid" sounds like "liver."

Adjournment

The chair or another leader closes the meeting with a song, prayer, or parting word. Outline the next steps in the campaign and the next event the organization is holding. Everyone should leave with an assignment of something to do-a petition to circulate, a letter to write, leaflets to give out, or posters to put up. Try to avoid having announcements about upcoming events of other groups. A barrage of meeting notices tends to diffuse the impact of the ending. Anyway, half the announcements are usually silly: "Citizens Opposed to Canned Food is holding an international convention to form a world-wide third party at the Parks Department field house."

Key Roles

Part of the process of leadership development is training leaders in visible, public roles. Generally, it's better to have more roles and jobs than less. Here are some of the key roles you will want in the meeting:

Chair. The person who chairs the meeting should be a respected leader of your organization. The job requires being prepared to keep the audience focused on the issue, and to keep the target from taking over the meeting. The chair should have a detailed agenda that includes who is speaking and what group they are from, the exact demands from the panel, and the times for each part. The chair needs to be able to jump in and improvise if something slips. The chair is assigned a small staff during the meeting.

- *Chair's Messenger:* Particularly if the room is large, the chair needs a way of communicating with other leaders and staff, finding the next speaker, and dealing with unanticipated problems. The messenger, who needs to be able to recognize everyone, stays near the chair.
- *Score Keeper:* If a scoreboard is used to record the targets' responses, a score keeper is assigned to the chair and marks the board *only at the chair's direction.*
- *Chair's Organizer:* An organizer should stay close by to discuss unexpected agenda changes.

General Organizer. The general organizer should remain in the back of the room dealing with problems. This person can double as the "celebrity spotter," looking for other elected officials and leaders of organizations whose presence the chair should mention.

Panel Members. The members of the panel who make the demands should be people from your planning committee who are familiar with the issue and politics of the situation. If the meeting is a coalition effort, they can come from different organizations, but this increases the need for a group rehearsal.

The Official Target Greeter. One person should be assigned to greet the target and keep her occupied until the meeting begins. This prevents the target from working the crowd, shaking hands, and acting nice. Ideally, the greeter should have met the target before. The greeter should not be on the panel. It's too hard to lean on someone after chatting with them for half an hour.

Press Contact. If you expect the press, assign one person to meet and greet them, and hand out a press statement. Some meetings have a press table to which press people are directed. It is fine for the press to interview people in the crowd, but the press contact needs to be sure that the organization's view of the issues is accurately expressed. The press greeter should make sure that the press are introduced to "our official spokesperson." Get a list of all press people who attend. Follow up with them as the campaign unfolds.

Ushers. A small group of people should be interspersed throughout the audience. They are responsible for starting clapping, cheering, or booing at appropriate times. They help people get seated, pass out any materials, and take the collection. Have an arm band or some identification for them. Ushers should be prepared for disruptive people. Sitting next to them or engaging them in conversation often distracts them. Don't actually touch anyone. That can quickly escalate into a fight or charges of assault.

Microphone Holder. Never leave a live mike unattended. It is a sure way to lose control. If you use a mike in the center of the room for audience participation, take away the stand, and assign a person to hold the mike for the speakers. This ensures control and allows the chair to maintain time limits.

Logistics and Spirit

As with any public meeting it's hard to anticipate all logistical matters, but the better planning you do, the fewer last-minute crises you will face. Consider the following.

Room Set-up. Map out where you want everything before you get to the meeting. (See the diagram on the next page.) Go to see and hear the hall in use and make a floor plan. If the chairs are moveable or the room can be partitioned, be sure that you have fewer chairs than needed rather than many empty chairs.

Generally, you want the Chair and the target in the front of the room with the target on the Chair's left. The panel members should be off to the side somewhat, and on the Chair's right.

There should be an easy way for the organizer to move from the Chair to other parts of the room.

Microphones. Do you need them? If so, where should they be placed? One for the chair, one or two for the panel, one for the target, and one for the audience adds up to more than many halls have. The cheap solution is to borrow small amplifiers. Even boom boxes have been used. Most have a mike jack. Buying the cheapest Radio Shack mike to plug in is still cheaper than renting. Test the equipment before the meeting begins.

Sign-In Sheets. Are there enough? Do you want special forms so you can get more information than just name, and address and phone number? Will the names need to be in a certain format to be entered into a computer database? If so, design the sign-in form to correspond to your database format. The goal is to get a complete list of everyone who comes, so you need lots of sign-in sheets to avoid a bottle-neck at the door.

Set up tables outside in the hall that everyone must pass, and assign a few people to stand next to them and steer people over. If you give out a name tag or program at the table, people are more likely to stop. Another method is to offer a door prize. People must fill out a card and drop it in a box to win.

Sign-in sheets tend to disappear. Make sure that they are given to the organizer as soon as they are filled out.

Handouts. Do you plan to hand out any materials? Will the agenda be printed? Do you need press materials? Who's responsible for preparing and printing (union label) the materials? Do you need signs on the front of the building directing people to the right room? Do you want posters hung around the room to express your concerns? (The practice of turning statements like these into questions was invented by a Greek named Socrates. If the answer to any of these questions is no, you are probably making a mistake. Call him and talk it over.)

Scoreboard. Often a huge scoreboard is placed next to the target. The demands are listed on it and next to each one are spaces to check "Yes,"

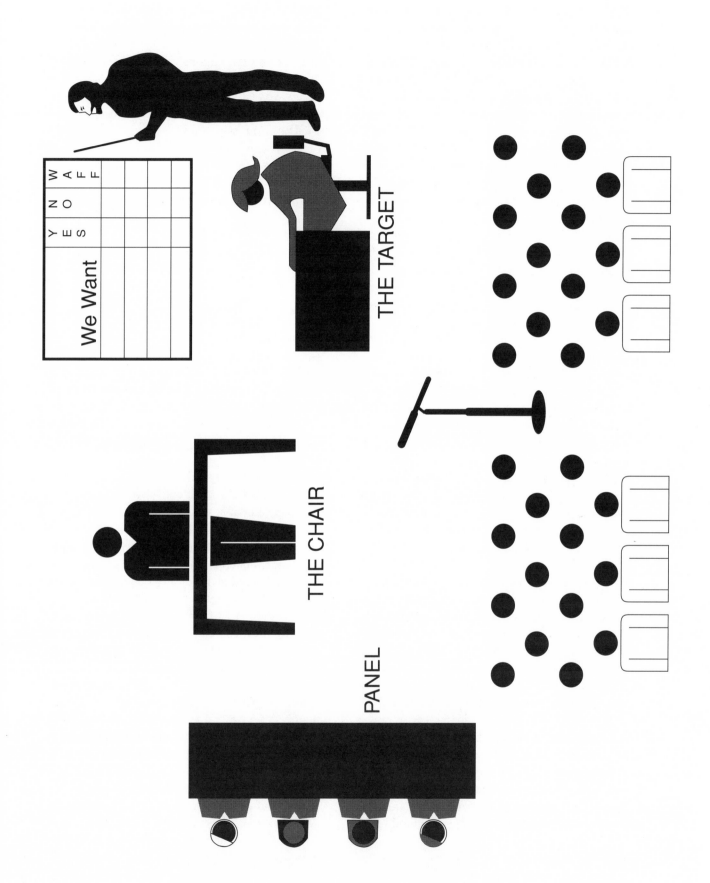

We Want

THE TARGET

THE CHAIR

PANEL

"No," and "Waffle." This device helps pin down the target. A scorekeeper marks the board at the direction of the Chair. An alternative is to print a score sheet and hand it out so that people can mark it themselves. The target knows that they will take it home and show everyone.

Fun Activities. Build in dramatic activities that also make a point. When a target waffled on a question, one group brought out a plate of waffles. Another group had a hugh cardboard waffle. A deputy mayor was presented with a small violin reminiscent of another politician who fiddled while Rome burned. After the head of a transit authority had finished speaking, an organization concerned with transit safety lowered a hugh graphic mural depicting a subway disaster. Visuals such as these are a key to getting TV coverage.

Other techniques include connecting in an out-of-town city council president through an amplified telephone to lend support. Very short, under five minute, slide shows and videos have also been used to help an audience visualize the problem. Longer slide shows have been used to everyone's sorrow. An organization fearing that the target would not show up hired a band to lead the audience to the target's house. The target came, but the band stayed to play "Happy Days Are Here Again" after the opening speech, and drum rolls to emphasize important points thereafter. Last, large bunches of balloons make great decorations.

You can think of better ideas than these. You want to be known as the group that puts on the greatest events that are still cheaper than a movie. Have fun while remembering that there is a fine line between clever and silly.

Money Collection. Bring cans or containers for the collection. Stop at a take-out Chinese food place and buy a dozen soup containers. Wrap leaflets around them, slit the tops, and tape them shut. Provide arm bands for ushers. In some African-American communities it is traditional to ask the audience to come forward and put their donations in a central collection plate. An experienced collection speaker is required.

Refreshments. Will there be any? If so, be sure that several people who have no other major jobs are responsible for them.

Fill-ins. What happens if your target is late or your panel needs a few minutes to discuss matters? Plan some "fill-ins" such as music, songs, or bird imitations. Try to use leaders for this who will be there anyway. There are few things worse than inviting a musician for a fill-in, and then having neither the need nor time for a performance.

Turnout, Publicity, and Transportation/Facilities

Turnout

Getting large numbers of people to the accountability session is critical for demonstrating your power. Of course, the meaning of "large numbers" varies greatly based on the size and nature of your community. Getting 200 people to an accountability session in a small town might be terrific, whereas getting that many to an accountability session with the mayor of a major city would be dreadful. On the other hand, getting 200 people to a session with a local city council person, even within a large city, is probably fine.

Whatever will suffice as "large" should be your attendance goal. Identify all the possible groups and people who might be interested.

The main goal of the turnout plan should be to make at least four times as many phone calls as you need people to come. Fewer calls may do if you have a particularly hot issue, or have been regularly turning out crowds. Every organization and individual has their own success rates with calls. The general rule is that of the people who have said twice that they will come, half show up.

The first step is putting together an adequate calling list. Start with your group's own membership list and ask allies for the use of theirs. Next, at a meeting, ask all your key volunteers to make a list of the people they will personally invite to the accountability meeting. Make copies so the organization can keep a list for last-minute reminder calls and changes. (This list is also a good guide for future leadership development because good leaders, or good potential leaders, are people who can get others to come.) Check back with each recruiter to see that the calls have been made.

Set up telephone nights in the office, and have volunteers come in to call organizational lists. If more phones are needed, get businesses or unions to let you use their offices. Avoid having people make cold calls alone at home. It tends not to happen, and it isn't any fun.

Remember, every person who says "yes, I'll come" must be called a *second time* to reconfirm within a week of the event. Once again, no matter what allied groups promise, your own organization should be responsible for producing at least two thirds of the minimum number of people needed from its own phone operation. By the end of the turnout campaign, you need to have a list of all the people who have said twice that they will come, and it must be twice as large as the minimum number of people needed. The rest of the crowd can be recruited by other groups and "off the street."

Save your list and check it against the sign-in sheets after the event. You need to know how many of those called actually came, and which of your leaders and allies really produced.

Publicity

Once your date is set and the general structure of your meeting is planned, you must quickly get out your promotional materials-flyers, letters and posters. You may not necessarily want to promote your event as an "accountability session" because most people won't know what it is. Instead, highlight the issues to be discussed in your promotional materials. Remember though, unless the issue is really major, few people attend public meetings just because they saw a flyer or heard an announcement. The flyers reinforce the phone calls and media publicity. The idea is to deliver the message to everyone several times.

Make lists of all the other community meetings that are being held, and send people there to make announcements. Don't overlook senior centers, political clubs, union meetings and "official" meetings like school boards. Try to get announcements made in churches. Leaflet and talk to people outside grade schools when school dismisses. If your organization has a door-to-door canvass, concentrate it in the area of the event a few weeks ahead of time. Canvassers should bring in names of interested people who you can write to and confirm their attendance by phone. Leaflet commuter lines, shopping centers, and malls. Combine leafleting with a petition or letter writing.

Transportation/Facilities

Is transportation a problem? If so, arrange for car pools or special transportation. Transportation is frequently a concern for some senior citizens. Sometimes social service agencies or churches are willing to loan their buses or vans to bring people to special community events.

You may want to offer child care if you hope to attract many families with young children. Make sure to arrange for adequate adult supervision of children, facilities for infants, and toys for children. You will want your child care providers to look at the space ahead of time to identify any possible difficulties. If transportation and/or child care are provided, be sure to mention these in all your promotional materials and announcements along with such things as accessibility for the disabled and signing for the deaf.

Press Plan

Your press plan should include:

1. Trying to get advance publicity if the issue is of city-wide interest. Sometimes releasing a study on the subject or even a clever media stunt will get the event mentioned, where a straight press release won't.
2. Sending a press release to key media contacts a week before the meeting.
3. Making follow-up calls to media people, city desks, day books, and assignment editors a day or two before the meeting.
4. Preparing a press packet for distribution to press people at the meeting. It should include another press release and background information on your issue and your organization.
5. Preparing visuals for photographing. Both newspapers and television prefer taking interesting pictures, rather than just pictures of talking heads. Prepare some visuals, charts, banners, or stunts that you think might be interesting. The visual should not just be "catchy," but should convey your

message. The name of the organization should be visible everywhere.

6. Talking with press people at the event. One person should be assigned to greet the press. Your planning group should clarify who are your spokespersons, so that the press greeter can direct them to the proper people for interviews.

7. Calling the press people who didn't come to tell them what happened, or sending a follow-up press release if you don't expect to get much media coverage.

8. Thanking the press people for covering your event, even if you don't like how they covered it.

If you expect lots of people and lots of press at the accountability session, you must be concerned with where they will be located. Consider roping off a special set of seats up front for the press and selecting a good spot for television cameras. Although much newer equipment is battery operated, be sure that the hall you are using has adequate electrical outlets. Pay phones should be available.

Consider inviting area college media classes to videotape your event, as a way to ensure decent video coverage of the entire event for your group and to make it appear that there are lots of media present.

If you expect the media to play a major part in your strategy, you will want to work closely with all your speakers to help them deliver tight messages in ten-second sound bites for television use. In some large media events, the television and radio press people are handed copies of speeches with the ten-second sound bites indicated, so the crews can be sure to have their television cameras running at the proper time.

Tone of the Meeting

The tone of the meeting should be upbeat but serious, professional but fun, and controlled but not too much so. It should always end positively, looking forward to future action.

Upbeat but Serious. The issue about which the meeting is organized is serious. The people who attend are serious about the issue. Nonetheless, the meeting must be run in a very positive fashion, assuming that a positive outcome will emerge from the meeting.

Professional but Fun. The meeting needs to be run professionally. There should be agendas, leaders should have practiced their speaking parts, the room should be set up, time limits held to, and logistics should run smoothly. No one should know about last-minute crises but the organizer and key leaders.

The event should not be conducted like a business meeting. It is a community accountability session. It should be fun. People should be encouraged to sing songs, hold up signs, join in chants, or participate in other "fun" activities that express concern about the issue and demonstrate the group's organizational ability. (Being organized enough to get everyone to chant the same thing is worth something.)

Controlled, But Not too Much. The Chair must control the agenda and is responsible for making sure that the meeting's goals are accomplished and that the target doesn't take over the meeting. However, sometimes Chairs feel so compelled to "control" a meeting that they become shrill and tyrannical. Control is important, but not too much control. Tyrannical Chairs cause audiences to sympathize with targets-not what you want.

End Positively with Action. Make sure that the close of a meeting is positive and leads to the next action. Prepare the meeting chair to give a rousing closing and send people off prepared to fight another battle-whether it be on this issue or the next.

Checklist for Holding an Accountability Session

_____ Are your key leaders on the planning committee?

_____ Have you used the strategy chart to plan the accountability session, being sure to take into account your power?

_____ Do you have main demands (usually substantive), a list of escalation demands, and some fallback demands (usually procedural)?

_____ Are the proposed date and time for the accountability session suitable for your constituency?

_____ Have you confirmed the date and time with the target?

_____ Do you have an appropriate site that is accessible, centrally located, and equipped to handle your needs?

_____ Have you made a realistic turnout plan? Are there enough people assigned to work on turnout?

_____ Is there a good press plan? Have you arranged for the:

- _____ Initial press release
- _____ Follow-up calls to media
- _____ Press packets at the session
- _____ Visuals for photographing
- _____ Press table and person staffing it
- _____ Special area for television crews
- _____ Post-session press release
- _____ Calls to press people who didn't attend
- _____ Thanking press people who covered the session

_____ Does the agenda demonstrate power over the target and give your leadership visible roles?

_____ Does the agenda include the following components:

- _____ Welcome and purpose
- _____ Opening prayer or song
- _____ Community residents speaking
- _____ Collection
- _____ Demands and target's response
- _____ Summary statement
- _____ Adjournment

_____ Have you taken care of logistics? Have you arranged for:

- _____ Refreshments
- _____ Room set-up
- _____ Room decorations (posters, banners)
- _____ Music or entertainment
- _____ Baskets or buckets for collecting money
- _____ Words for chants or songs
- _____ Demands scoreboard
- _____ Audiovisual equipment
- _____ Microphones

Checklist for Holding an Accountability Session *(Continued)*

_____ Extension cords
_____ Sign-in sheets and sign-in table
_____ Room clean-up

_____ Will you provide child care? Is there a good room available?

_____ Are there carpools or transportation arrangements available?

_____ Do you have a dress rehearsal scheduled?

_____ Is someone assigned to greet the target as she or he enters the building?

_____ Are your key leaders and staff assigned to the following roles:

_____ Chair (leader)
_____ Chair's messenger (leader or staff)
_____ Scorekeeper (leader)
_____ Chair's organizer (leader or staff)
_____ General organizer (leader or staff)
_____ Target greeter (leader)
_____ Press contact (leader or staff)
_____ Press spokesperson/s (leader)
_____ Speakers on the program (leaders)

_____ Have you recruited other volunteers and emerging leaders for the following roles:

_____ Ushers
_____ Microphone holder
_____ Person with the sign-in sheets
_____ Person to distribute handouts
_____ People to collect money
_____ Refreshment servers
_____ Music or entertainment fill-ins
_____ Child care
_____ Applause and audience participation starters

_____ Does your followup plan include:

_____ Sending a confirmation letter to the target
_____ Sending thank you notes to everyone who helped
_____ Celebrating with key people
_____ Checking attendance lists against those who said they would come and/or deliver people
_____ Meeting with the planning committee to evaluate the session

Midwest Academy
225 West Ohio, Suite 250
Chicago, Illinois 60610

New York Transit accountability session against the building of Westway Highway.

9

Wouldn't It Be Loverly? If you find yourself humming this tune as you think about building a coalition, Beware! Coalitions are not built because it is good, moral, or nice to get everyone working together. Coalitions are about building power. The only reason to spend the time and energy building a coalition is to amass the power necessary to do something you cannot do through one organization.

A coalition is an organization of organizations working together for a common goal. An individual membership organization cannot technically be a coalition, although the term is used more loosely in common parlance.

Coalitions come in a variety of forms. They can be permanent or temporary, single or multi-issue, geographically defined, limited to certain constituencies (such as a coalition of women's organizations), or a combination of some of the above (e.g., a Midwestern coalition of farm organizations). A number of the Citizen Action state organizations are permanent coalitions. Their goal is to bring together the major elements of the progressive movement to build a base of power capable of winning on issues of mutual concern. On the other hand, an environmental coalition formed to increase funding for the state EPA might best be set up on a temporary basis. The reason is that, apart from common interest in this one issue, their programs and constituents could be very different. One might be working on wildlife preservation, another on blocking construction

Advantages and Disadvantages of Working in Coalitions

Principles for Successful Coalitions

Do You Really Want to Form a Coalition?

Questions to Consider Before Joining Coalitions

Working for and Building the Coalition: The Organizer's Job

Building and Joining Coalitions

of a dam, and a third on preventing the use of pesticides.

Advantages and Disadvantages of Working in Coalitions

In Midwest Academy training sessions, participants are asked about their coalition experiences. Below are some common responses:

Advantages

- *Win what couldn't be won alone.* Many issues require large numbers of people and many resources to win. Coalitions can pool people and resources to win important victories.
- *Build an ongoing power base.*
- *Increase the impact of individual organizations' efforts.* Not only does your involvement help win, but you make the work you do undertake more effective.
- *Develop new leaders.* Experienced leaders can be asked to take on coalition leadership roles, thus opening up slots for new leaders.
- *Increase resources.* If the coalition's issue is central to your organization, you may directly benefit from additional staff and money.
- *Broaden scope.* A coalition may provide the opportunity for your group to work on state or national issues, making the scope of your work more exciting and important.

Disadvantages

- *Distracts from other work.* If the coalition issue is not your main agenda item, it can divert your time and resources.
- *Weak members can't deliver.* Organizations providing leadership and resources may get impatient with some of the weaker groups' inexperience and inability to deliver on commitments.
- *Too many compromises.* To keep the coalition together, it is often necessary to play to the least-common denominator, especially on tactics.
- *Inequality of power.* The range of experience, resources, and power can create internal problems. One group, one vote does not work for groups with wide ranges of power and resources.
- *Individual organizations may not get credit.* If all activities are done in the name of the coalition, groups that contribute a lot often feel they do not get enough credit.
- *Dull tactics.* Groups that like more confrontational, highly visible tactics may feel that the more subdued tactics of a coalition are not exciting enough to activate their members.

Obviously, not all of the experiences are positive, but almost everyone agrees that when there is an important shared goal, the benefits can outweigh the problems. The rest of this chapter will look at ways to emphasize the advantages and minimize the disadvantages.

Principles for Successful Coalitions

Hire Experienced Coalition Staff

It must be someone's primary responsibility to work for the whole coalition, and that person needs to be politically savvy. Ideally, money should be raised to hire an impartial, experienced organizer. Limited resources, however, may make it necessary for the staff to be contributed by one of the member organizations. When this is done, the contributed staff member needs to make every effort to be impartial, and not to appear to be acting as the agent of one of the organizations. A staff person running a coalition part time out of a desk while working full time for another organization is headed for trouble.

Choose Unifying Issues

There needs to be a common issue, not just a desire to work together on each others' separate agendas. A shopping list of issues will result in chaos and bad feelings. For example, a coalition of groups representing people with particular disabilities can be built around issues involving the civil rights of all the disabled. But, an issue that meets the needs of people with only one type of disability may be of no interest to other participants in the coalition.

If your goal is to build a permanent coalition, there may be short-term compromises you would be willing to make. For example, you may decide not to work on an important progressive issue even though your coalition's involvement could be decisive, because it could divide the coalition's membership.

Develop a Realistic Coalition Budget

This budget should include all of the anticipated expenses and income necessary to carry out the coalition's agenda. If staff are being contributed by a member organization, their salary should be included on the expense side and listed as an in-kind contribution on the income side. This will give members a better understanding of the real cost of the campaign.

Understand and Respect Institutional Self-Interest

Each organization brings its own history, structure, agenda, values, culture, leadership, and relationships to a coalition. It is important for all members of the coalition to understand each other in order to build on their strengths and avoid unnecessary conflicts.

Agree to Disagree

Seldom do all member organizations of a coalition agree on all issues. Focus on your common agenda, the issues on which you agree. Agree to avoid the issues on which you do not agree. If disagreements are so fundamental that they color everything else, then working together may be impossible.

Play to the Center with Tactics

When developing tactics for a coalition, it is usually necessary to play to the groups that are toward the middle. At certain points in an issue campaign, the coalition's strategy may be to encourage the appropriate organizations to act independently and in their own names, utilizing more militant tactics. This can make the coalition appear more reasonable. Such "independent" action should only occur with the consent of all the coalition partners.

Recognize That Contributions Vary

Organizations will bring different strengths and weaknesses to the coalition. As long as each member understands and accepts what other members bring, problems should be minimal. For example, one organization may be able to contribute large sums of money but be unable to turn out its membership, while the opposite would be true of another member organization. Both can be essential to the success of the coalition effort and should be valued for the resources they bring.

Structure Decision-Making Carefully

Unless all groups contribute relatively equally, decision-making cannot simply be one vote per organization. Those contributing the most must have the most say in decisions.

Help Organizations to Achieve Their Self-Interest

Organizations need to believe that they are benefiting from a coalition. Many organizations' self-interests are relatively easy to accommodate if they are clearly understood by the coalition's staff. For example, a neighborhood organization working to better its local schools may find it beneficial to join a statewide tax reform coalition in return for the coalition including increased school funding as part of the agenda. All groups want media coverage. Find ways to get coverage for as many groups as possible, assuring that the largest contributors to the coalition are included.

Achieve Significant Victories

Although its obvious, coalitions must achieve important victories if they are to be successful. Groups will only continue contributing if they see concrete, measurable results.

Urge Stable, Senior Board Representatives

As organizations join the coalition, their choice of representatives to the board is an indication of how seriously they take the coalition. If the presidents of the respective organizations do not participate, they should send a high-ranking board member or staff person as the regular representative. Some coalitions make participation dependent on sending an "important" representative.

It is very disruptive to have a series of individuals "fill in" for the president. It is enough of a problem that organizations in a coalition may be of very unequal strength, and that their level of participation may vary widely, without compounding that difficulty by having inappropriate people attending board meetings.

If high-ranking officers of major organizations don't see their peers at the meeting, they will drop out and start sending lower-level staff or interns who lack the power to represent the organization. This in turn lengthens the time it takes for the coalition to make a decision because many board members must report back to someone in authority and wait for an answer.

Clarify Decision-Making Procedures

Depending on the level of the coalition, different working arrangements are necessary. For example, in a large national coalition, and even in statewide coalitions in large states, it is very cumbersome and expensive to bring the whole board together regularly. Such coalitions often choose a working group or committee to meet with the staff to develop strategy. As long as the board is clear on how policy is set and

trusts the working group to check back at appropriate points, this method can be useful. Whatever the structure, it should be clear to all coalition board members.

Distribute Credit Fairly

One of the most frequent problems of coalition building is that of giving and receiving credit. To those who haven't had the experience of working in a grassroots organization, all of the fighting and jockeying over who gets recognition and for what, often seems petty, vulgar, and mindless. Some coalition organizers may feel that this is something that groups need to be cured of, and that the proper "attitudes" will make it go away. Quite the contrary, these problems are rooted in basic survival instinct. They will never go away, nor should they. An organization's ability to raise money, recruit members, build power, attract staff, develop leaders, and fulfill its mission depends directly on the amount of public credit it receives, particularly in the media. Coalitions that lose sight of credit concerns don't last long.

When the issue of the coalition is of only secondary importance to a particular affiliate, then credit is less of a problem. But when the issue of the coalition is also the main issue of the affiliate, then credit is a big problem. The program needs to be structured so that there are some things the affiliates do jointly as a coalition, and other things that the coalition helps them do in their own names. For example, a study done by the coalition can be released to local papers by local groups in their own names, at the same time that it is released to the statewide media in the name of the coalition. Each local release features the impact of the problem on that particular area. This is much more work for the coalition staff, but it keeps the affiliates happy and above all, healthy. Organizational self-interest is legitimate, and there is a saying among organizers that "Groups join coalitions to gain power, not to give it away."

Do You Really Want to Form a Coalition?

Before proceeding with a coalition, determine if it is appropriate for what you want to accomplish. Will you be able to advance your own organizational agenda? If yours is a new organization that needs to establish an independent identity, avoid coalitions for at least a year. Instead, choose smaller issues that you can win on your own. This leads to a strong membership-based organization that can eventually work in a coalition when necessary.

Building a coalition creates another level of organization or bureaucracy that requires separate resources. It is certainly not in your organizational self-interest to develop a separate entity with which you will later have to compete for resources. Nor do you want to devote scarce staff time to building a coalition instead of your own organization.

When a state-wide permanent coalition sets up and staffs a separate issue coalition, complete with its own board, letterhead, and resources, disaster looms. Inevitably, this new coalition will compete with the permanent one. Because the new coalition is working on the most exciting issue, it will draw more interest and resources than the existing permanent coalition. It would be preferable to set up a special issue campaign, clearly recognized as "under" the permanent coalition, that can draw new people and groups who might not otherwise join the coalition.

Permanent or Temporary?

When you do decide that your group should form a new coalition, determine whether it should be permanent or temporary. If temporary, consider calling it something other than a coalition. Using a more temporary sounding word like "campaign" or "countdown '96," connotes a shorter lifespan. The reason for giving a temporary coalition a temporary sounding name is that coalitions tend to take on lives of their own. This is particularly true of coalitions with full-time staff who will find new functions to keep the group alive after its initial purpose has been served.

The Midwest Academy believes coalitions are essential to achieve real social change. Unfortunately, many people and organizations use up valuable resources creating coalitions for which there is no need.

Questions to Consider Before Joining Coalitions

Organizations do not have to join every coalition that is formed. Many organizations develop formal policies for joining coalitions and criteria for different levels of participation. Some organizations will agree to participate in a coalition only if they are actually prepared to work on the coalition's issues. Others are willing to endorse a coalition, by lending it their name and stature, without participating in its program. Below are some questions to consider before joining a coalition.

Who Is Behind the Coalition?

If you have been invited to participate in a coalition, approach the table understanding that you will have to give something to get something. The question, then, is to whom are you giving it, and who is responsible for what you get back? Look around. Who else is participating? Who called all of you to this meeting? Why? Who covered the expenses (i.e., staff time, travel, room rental)? It is important to know the driving force behind the formation of the coalition. If it is funder driven, is the funder committed for the long haul or just willing to give enough to get things started? If led by a few organizations, will they get the bulk of the benefits and credit? In return, will they do the bulk of the work? All of this helps to determine not only if the effort is worthwhile but also if an organization of your size can benefit by being in it. If you are participating in a coalition you consider a priority, make sure that a critical number of other organizations are also participating so your efforts will not be in vain.

What's Your Organizational Self-Interest?

It is important to assess whether you should play a leadership role or merely be a member. Both are essential, but decide where you want to fit in. If you intend to be a leader of the coalition and to have your own members participate in its program, then make sure the coalition issue(s) affect your membership deeply.

Be upfront and clear about what you expect in exchange for your participation. For example, a local community group in a large city joined a city-wide coalition to improve mass transportation. The group set the following conditions for joining the coalition: 1) It was to be the only affiliate in its area. This gave it a sort of exclusive franchise on city-wide transit activity. People wishing to participate in the campaign had to join this group in order to do so. 2) Its leaders were to be among the principal spokespersons for the coalition. 3) It was to be the host organization for the coalition's first major city-wide event, with people from other neighborhoods being bussed into its community. Needless to say, the community organization had to be quite strong, and capable of significant turnout in order to negotiate this bargain.

How Can Your Members Participate?

Make sure that coalition tactics or activities will be designed so that your members can and will want to participate. Decide where you are most comfortable in the range, from low-key to militant, and make sure there is agreement from the other organizations that they will stay within that range.

How Will Participating in the Coalition Build Your Organization?

Because participating in a coalition will mean more work for your organization, it should also help you build your organization. Whenever possible, you want credit for your work. If your members will serve as spokespersons, you will want their organizational identity made known. In reality, all members of a coalition can't and won't get equal credit. The media, always reluctant to use the names of organizations, may pick up the coalition's name, but will rarely list all its members.

For example, when two prominent state-wide organizations agreed to combine in a coalition to win auto insurance reform, the subsequent campaign received a flood of media coverage. But, a survey of the newspaper clips showed that in articles where the name of the coalition was mentioned, the names of the two coalition partners were mentioned only 40 percent of the time, despite the fact that all coalition materials consistently used the names of the partners in conjunction with the name of the coalition (i.e., "Citizens Auto Revolt, a joint campaign of New Jersey Citizen Action and New Jersey Public Interest Research

Group"). This problem would have been compounded in a coalition of ten groups instead of only two.

Generally, the organizations that are the strongest and have the most visibility independent of the coalition will also tend to get the most recognition. If your organization has a spokesperson who is clearly identified with you in the public mind, you will get some indirect credit when that person appears for the coalition, even if your group's name isn't mentioned by the media.

Is It a Letterhead Coalition?

Often the board members of a coalition represent no one but themselves. This is what is known as a letterhead coalition. The telltale indicator is an asterisk after the board members' names that indicates "organizations listed for identification purposes only." There is nothing wrong with a letterhead coalition; however, it usually means that resources will not be coming from the coalition members, and there needs to be another plan in place. Your organization's participation should be on the same basis as the other groups.

Working for and Building the Coalition: The Organizer's Job

There is a difference between organizing an individual membership organization and a coalition. With a coalition, you are not creating an entity in which anyone who so desires may participate. You are carefully pulling together the appropriate groups, in the appropriate order, to ensure that all who "should" be in "on the ground floor" are invited, seemingly simultaneously. This must be done carefully, and it requires a skilled organizer who can juggle a number of things at once. You must talk to all the key players at about the same time to avoid anyone feeling as if they are "the last" to be consulted or invited.

Staffing a coalition board is different from staffing a community organization's board. Your job is not to develop "new leadership." Rather, it is to figure out how to work with the leaders who are sent from the member organizations and help them participate fully. It is also to minimize tensions among board members. Most of the people you will deal with already know how to be leaders. What they may not know is how to work with each other, and how to function in a coalition so that it both builds the coalition and builds their own organizations. Often you will need to demonstrate how to do this.

Never Become Involved in the Internal Politics of Any Coalition Member Organizations! This is a cardinal rule. You can only lose. Because you will have to work with the winners, stay neutral during members' internal election campaigns or fights. Be particularly careful not to become involved in jurisdictional fights between rival unions on your board, or in turf battles between community groups. If you are unaware of these problems, it is easy to fall into the trap of having the coalition take an action which favors one side or the other (or which the other side thinks does).

The program of the coalition should be carried out by and through the affiliates. The staff should be getting information to the affiliates, and helping them to mobilize their own members to support the issue. Staff should avoid the temptation to set up another operation on the side, or to start organizing individuals unless this is explicitly part of the strategy. (Canvass members are the exception.)

In addition to knowing the principles of building successful coalitions and guidelines for joining coalitions, there are other things you should know to be an effective coalition organizer. Before beginning your organizing, ask yourself the following questions:

Who Hired You? If your answer is "the coalition board or steering committee," then who is on the steering committee? How did they get there? What do they want collectively and what is the organizational self-interest of each member? The mere fact that there is a beginning "core" group will give you some sense of who will control it. If the "core" is too narrow and you must broaden the base to win, will the founding board agree? All organizations are not created equal. Which organizations are playing the leadership roles in the coalition? The lead organizations will probably have the most to say. You have to decide if you agree with their

perspectives and will be able to work with them.

Who Makes Decisions? Does any one organization have an exclusive veto? Why? In some coalitions things look fairly equal on the surface until you discover that one group has a veto. This veto power is usually not a formal arrangement or in the bylaws. It usually indicates that one of the member groups is making extraordinary contributions and therefore wants some ability to control the direction of the coalition. This may be fine, but you need to understand the self-interest of this controlling member if you are to help build the coalition.

To Whom Do You Report and Why? Who's the boss? It is almost inevitable that you will be getting requests from many board members to do too many things, some of them conflicting. It should be made clear to all board members to whom you report (to the executive director if you are the staff, or to a top officer, if you are the director). All requests for your time should go through that person. A written campaign strategy and clear workplan will ensure that all board members understand what you are doing.

All too often, a coalition board member will try to involve the coalition staff in some extra project for the member's own organization. This amounts to a subsidy from the coalition as a whole to that group. The group may feel justified in making such requests because of what it gives to the coalition, but this practice should be against the rules. An executive committee that meets at least monthly and reviews the staff's work can protect against this to some degree.

What Competing Organizational Self-Interests Exist Between Members? This is important to know before any strategy decisions can be made. For instance, some homeowner groups may want to defeat a proposed property tax increase, but the public employees union may be for it because the tax increase will provide money for better salaries.

Which Organizations Are Contributing the Most and Which Are Gaining the Most by Participating? If those contributing the bulk of the resources are not getting what they want, eventually they will resent seeing their resources go for things that are not a high priority for them and will stop participating.

Where Is the Money Coming From? All of the questions surrounding money are critical to understanding who has control over the coalition. If the bulk of the income is raised from the coalition partners, they will have the most control. More often, additional money will have to be raised to support the coalition.

If the money is coming from outside (e.g., a foundation), whose money is it? Who is actually raising it? What is the interest of the funding source, and what role will they have in the coalition, both formally and informally?

Who is Being Excluded and Why? If certain groups are being excluded, you want to understand why, to help you better understand the politics and self-interest surrounding the issue.

Coalition building is a skill that an organizer can develop. If there is adequate commitment to a coalition and clear understandings of the self-interest and relationships of the member organizations, one can build powerful coalitions capable of accomplishing what none of the parts can alone.

Coalitions in and of themselves are not "the answer" for progressive politics. Strong individual membership organizations must be built that mobilize large numbers of citizens on progressive issues. Nonetheless, there are major social issues, particularly at the state and national levels, that require broad-based coalitions, built upon those membership organizations, in order to win.

Building coalitions that are strong enough to challenge societal structures, and making them work effectively requires tough analytical strategic thinking, clear understandings about how coalitions work, savvy staff, hard work, and tender loving care. With such attention, coalitions can change the political landscape for the next century.

10

How come I do all the work around here? Well, either you're being punished, or you're not recruiting members and volunteers. Every task that an organizer does alone—every envelope stuffed, every phone call made, every page typed—is a lost opportunity to recruit someone else to do that job. Many organizations would be far stronger if their staff and leaders resolved to do nothing else but find others to volunteer for all the jobs.

In some ways recruitment is the most important subject we deal with in this manual. If we had entitled this chapter "Organizing" instead of "Recruitment," that would have given it the proper emphasis. We know organizers who are always surrounded by people because they instinctively draw people into their work. Other organizers function alone. Perhaps they are excellent at all the technical skills, but they don't involve anyone. Indeed, they often consider members a bother, and seem to believe that the goal is to present the perfect testimony at a hearing, or to write the world's finest press release. What such people do may be very valuable, but it isn't organizing. Recruiting and involving people comes naturally to some, but all can learn to do it by incorporating the techniques outlined here into their organizing personalities.

This same principle applies to such organizational responsibilities as speaking to the press, interviewing candidates, doing research, or tracking legislation. In coalition organizations

Basic Recruitment Principles

Your Image as a Recruiter

Six Steps Toward Successful Recruitment

Tips on Keeping Volunteers

Practice Makes Perfect

Recruiting

every activity carried by the central staff is a lost opportunity to involve the affiliates.

The essence of being an organizer is that you get other people to do things. Of course, this isn't a contest to see how much work you can get out of doing; it is the way that organizations are built. More and more people take on more and more responsibility (including financial responsibility). This makes them feel that they own the group and that it is the product of their efforts. The more that the staff does for members, the less ownership the members feel and the less commitment they have. You can produce the world's finest array of services, projects, activities, or publications for your members, but if they haven't been involved in planning it and paying for it, they will say, "Is this all"?

Basic Recruitment Principles

In addition to recruiting individual members, door-to-door canvassing, fundraising and coalition building are forms of recruitment. This chapter deals with recruiting individual members, but its basic principles apply to all forms of recruitment.

Often, but not always, the first step in getting new people or groups to do things is asking them to join. People want to join and to be active; they want to put time and effort and money into useful projects.

In 1832, when the Frenchman Alexis de Tocqueville came to America to chronicle life in the "New World," he marveled at the way Americans set up voluntary organizations for every form of social betterment. "Americans of all ages, all conditions, and all dispositions constantly form associations," he observed.[†] Comparing America to Europe, de Tocqueville noted that projects undertaken by the government in France, or the nobility in England, were done by citizens' associations in America. This tradition is no less strong in America today. So much so, that when George Bush spoke of replacing government programs with volunteer activities, many people actually believed it could work. (Volunteer activities are vital to building strong community organizations, but cannot be viewed as a replacement for government programs and planning.)

Your job as an organizer isn't as hard as it may seem. You don't have to figure out how to get people to be active, to care about their community, or to be concerned with larger issues. They will do that anyway. Your job is mainly to make sure that your organization gets its fair share of all the volunteer activity. Yes, that requires a special skill, but you don't have to change human nature, which is working with you on this one.

There is no indication, however, that organizations have the same natural

---

[†]*Democracy in America,* vol. II. New York: Vintage Books, 1945.

predisposition to join coalitions that individuals have to join organizations. Coalition recruitment is based on precisely the same factor as individual recruitment: self-interest.

Appeal to People's Self-interest

> If I am not for myself who is for me? And if I am only for myself, what am I? And if not now, when?
> —Hillel

Giving time, money, and loyalty to an organization involves giving so much of one's self that saying it is motivated by self-interest seems not only a contradiction, but ever so slightly mean. In fact, it is neither. People do the most selfless things out of self-interest, including joining unions, voting, inventing transistors, and walking dogs. Indeed, self-interest generalized becomes class interest, and few things beat class interest for making history, but that is another story.

When recruiting people, always appeal to their self-interest. This is very different from telling them why it is in your self-interest for them to help you. (In truth, there is a certain kind of person who you can recruit just to help you, but they are more like groupies than members. The problem with groupies is that they get jealous if you have more than five.) Self-interest takes several forms, which together with values, vision, and relationships underpin most organizational involvement.

Personal. People join organizations working on issues that personally affect them. Lower utility rates or lower taxes are examples of immediate self-interest, while global warming or disarmament exemplify longer-term self-interest. People join to stop the oppression, prejudice, and discrimination that affect their lives. Such activities are often accompanied by the feeling that they are doing it for their children or grandchildren, which brings a kind of satisfaction beyond the issue itself.

Senior citizens often join groups for companionship and a desire to continue to be useful after retirement. They enjoy an opportunity to apply the skills of their former occupations. They often seek activities that are multi-generational, rather than confined to seniors.

Then, there are people who volunteer for such additional social self-interest reasons as meeting people, making new friends with similar values, getting out of the house, taking a break from young children, just having fun, or even dating. A few people join for all of these reasons.

People also volunteer because organizations are fun. They are exciting, and particularly with direct action, very often a form of theater.

Professional. Many people volunteer for career self-interest reasons. They want to develop new skills that can enhance their resumes, or they want to test out possible new career options. They may want to make contacts that lead to jobs. Members of certain professions sometimes join organizations in the hope of finding clients. You will also meet people who are looking for work experience, such as students, or homemakers trying to get back into the workplace. A chance to learn word processing or spread sheets, which may be a chore for you, can be a real inducement for them.

Power. Some people volunteer for the power that comes from being part of an organization. They are interested in revenge against political crooks, landlords, and polluters of the environment. They enjoy the opportunity to be a spokesperson, to get on TV, or to speak at a rally.

Moral. To sustain commitment, people must volunteer based on their values and vision. They believe that using their time to help bring justice to the world is the right thing to do. Many people feel that they have a civic responsibility to do something for their community, and that this is indeed a life-long obligation, along with voting or paying taxes. In fact, moral values usually go along with all of the other reasons that people join groups. Moral values can be religious, ethical, or ideological.

Negative Forms of Self-Interest. Individuals become identified with an organization in order to sell out for a price, to promote their own interests against those of the community, or simply to provide themselves with an audience for crackpot ideas or abnormal behavior.

Ninety-nine percent of the time, however, self-interest works on the side of the organization, and if you understand what it is that people desire, you can structure your recruitment appeal and your program to those particular things. Self-interest is rarely one dimensional. People are motivated by combinations of needs, wants, and rewards. They join and stay with the organization that reflects their humanity and values and addresses specific forms of self-interest.

Fire a Shot Over the Water

Outreach needs to be built into every aspect of an issue campaign. An organization should be regularly doing things that raise its public visibility, and at the same time give people an opportunity to join. In fact, in any place on any issue, there is some number of people who are actually looking for you.

Mark Twain, in writing about his boyhood on the Mississippi, spoke of the practice of firing a cannon over the water to raise the victims of drowning. Something similar also applies to those still swimming. Particularly at the beginning of a campaign, but also later on, the organization should fire a shot over the water to bring in those who are just looking for a chance to participate. This takes the form of holding publicly advertised events such as hearings, teach-ins, accountability sessions, rallies, and marches. People will come to support the issue, but also to check out the group. Sign-in sheets and follow-up recruitment calls should be standard procedure.

Smaller activities also work well. Petition drives and letter writing campaigns can bring the organization into contact with hundreds of people in a short time, and each person should be asked to volunteer. Experience indicates that if one out of ten who volunteer actually shows up, you are doing well. The point is to have an ongoing activity that generates a constant inflow of new people.

Recruit to an Activity, Not a Business Meeting

Organizations often try to build their recruitment around meetings. This is probably the least-effective method for drawing people in, and if meetings are the only activity of your group, they may be a cause of dwindling membership.

Most of the time we are looking for people who want to do something more than come to a business meeting. What organizer has not offered prayers to be saved from the person who says, "I have no time to do anything, but I'd love to help you make policy. When is your next meeting"? By recruiting to an activity, you get action-oriented people rather than professional meeting goers.

Some very successful organizations rely on a program of house meetings as their major outreach method. This is not at all the same as recruiting to a business meeting, and has produced dramatic results. House meetings are action oriented. Those attending hear a brief talk on the issue, then they are asked to write a letter, give money, and sponsor a meeting in their own home. The follow-up involves recruitment to other activities. People are given little opportunity to settle into a pattern of just coming to meetings and talking.

Have an Ongoing Entry-Level Program for New People

A major obstacle to successful recruitment is that new people feel that they are arriving in the middle of the party. Everyone knows so much about the issues, and has learned all the jargon. They can talk about the "bi-modal split," "Mr. Parker at C.H.A.," or "parts of particulate matter per billion." No one wants to be around folks who talk in code. It creates an instant in-group, with all the new people automatically excluded.

When you recruit new members, it is important to involve them in something in which they can feel useful. For example, one successful community organization maintained a regular program of weekend letter writing at street tables. Because the issue was very popular and the tables were highly successful, working at them was a fine entry-level activity. Anyone could do it. New volunteers worked as equals along-side the organization's veterans. Passersby put dollar bills in the can, the weather was fine, and everyone felt good. Every letter writer was also asked to volunteer for an hour. They knew what would be expected of them because they saw the activity going on. They knew that they could successfully get others to write letters because they themselves had written one. Maintaining this operation required that several nights each week be spent contacting volunteers. Coming in and making calls was seen as a next step of organizational involvement. Although this particular issue campaign dragged on for ten years before victory, the outreach program ensured a small but steady stream of recruits.

Offer Child Care

Increasingly, the strongest volunteer programs in the country are addressing the obstacles to volunteering and adjusting to reach the changing face of volunteers. A key issue is child care. Consider if there are ways your organization can coordinate a child care program at certain times to enable parents of small children to participate as active volunteers. Some volunteers (probably without children) may be interested in volunteering child care.

Your Image as a Recruiter

Because the best recruitment is done in person, your image is important. Try to look as much as possible like the people you are trying to recruit. If this is impossible, then try to look like someone they would want to bring home to dinner. The rule of thumb on appearance is that people shouldn't be able to remember what you looked like. Remembering, regardless of whether it was good or bad, means that your appearance distracted from the message instead of blending in with it.

> "What did that young man in the three piece suit want?"

> "You mean the young man in the pin stripe and red tie?"

> "Yes, the one with the crimson pocket handkerchief and alligator Guccis."

> "I don't know, something about the world coming to an end. I didn't really get it."

Of course, eye contact is important, and language, like dress, should be appropriate. There are no guidelines for any of this. In fact,

in some ethnic communities averting the eyes, not eye contact, is a sign of respect. So do what everyone else does.

Sound confident by knowing the subject, but don't try to impress with a blizzard of facts. Most important, be enthusiastic. This will happen naturally if you are recruiting to an important activity. To convey urgency, avoid starting with history. Don't say: "Our organization was formed in 1982 because in 1973 the City Council passed a plan for the year 2000. In section III (b) there was a major flaw which wasn't noticed until 1981 during the Streetfogle Commission hearings when ..." Instead, start with the main point. "They are building a sewage treatment plant right in this community, and our homes won't be worth ..."

Practice explaining your organization's issue in a concise, up-beat fashion. In a few sentences, you should be able to convey the essence of the organization, the issue, and how you intend to win.

Six Steps Toward Successful Recruitment

Be Prepared

Recruitment requires solid preparation. Have in your mind a mini-strategy consisting of how you will explain your goal and what you want the person to do. Then add tactics and the areas of self-interest to which you will appeal. Have a few fallbacks as well. These are jobs that need to be done, but require less of a commitment: "If you can't chair the newsletter committee, can you help with the layout? Of course we can list you on the masthead, Layout and design by ..."

When you are acquainted with your potential recruit, review what you know about the person, his or her interests, experience, past activities, family, and anything else that will help you identify self-interest. If this is a "cold contact," someone you have never met and don't know anything about, then prepare some questions to bring up in the conversation that will get the person talking about him or her self. Look for visual clues, for example, parents of small children always have food stains on their clothing. This can lead you into a discussion of day care, baby sitting, public schools, taxes, playgrounds, traffic lights, crime, housing, and almost anything else. The clothing of cat owners is often covered with hair, although this leads to a more limited range of issues.

Of course, if you are recruiting an organization to join a coalition, research its history and program. Know its funding sources and tax status.

Legitimize Yourself

Particularly with people you don't know, you need to gain quick credibility. There are several ways to do this.

First, if it is true, explain that you are from the same community, workplace, school, ethnic group or whatever the appropriate division is, and that you have the same problem that they do. It is important to show that you are not using their problem to advance some other agenda (e.g., "We can get this toxic dump cleaned up if all functions of government are assumed by one big industrial union for all workers, regardless of craft").

Second, be able to say that you got the person's name from a mutual friend, church leader, or public figure in the community who suggested that you contact him or her.

Third, mention other people on the block (in the office, etc.) who have already agreed to join, sign, or come to the event.

Last, remind people that they really have heard of your organization. You were the group that blocked McDonalds from coming in.

A key part of your recruitment strategy is explaining why that person's participation will make a difference. What is the unique role they can play that someone else can't? Even if it is just a matter of boosting turnout, explain why turnout is important. "Representative Smith only won by 150 votes. If 76 votes had gone the other way, she would have lost. We need 76 people who voted for her to get up and say that they are now ready to switch. We have 75. Will you do it?" (Ok, so things really aren't made to order like this, but you get the idea.)

Listen

Draw people out, identify their self-interest, clarify their concerns, and establish rapport. If you are whizzing along telling your story, you won't be able to do any of this. Listening is how you get information and show your concern. It is

not simply the absence of talking, it is asking people good questions, and providing encouraging remarks and body language to convey your interest in them. It is also polite.

Listen to the response when you legitimize yourself. If you mentioned a person, what was the reaction to that name? If you mentioned a past campaign of your group's, had the person really heard of it? If you feel that you are not connecting, ask an open-ended question like "How long have you lived in the neighborhood?" Or ask about children or grandchildren.

Other things to listen for include special skills the person might have, useful contacts, and organizational networks such as a civic club or synagogue. Perhaps a meeting can be arranged for you.

Agitate

When you agitate, you are trying, as Webster's defines the word, "to stir up people so as to produce changes." You are not trying to offend or be obnoxious, but neither will you passively except excuses for people not getting involved.

When someone says "Oh well, I don't like the idea of a gas pipeline coming through here, but it has to go someplace, and we all have to accept these things. That's progress." Then you agitate by saying: "Yes, but it was originally designed to go through vacant land that happened to belong to a wealthy contributor to U.S. Senator Jones. The contributor went to Jones, who leaned on the gas company to move the pipeline into our neighborhood. That guy didn't think it was progress, and he's a millionaire, so he should know. Here is the clipping that tells the whole story."

By agitating, you make people angry. Not only is the thing bad, but it's unfair. You say: "No, schools aren't closing all over town, just in certain places. There are schools with far fewer students than we have that will stay open because those communities have more pull than we do. Is that fair to our kids?"

Get a Commitment

Don't leave a conversation open ended. Get a commitment. Remember, you are trying to match the organization's needs to the person's self-interest and talents. If you can't get an actual agreement, at least try for a date by which the person will decide. If you do get an agreement, it should be to do a specific thing on a specific day. Write it down. Make a note to call and remind the person. Clarify what will happen next, who will call, who will drop off the materials, and when the briefing will be.

Follow Up

Nothing impresses people more than timely followup, because few of us actually do it. Make sure that your administrative systems are in place to keep track of people and get back to them as scheduled. When people you recruited do come to an event or meeting, be sure to greet them and introduce them around. There is nothing worse than making a big fuss over people while recruiting them, and then ignoring them when they actually show up. If you worked on turnout for an event, try to free yourself from logistical responsibilities on that day, so that you can pay attention to the new people.

Tips on Keeping Volunteers

Recruitment has to be backed up by an organizational plan, with clear goals and expectations of what volunteers will do. For this, training and supervision are needed. People should be set to work as soon as they arrive, but first, take the time to explain the organizational importance of the task and how it fits into winning on the issue. Ask people how long they can stay and assign tasks accordingly. Never allow people to feel that you wasted their time, or didn't really need them. Have a variety of things to do. Provide coffee. Celebrate birthdays of office regulars. Bring in champagne to toast even small victories. Provide ways that those who want to, can move up in the structure of the organization, and don't high pressure those who are happy with the level they are at. Maintain regular volunteer hours at different times of the day. Keep the schedule the same so that people can plan around it. Thank people and give public recognition. Don't look disappointed when they go home. In short, make an evening in the office more interesting than staying home and watching TV.

Practice Makes Perfect

At the Midwest Academy, students often role play situations in which they recruit people. Consider having your staff and leaders practice on one another. Work on a few opening lines because getting started is the hardest part. Don't forget, most normal conversations begin by talking about the weather, sports, kids, or some other everyday subject. Practice answers to typical questions that you will be asked. If you can't adequately explain the program in role playing, consider the possibility that you don't have a recruitment problem, but an organizational problem, because your program, solution, or strategy really isn't clear enough to appeal to anyone.

Recruitment is the life blood of an organization. What kills groups fastest is that they stop recruiting new people. Growing, thriving organizations must train staff and leaders on how to recruit others and build recruitment strategies into their ongoing program work.

Ohio Citizen Action (formerly Ohio Public Interest Campaign) canvasser delivers over 100,000 petition signatures—all signers are potential recruits.

11

All organizing is about the development of leadership, although this takes place in many different ways. Some organizations, particularly community- and church-based groups, consider leadership development to be the real purpose of their work. To them, while issues are important, they are only a means to developing a large pool of skilled leaders, without which the organization can never win power for itself. In some organizations, state and national coalitions, for example, the leaders are often people who have risen to the top of another organization, such as a union, and who have many years of experience in a position of some power. In a network of progressive elected officials, the leaders are all elected.

While the experience level in each of these situations is very different, leadership development is nonetheless the critical element in making the organizations work. Community people may need to learn such basic leadership skills as writing a press release, analyzing the strength of an elected official, public speaking, and running a meeting. The union leader may have learned those thing many years ago, but is unaccustomed to working in coalition with environmentalists and consumer groups, or integrating direct action campaigns into the union's electoral agenda. The elected officials are grappling with such problems as working together as a team inside a system that can force them to compete with each other. All of this is leadership development.

For most community organizers, leadership

Principles for Leadership Development

The Leadership Development Process

Guidelines for Leadership Maintenance and Growth

Leaders and Organizers

Developing Leadership

development poses a set of basic questions: how do we get people to feel that they own this group, raise money for it, recruit to it, and work to keep it going? We will address the subject of leadership development on this level, knowing that the larger elements can't be attended to unless the organization has a sound foundation on which to begin.

Principles for Leadership Development

In established organizations, paid staff are responsible to their elected leadership or to a board chosen with input from the members. In new organizations, the staff are often out looking for potential leaders. In both types of groups, the task of replenishing the leadership core tends to fall mostly to the staff. This actually puts the staff in a more powerful position than is implied in the group's by-laws, and the success of the organization very much depends on the good judgment of the staff in finding potential leaders.

Leaders Have Followers

How do you know who is a good potential leader? Who among the membership should be encouraged to be more active and take on more responsibility? The basic guideline is that leaders have a base. They can bring people to events. It might be a neighborhood person who can bring friends from her building, or, in a coalition, the head of another organization who can bring his members. In any case, a leader has followers. Not only that, but the followers are typical of the community or constituency that your organization represents. The person who brings people from the Society for Freeze-Dried Pets may not be who you are looking for.

The importance of the principle that leaders have followers can't be stressed too much. It builds a reality principle into the organization. People who can motivate and move others are basically in tune with the community or constituency. They talk the language, they are trusted, they understand what others want or expect, they know how to get along. Therefore, the decisions that they make as leaders are more likely to be sound ones, and the organization is more likely to grow. The person who comes to every meeting and has a strong opinion on every subject, but who never can bring another individual is likely to be out of sync with the community.

In the course of time, it may be useful to add to the leadership people who have special skills or special training the organization may need (e.g., someone who understands the banking regulations on community reinvestment). But these folks, useful as they are, should not make up the majority of the leadership.

To develop the leadership of people—those who can bring out other people—the organization needs a program that includes many public events and opportunities to do turnout. It also needs to find ways to spotlight those who do the best turnout, such as praising them at meetings.

Unless this principle is followed and events are managed to encourage leadership by people with a base, top positions will end up going to those who talk the best game at meetings, or who are known because they run a local business or have ties to the political machine. A few such people are fine, but if they are the majority of an organization's main leaders, it can be a problem. (There are exceptions, however. One of our staff recalls organizing in rural Kentucky where, in three communities, the owners of the general stores became the main leaders. It worked out well. Meetings were held in the stores, people were used to coming there, they all knew the owners, and they all owed them money. Those store keepers had a real base.)

In coalitions, the principle of having a base takes on an added dimension. One leader may represent an organization with 7,000 members, none of whom ever come to anything, while another may have 70 members and brings 20 of them. Who gets a seat on the executive committee? Well . . . they both do, but the bigger group goes on first. There are many ways that the power of such an organization is both important and useful, even if the members are not seen. Perhaps later you will find the key to involving some of them.

Start with a Balanced Ticket

The balanced ticket is an old urban political concept. To get the votes of all ethnic groups, have one candidate from each group running on the party ticket. The same applies to organizations. If you want racial, ethnic, gender, and class integration, the leadership must reflect this from the very start. Once the leaders are established as being one kind of person, other people will stay away.

Many groups don't have an integrated leadership, just as most institutions and communities in our country are not integrated. We don't only mean racial integration, although that is often the case. Avoid trying to remedy this with tokenism. If people of a particular race, ethnicity, gender or class are staying away in droves, don't go out and find the one person from that constituency who is so atypical that he or she agrees at once to become a leader in your group, *unless that person has a real base and can bring other people along.* Instead, change your issues. Find out what is of concern to the

group you want to recruit, and start a campaign that will bring you in contact with its real leaders. If recruitment still isn't working out, consider a coalition approach instead.

Don't Rush the Leadership Process

Because of the need for balance, and for knowing who can bring out folks, it is wise for a new group to delay its first elections for six months or even a year. Set a date, of course, but in the meantime operate with a temporary steering committee open to all.

A pattern we have seen repeatedly is that at the first meeting of a new group, someone says, "We can't operate without by-laws." There are always a few people whose main interest in life is by-laws. They immediately start a series of long and boring debates on the subject, which drive away everyone else. Months later, when the by-laws are finished, there is no one left to run for office but the by-law crowd. Once in leadership they say, "The reason that no one comes to meetings anymore is that we need to revise the by-laws." Start with action. Stay flexible.

Both Task and Maintenance Leadership Are Needed

One helpful social work concept is that of task leadership and maintenance (sometimes called emotional) leadership. Task leadership is the kind of leadership that gets "tasks" accomplished. Maintenance leadership is the kind that cares about the emotional strength/maintenance of the group and the people involved in the group. Every successful organization has a healthy balance of both.

While most of us consciously try to develop skills in both areas, our personalities and innate characteristics lead us to be stronger in one area than the other. Someone who is stronger in task leadership is probably pushing through programs, but making people mad all along the way. Someone stronger in maintenance leadership probably gets along well with everyone, but has trouble moving a program forward. The point is not that one kind of leadership is better than the other, but that both are needed for a healthy organization.

If this concept is unclear to you, think about any group with which you are familiar that has functioned well together over a long period of time. See if you can identify a mixture of people who provide task and maintenance leadership. Or, you can observe any meeting. Typical task leadership functions are:

- Preparing an agenda
- Recommending objectives
- Determining key questions
- Suggesting ways to accomplish specific objectives
- Clarifying information
- Moving the group to action or decision-making
- Recording information and decisions
- Opening and closing meetings.

Typical maintenance (emotional) leadership functions are:

- Welcoming and introducing people
- Actively listening to people's ideas
- Including everyone in discussions
- Encouraging shy and quiet people to speak
- Thanking people for contributions and coming to meetings
- Giving positive feedback to speakers.

If you suspect that your organization does not have a good balance between task and maintenance leaders, watch a few meetings to observe the dynamics. If it seems to be short on one kind of leader, actively seek people who provide a balance.

Seek Qualities and Develop Skills

All good leaders possess both personal qualities and specific skills that make them respected. The easiest way to distinguish between skills and qualities (or characteristics) is to say: "Susie is _____" (a quality) or "Susie is good at _____" (a skill). A quality is something you "are" intrinsically. Usually, your inclination toward being a task or maintenance leader is one of your qualities. A skill is something you learn.

It is important in identifying potential leaders that you learn to distinguish between skills and qualities. We have to look for people with the qualities that are needed. We can then train people in particular skills.

For example, if we are looking for a volunteer treasurer, we are looking for someone with the characteristics of honesty, attentiveness to details, thoroughness, good follow-through, and commitment to the organization. These characteristics can't be "taught," at least not very easily. We must find someone with them. Obviously, we'd like to find someone with bookkeeping experience. If we can't, we can train someone in bookkeeping.

Although the qualities and skills needed for every position vary, there are some typical ones that leaders need in most roles. The qualities all leaders need are:

Commitment. If they are not committed to what they are doing, it will show. The leader needs a commitment to the particular organization, a long-term commitment to social change, and a vision of what the future can be.

Honesty. Honesty, tempered with tactfulness, is always the best policy.

Positive Outlook. The world is full of negative people and negative situations. A leader must radiate a positiveness that looks for solutions to problems instead of focusing on the difficulties.

Confidence/Self Assurance. A leader must have confidence in him/herself. This does not mean that the person knows everything, but rather that he or she is self assured enough to ask for help and to admit weaknesses. The confident, self-assured person accepts compliments as well as criticism.

Confidence is not only important in individual dealings and relationships, but also when the organization is facing an adversarial person who is representing an unjust institution. The leader must have the confidence to hold firm in a position based on the planned strategy.

Trust in People. Leaders must fundamentally trust and like people. They must draw out the best in people and urge them to live up to high standards, as opposed to waiting for people to falter. Most people live up to the high standards and trust placed in them.

Mistrust of Unaccountable Institutions. Although leaders must trust people, they must mistrust institutions that are not accountable to people. Leaders are frequently the people who ask, "why" or "why not?" A healthy skepticism is a useful quality for a leader.

Some of the skills almost all leaders need to develop include:

Listening. Leaders need to be able to listen to others. Good listening means not only opening one's ears but also really concentrating on what someone else is saying.

Diplomacy. All leaders find themselves in situations where they must use diplomacy. They must learn to be direct, assertive, and yet tactful, unless a group has consciously decided in a particular situation not to be diplomatic.

Recruitment. Almost all leaders need to recruit others to work with them in some capacity or other. Thus, they must clearly understand how to recruit and to develop experience in recruiting others.

Personal Organization. Leaders need to be personally organized. They need good systems for keeping track of meetings, following-up with people, making calls, and so forth. Without good administrative systems for organizing one's self, a leader does not follow through with tasks and commitments as promised.

Goal Setting. All leaders need to develop skills in setting measurable and realistic goals. Without such goals, we are unclear about where we are going. If we get there, we don't know to congratulate ourselves. Learning to set such goals helps avoid leadership burnout. The skills of goal setting are needed at all levels of the organization, from the board, to the staff, committee, and individual levels.

The Leadership Development Process

Start with Self-Interest

There is a saying in community organizing that leadership is developed, not found. There are very few "natural leaders" sitting around not doing anything but waiting for you to call. Your group may be lucky and find a person whose

leadership experience was developed in another organization, perhaps a church, or who is one of those rare people to whom others in the community turn in time of crisis. But for the most part, organizations develop their own leaders. (As noted previously, in coalitions, the people who come are already leaders, but they develop coalition skills.)

Developing leadership on any level starts with understanding the self-interest of the potential leader: A person who is going to put in long hours, hard work, and take real risks has to get something back in return. Of course, there is commitment to the issue itself, but issues are won and lost. There has to be more. Think for a moment about all the things a person can get out of being a leader in your organization. Here are just a few:

- Notoriety
- New skills
- Respect
- Excitement
- Social activity
- A chance to make history
- A seat on the dais
- An opportunity to start a new career
- The pleasure of sticking it to enemies of the community.

A coalition leader may already have all these things, but can gain:

- New allies
- A wider circle of influential contacts
- New ways to be more effective in her own organization
- Even greater contact with the media
- An opportunity to run for office.

Of course, not everyone wants all of this. The point is to listen and figure out what the potential leader's self-interest actually is, and then shape the position in ways that help the leader achieve those personal goals.

Create Positions in Which Leaders Can Develop

A true story illustrates this point. Many years ago a popular figure in both the women's movement and the peace movement ran for mayor of New York City. The campaign attracted hundreds of volunteers who where deployed on weekends at street tables up and down the main avenues. The volunteers, sometimes numbering as many as 300 in a single weekend, gave out literature, sold buttons and publicized issues.

The paid campaign staff ran the whole street table operation. There was no leadership among the volunteers until the staff decided to create it. They invented the position of "corner captain" and invited volunteers who had come regularly to be corner captains. Their responsibilities included arriving early to receive the table from the truck and then instructing other volunteers in their duties.

It worked. People began to take responsibility. Special training sessions were held at headquarters for the captains, and they felt more a part of the campaign. Later, the staff who had been supervising the weekly phone calls to all of the volunteers told certain captains, "We have six people for your location on Saturday. There are ten more volunteers living in your area, but we don't have the phone capacity to call. Could you call"? Before long, a number of the captains were calling their own volunteer lists.

A niche was thus created in which leadership could develop. There was a strong motivation provided by the candidate and the issues. There was a title, a short list of time-limited responsibilities, other people to help, and someone higher to step in if there were problems. It turned out that all the elements for beginning leadership development had come together at dozens of street corners.

In many organizations, the same type of niche is provided by a committee structure. People can start on the path to leadership by chairing a committee, and even a sub-committee, that has a specific task to carry out. It gives newer members a place to do something without being overshadowed by the older leaders. The reason for having a formal committee structure isn't necessarily that it is more efficient; it is a way to develop leaders.

We once saw the program for a dinner given by a congregation to honor a civil rights leader. The program listed the names of the members of all the committees. There was a committee in charge of floral arrangements for the head table, and another committee for floral arrangements for the other tables. There was even a committee to print the program listing the committees. In all, over a hundred names were listed on that program as having had some part in organizing the dinner, and you can bet that they all showed up at the event, and sold a lot of tickets as well. That's leadership development! In most groups, the organizer would just have picked up the phone and ordered the flowers, or more likely, there would have been no flowers.

As this indicates, one of the secrets of leadership development is breaking big projects down into manageable pieces, and then finding people to take responsibility for each piece. It will work if there are clear goals, the piece is really manageable, there are people to help, there is someone experienced to fall back on for advice or help, and doing the job brings some satisfaction and reward.

Guidelines for Leadership Maintenance and Growth

Practice Evaluations. Look for and give positive, as well as growth-producing feedback. Regular group evaluations at meetings are good.

Institute the Rotation of Roles, and Develop Systems for Training People for New Roles. Few of us want to remain doing the same job forever.

Make Sure Leaders Are Enjoying Their Positions. If leaders are not enjoying their positions, they will either get frustrated and quit, or they will make themselves, and those around them, miserable.

Use Strong, Skilled Leaders to Train Others. Every strong leader should be training others. No one should become "irreplaceable." Build leadership development into every position.

Ask Leaders to Set Personal Leadership Development Goals as Part of Your Annual Goal Setting Session. Provide needed support and training to help leaders achieve their goals, as long as they don't conflict with the organization's.

Leaders and Organizers

There are some schools of organizing that stress that a leader is one thing and an organizer is another. Conceptually, it is not quite clear that this is true. In a coalition, the leaders may all be the paid staff of other groups, and in many organizations that have no staff, volunteer leaders do much the same thing that paid staff would do. What is clear is that in local organizations with paid staff and volunteer leaders, there are certain roles that are appropriate for each.

One of the first things that most new organizers are taught is that in the absence of a salary, there are certain "perks" that leaders get: being quoted in the newspaper or interviewed on TV, representing the organization publicly, and receiving praise and recognition. This is not just a matter of rewarding leaders. It is important to the organization as a whole that its leaders become widely known personalities who enhance the group's power. For that reason, organizers are warned not to get in the spotlight themselves. Every time the paid staff are interviewed on TV, an opportunity is lost to strengthen the leadership. Worse, resentment is created and leaders ask, "Why should I help her run her organization; that's what she's paid for."

The situation is somewhat different in statewide and national coalitions. It is not always possible to have volunteer leaders on hand where and when the media want them. There is also a need to have the coalition as a whole receive a large amount of the recognition, rather than have it go to the head of one group within the coalition. In such situations, executive directors and other staff more often play the role of spokesperson.

The second thing that organizers should be taught, but many aren't, is don't do anything for leaders that leaders can do for themselves. The job of leaders is to do things to build the organization. The job of organizers is to get others to do things to build the organization.

There was a community organization that at one time had no staff. Often, leaflets had to be taken to the printer who was located in another neighborhood and closed at five o'clock. The leaders worked out a system to get their copy to the printer. The woman who did the layout brought it with her when she took her child to school. There, she gave it to another member who had a child in the same class. That member took the layout home and gave it to his wife who, the next day, brought it to work. At lunch, she gave it to a another member who worked near her. He took it home, and the next day, his wife, who worked near the printer, brought it in on her lunch hour. Now, it was true that getting the leaflet to the printer took two days and involved six people, but that was really fine. It kept the people in touch with each other, and with the organization, and it gave them a way of helping the organization that didn't take them much out of their way.

Later, when the group hired an organizer, he said, "I'll just pick up the layout at your house, and take it to the printer." Wrong!! The organizer is a paid professional. His job is to get people to do things to build the organization, not to run errands. That organizer was taking roles away from members and wasting time that he should have spent finding new people to do more things.

Here are some of the roles that are appropriate for paid organizers and for volunteer leaders. For most community organizations, organizers should:

- Make proposals for action
- Develop workplans based on board decisions
- Identify leadership roles and training needed
- Help recruit new leaders
- Ensure honest evaluations
- Help people assume leadership tasks
- Coordinate information flow between boards and committees

Volunteer leaders should:

- Represent the constituency, which means speaking in public forums and providing interviews for the media
- Lead in actions
- Maintain the organization by forming a board that is responsible for raising money, setting policies, hiring and evaluating the executive director (firing if need be)
- Doing as much of the actual physical work of the organization as possible.

Sometimes problems arise within organizations that hire community leaders to serve as organizers. Even if the leaders have good organizing skills, they many not understand that their roles have changed, and that they are now to develop the leadership of others and drop the up-front spokesperson role that they might have played in the past.

Another problem arises when people are hired to function as organizers, but really have no experience in organizing. Leaders become frustrated and wonder why they aren't getting paid if that person is. If the organizer is not looked to for providing professional organizing skills, then the leaders will tend to give the staff all the jobs they don't want to do. The organizer gets frustrated because he doesn't enjoy the work and is learning few skills.

If your organization is in this situation, consider raising additional funds in order to hire a professional, skilled and experienced organizer. Perhaps a person could be hired to train and develop your inexperienced staff, or perhaps the person could be shifted to another position. If you are not able to hire a professional organizer, be sure to provide intensive training and support from an experienced organizing consulting group. A few foundations set aside special technical assistance funds to ensure that community organizations get proper training and consulting.

In ending this chapter, allow us to restate what is really the only point, just in case anyone missed it. Volunteer leadership development is about the most important thing an organizer does. If you are not developing leaders, then you are not building the organization.

Senior leaders, Ms. Chertock and Mr. Fuchs, pressure doctors to accept Medicare Assignment.

12

Meetings can make or break an organization. If your meetings are well prepared, focused on planning for action, and facilitated in an efficient, yet involving and upbeat manner, they help build your organization. On the other hand, if your meetings are poorly planned, poorly run, and don't focus on planning for action, it will be difficult, if not impossible, to build an organization.

All meetings should help meet the basic principles of direct action organizing. First, the meeting should help the organization win concrete improvements in people's lives. Thus, all meetings must have concrete goals that matter and that are accomplished. If you are meeting with your organization's leadership, your goal is to plan, to make decisions, or to involve people in the work at hand. Few people want to attend a meeting, just to be meeting.

Second, the meeting should give people a sense of their own power. Meetings must be run efficiently and well so that people will gain a sense of their own power through participating. Make sure that meeting participants are encouraged to speak, ask questions, and gain confidence in their abilities.

Finally, the meeting should begin to change the relations of power. You do this when you build or strengthen your organization. Every meeting should strengthen your organization by making plans for raising funds, recruiting volunteers, training your board to function more effectively, or setting other plans for building your organization. Making sure that your

Preparation

Meeting Facilitation

Follow-up

Participating in Meetings

Planning and Facilitating Meetings

organization grows and develops enables you not only to win immediate issue victories, but also to build an organization that has real power in the community.

Preparation

Well run, effective meetings require solid preparation. Too many organizers underestimate the time needed to plan and organize a good meeting. The hardest part, and certainly the most time-consuming aspect of a meeting, is the planning. Consider the following:

Goals. It is critical that the organizer and key leaders have clear meeting goals in mind. Without them, it is difficult to figure out an agenda and hard to know who should attend. Every meeting should have concrete, realistic, and measurable goals of things you want to accomplish. Avoid goals such as:

- To have a meeting. A meeting is not a goal in itself.
- To educate people. It's tough to measure whether or not you've "educated" people. In addition, if your meetings consist primarily of educational programs, you will attract a different group of people than more action-focused meetings would.

Because most of your meetings, especially internal ones, should be used to plan action, make decisions, and build the organization, your goals should be such things as:

- To develop a strategy and timeline to implement an issue campaign.
- To develop a strategy and timeline for a specific tactic.
- To recruit volunteers or new members.
- To evaluate goals or programs and to plan for the future.
- To decide upon organizational positions.

Site: The choice of meeting site will affect who comes to a meeting. Criteria for choosing a site include:

- *Familiarity.* Is it a place with which people are familiar and comfortable?
- *Accessibility.* Is the meeting site accessible for those you are trying to reach? Make sure that the room is accessible for disabled and elderly people. Central location is important and accessibility by public transportation may also be important.
- *Represents Constituency.* Is the site perceived as a representative one for those who you want to participate? For example, if you are trying to build a multi-racial organization and your meetings are only held in an exclusively White church, your choice of site would not represent your constituency.
- *Adequate Facilities.* Different meetings require different facilities. Small meetings need a small cozy room, while larger meetings need larger rooms with more elaborate facilities. Meetings of senior citizens need a good loud speaker. Meetings

for young families need a safe space for child care. Be sure to consider all the things you might need before you choose a site.

Timing. Set the meeting at a time that is most convenient for those you want to attend. You may need to call several people and suggest possible options.

Chairperson. Every meeting should have a Chairperson whose main job is to facilitate the meeting. It is best to have someone who does not need to present program suggestions or answer lots of questions to serve as the Chairperson, who should be free to focus on facilitating the meeting instead of talking. The Chairperson should be involved in setting the agenda so that he or she understands it and thinks it is workable.

Agenda. Who actually plans the agenda depends on the situation. In most organizations' regular membership meetings, the organizer works with the Chairperson to plan the agenda. For board meetings, the organization's director works with the board president to plan the agenda. In general, it is a staff organizing function to work with leaders on developing agendas.

Whoever works on the agenda should assure that participants receive a printed agenda, which should list the topics and provide some background on the discussion. Many facilitators and agenda planners find that it helps them to list the objective of the discussion on the agenda (e.g., "the objective of this discussion is to decide upon which direction to proceed"). Another helpful tool for the Chairperson is to assign suggested time limits for each agenda item. The board president of a public housing residents' management organization in Chicago was having trouble chairing the organization's board meetings. People talked for long periods of time and the meetings went on forever. By placing times on the agenda, this Chairperson was able to keep the meetings to their allotted times, and their overall tone changed dramatically.

Every organizer wants commitment from every meeting. Getting commitment for work and participation builds the organization. Because this commitment is important, don't skimp on time for this section of the agenda. If

this part of the meeting has to be dropped due to lack of time, you probably won't meet your goals. Every organizer has attended day-long seminars where the most important part of the agenda, the planning for action session, was so late in the day that everyone had either left or was exhausted. Make sure that everyone leaves with something concrete to do.

For organizational meetings where many decisions will be made, such as board meetings, consider ordering the decisions as follows:

- Easy decisions—Ask the group to make a few easy decisions; it gets people off to the right start.
- Hard, controversial decisions—Next, put the hard decisions that require lots of discussion.
- Moderate, non-controversial decisions—At the end, put decisions that are of moderate importance, but upon which most people will probably agree. People are tired, so they don't want to debate things. And, you want to end the meeting on a harmonious note, if at all possible.

Once an agenda has been developed, review it to ensure that it meets the goals of the meeting. Change it if necessary.

Background Materials/Proposals. Whoever plans the agenda should identify materials and proposals that would provide the necessary background for people to make good decisions and would save the group time. In general, people find it easier to respond to proposals than to create programs from scratch. Written proposals enable people to identify the points of disagreement or concern. The larger the meeting, the more important it is that proposals be recommended for groups to choose from and alter. Small groups can create strategies and develop plans, but large groups can only alter and choose. Plan an agenda that fits the group size you expect.

Meeting Roles. Assign all meeting roles before the actual meeting. There are at least five reasons for people having particular leadership roles in a meeting. The first is that someone is good at something—leading a song, facilitating discussion, welcoming people, or whatever. The second is that the responsibility is part of someone's role. It is the treasurer's job to give the financial report. Not to have the treasurer give the report would be a slight to the person. The third reason for assigning a particular role is political. It would be politically good for your organization if a particular person played a leadership role in the meeting. The fourth reason is to develop leaders. People need experience in making presentations and leading discussions in order to develop. The fifth reason is to get people to attend. People will come if they have a role to play; thus, the more roles you have, the better.

Typical roles in meetings include:

- *Facilitator/Chairperson.* This person sees that the meeting moves forward and follows the agenda, unless the agenda is changed by a vote of the group.
- *Notetaker.* This person takes notes about the meeting. This person or the facilitator may also write the meeting's main points on a newsprint, which is placed so that everyone attending can see it.
- *Timekeeper.* A timekeeper reminds the Chairperson about the time constraints.
- *Presenters.* A variety of people can present various programs, ideas, and reports, as appropriate to the group. These people should be different from the facilitator/Chairperson.
- *Tone-Setter.* This should be a person who can open or close a meeting with a prayer or song.
- *Greeter.* In large organizational meetings, ask at least one person to welcome new people and get their names and addresses as they enter.

Room Arrangements/Logistics. Before the meeting, assess the actual room you will use in order to plan the room arrangements and logistical details. Possible items to consider include:

- *Chair Arrangements.* Chairs in circles or around tables encourage discussion and cohesiveness. Podiums and theater arrangements encourage formality. Decide which arrangements are best. Set up fewer chairs than the number expected. It's better to add chairs than have chairs sitting empty.

- *Places to Hang Newsprint Pads.* Will tape damage the walls? Is an easel available?
- *Outlets for Audio-Visual Equipment.* Will you need to bring extra extension cords?
- *Place for People to Sign In.* Where can you place the sign-in table to assure that you get names, addresses, and phone numbers for follow-up?
- *Refreshments.* Do you plan to have refreshments? If so, who will bring them? Can someone else bring the plates or cups? Do you need outlets for coffee pots? Is there a room arrangement whereby people can get food without disrupting the meeting? Who will handle cleanup?
- *Microphone Set-Ups.* Will you need microphones? Will someone be available to set up and test the equipment? Is there a way to adjust the volume from the back? Is the equipment height adjustable?

Asking people to bring items or to help arrange things for the meeting helps to assure their attendance. Assign people to bring coffee, cups, cookies, tablecloths, agendas, posters, sign-in sheets, tape players, or flowers. Ask different people to set up chairs, sound equipment, or informational displays. Delegating tasks ahead of time may seem more trouble than it's worth, but it gets people involved in the meeting and the organization. It also makes the meeting run smoothly, which people appreciate.

Turnout. If you want your large membership meetings well attended, make plans to remind people. Do not rely on mailings to get people to a meeting. If your meeting involves only a few people, one person can call everyone a day or two ahead. If you are hoping for larger numbers of people, recruit a number of people to help call those you want to attend. Calls should be made no more than three days before the meeting, although written notices or public announcements should be made as far in advance as possible.

These calls have an organizing function as well as aiding turnout. Explain the issues that will be discussed at the meeting, why they are important, and identify points of controversy. Because the leadership has already set the organization's program, the function of this type of meeting is to carry the program into action. It is the responsibility of the organizer to ensure that people come to the meeting prepared to do so.

For many groups, child care and transportation are barriers to people's participation. If you can make arrangements for both, you can increase your participation. Be sure to mention these in calls if they are available.

For large organizational meetings, keep track of what percentage of those who agreed to come actually showed up. This will give you a figure on which to base future turnout projections.

You can also compare sign-in sheets with lists of people, leaders, or groups who agreed to recruit to the meeting. You will then know who the real leaders are or what organizations are most effective in recruiting people.

Needless to say, once you have prepared for the meeting, most of the work is over. It's like producing a play. The time-consuming part is the rehearsing, not the actual performance.

Meeting Facilitation

Every meeting should be enjoyable, run efficiently, and build organizational morale. Although these characteristics may be difficult to measure, they are terribly important. No one wants to attend meetings that are boring or poorly run. Efficient meetings respect people's time as their most valuable resource. They also build organizational morale by generating a sense of unity and helping people respect and support one another.

Every meeting needs a facilitator, a person who helps the meeting accomplish its goals. In order to be adequately prepared, the Chairperson must know ahead of time that she or he will facilitate the meeting. There's nothing worse than arriving and asking, "Who's chairing this meeting"? If no one has prepared to facilitate, the meeting will probably be poorly run.

Being a good facilitator is both a skill and an art. It is a skill in that people can learn certain techniques and can improve their ability with practice. It is an art in that some people just

have more of a knack for it than others. Some positions in organizations, such as board presidents, require them to facilitate meetings; thus, board presidents must be trained in how to do this. Because other meetings don't require that particular people act as facilitators, you can draw upon members with the requisite skills. Facilitating a meeting requires someone to:

- Understand the goals of the meeting and the organization
- Keep the group on the agenda and moving forward
- Involve everyone in the meeting, both controlling the domineering people and drawing out the shy ones
- Make sure that decisions are made democratically.

The Chair must assure that decisions are made, plans are developed, and commitments are made, but in a manner that is enjoyable for all concerned. A good Chair is concerned about both a meeting's content and its style. By having the other roles suggested, such as notetakers and timekeepers, the Chair has some assistance in moving the agenda along. Here are some guides for meeting facilitation:

Start the Meeting Promptly. Few meetings actually begin on time these days, but you do not want to penalize those who did come on time. For large group meetings, plan to start within ten to fifteen minutes of the official beginning time. For smaller meetings, particularly regular organizational meetings, start exactly on time.

Welcome Everyone. Make a point to welcome everyone who comes to the meeting. Do not, under any circumstance, bemoan the size of the group. Once you are at a meeting, the people there are the people there. Go with what you have. (You may want to analyze the recruitment plans after the meeting.)

Introduce People. If just a few people are new, ask them to introduce themselves. If the group as a whole does not know one another well, ask people to answer a question or tell something about themselves that provides useful information for the group or the Chairperson.

The kinds of questions you should ask depend upon the kind of meeting it is, the number of people participating, and the overall goals of the meeting. Sample introductory questions include:

- What do you want to know about the organization? (if the meeting is set to introduce your organization to another organization)
- How did you first get involved with our organization? (if most people are already involved, but the participants don't know one another well)
- What makes you most angry about this problem? (if the meeting is called to focus on a particular problem).

It is important to make everyone feel welcome and listened to at the beginning of a meeting. Otherwise, participants may feel uncomfortable and unappreciated, and won't participate well in later parts of the meeting. In addition, if you don't get basic information from people about their backgrounds and involvement, you may miss golden opportunities. For example, the editor of a regional newspaper may attend your meeting, but if you don't find out that person's connections, you won't ask for an interview or special coverage.

The Chair of a meeting may need to introduce him or herself and tell why he or she is speaking or facilitating the meeting. This is especially true when most people are unfamiliar with the Chairperson. It never hurts for Chairpersons to explain how long they have been a part of the organization, how important the organization is to them, and what outcomes they hope for from the meeting.

Review the Agenda. Go over what's going to happen in the meeting. Ask the group if the agenda is adequate. While it will be fine 90 percent of the time, someone will suggest an additional item in the other 10 percent. Either the item can be addressed directly in the meeting, or you can explain how and when the issue can be addressed.

Explain the Meeting Rules. Most groups need some basic rules of order for meetings. If you choose to use a formal system, such as Robert's

Rules of Order, make sure that everyone understands how to use them. If not, a few people can dominate the meeting solely based upon their better understanding of Robert's Rules.

Encourage Participation. Every meeting should involve the people who come. Encourage leaders and organizers to listen to people. Seek reports on what people have done and thank them. Urge those with relevant background information on past decisions and work to share it at appropriate times. Draw out those who seem withdrawn from discussions.

Stick to the Agenda. Groups have a tendency to wander far from the original agenda. When you hear the discussion wandering off, bring it to the group's attention. You can say, "That's an interesting issue, but perhaps we should get back to the original matter of discussion."

Avoid Detailed Decision-Making. Frequently, it is easier for a group to discuss the color of napkins than it is the real issues it is facing. Help a group not to get immersed in details, suggesting instead, "Perhaps the committee could resolve that matter. You don't really want to be involved in this level of detail, do you?"

Move to Action. Meetings should not only provide an opportunity for people to talk, but should also challenge them to plan ways to confront and change injustice, in whatever forms it takes. Avoid holding meetings just to "discuss" things or "educate" people. Meetings should plan effective actions to build the organization.

Seek Commitments. Getting commitments for future involvement is usually a goal of most meetings. You want leaders to commit to certain tasks, people to volunteer to help on a campaign, or organizations to commit to support your group. Make sure that adequate time is allocated to seeking commitment. For small meetings, write people's names on newsprint next to the tasks they agreed to undertake. The Chairperson may want to ask each person directly how he or she wants to help. One rule of thumb, especially for meetings of less than ten people, is that everyone should leave the meeting with something to do. Discourage people from "observing" meetings. You need doers, not observers. Don't ever close a meeting by saying, "Our organizer will get back to you to confirm how you might get involved." Seize the moment. Confirm how people want to get involved at the meeting. There will be more than enough other follow-up work to be done.

Bring Closure to Discussions. Most groups will discuss items ten times longer than needed, unless the facilitator helps them recognize that they are basically in agreement. Formulate a consensus position, or ask someone in the group to formulate a position that reflects the group's general position and then move forward. If one or two people disagree, state the situation as clearly as you can: "Tom and Levonia seem to disagree on this matter, but everyone else seems to be in agreement to go in this direction. Perhaps we should decide to go in the direction of most of the group, but maybe Tom and Levonia can get back to us on other ways to accommodate their concerns."

Some groups feel strongly about reaching consensus on issues. If your group is one of these, be sure to read the book on consensus decision-making listed in the resource section on meetings. Most groups, however, find that voting is the most appropriate way to make decisions. A good rule of thumb is that a vote must pass by a two-thirds majority for it to be a good decision. If only a simple majority (fifty one percent) is reached, it does not have strong enough support to make it a good decision. For most groups to work well, they should seek consensus where possible, but take votes in order to move decisions forward and make leaders accountable.

Respect Everyone's Rights. The facilitator is the protector of the weak in meetings. He or she encourages quiet and shy people to speak, and does not allow domineering people to ridicule others' ideas or to embarrass them in any fashion. Try one of these phrases for dealing with domineering people: "We've heard a lot from the men this evening, are there women who have additional comments?" (assuming the domineering one was a man). Or, "We've heard a lot from this side of the room. Are there

people with thoughts on the other side of the room"? Or, "Let's hear from someone who hasn't spoken yet."

Sometimes people dominate a discussion because they are really interested in an issue and have lots of ideas. There may be ways to capture their interest and concern, without having them continue to dominate the meeting. For example, consider asking them to serve on a taskforce or committee on that matter.

In other situations, people just talk to hear themselves. If a person regularly participates in your organization's meetings and regularly creates problems, a key leader should talk with him or her about helping involve new people and drawing others out at meetings.

Be Flexible. Occasionally, issues and concerns arise that are so important, you must alter the agenda to discuss them before returning to the prepared agenda. If necessary, ask for a five-minute break in the meeting to discuss with the key leaders how to handle the issue and how to restructure the agenda. Be prepared to recommend an alternate agenda, dropping items if necessary.

Summarize the Meeting Results and Follow-Up. Before closing a meeting, summarize what happened and what followup will occur. Review the commitments people made to reinforce them, as well as to remind them how effective the meeting was.

Thank People. Take a moment to thank people who prepared things for the meeting, set up the room, brought refreshments, or typed up the agenda. Also, thank everyone for making the meeting a success.

Close the Meeting on or Before the Ending Time. Unless a meeting is really exciting, people want it to end on time. And remember, no one minds getting out of a meeting early.

Follow-Up

There are two main principles for meeting follow-up: Do it, and do it promptly. If meetings are not followed up promptly, much of the work accomplished at them will be lost. Don't waste people's time by not following up the meeting. There's nothing worse than holding a good planning meeting, but then allowing decisions and plans to fall through the cracks because follow-up was neglected.

Make sure that your notetaker prepares the meeting notes soon after the meeting. Otherwise, he or she will forget what the comments mean, and they will be useless later. Organizers should work with the notetakers to assure that these notes are clear and produced in a timely fashion.

Call active members who missed the meeting. Tell them you missed them and update them on the meeting's outcome. If you are actively seeking new people, call anyone who indicated that he or she would come, and not just active members.

Thank people who helped make the meeting successful, including people who brought refreshments, set up chairs, gave presentations, and played particularly positive roles in the meeting. Don't forget to thank the people "backstage," such as the clean-up crew, child care workers, or parking lot security guards.

Call the Chairperson. Thank him or her for chairing and review the outcome of the meeting. If appropriate, discuss ways to improve the meeting for next time.

Call new people who came to the meeting. Thank them for coming and see about setting up one-on-one meetings with people who look like potential leaders. Be sure to follow up with people while their interest is still fresh.

Once the minutes are prepared, write relevant reminder notes in your calendar. For example, if someone agreed to research something by March 15, jot down to call the person on March 7 and inquire about how the research is progressing.

Before the next meeting, the officers and staff should assure that tasks that were agreed to at the last meeting are accomplished. Reports should be prepared for the beginning part of the next meeting.

Place a copy of the meeting notes in an organizational notebook or file so that everyone knows where the "institutional memory" is kept. For meetings of your board of directors, the minutes are the legal record of the corporation. Minutes record important legal decisions and are reviewed as part of the annual audit.

Participating in Meetings

Everyone who participates in meetings has a responsibility to help make them a success. We can't always control others, but we can control ourselves. Below are some do's and don'ts for participating in meetings:

Do

- Personally welcome new people
- Actively listen to others
- Support the facilitator in moving the agenda ahead
- Recommend ways to resolve differences
- Participate in discussions
- Encourage new people to speak and volunteer
- Help set up and clean up the room
- Be positive and upbeat throughout the meeting
- Tell a joke or add a light comment to ease the tension in a difficult discussion.

Don't

- Dominate the discussion
- Bring up tangents
- Dwell on past problems
- Insist that people support your ideas.

Every meeting is important and must be planned with great attention. With solid planning, good facilitation, and strong follow-up, an organization can move forward in ways that win real victories, give people a sense of their own power, and change the relations of power. Meetings play a significant role in achieving your goals and deserve your utmost attention. Make your organization the one with the fun, productive meetings.

Meeting Checklist

_____ Have you set concrete, realistic goals?

_____ Is the site familiar, accessible, representative, and adequate?

_____ Are the date and time good for those you want to attend?

_____ Do you have a chairperson for the meeting? Has the chairperson been involved in preparing the agenda or been fully briefed?

_____ Does the agenda:

      _____ Accomplish the goals
      _____ Encourage commitment and involvement
      _____ Provide visible leadership roles

_____ Do you need:

      _____ Printed agenda
      _____ Background materials
      _____ Proposals

_____ Have you asked people to serve as the:

      _____ Chairperson/facilitator
      _____ Notetaker
      _____ Timekeeper
      _____ Presenters
      _____ Tone-Setters (open and close meetings)
      _____ Greeter (welcome people and get names and addresses)
      _____ Refreshment servers

_____ Have you considered the following logistical matters?

      _____ Chair arrangements
      _____ Newsprint and markers
      _____ Easel or chalkboard
      _____ Outlets for audio-visual equipment
      _____ Sign-in sheets and table
      _____ Refreshments
      _____ Microphone set-ups

_____ Do you have a turnout plan and enough people working on making turnout calls? Do you have a system for comparing those who said they will come with those who actually come?

_____ Have you arranged for childcare?

_____ Do you have transportation for those who need it?

Midwest Academy
225 West Ohio, Suite 250
Chicago, Illinois 60610

New Jersey Citizen Action statewide meeting

13

There are two astonishing facts about public speaking. First, it is easier to speak to fifty people than to five. When you speak to a very small group of people in an informal setting, each of them expects personal communication from you. You may be giving a report to a committee, but each member wants it to be like a private conversation. You are supposed to have rapport, to know what's on each one's mind, and relate to that. Although this is very difficult, most people do it and feel comfortable with it. You have probably done it lots of times without even thinking about it.

On the other hand, when speaking to a large group (from 20 to 20,000), no such personal expectations exist. People know that they are going to hear a speech, and that you have something important to say. Otherwise, you wouldn't be up there in the first place. They know that they would just die if they had to speak to a group that big, so as long as you don't go blank or throw up, you can't lose. It is only necessary that the material be clearly presented and that you can be heard.

Second, it is easier to speak to strangers than to friends. The trouble with friends is that they know you. They know that you can't remember figures. They know that you have a rash behind your knee. They know that you can't pronounce "thesaurus," and that your son won't bathe. Everything you say is evaluated in light of these facts.

The great advantage of speaking to strangers is that they know none of this. They form a quick first impression, and then the speech

Being a Great Public Speaker

stands on its own. You and it are taken at face value. You are even free to do things that you wouldn't do with close friends—to be more forceful, more emotional, or more poetic. The audience will think you're like that all the time. Anyway, you'll never see them again, so who cares? Yet, how often have you said, "I can't get up there and talk. I don't know those people"?

A Speech Moves People to Act

Unless you are simply giving information to people who won't or can't read, the purpose of a speech is to move people to action. This doesn't necessarily mean exhorting them to storm the Bastille, although that has been done successfully. The activity might be something as everyday as buying a raffle ticket or coming to the annual picnic.

In general, the more immediate and concrete the activity, the easier the speech is to prepare and deliver. The Germans have a word "weltverbesserungswahn," which means "world-betterment-craze." Speeches on this subject are often dreadful because no amount of brilliant analysis can compensate for the advocacy of distant, uncertain, and murky solutions. So, before you prepare your speech, make a decision about the action that people are to take. Construct the speech using that as the goal. Don't be vague. It's not enough to say "Go home, tell your neighbors, write your congressman and help in any way you can." Tell the neighbors what? Ask them to do what?

Describe the message to the congressman, and just how many letters are needed, and by when. List three ways that people can help, one of which is always asking them to give money.

Speaking to Create a Mood

One way a speech moves people to action is by creating a mood. The mood may be one of anger or indignation, making people despise their opponents or hold their enemies in contempt. It may be one that expresses people's confidence in themselves, their organization, and its leadership. There are moods of faith, determination, or perseverance. There is the exhilaration that people feel when they first see their way through to the solution of a difficult problem. The specific content of the speech is secondary to creating the mood. The very best speakers can take people through a series of moods or emotions.

Creating a mood by speaking is something that we do naturally all the time. Try saying to your child, "Stop that at once, and go to your room," and watch her mood change. A mood can also be created by playing a violin, but that is much more difficult. Even the lowly treasurer's report creates a mood. The organization is in debt, and everyone must help! The raffle was a great success, this is a great organization, and I'm a great treasurer! The organization is out of debt! The actual numbers in the report will back this up. Mention a few in the speech, but hand out the rest.

Think of a speech as being like a song. You sing to create a mood, not to transmit data. (The one exception to this is the song, "Ninety-Nine Bottles of Beer on the Wall.") The written word creates a mood, but a speech is not merely an extension of the written word. It is not the written word read aloud. It is its own separate form of creating and communicating emotion. A speech can be reduced to writing, but it is not the same as writing.

But, you cry, I don't want to create a mood, I just want to announce the annual picnic: "The picnic will be August third in Riverside Park. Admission is five dollars. Bring your own food, charcoal, starter and matches. No alcoholic beverages, unleashed pets, or unsupervised children by order of the Park Department please. Senior citizen discount is 50 percent. Thank you."

Well, OK, but remember that with us humans, speaking is always an emotional business. You will create a mood whether you want to or not; it can't be helped. Pay attention to it or the mood will come across as "This picnic is organized by a dull and nervous person who will probably forget to bring the park permit, so don't spend a lot on food."

Now if you were to get up, raise a big striped umbrella, open a huge picnic basket, and with each word, place on the table a delicious looking item, this would create a wholly different mood. It wouldn't even matter if you were nervous because people don't notice that when you are waving a ham at them. The purists will argue that this is an example of theater, not speech making. We reject any such distinction. Of course, it is true that in the theater it may be considered sufficient if the audience has a good laugh or a good cry, and goes home. But the purpose of a speech is to produce a result, not just a reaction.

Preparing Your Speech

Research the Audience

If there is one single key to success, this is it: Before even researching your topic or sitting down to write, you must know who will be listening. Where do they live, and in what kind of houses? What do they do for a living? How old are they? What kinds of families do they

have? How much money do they earn? How are they the same as, or different from, the majority of people living in the area, state, or nation? How much school have they attended? What is their race or ethnicity? What has their organization done? What issues is it interested in?

Most of you will be speaking to your own organizations in your own community, and will already know all of these things, but perhaps not be conscious of them. Think about them anyway. Ask yourself two sets of questions: First, how am I the same as everyone here? What do we all have in common that I can mention in the speech to draw us together? Second, how am I different? Am I the only person who has or hasn't a job, did or didn't go to college, is or isn't rich, does or doesn't speak with an accent? Are their goals and aspirations and life styles the same as mine? Am I taking the same risks that they are? When you call on common experience, make sure it really is common. Once, at a government hearing on a land development project, a Midwest Academy trainer attacked a representative of the real estate board saying, "Why should we listen to him, he represents our landlords"? The audience laughed. No one else in the room was a renter.

For those speaking to groups outside your own community, gathering this preliminary information is important for both style and content:

- *Language should be appropriate and geared to the audience's actual vocabulary.* Books, songs, or people quoted must be known to the group. (The Bible is almost always safe when done respectfully.)

- *Humor must be tailored to the audience.* The clever word play or double entendre, much prized by urban intellectuals, falls flat elsewhere.

- *Even factual information is transmitted differently according to class and region.* Some people don't quote statistics to each other; they tell anecdotes that illustrate, in non-quantitative ways, the point being made. Others expect statistics from unimpeachable authorities.

- *The life experience of the audience matters.* The annual convention of an industrial trade union will be little moved by speeches on the promise of trade unionism; the delegates have been hearing them for many years. The same speech delivered on a picket line or to a newly organized unit of service workers gets an entirely different reception.

- *The geographic location changes the impact of the speech.* Using the insurance industry as an example of corporate greed goes over well in West Palm Beach, Florida. It bombs up in Jacksonville, headquarters to many insurance companies.

- *Age changes perspective.* An audience of second-generation Cubans has social views different from those of the immigrant generation. Even within the same generation, the separation of class position can be critical. The self-interest issues to which a speaker at a private university might appeal are very different from those at a public university.

In summary, the more factual information you have about the audience, the better the speech will be. It even helps to know something of the organizational background of the particular event at which you are speaking. A speaker ought to know what brought this particular audience together. How was the turnout done? Are these the organization's regulars, or did they come off the street in response to a particular crisis? Assume nothing. One of our staff was the after dinner-speaker at a fundraiser for a local community group. The speech was addressed directly to the members of the organization, but it turned out that few of them were actually in attendance. Tickets, priced out of their reach, had been sold instead to area service agencies, which passed them out to staff. The audience, presumed to be low-income neighborhood people, were really professionals and not exactly, "united in our common struggle to save our homes."

Ask about the details of the program. How big is the audience? How long are you expected to speak? What is the rest of the program? It is one thing to be the opening speaker, something else to be on the agenda near the beginning, and a different matter altogether to be the last speaker before dinner. If you are standing between people and their dinner, keep it short. While you're asking, find out who else is on the program and what topics they are covering. Are

you the only Black speaker or the only woman? Are you one of five lawyers? Shape your remarks accordingly.

Ask those who know, and ask yourself, what the audience expects you to say. What do they want to hear, or hope to hear? Show that you are in tune with this. "I know that you are expecting a talk on sericulture (the raising of silk worms), and I'm not going to disappointment you." Or, "I know that you want to hear more about sericulture, but allow me to read a poem instead." More to the point, use this information to strengthen your message. "I know that you all expect me to come before you to urge endorsement of the Democratic candidate, so you will realize how serious it is when I say that this year, we should not take a position."

Research Your Topic

"What, more research? But I heard that if you prepare too much, the speech will go flat." If you don't prepare, you'll go flat. The point is that you are going to have to condense the topic to bring out just two or three essential points. That means you must know a lot, just to figure out what those few essential points are. People who know only a little can still fill a speech with facts, but they can't focus it properly. What's worse, they are so afraid of leaving out something important and not knowing it, that they try to cram in everything just to be safe.

Researching and writing a speech are two separate steps. Many people try to combine them, mistakenly thinking that the speech is merely the written word read aloud. That really does make the speech flat. If it were a documentary movie, and not a speech, the difference between the steps would be clear at once. First you would assemble the information, and then start filming.

It doesn't matter whether your topic is "The Sorry State of World Trade" or "The Annual Picnic Announcement"; the research process is essentially the same. How do you research the picnic? Start with the location, Riverside Park. Go over and take a good look at it. Are there bathrooms, drinking fountains, charcoal grills, and ball fields? Are there picnic tables or should people bring blankets? Is there a concession stand to buy soda? What about slides, swings, and a sandbox for the little kids? Is there parking or public transportation nearby? Look for beauty as well. Can you see flowers, and how is the view of the river? Take notes. Of course, all of this information won't be in the speech, just a few essential facts.

Even if Riverside Park is right in the neighborhood and everyone knows exactly what it is like, go and do the research anyway. It helps just to be able to say "I was over there yesterday. The grass is bright green, and covered with beautiful yellow dandelions. The river was a deeper blue than I ever remember it. We're lucky to have such a great spot for our picnic."

Next, research the organization's program. Five bucks is a lot to charge for a bring-your-own-food type of picnic, so find out what the money is for. It better be going to fight an important issue campaign, and not to pay the electric bill or your salary. (See Chapter 20 on grassroots fundraising.) You'll need to know enough about the issue so that you can explain its importance in one or two sentences.

If you haven't already researched the audience, do it now. Is this a ball playing crowd? Are there many seniors present for whom the discount is important and transportation likely to be a problem? Are there lots of parents with young children in the group? Now that all the information is together, you can start to write the speech. Of course, had the topic been "The Sorry State of World Trade," the research methodology would be a bit different, but the process is basically the same.

Write the Speech

"Never mind, I'll just get up and wing it." Oh yeah? Did you ever sit through a rambling speech, and just when you could stand it no longer, the speaker said, "Now I'll pull all these ideas together"? Then he pulled and pulled, but it never did come together. Weren't you insulted that the speaker took your time and hadn't bothered to prepare? Whether you actually deliver the speech by reading it, memorizing it, or something in between, is a different matter that we will come to presently. You should have a fully written out second draft. A few really great orators can come with nothing but three points on the back of an envelope. They know who they are, and may ignore this advice.

Every speech has a beginning, a middle, and an end. Plan each of them separately following

the old advice that you should tell the audience what you're going to tell them, then tell it to them, and then remind them of what you just told them. Putting it another way, a speech isn't like a report. A report starts out by stating facts, and then logically works toward a conclusion that comes, appropriately, at the end. If you wait until the end of a speech to get to the point, you are likely to lose the audience.

Start with an outline. Write in the headings "Beginning, Middle, and End," then list the points to be made under each. You can break it down into smaller parts. For example:

1) Beginning   Half page
   a)
   b)

2) Middle   Two–Three pages
   a)
   b)
   c)

3) End   One page
   a)
   b)
   c) Closing   Half page
      1)
      2)

A trick is to write the beginning last, after you have had a chance to see how the speech unfolds. This lets you use the introduction to focus what you are actually going to say, not what you thought you were going to say. Through the miracle of word processing, you can take the closing, and move it to the beginning, and then write a new end with more flourish than the old one. None of this is logical, or what you are "supposed" to do, but it works.

The beginning or introduction is really a summary of the whole speech. It states the problem and the solution, and it tells people what they have to do to achieve the solution.

The middle of the speech adds more detail. The detail might be supplied by making factual arguments, or by telling stories of people's personal experience with the problem. The goal here is to make the problem real to the audience. This is also a good time to go on the attack against either the person who caused the problem or the person who holds the key to the solution but won't use it. This might be overkill in the speech about the picnic, but since you are going to mention the issue campaign to which the money is going, it could be worked in at this point.

As you move into the end of the speech, start building the case for the solution you are going to advocate. No solution to any problem should be considered self evident. If it was, everyone would have hit on it long ago, and you wouldn't be explaining it now. Try to anticipate some of the major objections that will crop up in the minds of the audience and head them off. It is better to acknowledge up front that there might be questions about what you are proposing. If you talk to enough people beforehand, you can anticipate the questions. "Some of you remember that at last year's picnic, there was certain evidence that dog walkers had been in the area. This year, our super-heroic-volunteer-clean-up-crew will sweep through just before starting time." If you haven't been specific about what needs to be done, now is the time. "Each person in this room must sell five picnic tickets each week for the next two weeks. That's only one ticket a day. I know you can do it."

The closing section of the speech quickly summarizes the steps the organization has to take to make the solution happen. Then it moves on to its real purpose, which is the charge to the audience that closes the speech. It goes along the lines of "We have never failed our community before, and I know that if we each do our part, we will win." Or, "Our allies in labor have always stood by us. Now is the time to walk with them." Or, "This picnic can break all records, and all you have to do is be there."

Ending the speech can be a combination of words and gestures. Sometimes words alone don't quite convey that the speech is now over. You have heard speakers go through three endings and not be able to figure out how to stop. Use gestures. Step back. Take your notes off the podium. Make a dramatic gesture with both arms. Simply sit down; you can stand up again in a moment to acknowledge applause. Many speakers end by saying, "Thank you." This is fine for closing all but the most emotional or dramatic speeches. In any event, don't overstay your welcome. You will be appreciated as much for being brief as for the content of what you said.

Each speaker has a personal speaking rate and you should know exactly how long it takes to say the equivalent of one double-spaced typewritten page. Time yourself until you know this precisely. Then you will always know how long a speech will run.

Use the outline to write the first draft. Plan on writing at least two drafts. The first is just to get the information down and sort out the order of your points. It is like making the initial sketch for a painting. In the second draft you start adding the color, or in this case, the colorful language. Your mind must first be relieved of worrying about the content before you can focus on mood and style. Many will be tempted to simply edit the first draft, and call it a second draft. Don't. Start a new file and begin to type in the speech all over again, copying from the first draft. With each sentence ask, how can I say this better? Should I say it at all? Should it go someplace else? Does it need an example? Rewrite as you go. Too many facts and too much detail are the most common problems.

A good book of quotations is useful for speech writing. Use quotes as in a sermon. Start with the quotation, explain what it has to do with the subject, then come back to the quotation several times to emphasize points. Get it right. Remember the mess that Vice President Quayle made when he addressed the United Negro College Fund? Trying to quote their motto, "A mind is a terrible thing to waste," he said, "What a waste it is to lose one's mind—or not to have a mind—how true that is."

A prize winning painter of landscapes said that he starts by squinting at the scene to be painted. This breaks up the detail so that only the boldest colors and shapes stand out. Mentally squint at your first draft. Let the boldest colors and shapes stand out in your mind. Then find words to express them. Another term for this is "style."

Style

Images and Pictures

Abraham Lincoln once said of an opposing lawyer, "He can compress the most words into the fewest ideas." In public speaking, of course, the goal is to do the opposite. It is to use the fewest words to represent your ideas. A speech is a picture painted with words so that the picture tells the story. The words don't tell the story, they create the picture. The words are like the brush. The brush makes the painting, and the painting tells the story. You can use a very small brush and put in many brush strokes (words) in order to fill the picture with a lot of fine detail, or you can use a broader brush with fewer strokes to give the impression of your subject with fewer words. The imagination of the listener will then fill in the details, which makes the details more vivid and the listener more involved. This happens when you read a book and build pictures of the characters in your imagination. Often, when the book is later made into a movie, you are disappointed with the characters as they appear on the screen. The ones in your imagination were more real and vivid.

If you were using a very fine brush, you might say,

> Between 1990 and 1995, the number of poor people in this town rose from 10,153 to 11,239. That's an increase of 10.7 percent. During the same years, 1990 to 1995, the number of homeless rose from 50 to 638, an increase of 963.3 percent. Of those, only an estimated 349 are in charitable facilities, the rest are on the streets.

If you were painting with a broader brush to create a picture and a mood, you could say,

> When I left here to start college, I saw just one homeless person sleeping on a bench at the train station. Coming back four years later, every bench was filled, the washroom was filled, even the news stand had become a refuge for someone. In that short time homelessness had increased by nearly one thousand percent.

Of course, this is much less precise, but that is just the point. The exact statistics don't really matter, they are undoubtedly wrong anyway.

The years don't matter either, a rise of 850 percent between 1989 and 1994 would be no different. Drop the numbers, and paint a picture of the human magnitude of the problem. (But, have the numbers on a card in your pocket, because someone will ask during the question period. The picture should be an interpretation of information you have, not a coverup for what you don't know. People who do that eventually get caught.)

Abraham Lincoln himself was a master at painting pictures with words. In the opening of a speech that he thought the world would "little note nor long remember," and that doubtless would not be gender-specific if made in modern times, Lincoln said,

> Four score and seven years ago our fathers brought forth upon this continent a new nation, conceived in liberty, and dedicated to the proposition that all men are created equal.

That was one sentence of thirty words, and yet it flashed to the audience four broadly painted, mood setting pictures:

1. "Four score and seven." Simply saying 87 years ago would have been more direct, but Lincoln's audience read the Bible more than most do nowadays. They knew that each person's allotted time on earth is "three score years and ten." Four score and seven, then, starts to paint a picture of the previous generation, and separates it from the present one. The words lead directly into "our fathers"—not the founding fathers, not some remote group of people, but the actual parents and grandparents of that very audience. The image Lincoln was conveying was that the audience and the nation were literally brought forth by the same parents.

2. "Conceived in liberty." The phrase takes first prize for the grandest picture painted with the fewest words. The words themselves, taken literally, don't actually make sense. Only the picture they paint makes sense.

3. "Dedicated to the proposition," paints another picture, one with blurred edges. This picture helped Lincoln to solve a political problem in the speech. He was heading toward painting the Civil War as a war for equality and wanted to link that idea with the heritage of

1776. The problem was that while the Declaration of Independence had said that "all men are created equal," the Constitution had not. Equality was not one of the founding principles of the Republic, and everyone knew it better then than we do today. The word "proposition" can be read as meaning a proposal, not yet a reality, or an undertaking, not yet an accomplished fact. Thus, in only four words, Lincoln resolved (and fudged) the ambiguity of the founding of America, which involved forces both for and against universal freedom. Again, the words taken literally don't quite make sense. A nation can be dedicated to a principle, but exactly how is it dedicated to a proposition? As a picture, however, it makes perfect sense.

Lincoln might have tried to explain, using a finer brush and more words, that if Madison had been more of this, and Hamilton less of that, and the northern states gone more this way, while the southerners went some other way, it all might have been as we wish it had been. But that would not have been painting pictures and creating a mood, it would have been writing a report.

4. By saying, in effect, that all people are created equal, Lincoln again accomplished a fine picture. The Declaration had held that common people and kings were equals; slaves were now to be included in that equation. It was only ten months since the Emancipation Proclamation had gone into effect. Before that time, the war was justified as being fought to preserve the Republic. Now, new dimensions of freedom and equality were officially added. This entire conception was boldly sketched into the speech with only five words.

The entire address is worthy of study. It is like watching a slide show. Image after image flashes by. They are created by words, but are more than words. The desired action, of course, was that the audience rededicate itself to winning the war. Toward that conclusion the speech moved with the cadence of a march, "We can not dedicate, we can not consecrate—we can not hallow—of the people, by the people for the people." It carries the audience up past the endless rows of graves which surround them, and on to the most lofty aim of the war: the new birth of freedom. So pronounced is the rhythm of the speech that the closing lines were actually set to music and sung as a march in the stirring "Ballad for Americans," recorded by both Paul Robeson and Odetta.

Humor

It is customary to begin speeches, other than those dedicating cemeteries, with a joke. Follow this tradition, as long as the joke has something to do with the topic, is non-offensive, isn't about making a speech, and you can tell a joke well. Telling the opening joke is a little like bribing the audience to like you, but that's OK.

Humor has a number of functions in a speech. Most important, it really does make people like you. Speeches in which you take an unpopular position are best cloaked in humor. Getting a group to laugh with you at itself is a good way of giving criticism. Laughter keeps the audience alert. Jokes are the one part of the speech that no one wants to miss. If they know jokes are coming, they will listen for them and catch more of what you are saying. Humor quickly changes the mood, which makes it a good transition from one part of the speech to the next. It also relieves tension. If you are a speaker good enough to create tension, you should also break it occasionally. Laughing wakes people up by causing them to breath deeply and rapidly, thus getting a shot of oxygen to the brain. (In smoke-filled rooms it just gets smoke to the brain, so be careful.) This is why a joke at the start of the speech is not enough. Work humor right into the text. Here are a few things that are funny:

An Unusual Invective. When aimed at an opponent, this can be funny. "I have always considered him to be the short end of nothing shaved down to a point." Playing with your opponent's name is funny. "Here comes let-them-eat-cake Drake." Or, "Doctor Jones, I don't think he ever went to medical school. His mother just named him Doctor to make him rich." (But be careful not to come off as mean by making fun of everyone but yourself.)

An Allusion to the Forbidden. References that come close to forbidden subjects are funny. "I saw Limburger cheese once. I didn't know whether to eat it or step in it."

Word Games. Word games are funny if people get it. "We stopped at a little village called Hadem on the Hill." But not funny if they don't.

Informality. Being less formal in speech or manner than previous speakers, or than the occasion seems to demand, is funny. (But, there is a thin line between funny and silly.)

Storytelling. Telling a story about a personally embarrassing situation is funny. "There I was with the grease oozing out of my button holes, the Mayor coming toward me, and the police behind me, and I know I don't have to tell you what happened next."

The Absurd and the Unexpected. "You should have been at last year's picnic, a parrot won the raffle. I called the number, and this bird flew up with the ticket in its beak. I said, 'Just what are you going to do with a weekend for two in Atlantic City?' The parrot shot back, `What's the matter, you don't think I can get a date?'"

Of course, the best jokes are the ones you make up, but it helps to clip jokes or funny situations out of papers, or to keep books of jokes. Don't use jokes straight from the book, just the idea. Change the situations and names to fit the speech.

Sharing Yourself

In course of the speech, you need to project yourself as a believable character, someone the audience feels they know. There has to be a personal reason why you are so concerned about the subject. It can't be your job to just get up and say certain words. Talk about yourself, your experience, and how the problem affects you. Tell stories about people you know who are in the same situation, and what happened to them, and how you felt about it. Why did you decide to get involved with this? Mention your family, and how the situation had an impact on them. Quote your child or your Great Aunt Tilly.

Delivering the Speech

Decide How You Will Give the Speech

There are very few guidelines for this. It is an individual matter. Some people actually read every speech word for word. It works if you write the way you speak, although it can sound stilted. Most people use an outline, filling in the actual language from memory. A few speakers actually memorize the whole presentation, but they are often people who use the same material over and over. It is probably easier to learn to read well than to memorize, but it is hard to write the way you speak if you have been encumbered by formal education.

Go back to your outline and try using it to jog your memory while you plug in the language from the final text. If you don't feel comfortable with this, take the fully written out speech and highlight the key points. This way, the highlighted points serve as an outline, but the whole text is there if you need it. If you speak from index cards, number them. If you ever drop your cards, you will thank us for telling you this.

You still don't feel that you have it? OK, just read the speech word for word. If you practice, it will come out fine.

Practice

Start with a tape recorder. Rig up a podium to rest the text on. Put it six feet from a full-length mirror. Stand up and blast away at yourself. Use the mirror is to practice eye contact with the audience as well as hand gestures and, of course, your smile. If you are a beginner, don't worry about gestures a first, but build up to using your whole body in a speech. That's why you were given a body. During practice, look at yourself in the mirror more than at the speech. Read a sentence or two without speaking. Put your finger on the next sentence to be read. This holds your place. Look up at the audience and speak the sentences. Quickly look down at your finger, read, move finger, look up, speak, read, move finger, look up speak, etc. If you are memorizing the speech, you can practice with a tape recorder in your car on the way to work. Don't practice on public transportation. There are too many people doing that already.

Play back the tape, listening for the timing. Most speeches are delivered too fast. Slow down for clarity, and slow down further at certain parts for emphasis. For still greater emphasis, try saying a sentence at normal speed, and then repeat it at half speed with your voice slightly lower. Mark the margins of the speech to indicate slowing down and raising or lowering your voice. As you listen to the tape, think of where you want the audience to participate in the speech by laughing, clapping, or even shouting. Mark pauses in the margin to allow time for this.

Listen for sentences that are too long or involved. Remember that when you speak, the audience can't see the punctuation marks. Don't use anything more complicated than a comma. You can always pause for a comma, but what do you do for a semi-colon?

Listen for even volume. You do not want to say everything with the same degree of loudness; but, before you can control that, you must eliminate spots where your voice falls off. These are usually caused by running out of breath on sentences that are too long. After shortening all your sentences to a length you can say without gasping for air, look for phrases that should be emphasized by speaking more loudly or more softly.

Put speaking directions in the margin or in the text. A favorite speaking direction is "Pound table, logic weak." When finished, your text might look something like this:

Pause *Between* *Words*	Sometimes it is said that man can not be trusted to govern himself.
Regular	Can he then be trusted with the government of others?
Hit *"Kings"*	Or have we found angels in the form of kings to govern him?
Soft/ *Slow*	Let history answer this question.

Jefferson's First Inaugural, 1801

An effective speaker we have heard uses a different method. She writes in the margin the type of emotion she wishes to evoke at that point. Anger, fear, sadness, or joy, among others. Just seeing the word puts the right tone into her voice. She doesn't know why it works, but we can attest that it does.

Audience Involvement

Large Groups. The audience should be as much involved in the speech as you are. In large groups, this will occur naturally if you pause to give them a chance to clap after lines with which you know they will agree. Take this a step further and write in applause lines that state the group's sentiment in ways they will want to support. "Year after year we have seen the Legislature sold to the highest bidders. Laws were made by people who were nothing but the hired servants of corporate wealth. Today, with Democratic Election Financing we can get the big money out of politics."

Enjoying humor is another form of participation. Pausing for laughter not only encourages it, but also keeps your next words from being drowned out.

Beyond this, if you want still more participation, you have to build it into the text. In general, the larger the audience, the easier it is to get people participating because they enjoy the feeling of power that comes from doing something together. A line such as, "Will we let them get away with it again?" will bring a resounding "No!" Or, "Is it time to fight back?" "Yes!" "I can't hear you." "YEEES!!"

Any response other than a simple yes or no must first be taught.

> "We can't pay these bills. We've got to roll back rates. We're going to tell the Governor—roll back rates. What do we want?" "Roll back rates." "Say it so he can hear it." "ROLL BACK RATES!"

Make sure that even yes or no questions are clearly put so that the audience knows how to respond. Avoid such often made errors as, "Should this war go on, does it have to stop?" Even worse, "We either sink or swim or we don't. What do we want?" Avoid trying to get an audience to shout a slogan in a foreign language, no matter what country or movement you are in solidarity with. Be flexible. If you are the third speaker and the other two have solicited a lot of audience involvement already, cut down and save it until near the end.

Small Groups. Start by asking people to introduce themselves and tell one thing about themselves such as a recent victory of their organization, or what they hope to get out of the meeting. Why are they concerned about the issue? Think of a question that is both an ice breaker and has something to do with the subject. In the course of the speech, direct other occasional questions to the audience. "Has anyone had experience with this?" "In a minute I'm going to call on Lynn and Dan and ask them to respond to the points we have been discussing, but first I want to say. . ." (This gives people a minute to collect their thoughts.)

Here are a few tips for speaking informally to small groups when you are unexpectedly called on, or have had no time to prepare, and are casting about for something to say. Size up the group and decide on three points to make. No more, no less. If you are being introduced for the first time and will have an ongoing relationship with the organization, then what are the three things about you that are most important for them to hear? Otherwise, what are the three most important things to do about the issue or the campaign? What are the three most important things to tell them about your organization? Who in the group should get praise or recognition from you? What can the group as a whole be praised for? Is there an unstated sentiment in the room that needs expression? "We are all frightened." We are all fighting mad." "We are all relieved, but this must never happen again." Any combination of these will give you a fine off-the-cuff speech.

Being Introduced

"How would you like to be introduced?" "Me? Oh don't bother, I'll just get up and speak." Bad idea! Of course, most of us are modest; we don't like being talked about or praised in public, and we certainly don't like telling someone else how to do that. Nonetheless, the introduction matters. As in recruiting volunteers or members, you need to legitimize yourself. The introduction can even make or break the speech. It sets you up with the audience. "Last March was bleak. The organization had debts, and I couldn't find anyone to head up the Picnic Committee. Then I called on Fran. Even though she was home with a new baby, she volunteered, and she has been on the phone every day since, selling tickets and making arrangements. Lets show our appreciation to Fran."

When speaking to a group you don't know, a warm introduction from one of its leaders is like a license to speak. If the leader stumbles over your name and forgets which organization you are from, the audience gets the message that you aren't very important. If the leader says that she met you ten years ago and mentions the helpful things you have been doing ever since then, it's a different story. But even someone who really has known you for ten years can stumble over your name if they are nervous or unprepared. Most of the time you will be asked for material for the introduction. If not, then offer it. Write it down. Print your name, the name of your group, and one or two things about the importance of the issue, and one or two things that qualify you to speak on this issue. Don't try to pull rank on the audience with your qualifications. "Dr. Max has done post-graduate work in astrophysics, and speaks seven languages. He was sent to Europe with the team to save Venice from sinking. His topic today is 'The Challenge of Community Gardening.'"

If, after being introduced, you feel that there are still important points about who you are or why you are there, you can always add them. Don't assume that everyone knows you, no matter how famous you are. Don't let the chair get away with saying, "Now, someone who needs no introduction." Every speaker needs an introduction.

Actually Doing It

The rule of thumb in speaking publicly is to dress slightly more formally than the group you are addressing. For many groups, looking more formal and business-like is a sign of respect for the audience. In any event, you want people to remember what you said, not what you wore.

Nervous? Good. You should be a bit nervous. The old fight-or-flee instinct will pump you up, and make your voice sharper and more energetic. If you are completely calm, go out and make yourself nervous by worrying about what can go wrong. If you are too nervous, actually shaking, talk to a friend about something else until you hear yourself being introduced. It helps to arrive early, and stand in the place you will be speaking from. Once you have tried it out, you will feel more comfortable.

Listen carefully to the introduction or to previous speakers and try to see what distance from the microphone works best. Beware of getting too close to the mike, it distorts the sound. Ask a friend in the audience to stand in the back of the room and signal you if you can't be heard. If you are speaking from notes, arrange in advance for a podium. Otherwise, you will be standing up and looking down at the table, a distance usually too far to read comfortably. Worse, you won't be looking at the audience. A podium is a bit formal but necessary.

Always speak standing up. Your lungs won't function properly sitting down. Keep a glass of water on hand. Ask loved ones if you tend to sway back and forth, or to pace when speaking. Both are distracting. If you do, keep one foot on a leg of the podium. This throws you off balance and you have to stand still to keep from falling. Take coins out of your pocket to avoid jingling.

Stage fright, also called tunnel vision, can hit anyone. Your text goes blurry, you can't remember anything, and you freeze. If it does hit, drink water. That sometimes stops it right away. If not, it buys you some time. Take a tissue from your pocket or purse, and wipe your brow. Breath deeply and steadily. Say these words to yourself: "As soon as I finish here I can go to the bathroom." Look out at the expectant faces of your audience, which thinks you have paused for dramatic emphasis, and speak on.

Above all, never apologize for anything. Don't talk about how nervous you are. Don't say that you had to stay up all night and couldn't prepare. Don't say this is your first speech. One young activist opened a speech with a long sob story about how hard he had been working, how far he had traveled, how tired he was, and how he might be catching a cold. The next speaker was a wizened Vietnamese Buddhist monk who had been fasting for peace for eight months. He didn't apologize. His speech was a perfect jewel. (The activist was forgiven and now works for the Midwest Academy.)

Learn to listen with your third ear. What you hear when speaking is the sound of your own voice. But, hidden inside your head there is actually a third ear which is meant for listening to audiences. Although communication is going out from you to the audience, you need to keep open a channel back in. How is the audience responding? Are they all getting the jokes? Are they restless? If you stop connecting and start to bore the audience, they will begin moving their chairs and coughing.

Once the audience's attention goes, it must be brought back. Check your speed and slow down. Going too fast is the easiest way to lose a group. Try speaking very softly so that people strain to catch your words. This usually quiets a room. Slip in a joke if you are able. Try an audience participation gimmick. If all else fails, skip to the last page and get out of there quickly. They won't even notice.

A very experienced speaker learns to make changes in mid speech according to the feedback coming in. Perhaps people are tired and the speech needs to be shortened, or the vocabulary is wrong for the audience, or there is more disagreement than you thought and longer discussion time would be useful. It takes quite a while to develop this ability. Keep it in mind as a goal.

After your speech, no matter how good it was, and it was probably very good, you will feel awful. You will think you did a terrible job, made a fool of yourself, and had a spot on your clothing. This is a natural feeling that always comes when anything taking a great deal of energy is over. The adrenalin goes out of your blood and you feel a letdown. The feeling goes away overnight. Wait until tomorrow to critique your speech or play back the tape or video.

Your speaking will be improved by critique and practice. Look for speaking opportunities, volunteer, and seek larger audiences. The ability to move an audience to action is one of the most valuable skills you can learn.

Now let it work. Mischief thou art afoot. Take thou what course thou wilt.
      —Anthony's Funeral Oration

14

From the time of the town crier to today's 6 o'clock news, good organizers have figured out how to use the available means of communication and technology to their advantage. One Citizen Action state director has a pilot's license and flies from city to city within his state, holding airport press conferences on the newsworthy events of the organization. Within the same state, a local tenants' organization hand-writes press releases and volunteer activists call reporters. Both organizations get excellent newspaper and television coverage. Why? Both have clear issue strategies that include plans for how and when to use the media.

An organizer's job is to make sure that there is not just media coverage, but a plan for utilizing the media as well. Approach the job of getting media coverage like any other aspect of organizing. Getting media coverage should meet the three principles of direct action organizing. It should help win real improvements in people's lives, give people a sense of their own power, and change the relations of power.

Using the Media to Win Real Improvements in People's Lives

Media work is not done just for the fun of it. Media coverage can help win real issues. As you think about your issue strategy, figure out how best to use the media to help win your issue. Media coverage is a secondary aspect of

Using the Media

political/electoral power and consumer power, because it influences both votes and consumer purchasing.

When you make your issue campaign timeline, include media work where it will be the most strategically effective. Sometimes groups focus on media work at the beginning of a campaign in order to garner enough support to get a bill introduced into a legislative body. For example, one Citizen Action state organization was working on an auto insurance campaign. As a means of building broad-based support for the campaign and generating enough interest among legislators to introduce strong legislation, a three-month media campaign was developed. The organization held press conferences, employing photo stunts like a toilet in a car trunk to denounce insurance rates that are so high that people are forced to live in their cars because they can't afford both their homes and their car insurance. This series of media "hits" (stunts, press conferences, releases of studies) helped build the momentum necessary for getting legislators to introduce legislation on car insurance rates.

Frequently, groups seek media coverage in the middle of a campaign to discredit or embarrass a target. This is usually done in the context of political/electoral power. For example, during one of the attempts to cut Social Security benefits in the Reagan years, a local chapter of the National Council of Senior Citizens in Peoria, Illinois participated in the national campaign to stop the threatened cuts.

All the seniors were directed to contact their Congressional representatives and make their position known.

The Peoria group was creative and strategic. Their Representative, Bob Michael, minority leader of the House, was leading the floor fight in Congress to cut the Social Security increase in the cost of living allowance. The Peoria seniors felt they had both a local and national story. After all, it was Peoria (as in "will it play in Peoria").

The Peoria Council notified the media that they would form a human billboard outside the hotel where a fund-raiser was scheduled for Congressman Michael. National dignitaries were expected and the media were planning to cover the congressman's event. As seniors stood in line displaying letters that spelled out "TELL RON [Reagan] IT WON'T PLAY IN PEORIA," local and national press photographers snapped away. Television cameras rolled. Twenty-six Peoria seniors appeared on the evening news, in local and national papers, and even in some weekly news magazines. All who participated had fun. The organization made its point and got loads of free publicity. The media got a good story and great pictures. The only one who probably wasn't happy was Congressman Michael. The group's use of the media not only challenged Michael, but also helped reach voters in other districts and thus put pressure on all legislators. This press event helped overturn the threat to Social Security.

Using Media to Give People a Sense of Their Own Power

People love seeing their names in print. Pictures are even better. Nothing gives leaders a stronger sense of power and a conviction that what they are doing is important, than to see themselves on television or in the paper.

Who gets interviewed and who is photographed matter greatly. For community organizations, the volunteer leaders, not the staff, are usually the people who speak before the media. Leaders sometimes resent staff who "hog" the media.

The person who speaks before the media or gives an interview should be a leader in your organization, someone who does real work, and not simply an articulate person. Don't allow people who do little work to "volunteer" to be the media spokespersons.

Some leaders may be bashful about working with the media, but they should be encouraged to practice (perhaps in special training sessions that are videotaped) and then supported in their initial efforts. Everyone who is good at working with the media was scared the first time. Besides, getting in the media is a small "perk" for longtime committed leaders.

One public housing group was demanding that lead paint be removed from their development. As part of the campaign, the health department was asked to test children in the development for lead poisoning. The media were called and asked to cover the testing. The testing and the issue got excellent print and television coverage. The few leaders involved were surprised to find themselves quoted in the paper and began to take their work and the issue much more seriously. The coverage enhanced their self image and enabled them to talk more freely with their neighbors about the importance of the issue.

In some large organizations, particularly national or large statewide coalitions, the director is often the spokesperson because it may be impractical, if not impossible, to have the volunteer leaders play this role. In large organizations where press releases are sent to numerous places throughout the country or state, quote local leaders in the releases to media in their area. Be sure to get the leaders to approve the quotes first. This takes a little longer, but is

well worth it. The local media are more likely to pick up the story and your leaders and local membership will feel better about being part of a larger organization.

Using Media to Change the Relations of Power

The key aspect to changing the relations of power is building strong organizations. Media coverage can help you do this.

Too often news coverage is generic. How many times have you groaned as you read in the paper "a local citizens group said..." The name of the organization was left out!! An organizer's goal is to prevent this from happening. Figure out how to get the organization's name listed or shown in the media as many times as possible. Become a source to whom the media turn for public comment. You won't always be successful, but it's worth trying to improve your batting average.

In one national membership organization, the volunteer media coordinators were trained on how to get the organization mentioned and how to push membership. Its leaders knew that in the last minute of radio or television interviews, they should give out the organization's address and toll-free membership number. In talking with reporters for print media, they would specifically ask if the address and phone number could be listed at the bottom of the article. Only about a third of the time would they actually be included, but it would never have happened without pushing.

In press releases, mention the name of the organization as many times as possible, in case the release is picked up "as is." At press events where photographers are present, make sure that signs are everywhere with your organization's name on them. Hang banners behind speakers. Ask people throughout the crowd to hold signs. Place placards on the podium. It is a good investment to have small neat signs made up that fit at the top of a podium displaying the name of the organization. Spokespersons can also wear buttons with the organization's name. If you don't have buttons, bright sheets of paper bearing the organization's name and worn by all attending can be quite noticeable when the cameras scan the crowd.

It's preferable to get positive media coverage, but don't fret too much if the coverage is not completely flattering (unless it's a complete exposure on how your organization has mismanaged funds). Name recognition is useful to your organization for recruiting people and raising funds. Some people even suggest that "all coverage is good coverage." If the media's coverage is not to your liking, use it as an opportunity to get more coverage. Organize people to respond via letters to the editor or hold a press conference clarifying your position.

Options for Using the Media

There are many ways to get media coverage. Some are more appropriate than others for particular issues and particular times during an issue campaign. As you plan your organization's issue campaign, consider various ways to use the media throughout to help you win issues, develop leaders, and build the organization.

Events. Sometimes groups plan events or demonstrations staged solely for the media's benefit. Other times, the media are invited to cover an action or an accountability session in which real demands will be made on a target. Regardless of its type, the event is the chance for the organization to make itself and its position known in the community.

Before the event, practice with the leaders. Assign someone to play the press roles and ask questions. Develop short statements with quotable lines. Encourage people to stick to the script. Remind them that they are representing the organization and should only give the organization's position. If they don't agree with the position, they shouldn't act as spokespersons. They also don't have to answer every question, particularly ones for which they don't have an answer. It's OK to say: "I don't know" or "our organization has not taken a position on that issue." Anticipate the obvious questions and make sure that all spokespersons have answers.

Everyone should be prepared to mention the name of the organization in their answer. When asked the question, "Why are you here today?" all organization spokespeople should respond

"As a member of (organization name), we are here today to...."

Be in control at the event. You don't have to be a career public relations person to appear professional. Have a press table where reporters, photographers and camera crews sign in (so you can add them later to your press list). Hand out press kits containing a press statement and background pieces on your organization and the issue. Assign someone to greet the press and direct them to your spokespersons (everyone should know who these people are). Distribute a list of all spokespersons with names spelled correctly and, if part of a coalition, their organization identified. Assist media people in locating phones, electrical outlets, and building technicians. Keep extra paper, pens, tape, batteries, and extension cords on hand.

Friends of the Earth sponsored a press event on the first anniversary of Chernobyl to help build public support for legislative efforts to strengthen regulations on nuclear power. A "nuclear lottery" was held in a U.S. Senate hearing room, complete with lottery bin and racing lights. Spokespersons at the event had carefully scripted speeches, with tight ten-second sound bites. In the press packets were copies of all speeches, including the underlined sound bites so that camera crews knew when to have their cameras rolling. Dozens of reporters and camera crews packed the room, and shots were used on stations across the country.

Press (News) Conferences. A press (news) conference is similar to a media event, except that it relies primarily upon talking heads. Many groups find it difficult to draw press to a press conference unless their issue is really in vogue. Nonetheless, when your issue is "hot," call a press conference even if you haven't tried it before.

During one of the famines in Africa, Bread for the World had been lobbying for increased food and development aid to needy countries for over a year, with limited results. All of a sudden, the media "discovered" the famine, and millions of people wanted to donate money to help starving Africans. As important as donations are, Bread for the World knew that it was critical that the U.S. government respond as well and decided to use the opportunity to focus the public's concern on the U.S. government's miserly response.

Despite the fact that no local Bread for the World chapter had ever held a press conference before, twenty-five chapters volunteered to organize local press conferences within the week. Key religious and Bread for the World leaders were recruited to speak, statements were drafted, media contacted, and successful press conferences held. Every press conference generated media coverage, most in both print and television. The conferences focused attention on the issue and helped Bread for the World further its strategy to triple the government's contribution to the international relief effort.

The logistics of a press conference are similar to those of a media event (see the checklist at the end of this chapter). If possible, have only a few speakers. One main spokesperson should make a statement and then introduce the others who are making statements. If you need others present for political reasons, have them stand in the background so as to be visible in pictures.

Features. All media regularly run feature stories on specific people and issues. If you are engaged in an issue campaign that you expect to run for several months, check with the local media to see if they have any features scheduled that relate to your situation. You could end up becoming the subject of a lengthy special.

A suburban Chicago group was trying to get a local school board to start an afterschool daycare program in the public schools. Calls were made to local television stations and one station indicated that it had a feature on parenting planned for the next month. The station was eager to cover the group's work and provided an in-depth report, with little work on the group's part. The media coverage both strengthened the resolve of the leaders and assisted in their victory with the school board vote.

Interviews/Talk Shows. Both radio and television talk shows are always looking for interesting new angles, people, and issues to cover. Many Citizen Action and other progressive citizen organizations have been on national media, such as *The Today Show, Donahue, The MacNeil Lehrer Report,* and *Nightline.* Local television and radio talk shows are even more accessible.

Get to know the producers and/or assistants, even if only by phone. If you provide interesting guests and material, you may be asked back regularly. Try to cultivate a relationship that causes them to call you when they are looking for the "consumer" or "citizens'" response to events as they happen. Some publications will also interview people for "human interest" angles on stories.

Letters to the Editor. Don't forget letters to the editor. This is the most widely read section of the newspaper, except for the front page. Work with leaders at a meeting to draft letters to the editor in response to an article. And especially, write them in response to articles about your organization.

Meetings with Editorial Boards. Small papers have an editor who writes the paper's editorials. Large papers have an editorial board who share the editorial responsibilities. Although these editors are seldom the most progressive characters, it is worth scheduling a time to talk with them about your issue. This is the time to pull out the academics and researchers who support your positions. Once you build a relationship with editors, send them your press releases. Sometimes they will write an editorial that looks remarkably similar to your release.

Announcements/Bulletin Boards. Both publications and radio stations offer free community bulletin boards or meeting announcement sections. Don't rely on them to draw people, but consider them another means of building name recognition for your group. They will also make the recruitment work easier because some people may have read or heard about the upcoming event.

Tips for Using the Media

Develop Relationships

All organizing is about developing relationships. When dealing with the media, you need to think about developing the necessary relationships to make your and their jobs easier. These relationships are always professional.

Honesty is crucial. The media do not have to like you, but they must respect you. You want them to know that when your organization seeks press, it is about something newsworthy and it is true.

No matter how friendly a press person is, no matter how well you get along, you can't ever assume that it is a private friendship. Nothing should be said that you don't want to read in the newspaper. If you speak off the record (we don't recommend it), it should be very clear exactly what is off the record. It is better to always assume that nothing is secret, and act and speak accordingly.

In dealing with your daily and weekly newspapers, it is definitely worth the time to cultivate a relationship with the reporters who cover your area (geographic and issue) and the papers' editors.

When you offer to get back to a reporter or editor with additional information, do so promptly. Develop a reputation for providing reporters with solid, timely information. Media people appreciate those who make their work easier.

Develop a Media (Press) List

You should not have to compile a new list each time you contact the media. Ideally, your press list should be computerized in such a way that you can generate mailing labels at a moment's notice. If you don't have the list computerized, at least have the list on labels and keep a couple of sets on hand for when you have to act quickly.

Divide or code your lists by category. Make sure you have included the personal contacts described above, news reporters, specialty editors or "city desks" for television (local, network, and cable), radio, daily newspapers, weekly newspapers, ethnic newspapers (Black, Hispanic, or others), student newspapers (if you are in a large college town), and religious and union publications. In large cities, there will probably be an AP and UPI reporter and a "daybook." The daybook lists all scheduled events for the day and is used by most media.

At first, your media list may not have all the correct names on it. Update it with the proper names and phone numbers to ease follow-up calls. Keep track of personal contacts with reporters so that if staff change, there is an "institutional" memory for press work.

Think Pictures

When press coverage is likely, think pictures, both TV and newspaper. Notifying the press that there will be "photo opportunities" can increase the likelihood of media coverage. Use your group's creativity to develop visuals and symbols that support your message. Remember the fine line between clever and silly.

Before the start of a press conference or event, cup your hands around your eyes and pretend you have a camera. What do you see? For a press conference, focus in on the speaker. Too often, the sign you placed behind the speaker is too high to be seen. Or, all that is visible are two or three letters surrounding the speaker's head and the "Holiday Inn" plate on the front of the podium. Adjust the room before the media arrive.

Mail or Fax Press (News) Releases

The object of the press (news) release is to get the media to cover your event or to write a story, not to pack in as much information as possible. (Even though it is called a "press" release, it is standard format for communicating information to all forms of media.) The release should serve as a "hook" to pique their interest. If your press conference, story, or event is interesting enough, they will attend or call about the story.

Press releases to the wires, daily papers, television and radio stations should be received two to four days before an event. Weekly newspapers usually have deadlines of three or four days before publication, so check beforehand. If you have control over your timing, schedule your event to maximize coverage.

Follow Up Press Releases with Calls

No matter how good your press release is, you will have a better chance of getting covered if you follow up the release with a phone call. Frequently, the release has been lost or given to the "wrong" person. Your calls allow you to answer questions or concerns that might have prevented the media from covering your story.

Recognize Who Controls the Media

No matter how good your work in getting stories out, you may have trouble if your target is an ally of owners of the media. Sometimes it is unclear why certain stories appear to be blocked.

For example, during the Pittston coal miners' strike, when the strikers took over a breaker building, the story was not covered for three days, despite an entire team of professional media people working on publicizing it. The story was effectively squelched in the national media. We may wish we controlled the media, but we don't.

Recognize Luck

As in all of life, luck plays a role, good and bad. You may have the greatest story to tell or the best event in town, but if there is an earthquake in San Francisco or dancing on the Berlin Wall, you won't be covered. On the other hand, you may schedule an event on a slow news day and be the star of the evening news. Such is life.

Peoria citizens say "Tell Ron it won't play in Peoria."

Checklist for Press (News) Releases

_____ Is the release on organizational letterhead?

_____ Is the release dated and marked for immediate release or embargoed until a specific day and time?

_____ Is the contact person's name and phone number (day and evening) listed at the top of the release?

_____ Is the headline short and pithy? (Don't struggle too hard in coming up with a headline. The media probably won't use yours anyway.)

_____ Is the copy double spaced?

_____ Does the first paragraph explain who, what, why, when, and where?

_____ Have you quoted key leaders in the second and third paragraphs? Have you cleared the quotes with them first? (Remember, who you quote is an organizational decision.)

_____ Have you listed your organization's name several times?

_____ Are all names, titles, and organizations spelled correctly?

_____ Is each sheet marked with an abbreviated headline? (Try to keep your release to two pages. One is better.)

_____ Is PHOTO OPPORTUNITY mentioned if there is one? (If so, send a copy of the release to the photo editor.)

_____ Did you put "-30-" or "# # # #" at the end of the release? (Why? Because "they" say so.)

_____ Have the date, time, and place been cleared with all the speakers?

_____ Are there other media conflicts (e.g., another major event or press conference)?

_____ Is the room large enough?

_____ Are there pay phones nearby?

_____ Will you need a public address system?

_____ Have volunteers been recruited to set up and clean up the room before and after the press conference?

_____ Do you plan to serve refreshments? If so, have people been asked to bring them?

_____ Who is sending the press releases?

_____ Who is making follow-up phone calls?

_____ Is there a script available for those making follow-up phone calls to the media?

_____ Are visuals, charts, or graphs needed at the press conference?

_____ Who is writing each person's presentation? Are there good quotable sound bites?

_____ Is someone drafting a question and answer sheet for anticipated questions at the press conference?

_____ Is a time set for speakers to rehearse their presentations and answers to the anticipated questions?

_____ Are materials being prepared for the press kit?

    _____ Press release

    _____ Background information on speakers

    _____ Fact sheet

    _____ Organizational background

    _____ Copies of speakers' statements

_____ Will your organization's name be projected well through signs, posters, buttons, and so forth?

_____ Who will greet the media and staff the sign-in table?

_____ Is someone in your group going to take photographs?

_____ Who is assigned to assist the speakers with details at the press conference?

_____ Who will send releases to those who don't attend the press conference?

_____ Who will call reporters who don't attend, but would need the information immediately in order to use it?

_____ Are volunteers assigned to watch for stories in various media?

_____ Will thank you notes be sent to all spokespersons and volunteers?

Midwest Academy, 225 West Ohio, Suite 250, Chicago, Illinois 60610

15

So you've been called on to lead a workshop. Well, that should be easy, everyone has been to a workshop and knows just what it is. It's about twenty people sitting all day in the most uncomfortable chairs they can find. The workshop leader gets up and says, "For the next seven hours I will speak about international woolen garment shipments." Or, someone says, "Let's break down into groups of three and spend the next seven hours really getting in touch with our feelings about international woolen garment shipments." Whichever style is chosen, the result is the same. Little good comes of it, and given what Freud said about woolens, one should never get in touch with them in public.

A workshop can be great or it can be dreadful. If your organization has a reputation for conducting good workshops, people will come, and they will develop into stronger leaders, candidates for office, or coalition partners. If you are known as a good workshop leader, you will get requests all the time, and you will find that it sure beats working.

The starting point for a great workshop is understanding the strengths and weaknesses of the workshop format as a tool for educating people. By workshop, we mean a group of ten to thirty people meeting for several hours, a day, or at most, a weekend.

A word on time. Unfortunately, too often you will be asked to lead a one-hour workshop. Little can be accomplished in this short period. Urge groups to set aside longer periods of time for workshops; three hours is preferable.

Advance Planning

Conducting the Workshop

Designing and Leading a Workshop

A workshop is very good for accomplishing five things.

Giving People a General Orientation, Conception, or Overview of the Subject. For example: This is how the campaign for public election financing will work. This is how you set up an election day operation. This is how a group chooses an issue. People can work out the details of their own specific situations later.

Teaching People to Do One Thing Well. This is how to talk to your legislator about state aid to education. This is how to hold a press event about state aid to education.

Creating a Common Language, Attitude, or Approach. By doing exercises and planning strategy together, people learn a system for analyzing and solving problems. They come out of the workshop better able to communicate and work with each other because they are speaking a common language.

Creating Enthusiasm. When passing the bill in the legislature requires forming a committee in each of nine legislative districts, for example, hold a workshop, bring in people from the districts, and discuss how to do it. They will go home committed to the idea and to each other. If you just sent the information by mail, even with follow-up phone calls, the results would not be as good.

Building Confidence. Most people lack self confidence. Role playing a situation gives people confidence in their abilities, especially when the workshop leader and other participants praise and support them. Frequently, people "know" how to do something, but they need the confidence that they know it.

Workshops are bad tools for teaching involved subjects such as nautical navigation, Latin, word processing, and solid geometry. Think back to grade school when you learned long division. You really learned it from a skilled teacher, and there wasn't much a group could do to help you.

Now, contrast learning to *do* long division, with learning to *explain* long division to the community. There is actually a great deal that a group can do to help you learn to explain long division. People can brainstorm ways to put across a complex concept in simple terms. Some can role play community members, while others practice explaining long division. You can improve your own technique by listening to others practice theirs. Watching video tapes of people explaining long division to the community might also be helpful. On the other hand, a video actually telling you how to do long division belongs in a workshop on insomnia.

O.K., here comes the point! *Workshops are best for subjects where group participation aids the learning process*. They work less well when they are a substitute for old fashioned one-on-one teaching. So, plan the workshop to make the best use of the group. Use methods in which the group is a necessary part of the learning process. Avoid methods in which a group is actually a hindrance. If people want to learn nautical navigation, send them to the Coast Guard.

Advance Planning

Leading a good workshop takes time for preparation, as well as skill in leading it. The "safest" workshop is usually a presentation followed by a discussion, but it is also the least interesting. Think creatively about the main points you are trying to convey. Find ways to convey the material that would help people better grapple with or absorb the material.

The danger in trying to design an innovative workshop is that it becomes cutesy and/or cluttered ("We will now all skip rope to demonstrate the relationship between economic growth and full employment"). Ask several people for their feedback on the workshop design. Does it make sense to them? If so, try it. If what you designed doesn't work, revise it for next time. In this section, we present some of the basic elements you should take into consideration in planning a workshop.

What Are Your Goals?

Clarify your specific goals, taking into account the areas in which workshops are most helpful. Consider the overall concept with which you want people to leave. Then identify no more than three things that you want people to learn at the workshop. Think about developing a common language and enthusiasm for the issue or project.

Often, the main goal is to build up the confidence of the group members so that they feel able to understand, talk about, or try out some new idea. A confidence building workshop is going to require a different design than an informational workshop. People always say that they don't have enough information, but it is rarely a lack of information that causes a lack of confidence. Think back to your first date (or your fiftieth).

The workshop must reflect the overall goals and strategy of the sponsoring organization. There is no such thing as just teaching skills independently of an organizational context.

Perhaps if the topic were, "how to eat a good breakfast," you could discuss it without any organizational considerations. But, the moment the topic becomes "eating a good breakfast at your desk," you must put it in an organizational context.

Who Should Come?

The selection of participants greatly affects the success of the workshop. Even if you are leading a program for another group, make it clear that you want to be consulted about who is invited. Not all workshops are appropriate for everyone.

For example, a tenants' group sponsored a workshop on organizing through direct action methods. The group's leaders debated inviting people from other housing organizations. The workshop leader urged them not to, knowing that a frank discussion of their own problems would be impossible with others present. The leaders also considered whether to invite only board members or all active members. It was decided that because expanding the board was a major organizational goal, they would invite the most active members. But some board members objected, saying that the portion of the workshop on strategy was so specific that it was really making policy, which was the board's function. It was then decided to hold a formal board meeting shortly after the workshop to ratify the plans. Details like these have to be considered, and will make a difference in the success of the workshop. Here are two guidelines for who should come.

Participants Should Have Similar Backgrounds or Levels of Experience. Unless it is a workshop on intergroup relations, the more homogeneous the participants, the better it will be. Without even meaning to, college educated people tend to push others out of the discussion. Younger people often race ahead of seniors. Native born people use slang words that foreign born people don't understand. People with a lot of experience use jargon and acronyms that make inexperienced people feel dumb. If your audience is heterogeneous, you can always hold more than one workshop.

Participants Should Have the Same Relationship to the Organization. When the workshop is about something specific to your organization, there is still a question of who should come. Discussions with leaders, staff, members, allies, or people off the street are going to be different. Members may be more interested in discussing the issue, while staff will be more interested in the details of strategy. Leaders will be called on to do one set of things, allies another. Not every discussion is appropriate for everyone. The more types of people who attend, the more difficult it becomes for you to establish a perspective from which to speak, and the more disjointed the discussion.

What Are the Participants' Backgrounds?

What do people already know? Have they received previous training or had experience in the area? What are their ages and backgrounds? Is everyone literate? Are there particular problems or issues people want addressed in the workshop? If there is no one who can answer these questions, mail a short questionnaire or application form ahead of time to the participants. Use the answers to these questions in designing both the content and the style of the workshop.

What Is the Organization?

If it is not your own group, learn about it as much as you can. Learn its history, style, and program by looking over its literature, newsletters, and press clippings, and talking to officers or staff. If the group's leaders are participating in the workshop, should they have some special function? How free are you to disagree with them? Be sure that your goals for the workshop and the organization's are the same. Are there particular problems that the leadership is trying to solve by holding the workshop? Are there major divisions in the organization over the problem? Will they be brought out at the workshop?

Preparing the Workshop Program

Adults learn best by "doing." So, seek hands-on "doing" opportunities. The second-best way adults learn is by both seeing and hearing. If you can supplement presentations with visual aids, they will retain more information.

The worst way for people to learn is just by listening to a presentation. Few of us are so

interesting that people want to listen for much longer than 30 minutes.

Most really good workshops are a combination of presentation, exercise, role playing, and discussion. The form of a workshop and how material is presented are as important as the actual content.

Develop an outline of time use for each section of the workshop. Start by estimating the time slots. Then write a separate content outline that includes exactly what you will say, what the group will do, and the points to be made. Now go back and see if it all fits into your original time estimate. The time outline for a workshop on writing a press release might look like this:

Press Releases	*3 hours*
Introductions	15 minutes
Presentation	20 minutes
Discussion	10 minutes
Exercise	30 minutes
Evaluation	1 hour
Wrap up	15 minutes

The assumptions here are that you have fifteen people in the workshop. The exercise will consist of each person writing a short press release from a longer background paper that you will give them. In the evaluation, each person's release will be read to the group and commented on. This is a tight schedule, but an extra 30 minutes is built in.

Using Exercises and Roleplays

Exercises. Exercises can be practical, such as actually designing a newsletter or making a one-minute speech. They can also be more conceptual.

A problem solving exercise is usually done in small groups. Participants are given the factual background of a problem and are asked to come up with a solution, plan, or strategy. This provides opportunities to reinforce the principles and guidelines you've explained in the presentation part of the workshop and helps people grapple with the crux of the material. Sometimes exercises are used to demonstrate how much people already know, which builds confidence.

The key to success is to keep the exercise simple and make its problem true to life. The more it is based on actual situations in which you were involved, the more real it will sound, and the better able you will be to lead the discussion. Don't use situations with which some members of the group have actually had experience. They will short circuit the reasoning process by stating what actually happened, and then argue with people who have a different idea. The goal is not to have people reconstruct the original circumstances, but to learn a method for finding a workable solution.

Roleplays. Like exercises, roleplays can be more practical or more conceptual. A roleplay is a way of recreating a bit of outside reality within a workshop. An exercise is really the first step in a roleplay. After solving the problem on paper, the group acts out the solution as a way of testing it. If you are using the workshop to prepare people to sell raffle tickets, for example, they can write a short sales pitch on paper. Roleplaying the sales pitch shows who mumbles, looks at the floor, and plays with his ears—problems that you wouldn't spot from the writing.

In shorter workshops, usually only short one-on-one roleplays are used. Larger team roleplays, where the goal is to develop a strategy and reproduce an event such as an action or accountability session, take a great deal of time to prepare, produce, and debrief. Two-and-a-half to three hours are required. If people are being prepared for a specific meeting with certain elected officials, then use a roleplay to simulate the meeting, even if it takes up half the workshop time. Nothing else will better prepare people.

Most adults complain about having to do roleplays, but really enjoy them once they get going. Their main concern is that they don't want to embarrass themselves in front of others. The purpose of a roleplay is *not* to demonstrate how ignorant someone is. Roleplays done well give people experience and build their confidence. Make sure that everyone is given adequate information. All materials to be handed out in connection with exercises and roleplays should be color coded. It is the only way to make sure that everyone is looking at the right sheet of paper, and that one team isn't walking off with another team's background information.

With team roleplays, assign major parts to strong people who will make the roleplay work well. Listen to the teams prepare. Prompt if necessary, but be sure to be impartial and give the same information to both teams.

Roleplays should always be debriefed. Begin by asking people who played key roles what their strategy was and how they felt they did. Explain to people what was done well, and what could be improved upon. With few exceptions, as long as your comments are generally encouraging and supportive, people are eager to hear things they could do better. It is very bad form to set up a roleplay that doesn't work, so that you can sound smart when you debrief it. If you do that, we will publicly deny that you read this book.

Handouts

Workshop participants love receiving handouts. Use them to provide the details and backup information that would otherwise make your presentation long or boring. Also, be sure to provide detailed information in handouts about how to get a more in-depth knowledge about the subject material. An annotated reading list is always helpful.

Many workshop presenters like to save handouts until the end, because they don't like people to read things during a presentation or discussion time.

Conducting the Workshop

Atmosphere

People care about how things look and feel. They appreciate rooms that are comfortable and attractive. The setting in a room will greatly affect the tone and outcome of a workshop.

Place tables in a big square or horseshoe with chairs around the outside, so that the participants can see one another and the charts, videos, or overheads. If tables are unattractive, cover them with tablecloths or sheets to improve the setting. Remove unneeded chairs.

Clean up a room before you begin any session. Make sure that coffee cups or napkins from previous groups have been cleared away. You might put a hard candy or piece of fruit at every participant's spot to welcome people to the workshop.

A bouquet of flowers adds a "touch of class" to any workshop. Set the bouquet in a vase near the podium or table for the workshop leader.

Adjust the temperature before you begin the workshop. It should be a bit cool before everyone enters the room. If there is noise from adjacent rooms, try to have it stopped or muffled.

If you are working alone, recruit someone to assist you in setting up for the workshop. That person can serve as the "staff" during the workshop and assist you in handling logistical difficulties and equipment.

Making Introductions

Unless the workshop is very large, take a few minutes to get to know people's names and backgrounds. People are more comfortable in a room if they know others or something about them.

Ask participants to answer a question that gets them talking, and that provides you with useful information about their experience. For example, if your workshop is about press releases, ask how their organizations use press releases or if they have ever written one. Resist the temptation to ask questions like, "What animal do you wish you were?" unless it is one of those touchy-feely groups.

You may choose to use your introduction period as a way of getting into the material. For example, in a workshop on how to lobby elected officials, you might ask participants to explain when they feel that they are being good lobbyists and when they are uncomfortable lobbying. Then use that information to develop a profile about when all of us are good lobbyists (when we're knowledgeable, prepared, have numbers of people and power) and when we are uncomfortable (we don't know the bill number, or we can't remember who our representative is, or there are very few of us and we don't have power). The key point is that the introduction period should be used to gather information and not just to get names from people.

During this time, draw a rough sketch or diagram of the room and put people's names on your drawing in the approximate spot where they are sitting. This map will help you call people by their names. Another suggestion for getting names is to ask people to make name cards to place on the table in front of them.

Your Presentation

Even though adults learn least well from just listening to a presentation, it usually can't be avoided. Use the presentation time to lay out principles, steps or guidelines to your subject materials. (Sometimes good films or slide shows are available that can be substituted for your presentation. If you can use them, participants will learn from both seeing and hearing.)

Use whatever outline, notes, or script that makes you feel most comfortable. If you like having every sentence written out, do it and then practice giving the presentation without appearing that you are reading it. A few especially talented people can conduct workshops without notes and outlines, but most of us need meticulous preparation.

You may want to write an additional sheet of notes for the discussion period with questions you will ask in order to start the discussion or keep it going. Put down additional points to make or statistics for people who request them.

Most inexperienced presenters tend to provide too much detail and information on a subject. After you have written your first draft of a presentation, go back and cut out the extraneous material. Add in examples and stories that illustrate your main points. Keep it lively and entertaining. Frequent jokes or funny stories are helpful in keeping people's interest. Don't just stand there rattling off statistics. If you feel you must, at least speak very rapidly and end the workshop before lunch.

Feedback During the Workshop

Workshop leaders are always wondering, "Is anyone getting this"? Exercises and roleplays will give you a clue. Check with other staff or officers frequently during the session. Ask the group questions that will help you figure out what people have learned.

One tool that Midwest Academy trainers use is a written one-page multiple choice or fill-in-the-blanks quiz distributed at the end of a workshop. Names are not put on the quiz. The quiz is really more a test of the workshop leader's communication skills and the structure of the workshop, than of the participants' comprehension skills. For example, if most people missed two particular questions, then the material related to those questions wasn't presented clearly or wasn't presented in a manner that helped people retain it.

Note-Taking by Participants

With one exception, which we shall discuss, encourage note taking during presentations. When you put key ideas on a board or newsprint, you get the triple effect of the participants hearing the words, seeing them, and writing them—a great boost to memory. Note-taking can be encouraged by handing out paper or yellow pads.

There are two options for displaying the key ideas. You can write them as you speak, which has the disadvantage of slowing you down and placing your back to the group much of the time. It also leaves you at the mercy of spelling fanatics. If you chose this method, a good trick is to prepare all the notes beforehand, writing them in light pencil on newsprint. They can be read by you, but will be invisible to the group until you trace them with your marker. The second way is to prepare the notes beforehand, either on newsprint or overhead projector transparencies. The disadvantage is that as soon as they are displayed, the group will start to copy them without waiting for your explanation. There is no ideal method.

College graduates and professionals instinctively take notes. Those with very little education will do the same, particularly if they see others taking notes. Unfortunately, for very poorly educated people, the effort of writing may be sufficiently difficult to distract them from what you are saying. With such groups consider discouraging note-taking. One method is to hand out a bare bones outline of your remarks. Tell people to follow along with it, take it home, and that they don't need to take notes unless they want to.

Audiovisuals

Audiovisuals are used in a workshop to support a presentation. Slides or overheads are relatively easy to make and use, especially with computers. While slides are often clearer and more colorful than overheads, they have the disadvantage of placing you in the back of the room with the lights out. Overheads allow you to stand up front with the lights only dimmed. Films (16mm) also work well. Videos shown on a TV-size screen are fine with small groups, but lose a lot with larger groups. A few well-equipped training facilities have video projectors that enlarge the picture. The most frequent problem encountered by Midwest Academy staff is rooms that cannot be darkened. Inquire about this well in advance.

Murphy's law, "If anything can go wrong, it will," certainly applies to audiovisual equipment. Set up and check all equipment ahead of time. Get things arranged in the right position so that time is not wasted during the workshop. Have extra bulbs, batteries, fuses, extension cords, and three-prong adapters available.

In general, don't show slides or films and let it go at that. No matter how good the material is, the greater value is in the discussion. As with exercises and roleplays, audiovisuals give people an immediate common experience to which they can react. Sometimes it is the only thing a group has in common, so use the opportunity well. Plan the points to be made in the discussion. Ask questions to see if everyone has the same reaction to the material. Are there patterns in people's reactions that can be traced back to differences in their organizations, issues, jobs, or experiences that can lead to a deeper discussion?

Do not try to substitute a film for an exercise or a roleplay. It is not the same. A film does not engage people like a roleplay. A film may present material better than a speaker might, but it is still a one-way communication.

Discussion

Discussion in a workshop can be exciting and involving, but it needs to be focused on particular topics and facilitated by the workshop leader. Too often, workshop leaders use group discussion as a way to fill up time when they haven't really prepared well. We've all been a part of group discussions that are a collective sharing of ignorance.

Clarify in your mind what is the purpose and direction of any group discussion. Prepare the key points you want stressed, and then design questions for the group that will elicit responses around those points. Don't say: "Has anyone anything to say"? "How did you like the movie?" "What would you like to talk about?"

"Are you getting anything out of this?" Instead ask: "What was it that gave the group in the movie the courage to go on"? "What might have discouraged them?" "What power did they have?" "What leadership roles could you identify?"

When you set aside time for discussion, facilitate well. If not, one or two people will dominate most of the discussion. Groups appreciate strong facilitators who encourage broad participation while keeping them to the subject at hand.

Style

Your style is part of your personality. There are aspects of your "style" that are probably difficult to change. However, almost every good workshop leader conveys humor, enthusiasm, optimism, knowledge balanced with modesty, and structure. (If none of these are part of your personality, we suggest a long period of reflection.) Good workshop leaders are entertaining. They don't have to be able to tell jokes, but they do have to find ways of laughing at themselves or breaking the tension in a group, particularly with serious material.

Good workshop leaders are enthusiastic about their material. You must convey energy (particularly if your workshop is scheduled right after lunch)! Watch yourself on video sometime. If you are less expressive than you thought, practice being a bit more dramatic in expressing your points. It's often just a matter of raising your voice and speaking more distinctly.

Good workshop leaders are optimistic. Workshop participants want to know that they can do things. Workshops that focus on the negative aspects of a subject are debilitating. Workshop leaders must be realistic, but optimistic, and must find ways to convey that optimism in workshops. A good workshop leader praises the efforts of workshop

participants and maintains the group's energy and spirit.

Good workshop leaders are knowledgeable about their subject material, yet modest. If the participants are not familiar with your background and "expertise" on a subject, it is important to share why you were asked to lead the workshop. Giving yourself credentials for leading a workshop is similar to the legitimatizing that one does to recruit people. Simply introduce yourself, sharing a bit about why you are equipped to lead the workshop. Don't claim to know everything about the subject.

Good workshop leaders provide structure. If you've followed the outline suggestions made earlier in the chapter, you will have a good structure.

Evaluation

Without fail, prepare an evaluation sheet for participants to fill out at the end of the session. It can be as simple as asking people to list what they found more useful and less useful, or it can go over the workshop section by section for more detailed responses. Some leaders encourage oral evaluations. Others don't. In any event, the evaluation lets you improve your workshop method in the future. It also protects you when the one person who didn't like the workshop goes around saying that no one liked it.

No workshop is ever perfect; there are always things that can be changed or added to make it more effective. Think of your workshops as artistic products in process.

Obviously, the best measure of success is when a participant puts the workshop messages to use or acts on particular insights. Nothing is better evidence of achieving goals than having someone try something you suggested and having it turn out well.

16

At the most fundamental level, an organization needs a board of directors in order to incorporate as a tax-exempt organization. Legally, you must have a board.

But organizations need boards for other reasons as well. Boards are needed to help manage the organization effectively, helping to deal with administrative and financial questions, and building in accountability and feedback for the director.

A community organization board considers itself based in and representative of a community. Community boards fulfill the same legal and administrative functions as agency boards, but they also set the overall direction on programs and policies, and provide leadership, vision and energy in the community. The community board is the embodiment of and training ground for an organization's leadership, representing its diversity and strengths. In short, community organization boards are the heart and soul of community organizations.

Responsibilities of Community Organization Boards

Community Organization Board Composition and Structure

Executive Directors and Community Organization Boards

Typical Problems

Responsibilities of Community Organization Boards

Program and Policy Directions

Community boards decide the overall program and policy directions of the organization. Their responsibilities include the following:

Set Goals and Policies. All boards approve the organization's annual goals and set its general

Working with Community Organization Boards

policies or positions. The extent to which the board is involved and the level of detail with which they participate in these activities vary greatly.

Oversee Budget. The board must set or approve the organization's overall budget. All boards are involved in budget work at some level. Community boards should make the political decisions reflected in a budget, but should not focus too much on the details. A budget is the best reflection of an organization's priorities. No matter what an organization's goals or the promotional materials say, the real priorities are set forth in the budget by the way money is spent. A board thus sets the overall priorities of the organization by setting or approving the budget.

One good way to approach a budget discussion is to review an annual report, which helps the board reflect on last year's work, set goals for the coming year, and then look at the finances and the budget. New boards may agonize over every budget category, but this should be outgrown as the board and organization develop.

Analyze Power. Community boards must develop their ability to analyze power. How much power does the organization currently have? How much is needed to win on the issues of interest to the community? How can you develop more power? The amount of power the organization has or can build determines the kind of issues it can win.

Choose Issues. Community boards must be actively involved in selecting issues on which the organization will work. Most boards find it useful to develop a set of criteria, similar to those discussed in Chapter 3, for selecting issues. Once the criteria are developed, board members must carefully analyze each issue, as well as the overall package of issues on which the organization works.

Develop Strategies. Most community boards are involved in developing strategies for winning on the issues selected. Sometimes strategy development is handled by board committees, sometimes by issues committees chaired by board members but involving non-board members, and sometimes by the full board. It is important that the board is involved at some level, and that the full board reviews the strategies because all of its members will be asked to participate in tactics developed to implement the strategies.

Administrative Review

Community boards have the same kinds of administrative responsibilities as agency boards or other kinds of boards. They must work with the director to see that the organization is managed effectively.

Personnel. The board of directors is responsible for hiring, firing (if need be), and evaluating the director of the organization. The director, in turn, is responsible for hiring, firing, and evaluating other staff. If the board is involved in interviewing candidates other than the director, it should be clearly understood that the board's role is only "advisory" to the director. Whenever boards become involved in supervising all staff members, there are problems. The board must trust the director to deal with other personnel. If there are ongoing unresolved personnel problems, the board should work with the director, get training for the director, or hire a new director.

The board must assure that the organization has a personnel policy and that it is implemented fairly (applied equally to all staff). Without this, employees are unclear about expectations and benefits, and the organization can be subject to legal suits from disgruntled employees. Many suits in non-profit organizations are filed by the hardworking, conscientious, longtime employees who see a suit as the only means for addressing unfairness in personnel matters. Don't think it can't happen to your group. Frequently, a committee of the board is designated in the personnel policy to work out staff grievances with the director.

The board of directors not only needs to assess whether a policy is fair, but whether it is just. For many non-profits, a key question is the health care benefits offered. Every organization should arrange for heath care coverage for its employees. If an organization expects its staff to stay around for more than a few years, it also needs to consider staff pensions or retirement benefits. Sometimes, it takes an outside group of people, like a board, to think of what's best in the long run for staff.

Financial Management. Because the board is legally responsible for safeguarding the organization's resources, it must ensure that money is handled properly. Where there is money, there can be problems. The board needs to know that the accounting systems are in good shape in order to assure good management and to prevent theft. It is not enough to say that things are fine because Susie handles the books and Susie is trustworthy. Many boards insist on an annual audit in order to get an outside appraisal of the soundness of the organization's financial systems. (See Chapter 24 for more information on financial matters.)

A part of financial management is monitoring the organization's income and expenses, and altering the budget as needed. The board may need to assist the organization in preparing for cash flow shortages. Staff should have some flexibility on budget categories (i.e., how much can be altered without board approval), but not too much. The amount of flexibility depends on the overall size of the budget, the experience of the staff, and the trusting relations between the director and the board.

Legal Matters. A board of directors must make sure that the organization follows all relevant laws, paying special attention to Internal Revenue Service and Federal Election Commission regulations. Board members can be personally liable for an organization's problems, such as failing to deposit federal payroll withholding taxes within three working days. (See Chapter 24 for more detail on legal matters.)

Tone, Vision, and Community Leadership

Community board members set the tone, vision and leadership for the community. They provide these at board meetings, community meetings, and in their overall involvement in the community. In this capacity, they are responsible for:

Representing the Public's (Community's) Needs. All boards, at least on some level, are responsible for representing the public's needs and interests to the organization. This is especially true with community boards because the board members are also members of the community.

Representing the Organization. Board members are expected to represent their organization to the general public. This includes speaking with the media in public situations, and very often, fundraising. Thus, many organizations try to recruit people with fundraising or public relations expertise to serve on their boards. Because community organizations may choose to limit their board members to those who are also part of the organization's direct constituency, they may need to develop the fundraising and public relations skills of their board members.

It is not appropriate to lay the full burden of fundraising upon staff people, especially with community boards. Board members should be well situated to approach other community residents, agencies, congregations, and businesses about supporting the work of the organization.

Developing Relationships. Although it is helpful if community board members have expertise in particular issues or in financial or legal matters, it is essential that they be leaders in the community. As was discussed in Chapter 11, board members do not become community leaders by virtue of serving on the board. Rather, they become leaders by having or developing relationships so that people will "follow."

How do you know if a board member has a following in the community? See how many people that person can turn out for meetings or volunteer when asked by the board member.

Lead Activities. Community board members are actively involved in implementing issue strategies by leading activities. They are the spokespersons at events, the people interviewed by the press or quoted in press releases, and the leaders in community meetings. Community board members are involved in doing, not just directing others to do.

Tone and Vision. Most staff members focus on the details of their work and the problems they face (as they should). Board members must help set the positive, activist tone for the organization and provide vision for the future.

Community organizations are not just about winning on particular issues. They help bring grassroots democracy to the community.

Community Organization Board Composition and Structure

Who is on your board matters. Most boards have a nominating committee that oversees the process for nominating its members. (Some board analysts believe that the nominating committee is the board's most important committee because it helps determine who else

will serve on the board and thus who will serve on every other committee.) The ideal attributes of community board members are listed below.

Commitment. Members must be committed to the goals of the organization and the principles of direct action organizing.

Relatively Objective about Staff. Most organizations have found that problems arise when board and staff members are close relatives. Some organizations have guidelines saying that no person can be hired for a staff position if he or she is a relative of someone on the board.

Experienced. Organizing and grassroots fundraising experience are of particular importance for board members. A mix of people skilled in administration, finance, personnel, research, and public relations is useful as well.

Leaders. Community board members should have extensive relationships with people in the community. These relationships must be built upon trust and respect.

Willing and Able to Work. Community boards need workers: people who are willing and able to commit time. Community boards don't usually seek "big names" who might lend prestige to the organization, but are not willing or able to work for it.

Choosing the Board

Be sure that your by-laws clarify how someone gets on the board. Is there an annual election? Is there a nominations committee? If there is an election, who gets to vote? Even though a formal process may seem unnecessary at first, it is important to build in community accountability by having a clear and democratic process for getting on the board.

The actual number of members on a board varies a great deal, although everyone should be able and willing to contribute to the growth of the organization. A small board is able to discuss items thoroughly and work in a collegial fashion. Larger boards are able to draw in more diverse perspectives and reach more people in the community, but more decisions tend to be delegated to an executive committee. The size of community boards most commonly ranges from twelve to eighteen members.

The terms of office (i.e., the length of time for which someone is to serve on the board) vary as well. Unfortunately, many community groups do not have clear terms of office, so people can stay on the board forever. This is not healthy for your organization or the board members themselves. Develop a reasonable term of office, usually two or three years, and write it into your by-laws. Also, establish systems for rotating members off the board for at least a year after serving two or three full terms. Coalition boards are exceptions.

Some boards develop standards for board participation, including how many board meetings (excused or unexcused) can be missed before the person is dropped from the board. Others require board members to volunteer a certain number of hours per month and to keep careful track of their hours.

Usually, those on the board elect the officers, although sometimes the community or membership at-large elects the officers. All community organizations have a president, secretary, and treasurer. These three positions are required by most state laws. Additional leadership positions should be added as needed.

Committees

Almost every community board has an executive committee. It is composed of the board officers (and sometimes others) and frequently also functions as the personnel committee. Additional committees that are common for community boards include:

- budget and finance committee
- fundraising committee
- program committee
- nominating committee
- annual meeting committee
- various issue committees.

The board can decide about expanding issue committees to involve community residents who do not serve on the board. Do not establish a standing by-laws committee, or else you will deal with by-laws forever. By-laws, as well as special events and problems, should be dealt with by temporary ad-hoc committees.

Executive Directors and Community Organization Boards

Sometimes executive directors wait for their boards to provide the program and policy directions, administrative review, and tone, vision, and community leadership described above. If board members have worked together for a long time and are well trained, they will. If not, they won't.

One of the key jobs of any executive director is to "organize" the board. Most board members are eager to be helpful to the organization and to the director, but need guidance and training.

The first thing the executive director must do is to develop a personal relationship with each member on the board. The director must understand each person's self-interest, as well as his or her skills and characteristics. The director must help each board member participate as fully as desired and must assist the person in developing leadership skills.

It is essential that the board president and the director develop a good working relationship. Without a healthy relationship between these two positions, conflicts will emerge. They should be friendly, but not best friends, because the board president needs to be able to represent the concerns of the board as a whole, and not be perceived as the defender of the director.

Most boards need training on their roles and periodic workshops to analyze the board's structure. The executive director should work with the board president to assure that this training is provided. Outside trainers can provide assistance in this board training.

The director must work to involve every board member in the life of the organization. If someone on the board is not functioning well at meetings or not participating at all, the executive director should discuss the problem with the board president. Between them, they should develop a plan for approaching the person about the problem.

Part of working with board members, especially when they are new to the board, is helping them grasp the vision and excitement of the organization. Even though providing vision and tone is part of the board's responsibility, it is also the director's job to help the board develop and understand the broader vision. This is primarily done through one-on-one meetings and through the development of board members as leaders.

Typical Problems of Community Organization Boards

No institution involving human beings is without its problems and conflicts. Community boards are no exception. Below are some of the typical problems that community boards, as well as many agency and coalition boards, encounter.

Clarifying/Balancing Staff and Board Roles

Every community organization has to clarify what jobs are done by staff and what jobs are done by board members and other volunteers. This is especially problematic when a former board member or volunteer in the community becomes a paid staff person. Questions almost inevitably arise about "why is she getting paid?" It is less a problem when organizations hire an experienced organizer who is perceived as bringing in the necessary organizing skills.

Community boards and their staffs need to approach policy conflicts and strategy questions between board members and staff in an open manner. Don't assume they will go away. They probably won't. Schedule an open discussion at a board meeting, drawing on an outside facilitator if needed.

Hasty Budget Decisions

Especially in times of crisis, community boards can make hasty, short-sighted budget decisions unless they are properly trained and well-informed about the options available to them. Board members should listen carefully to the director and knowledgeable staff on budget matters, but recognize that they too may panic.

Another budget problem is that boards will allocate money for new projects without regard to where the money will come from. Community boards must learn that for every additional expense, there must be an additional source of income, or that money must be cut in another budget category. If board members are actively involved in fundraising, they will be

less likely to allocate money without considering where it comes from.

As an organization's budget grows, board members may be overwhelmed by the budget, especially new board members. Sometimes board members will focus on a relatively insignificant part of the budget because it is a part that they understand. Boards need to be encouraged to focus on the large financial items that are the organization's priorities, and not allow themselves to be diverted into less important, more easily understood budget categories.

Board Interfering in Personnel Matters

The most effective structure that organizations have found for handling personnel matters is for the board of directors to hire the executive director, who is then responsible for hiring, or firing, and supervising the work of other staff. The board's role is to set the personnel policy and ensure that it is followed. Beyond that, the board must allow the director to deal with staff. Interfering with personnel matters, such as trying to supervise other staff, only creates conflicts and difficulties. It is unfair for a staff person to have more than one boss.

The other common difficulty is that when a staff member is reprimanded by a director, he or she may complain to sympathetic board members. This is not a healthy process. If there are legitimate questions about how the staff person was dealt with, they should be raised with the director in accord with a grievance procedure, and then appealed to the board personnel committee if necessary. If a director has problems supervising staff, he or she should be urged to get additional training in that area, or the board must find a new director.

Lack of Clarity on Issues Before the Board

Many community boards deal with extraneous issues because the real issues that need decisions or discussion are not clearly stated or adequately prepared. It is important for board members to receive materials ahead of time and have agendas that clarify what needs to be accomplished at meetings. The director and board president must work together to assure that agendas are clear, background materials are adequate, and that meetings are chaired well.

Restricting Staff Attendance at Board Meetings

Many community boards restrict staff presence at board meetings. Sometimes these boards become unnecessarily rigid on the issue and rule that no staff member, except the director, can attend or speak at board meetings. This may be a backlash from situations in which staff members dominated board meetings. Regardless of the origin of this problem, community boards should develop a sensible approach to staff at board meetings. Staff members should attend parts of board meetings that make sense and should be able to speak if called on by the director or the board. Directors should ensure that staff provide solid background information, but don't dominate discussions. During personnel discussions about the director or salaries, all staff should be asked to leave the room.

Reluctance to Make Choices

Sometimes community boards are reluctant to make the important "hard" decisions. It may seem easier to foist the decision off to staff, but ultimately the board will resent whatever decision the staff makes.

Most community boards face difficult choices. The organization cannot take on all the important issues in the community. It must choose which issues to work on and what strategies to pursue. If you find your board fudging on these kinds of decisions and throwing them back to the staff, you need to stop and regroup. (One reason to pay for professional staff is to have someone to force the board to make hard choices.)

Director Evaluation Handled Poorly

An annual evaluation of the director is a board responsibility; however, if it is not handled delicately, the director will leave, even if the board thinks the director is doing a terrific job. The president of the board or a small committee should do the bulk of the work on an evaluation. A summary, leaving out gory details, should then be presented to the board. The entire evaluation process must be conducted confidentially, in order to remain supportive of the director. The evaluation must always be approached as a means for supporting and developing a director.

If there are some areas in which the director needs improvement (and most people need improvement in some areas), the board president or personnel committee should talk with the director and find ways to support the director's development in that area. The growth areas should be raised only in the context of overall positive leadership.

If there are major problems that would suggest that the director should be removed, the board must bite the bullet and get rid of the director. It is better to deal with firing a director than to watch a potentially strong organization stagnate or deteriorate. Be sure to review some literature on how to handle getting rid of a director, both legally and humanely (a few references are suggested in the bibliographical section on supervision).

Board Members Are Unclear About Roles and Responsibilities

Many new community board members are unclear about their roles and thus hesitate to take on responsibilities or speak up at meetings. Every community board should write down the expectations it has of all board members and its specific expectations for officers and committee chairs.

In addition, every new board member should receive an orientation. This should include background materials to read about the organization as well as information about board participation. The director and/or board president should arrange to meet with new board members to explain more about what is expected of them and to answer questions.

Most community boards find it useful to bring in outside trainers to assist in board development. The issues of roles and responsibilities are usually covered in most board training sessions; however, the board should identify its questions as clearly as possible prior to contracting with a trainer.

Function Like an Administrative Board, Not a Community Organization Board

Sometimes, community board members view themselves as "experts" or "advisors to staff" instead of community leaders. Community boards must build power in the community. This requires each board member to become a leader by developing strong relationships in the community. A community board cannot simply address the legal and management issues facing the organization. It must also organize. It must analyze power, choose issues, develop strategies, and lead in tactics.

Most community boards of directors are vibrant organisms. They grow and develop, but not without some conflicts and pain. Nurturing and developing your community board is not merely another job. It is essential to a community organization because the board is the embodiment of the organization in the community. A strong board is one characteristic that distinguishes a community organization from an agency located in the community.

Community organization boards provide program and policy direction, administrative review, tone, vision, and community leadership. These boards build and lead strong democratic community organizations that can control or influence decisions affecting the community. Effective community boards serve as a training ground for all those who serve on the board, and demonstrate models for decision-making and community control to government bodies. Community boards are a key component of citizen action and citizen control in a democracy.

17

Religious organizations are some of the more powerful institutions in most communities. They also are seen as offering moral leadership to both their members and the community at large. Organizers who are active members of religious denominations find it perfectly natural to work with religious organizations. Others, with more secular backgrounds, have concerns and questions.

In recent years, religious and non-religious activists have functioned in separate worlds, although many of their concerns are the same. As organizers, we need to bridge these worlds and help the religious and progressive communities to work together more closely.

Why Work Together?

Mutual Self-Interests

It is in the mutual self-interests of religious and non-religious groups alike to work together. Why do community and state organizations want to work with religious groups?

People. Lots of people are affiliated with religious groups. In fact, 42 percent of the U.S. population attends church at least once a week. Fifty percent of the Jewish community consider themselves "religious."

Organized Institution. Religious organizations are organized. They have volunteers and structures that can be mobilized for social justice.

Working with Religious Organizations

Resources. Religious institutions have lots of material resources in addition to their human ones. They have money, buildings, buses, office equipment, and many other financial and in-kind resources that are needed in organizing work. The largest recipients of donor dollars are religious institutions, and almost half of those funds are used on charitable activities and community service.

Respect/Credibility. Few institutions bring as much respect and credibility as religious groups. Many organizing campaigns need respect and credibility, especially at the beginning stages.

Values. Religious institutions provide leadership on issues of moral concern and provide arenas in which large numbers of people discuss their fundamental values.

Racial Diversity. The religious community as a whole, and some national denominations in particular, cross racial lines. Very few other national institutions reach all sectors of U.S. society. By working with religious organizations, progressive organizations increase their opportunities for working cross-culturally and building multi-cultural organizations and coalitions.

Why do religious groups want to work with community and state organizations?

Ministry. The most fundamental reason why religious groups want to work with community

and state organizations is that they share values and by working together, can help religious organizations meet their goals of ministry. Most religious denominations believe that part of their ministry is to be a witness in the world. Justice is a fundamental theme for most denominations. And yet at the local level, congregations are confused about how to act effectively on their concerns and values. State and community social action groups can provide concrete strategies for putting their faith into action.

Congregational Development. Local congregations are concerned about their own growth and development. Working with community groups helps them make the surrounding area a more desirable place to live. In addition, many congregations have found that social action and community involvement revitalize their congregations, and encourage more people to join.

Leadership Development. Congregations, like most institutions, are concerned about training and development for their leaders. Organizing provides opportunities for leaders to be trained and develop new skills.

Recognition/Visibility. Like most institutions, congregations want to receive recognition for the work they do. If a congregation is active on a particular issue, it will want the visibility that results from participating in a larger coalition or organization.

If you understand a congregation's self-interest, you are better equipped to address how your organization's work can assist the congregation. By all means, stress the moral aspects of your endeavor, but don't forget to mention the direct benefits to the congregation.

Involvement in Issues

If you haven't worked much with the religious community, you may be wondering if congregations really get involved in organizing and public policy work. A couple of examples follow for "ye of little faith."

A number of Illinois social service agencies and advocacy groups spearheaded a coalition, called Work, Welfare, and Families, to reform the welfare program and increase its benefits level. Most of these agencies had long histories of involvement in welfare issues, but had experienced difficulties in recent years in getting the state welfare agency to budge.

The group expanded their coalition to include a number of religious groups who actively participated in designing a new organizing strategy. A key component of the strategy was to organize congregations' letter-writing campaigns to state legislators. A congregational organizing packet and special bulletin inserts were prepared for the campaign. Dozens of state and regional denominational leaders were contacted about the campaign and offered to send materials to thousands of congregations across the state.

They responded, and record numbers of letters were sent to legislators about welfare reform in Illinois. A number of improvements were made in the welfare program and the first benefits increase in four years was granted. Churches and synagogues were major players in this welfare coalition.

Washington Fair Share, a Citizen Action affiliate, developed an exciting program called the Campaign for the Working Poor. The program built on congregations' and unions' mutual concern for just and fair wages. One particular campaign focused on fair wages and benefits for janitors working in downtown Seattle office buildings. A religious committee was formed that developed the strategies and tactics for involving the religious community. Clergy and lay leaders wrote letters to managers, or met individually, to urge them to negotiate a fair contract. A community hearing was sponsored by religious organizations. Fifteen religious leaders conducted an "Interfaith Prayer Service for Janitors" in the lobby of a major, anti-union office tower. Denominational leaders issued statements of support.

In the end, the union won a new contract, with no concessions, and wage and benefit increases. The religious community's involvement was a key component in the victory, and laid the groundwork for future coalitional work between the religious and labor communities.

Concerns/Possible Problem Areas

Working with religious organizations is not necessarily easy. Indeed, there are problem areas that you should prepare for and concerns that you will want to consider. However, most of these can be addressed or avoided.

Separation of Church and State. One of the first questions you will hear raised when you try to involve religious organizations in social justice issues and organizing efforts is, "Well, what about the separation of church and state"? (You will hear this issue more in White churches than in African-American churches or synagogues.) This phrase is highly misunderstood and misused. The proper response for an organizer to this issue is what is true: "Yes, we fully support the separation of church and state." You do not want the church controlling the state, nor do you want the state controlling religious groups. You support Article I of the U.S. Constitution, which says, "Congress shall make no law respecting an establishment of religion. . . ."

The "separation of church and state" phrase is sometimes raised to justify not getting involved in organizing or social justice issues, but no denomination except perhaps the Jehovah's Witnesses is consistent on this matter. Religious folks vote, and take their faith with them into the ballot box. Churches and synagogues are involved in a whole range of "political" issues, ranging from off-track betting, to abortion, to peace. The real issue is not whether religious groups are involved in political issues, but rather, how they're involved and on what issues.

Divisions Within the Congregation. Frequently, the real reason why congregations won't get involved in social justice issues is that people within the congregation disagree on the issue. A small segment of the congregation may work on the issue, like a peace committee, but the entire congregation doesn't because of the fear of splitting the congregation. Where there are major divisions on an issue in a congregation, it is unlikely that they will become involved. Congregational leaders cannot involve congregations in issues that will divide the congregation.

On the other hand, there are dozens of progressive issues that are not controversial for congregations, especially if presented properly. Most individual congregations are both racially and economically segregated. The more homogeneous they are, the more likely that the whole congregation would agree or disagree on a particular issue. Thus, there are clearly congregations that will want to work with you and congregations that won't. Go with those that do want to work with you.

Differences on Other Issues. A number of progressive organizers hesitate to involve congregations in organizing campaigns because they disagree with the congregations' positions on other issues, such as abortion or gay rights, or they maintain inaccurate stereotypes about religious people. Stick to the issues at hand and don't feel obligated to share your personal opinions on other issues, unless they actually are organizational positions. It is very unlikely that you will be asked about non-germane issues; however, if you are, simply respond that the organization does not have a position on that issue (assuming it doesn't).

You do not have to agree with everyone on every issue in order to work together on issues of mutual concern. Find the areas of commonality and move on. Avoid requiring litmus tests before you work with people.

Tax Concerns. Some congregations are concerned that by becoming involved or supporting an action organization, they will lose their 501(c)(3) tax status. If the organization is a 501(c)(3) or a 501(c)(4), it is almost inconceivable that there could be a problem. A congregation would have to devote more than

20 percent of its resources to lobbying before there would be a problem. There are some legitimate concerns about partisan electoral work, although nonpartisan electoral work is fine (such as nonpartisan voter registration). Tax-deductible funds, such as congregations receive, are not to be used for partisan electoral work (see Chapter 24 on legal matters).

Style. Frequently, the biggest barrier to involving religious congregations is not a matter of substance, but of style. All groups have their own language, dress, and appropriate mode of behavior. Religious organizations are no exception. Talk with people active in the religious organizations and get advice on how best to approach the denomination or congregation.

Stealing Leaders. Congregations may be concerned that your group wants to steal their active leadership. Find ways to support and develop the congregations' leaders. Help them involve and draw the entire congregation into your organization's activities in ways that build and unify the congregation.

Overworked Staff. Many small urban congregations are struggling for survival. Their pastoral staff and key lay leadership are overwhelmed. They may not be able to consider another issue, no matter how worthy, unless you can suggest simple ways the congregation can be involved that don't rely upon already overworked personnel.

Segregation. Even though the religious community as a whole is racially diverse, individual congregations are not. They tend to reflect the segregation of the community. Thus, if you seek racial diversity, you will need to select congregations and denominations carefully.

The Steps to Take Toward Working with Religious Organizations

Assessing Your Community

If you want to involve religious groups in your organizing work, you will need to assess which denominations are likely constituents (or allies) and whom you want to approach first. You can either try to involve those most important politically and numerically, or those most likely to become involved. Most groups do a combination of the two.

The easiest way to find out which denominations are numerically strongest in your community is to count the number of listings in the Yellow Pages under "churches" (synagogues are usually listed there as well). If the community you are trying to organize is the state, call the State Council of Churches (sometimes called the Conference of Churches or the Interfaith Council). Most counties are heavily dominated by one or two denominations, reflecting historical settlement and migration patterns.

Unfortunately, the most prominent denomination in an area is not always the easiest to get involved. They tend to be the most closely tied into the region's power structures, and consequently are reluctant to challenge the status quo. When a denomination is smaller in numbers (less powerful), they tend to be more open to coalitional work.

Some denominations have strong positions on social justice issues and good internal networks for activating congregations. These are likely to be the easiest denominations to involve. Try to identify the more active ones and approach their leaders on your issues—either at the regional or local level.

Even though some denominations may be the most likely to get involved, there are always congregations that are far more active and progressive than their denominations might suggest. Don't write off any congregation just because their denomination tends to be a more conservative one.

Most communities have a council of the religious leaders in the community. In fact, there are usually a number of these bodies. A standard set of councils is the Interfaith Council (primarily mainline Protestants, Catholics and Jews), the Black Ministerial Alliance, and the Evangelical Ministers Association. The first two groupings are more likely to become active, but talk with the Evangelicals if time permits (there are "Evangelicals for Social Action").

If you are in a small town, none of these councils will have staff; thus, the appropriate person to meet with is the president of the council. In large towns, the Interfaith Council (it may be called the Council of Churches, Ministerial Association, or another name) will have staff. These people can give you a good assessment of the denominations in the area and who to contact for your issue.

If you want to talk with the entire council, ask to attend one of their meetings (which are usually held monthly). Do not have high expectations for what you can achieve by meeting with these councils. They tend to be more networking groups for the clergy than agencies with programs. Appropriate things to ask for include endorsements, contacts within local congregations, and the names of ministers who would like to become involved. The councils themselves seldom "organize" things. Nor do they give money. Consider passing a sheet around the room during your presentation asking people to sign their names if they want you to meet with them and others in the congregation about the issue or the organization. Be sure to highlight any resources that are geared for congregations, like bulletin inserts or adult study programs.

Making the Right Request of the Right Person

Each denomination has its own regional structure, congregational decision-making body, style of worship, and committees for social action. The best way to learn about them is simply to ask people within each denomination. Ministers, in particular, like to talk about their denominations.

In general, most denominations have a regional structure. For some, it is a state; for others, it is a metropolitan area. For example, there is the Illinois Baptist Association for the Baptists and the Archdiocese of Chicago for the Roman Catholics. Other names for the regional levels are synod (Lutheran), presbytery (Presbyterian), and conference (Methodist). (See the charts at the end of the chapter for an introduction to terms.) At this regional level, many denominations have a staff person assigned to peace and justice, social action, community concerns or some such category. In addition, there may be a regional committee within the denomination, like the African Methodist Episcopal Conference Social Action Committee. These committees will be composed of lay and clergy members from across the region. Their members are usually some of the most active leaders within the denominations.

When you meet with regional social action staff or committees, ask for the following kinds of things:

- *Mailings*. Most regional groupings do mailings to portions of their denomination's membership. Ask them to include information about your group or issue in one of their mailings.
- *Money*. Regional denominations may have small amounts of money for local projects. Consider asking for money to cover the costs of involving their members or designing materials especially for religious groups.
- *Key People/Congregations*. Regional leaders can put you in touch with the people and congregations that would be most concerned and active.
- *Speaking Opportunities*. Find out if the grouping has any regional gatherings. If so, see if you can be on the program to present your issue.
- *Articles*. Ask if the denomination has a regional publication. If so, ask if they can arrange to have an article on your issue.

At the local congregational level, you almost always want to talk first with the minister, priest, or rabbi. Frequently, these are not the people who will be the most active in your organization, but you need their "blessing" to talk with others in the congregation. When you meet with these members of the clergy, find out about the general direction and programs of the congregation. Also, ask for:

- *Introductions*. Ask the pastor to introduce you to the key people in the congregation. Ask for suggestions on ways to involve the entire congregation. Find out about social action committees, women's committees and other active groups.
- *Prayers/Speaking*. Most members of the clergy like to speak in public. They are good people to open meetings (with a prayer), close meetings (with a prayer), or speak about the moral implications of an issue. You might also want them to participate in a press conference or press event.

- *Notices in Bulletins*. Ask if you can place announcements in the congregation's bulletin or newsletter. Find out to whom the notices should be sent.
- *Other contacts*. Ministers know other ministers. Get the names of other religious leaders concerned about these issues.

Occasionally the clergy are good organizers, but more often, they are simply too busy. Get the clergy's support, but work more closely with lay leadership within the congregation. Sometimes the social action committee (also called Church and Society, or peace and justice committee) members are the best people with whom to work. In other congregations, the social action people are perceived as unrepresentative of the congregation. In this situation, you may be more effective working with the women's committee, the parish board, or the adult education committee. Seek out the most powerful committees. Below are the kinds of things you can ask for from the lay committee members:

- *Announcements*. Congregations have various means for getting the word out to members about upcoming activities. Some means include bulletins, newsletters, announcement boards, telephone trees and "minutes for mission" (a short time during a service in which community announcements and congregational missions are mentioned).
- *Material Support*. There are many ways in which a congregation can support your organization or work. Some committees will have small pots of money over which they are responsible. Others have the authorization to request funds from the congregation decision-making body (board, vestry, council). Even if there is not money available, you can usually get some in-kind contributions. The dollar value of these can be enormous. Items in this category include buses, meeting space, photocopying/printing, supplies, refreshments, and donated goods for grassroots fundraising events.
- *Meetings*. In addition to asking for meeting space, ask for groups of people to talk with about your issue. Appropriate forums might be adult education classes, lenten studies,

family night suppers, women's meetings, and special forums. In some congregations, you or another member of your group might be asked to deliver a message (sermon, homily) in the regular service. If so, ask for additional time after the service to meet with people who have questions. This way you will know who really cares about your issue and will be able to answer questions they might have.

- *Letters/Calls*. There are a number of different ways to get congregations to write letters or make phone calls to elected officials. Standard techniques include: letter-writing tables in the vestibule or during coffee-hour, times set aside for letter-writing during committee meetings, activation of prayer chains for letters, "offerings of letters" during services, or requests for letters and calls in bulletins and newsletters.

- *Turnout*. If a congregation is really concerned about and involved in an issue, the leaders can help turn out people for community meetings and events.

Guidelines for Working with the Religious Community

Develop an Ongoing Relationship. Don't just approach religious leaders or congregations at a point of crisis. Develop a relationship with them. Get religious leaders on your board or other appropriate bodies.

Involve the Religious Community in Your Organizational Planning and Strategies. The religious community likes to help plan how to mobilize itself. Refrain from developing organizing campaigns for congregations without involving them in the planning.

It is also important to develop special materials and organizing strategies for working with congregations. You can't realistically expect a congregation to adopt your resources if they are not designed with congregations in mind.

Recognize Past Involvement. If you know of a congregation or denomination's past involvement, acknowledge it. If you know of

statements it has made on social issues that support your concerns, mention them; however, don't wait until you know this information to contact the congregations.

Be Aware of Religious Holidays. Purim, Passover, Rosh Hashana, Yom Kippur, Hanukkah, and Sukkot are important to the Jewish community. Please note that Sabbath begins Friday evening at sundown and runs to Saturday evening at sundown. Ash Wednesday, Palm Sunday, Maundy Thursday, Good Friday, Easter, and Christmas are important to the Christian community. Many congregations also have special events and services around Mother's Day and Thanksgiving.

Avoid Non-Germane Issues. Do not raise issues of controversy within the religious community, unless you are working on those issues. Do not discuss the Middle East in synagogues or abortion in churches.

Ask About the Order of Service and Appropriate Dress, If You Are Speaking to a Congregation. Go through all the details of things you might need to know, such as where to stand, appropriate things to begin and close with, usual length of time, and special procedures for entering and exiting.

Stress Basic Judeo-Christian Themes. Don't try to pass yourself off as a Bible or Torah expert; however, do stress basic themes of justice, charity, stewardship, and concern for the well-being of the whole being (both spiritual and physical).

Avoid Theological Issues. Avoid complex theological concepts such as sanctification, predestination, and any other big-word concept! Don't quote theologians unless you are sure they are acceptable (e.g., Martin Luther to the Lutherans or John Wesley to the Methodists).

Understand Scriptural Context. Too often, organizers unfamiliar with religious texts pull material and quote it totally out of context. Be sure to check with a member of the clergy if you have questions about a particular passage. (See *Cry Justice*, listed in the bibliographical section.)

Avoid Saying or Implying that "God Is on Our Side." Organizers hope God is on their side, but avoid claiming it, particularly in matters of public policy. Implementation of God's will is tough for mere mortals to assess, although groups certainly want the religious community's prayers and faithful guidance.

Pray at Appropriate Times. If religious people are involved in your activities, arrange to have prayers led at appropriate times, such as at the beginning or end of meetings or before meals. Avoid clapping at the end of the prayer, no matter how moving and inspirational. It is inappropriate.

Involve Key Jewish Organizations. In addition to the synagogues and denominational structures, try including:

— *National Council of Jewish Women,* 9 E. 69th Street, New York, NY 10021, (212) 535-5900. The Council operates programs in social and legislative action. Contact the local chapter in your community.

— *Jewish Federations.* There are approximately 200 Jewish Federations in the U.S. and Canada. All major metropolitan areas have Jewish Federations that coordinate programs for the community. Some are more socially active than others. Frequently, the Women's Divisions of the Federations contain some of the most socially active people.

— *Jewish Fund for Justice,* 260 Fifth Ave., New York, NY 10010, (212) 213-2113. The Fund supports organizing and social justice efforts, particularly ones that link Jewish communities with Black and Hispanic communities.

Involve Key Christian Organizations. In addition to the denominations, there are "parachurch" organizations. Some of them are quite active and can put you in touch with activist-oriented church leaders.

— *Church Women United,* 475 Riverside Drive, Room 812, New York, NY 10017, (212)

870-2347. Church Women United is a lay women's group with approximately 1,200 chapters across the country. This is one of the more racially integrated organizations among churches. It is a good source for active church women.

— *Call to Action,* 4419 N. Kedzie, Chicago, IL 60625, (312) 604-0400. Lay people, religious and clergy working together to foster peace and justice. They sponsor a large annual conference linking small faith communities and church renewal organizations.

— *Evangelicals for Social Action,* 10 Lancaster Ave., Winnewood, PA 19096, (215) 645-9390. This small organization is a good entree for finding evangelicals who are concerned about social action. There are local chapters across the country.

— *Sojourners,* 2401 15 Street, N.W., Washington, D.C., 20009, (800) 714-7474. Began as a magazine, now a network of people putting their faith into action.

The religious organizations are institutions, complete with bureaucracies, strengths and weaknesses. They may not always be as easy to involve as you would like, but they are important in most communities and can greatly strengthen your work. Some will support you. Others won't. Do your best to find the support. Identify the mutual self-interests between your organization and the religious institutions. Work with the congregations to put their members' faith into action. The fundamental values of justice and compassion are the ones we strive for in our world. Call on the religious institutions to join you in "loosing the bands of wickedness, undoing the heavy burdens, letting the oppressed go free, breaking every yoke, and giving bread to the hungry, shelter to the homeless, and clothes to the naked" (Isaiah 58:6–7).

Selected Forms of Address

Category	Written Form of Address and Salutation	In-Person
Archbishop (Roman Catholic)	The Most Reverend John Smith Archbishop of _____ Your Excellency:	Bishop Smith
Bishop (Episcopal)	The Right Reverend John Smith Bishop of _____ Dear Bishop Smith:	Bishop Smith
Bishop (Methodist)	The Reverend Jane Smith Bishop of _____ Dear Bishop Smith:	Bishop Smith
Bishop (Roman Catholic)	The Most Reverend John Smith Bishop of _____ Dear Bishop Smith:	Bishop Smith
Cardinal (Roman Catholic)	His Eminence John Cardinal Smith Your Eminence:	Cardinal Smith
Clergy (most Protestants)	The Reverend Jane Smith Dear Ms. Smith:	Reverend Smith
Dean of a Cathedral (Episcopal)	The Very Reverend John Smith Dean of _____ Dear Dean Smith:	Reverend Smith
Elder (some Protestants)	Elder Jane Smith Dear Elder Smith:	Ms. Smith
Monsignor (Roman Catholic)	The Right Reverend Monsignor John Smith Dear Monsignor Smith:	Monsignor Smith
Priest (Episcopal)	The Reverend Jane Smith Dear Ms. Smith:	Reverend Smith
Priest (Roman Catholic)	The Reverend John Smith Dear Father Smith:	Father Smith
Rabbi	Rabbi John Smith Dear Rabbi Smith:	Rabbi Smith
Sister (Roman Catholic)	Sister Jane Smith Dear Sister Jane:	Sister Jane

Midwest Academy, 225 West Ohio, Suite 250, Illinois 60610

Organizing for Social Change

Selected Denominational Terms

Denomination	National	Regional	Local	Hired Leader
African Methodist Episcopal Church	General Conference (President & Senior Bishop)	District (Bishop)	Church Congregation	Minister
American Baptist Churches in the USA	Biennial Convention (President & General Secretary)	Association (Executive Minister)	Church Congregation	Minister
Christian Church (Disciples of Christ)	General Assembly (General Minister & President)	Regional Office (Regional Minister)	Church Congregation	Minister
Episcopal Church	General Convention (Presiding Bishop & Primate)	Diocese (Bishop) Deanery (Dean)	Church Parish	Priest
Evangelical Lutheran Church in America	Churchwide Assembly (Bishop)	Region Synod (Bishop)	Church Congregation	Minister
Presbyterian Church (USA)	General Assembly (Moderator & Stated Clerk)	Synod (Synod Executive) Presbytery (Presbytery Executive)	Church Congregation	Minister
Progressive National Baptist Convention, Inc.	Annual Session (President & General Secretary)	Region (Regional President) State Convention (State President)	Church Congregation	Pastor, Minister
Roman Catholic	National Conference of Catholic Bishops (canonical) US Catholic Conference (civil)	Archdiocese Diocese (Bishop)	Parish	Pastor, Priest
Southern Baptist Convention	Annual Convention (President)	State Convention (Executive Director) Association (Executive Director)	Church	Minister Preacher Pastor
Union of American Hebrew Congregations	National Office (President)	Region (Director)	Temple Synagogue Congregation	Rabbi
United Church of Christ	General Synod (President)	Region Conference (Conference Minister)	Church Congregation	Minister
United Methodist Church	General Conference	Annual Conference (Bishop) District (District Superintendent)	Church Congregation	Minister

Please note: These are not parallel structures. The size, power, and structures vary greatly between denominations.

Midwest Academy, 225 West Ohio, Suite 250, Illinois 60610

18

Unions are valuable partners in many community and statewide coalitions. Both unions and citizen organizations seek to increase people's power through unity in order to improve the quality of their lives. Unions often have resources, members, political contacts, and power that can be essential to winning citizens' issues. Community and citizen organizations not only share with unions an interest in many issues, but can also lend valued support to labor's battles, both in the legislature and in the workplace.

It isn't necessary here to discuss why unions and citizen organizations should work together. That is already widely understood. This chapter, written for citizen organizers by a labor educator, will help you put theory into practice when developing relations with unions at the local level.

Understanding Each Other

If the reasons for working together are so clear, why do the alliances between labor and citizen groups sometimes fall apart or are never really reached? Generally it's not the issue that is the problem, but rather the relationship, or lack of relationship, between the organizations. One way to understand why local unions are sometimes reluctant to work with citizen organizations is to try reversing the usual roles. Think of a union organizer approaching you, a staff person for a citizen organization, and asking you to form an alliance with the union.

Organizing for Social Change

Working with Local Unions and Central Labor Councils

Imagine that for ten years you've been building up a local group. Despite conflicts among your leadership, high staff turnover, constant battles for funding, and attacks from Right-wing groups, you've built an organization that has won some real victories and has become recognized as a powerful group in the community. You have made personal sacrifices to see this happen. You've given up time with your family and haven't had a real vacation in years. Yet, despite all the progress, it is still a day-to-day struggle to keep the organization afloat, meet payroll, keep the members active and involved, and satisfy your board.

One day, while you are involved in a major campaign for the rehabilitation of abandoned houses in your area, a young labor organizer comes to meet with you. She explains an innovative and exciting campaign to organize low-paid clerical workers at a non-union company in town. Caught up with enthusiasm for her work, she explains that the only important organizing is workplace organizing—where you can really change the root causes of poverty and disenfranchisement. She says that community groups should put all of their resources into assisting real organizing, instead of fighting to get one more traffic light. Of course, she does agree that some community organizing is necessary and she has actually heard about a coalition involving labor and some other groups that fought for lower auto insurance rates, but she quickly reels off thirty ways that you can help her organizing drive. How would you react to this? After all, you are

equally as enthusiastic about your work, and equally convinced that it is the most important kind of organizing.

Despite the good intentions of the union organizer, you would probably feel insulted, patronized, and angry. Who is this person to come in and give the impression that your work is less important than hers? She knows nothing about what you and your organization have accomplished over the years. Even if you wanted to help, you can't shut down your own organization. How could you help her union while still meeting your own organization's needs?

Whether justified or not, many union leaders have a similar reaction when approached by non-labor organizers who, they believe, neither understand what it takes to run a local union or central labor council, nor give them credit for the importance of their work and what they have accomplished. At some time or another, union leaders have been involved in planning militant actions against their bosses, and organizing legislative or political campaigns, as well as running the day-to-day operations of their locals.

Labor leaders feel tremendous pride in labor's history and accomplishments. Despite incredible opposition, unions have won better wages, benefits, dignity, and justice on the job. Unions have been and still are very active in the legislative arena. They have fought for workers' compensation, unemployment insurance, child labor laws, and many other things that we now take for granted. Many unions have been in the

AMERICAN UNION STRUCTURE

Individual Union	AFL-CIO
National Level	
International union (e.g., Auto Workers, Machinists, AFSCME).	AFL-CIO. The federation of unions at the national level.
The members are individual workers who join through local unions.	The members are international unions. Each is an independent organization.
State or Regional Level	
The state or regional body of the international union (e.g., Region 9, United Auto Workers).	State labor federations which belong to the AFL-CIO. Called "State Feds."
The members are local unions of the international union.	The members are local unions and central labor councils in the state.
City, Town, or County Level	
Local unions, district councils, and joint boards (e.g., Local 101, Brown County School Employees; DC 37, AFSCME; Local 2804, XYZ Steel Co., US Steel Workers).	Central labor councils of the AFL-CIO.
The members are individual workers.	The members are local unions in the area.

forefront on civil rights, pay equity, child care and parental leave, as well as right-to-know legislation. Unions pioneered many tactics years ago that are now seen as new and creative. Tent cities, boycotts, sit-ins, sit-downs, civil disobedience, non-violent action and strikes are all part of union history.

Unions now face assaults from all sides. Employers and the government are working to weaken labor. As a result, membership and resources are down. Many unions are fighting just to survive. Unions are reexamining the strategies and tactics it takes to win in organizing and bargaining. A union's ability to assist a community campaign depends upon its own well-being.

Understanding Labor's Structure

The first step toward working successfully with unions on the local level is to understand labor's structure, or more correctly, structures. There are two main structures that run parallel to each other from the national to the local level. The first is the structure of any given union such as the International Association of Machinists or the Communication Workers of America. The second is the structure of the American Federation of Labor-Congress of Industrial Organizations. The AFL-CIO is not a union. It is a federation of unions, which is organized as a federation down to the local level. The two structures are depicted in the box on this page.

Labor at the National Level

Through its convention and executive council, the AFL-CIO makes policy for labor, and carries out a wide variety of functions in the political arena.

As of December 1995, there were 78 national and international unions affiliated with the AFL-CIO. (The word "international" means a national union. It is used because most unions have affiliates in Canada or Puerto Rico, such as the International Association of Machinists.)

In addition to belonging to the AFL-CIO as a whole, individual unions are affiliated with trade and industrial departments within the AFL-CIO structure. These departments serve the needs of particular groups of unions such as building trades, industrial unions, professional unions, or public employee unions. The AFL-CIO both supports and is supported by state labor federations in all fifty states. At the local level are over six hundred central labor councils which are themselves federations of local unions in a city, county, or region of a state.

It is unlikely that organizers learning about unions for the first time from this manual will have contact with the national leadership of either the AFL-CIO or its member unions. Most organizers will instead encounter international unions at the regional, state, or local levels, and the AFL-CIO at the state federation or central labor council levels.

State Labor Federations

State labor federations are voluntarily supported by local unions and central labor councils. Commonly called "state feds," these bodies coordinate labor's legislative, electoral, and community service work. They also support strikes, sometimes assist in organizing, and do public relations activities.

International unions may also have a state or regional structure, although many unions do not. A distinction should be made between state, regional or district structures, which are largely for administrative or political purposes, and district councils or joint boards, which are amalgams of local unions that are often too small to support their own individual staffs or facilities.

Local Unions

These unions usually operate in a specific city or geographic area, and have a "jurisdiction"; that is, a type of worker they represent (telephone workers, social workers, teachers, janitors, or carpenters). Local unions vary dramatically in size, resources, and community involvement. Some have a few hundred members and no full-time staff. Others have thousands of members, their own buildings, printing facilities, and many staff.

Joint boards and district councils are organizations of smaller local unions within the same international union. By pooling resources, locals that could not otherwise afford staff can share resources. These bodies have their own structure of paid officers elected by the members. The individual locals within them also have officers who are usually unpaid. The members of local unions are all usually in the same industry if not the same company. Joint board or district council members, on the other hand, can come from different companies and different industries.

Local unions elect their own officers. They have an executive board, committees, and a steward system at the work site. A steward is an appointed or elected union representative at the workplace, sometimes called a delegate.

A local union officer has a huge number of tasks to work on, from handling hundreds of workplace grievances, bargaining contracts, organizing to bring in more members, and paying bills, to implementing the international union's agenda. The first responsibility of a local union officer is to ensure that the day-to-day business of the local is completed. If that isn't done, the local will decline and the officer will be voted out.

Central Labor Councils

Local unions in cities and counties affiliate with an AFL-CIO central labor council in order to work together on political, legislative, and social issues.

The mission of the central labor council is to organize in the community to promote social justice for all working people. Local unions send delegates to their council's monthly meetings to share information about what is happening in their locals, support other unions if needed, and work together in committees to carry out the goals of the council.

Central labor councils are funded by dues from their local union affiliates. They may occasionally receive a small amount of money from a state labor federation for a special project, but they must meet their own expenses.

As is the case with state labor federations, there is no rule saying that a local must belong. An individual international union might have a rule that its locals must belong to central labor bodies, but the council itself can't make such a rule. They have no authority over the local unions in their areas.

Most officers of central labor councils are volunteers. Outside of large cities, few councils have paid organizing staff. Some councils have a building, others operate out of their presidents' homes. A central labor council president can often give you information about unions in the community.

The Whole Picture

The chart on the next page is a simplified view of the structure of the AFL-CIO (on the top and left) and an individual union (on the bottom right). COPE stands for the Committee On Political Education, labor's electoral and community service arm. The trade and industrial departments provide service to unions with particular types of members: "Industrial" is the Industrial Union Department, "Trades" is Building Trades, etc. There are many more departments than are shown here. The arrows give a rough sense of how international and

---

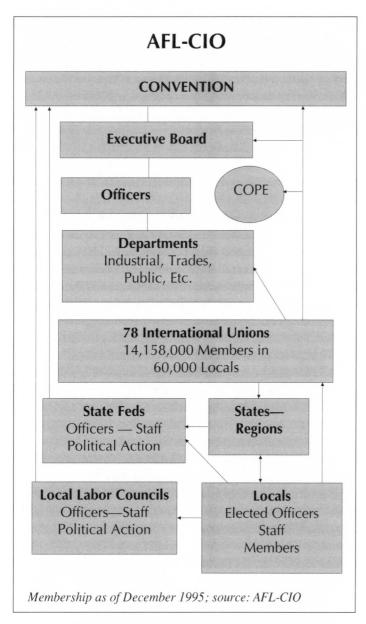

AFL-CIO

CONVENTION

Executive Board

Officers

COPE

Departments
Industrial, Trades,
Public, Etc.

78 International Unions
14,158,000 Members in
60,000 Locals

State Feds
Officers — Staff
Political Action

**States—
Regions**

Local Labor Councils
Officers—Staff
Political Action

Locals
Elected Officers
Staff
Members

Membership as of December 1995; source: AFL-CIO

local unions and central labor councils have input into the decision-making structure of the AFL-CIO. The chart does not attempt to show the policy-making structure of an individual union. Note that only in the bottom box on the right are there actual individual dues-paying members. The rest of the structure supports, and is supported by, those members.

Understanding Unions' Motivations

Political Interests

Labor organizations are highly political in two senses of the word. First, some play a very active role in local electoral politics: they endorse candidates and work in campaigns.

Citizen organizers should know the history here. Usually, elected officials who are strong supporters of labor are also good on other citizen issues, and vice versa, but this is not necessarily always the case. If your group has opposed or pressured a politician supported by local unions, it is very important to be aware of this when asking them to help you. It is also a problem when you ask unions to target elected officials whom they consider allies on labor issues. Of course, this is true of any group, including your own, only the issues are different.

The second sense in which unions can be political is that some have a very active internal political life. There are factions that vie for control of the organization through the election of officers. Stay clear of labor's internal politics. When approaching labor for cooperation on a local, district, or state level, go straight to the elected officers or top staff. Don't have dealings with people who want to involve you in intrigue. Someone wins and someone loses every union election. You should be able to keep on good terms with the union no matter who wins. Whether you are working with a local, state fed, or labor council officer, being on good terms also means respecting their agenda and realizing that they have responsibilities that must come ahead of work with outside groups.

Local Union Self-Interest

There are certain things that will make your job easier in approaching local union officers to cooperate with a citizens' organization. First, if your issue is one that higher bodies of the union or AFL-CIO have already endorsed and asked the local unions to work on, then the door is partly open. Often, local officers will be trying to find a way to squeeze another hour into the day for this issue. If you come with a plan that is very specific, and requires the union to do a set and limited amount, you will be welcomed. On the other hand, if you announce that you have come to "coordinate their efforts," and then propose several interminable meetings with people who don't know what to do, your reception may be less than enthusiastic.

Second, it helps if your issue is one that will materially benefit the union's members. It is easier all around if the officers can present it as an additional thing the union does to better the members' lives. Remember that unlike community groups that may get money from grants, canvassing, or even government agencies, every cent a local union has comes from the members' dues. (Dues are often several hundred dollars a year, depending on the member's pay scale.)

The members join unions primarily to win benefits on the job. Everything else is extra. If they feel that job-related issues are not being taken care of, or if they don't agree about your issue, they will be reluctant to see their dues money being spent to support it. Citizen organizations are often ambivalent about this point. On the one hand, they want union leaders to be accountable to the members. On the other hand, when the members disagree with the citizen group's issue, the group wants the union leaders to go ahead and support it anyway.

Third, you can help to promote a close working relationship with a local union if your issue is one on which labor-backed candidates can later campaign, or one that labor can use to attack opponents for not supporting. Many unions are not familiar with the type of issue campaigns that some citizen groups conduct, although this is rapidly changing. To a local union, political action usually means electoral campaigns. If you are in a position to talk with them about elections, you are immediately speaking the same language; other types of campaigns take some explanation. Unions do not work under the restrictions that apply to tax-exempt citizen groups. They are, however, prevented by law from spending dues money on electoral campaigns. Campaign work is done through political action committees, which they must fund separately. This money is contributed almost entirely by the members.

The key to working with local unions and central labor councils is thus the same as working with any other organization. *Understand their self-interest*. This means understanding the personal self-interest of the officers and staff, understanding the organizational self-interest of the union, and understanding its political self-interest as well.

As with other groups, whoever asks for help and gets it incurs a debt. Thus, you may be expected to help the union sometime in the future.

Approaching a Local Union

Here is a checklist of things to find out before approaching a local union. Having this information will help you to figure out the degree of interest any particular local union will have in your issue and what it can do to help. A little research will give you a better idea of what the local can gain by working with you, and how you can adjust your program to help the union's members. Local officers will expect you to know much of this. They will be impressed if you know a great deal.

- Number of members?
- Type of members?
  —occupation
  —income
  —sex
  —race
- Neighborhoods where members live?
- Location of work sites?
- Government or private sector workers?
- Growing or declining membership?
- Number of full-time staff? (Paid officers count as staff.)
- Active in politics or in the community? What issues?
- Facilities?
  —printing
  —meeting rooms
  —phones
- Who really runs the union? (It is usually the highest ranking *paid* elected officer. If, for example, there is an unpaid president and a paid elected business agent, the business agent is probably the person you would approach first. If no one is paid, then it is usually the president.)

Approaching a Central Labor Council

Central labor councils reflect the political complexion of the unions in their area. Often community organizations will have relations with those local unions that are most socially active. At the labor council you will meet the whole labor family, from the most progressive to those closer toward the center.

While central labor councils also have

intense internal politics, usually the unions in them have figured out how to work together on a common electoral and legislative program. Unlike local unions, labor councils are voluntary coalitions, and there are many lessons about coalition building to be learned from them. In developing a relationship with the central labor council, the first question to ask is who are the officers and what local unions do they come from? Is there a paid officer on the council? Are the top council officers also the officers of their own locals? Because you want to talk to the person who can actually commit the resources of the organization, find out who really has the power. Find out if the largest locals in the council are public employee, building trade, manufacturing, or service unions. The type of issues the council will be interested in will, to some degree, be influenced by this, and you will be better able to analyze its self-interest.

Assistance Labor Can Offer

Labor organizations can offer citizen organizations the following types of resources and assistance:

- Phone banks
- Meeting rooms, auditorium
- Printing
- Access to members
- Article in newsletter
- Political contacts
- Volunteers
- Officers to participate in press events
- Members with experience in activities, e.g., coordinating rallies or designing leaflets
- Members with specific expertise, e.g., teachers who know the school system

Ask the union for other ways in which it can help.

As with any successful coalition, the focus on the specific issues must reflect the self-interest of the organizations. Understanding

a union's self-interest and the demands that the organization is facing, its specific resources, its accomplishments, and its experience will produce a more positive relationship. Both unions and citizen organizations seek power through unity.

Glossary of Labor Terms

AFL-CIO (American Federation of Labor–Congress of Industrial Organizations). A federation of international unions in the United States, formed by the 1955 merger of the AFL (which consisted largely of craft or occupational unions) and the CIO (which consisted of industrial unions).

AFL-CIO Central Labor Council. In local areas, local unions may form central labor councils. These are active in city and county politics as well as the state legislative and congressional district levels. They are often directly involved in supporting strikes and in community services.

AFL-CIO Committee on Political Education (COPE). The political action arm of the AFL-CIO, COPE is primarily involved in electoral politics and political education among AFL-CIO members. COPE makes campaign contributions and coordinates the support of member unions for endorsed candidates. Many individual unions also have their own political action committees, as do some large locals. It is not legal in the United States to use unions dues for electoral campaigns. All electoral money is contributed by union members separately from their dues payments.

Agency Shop. The agency shop is a provision in a union contract that requires all non-union member employees in a bargaining unit, as a condition of employment, to pay the union a fixed amount, usually the same as dues, for services rendered by the union. Such provisions are rare. Where they exist, they greatly strengthen the union and insure its financial base. Agency shop means that the members don't have to subsidize services for nonmembers. Unions are required by law to provide the same services to nonmembers in a bargaining unit as they provide to members.

Agreement (Contract). A written agreement between an employer and an

The Midwest Academy thanks Marilyn Sneiderman for contributing this piece. She has had many years of experience in labor education and union work.

employee organization, usually for a definite term, defining conditions of employment, rights of employees and the employee organization, and procedures for settling disputes.

Arbitration. Usually the final step of a grievance procedure in which a dispute between a union and an employer is taken to an outside professional arbitrator for decision. In some contracts, the arbitrator's decision is binding; in others it is advisory.

Authorization Card (Cards, Card Drive). The process of petitioning for an election of a bargaining representative is begun when the employees sign cards designating a particular union as their representative. When a majority of the bargaining unit has signed cards, the National Labor Relations Board will, if asked, put the election procedure into motion.

Bargaining Agent. An organization elected by employees and designated by an appropriate government agency, or recognized voluntarily by an employer, as the exclusive representative of all employees in the bargaining unit for purposes of collective bargaining. The agency is usually the National Labor Relations Board, or a state labor relations board. By U.S. law, there can be only one bargaining agent per bargaining unit. In Europe and elsewhere this is often not the case, and several unions, often affiliated with rival political parties, will coexist in the same unit.

Bargaining Unit (Negotiating Unit). A group of employees recognized by the employer or designated by an authorized agency (e.g., the National Labor Relations Board) as appropriate for collective bargaining. Because all of the people in the bargaining unit can vote on which, if any, union will represent them, how the unit is drawn and who is included strongly affect the outcome of the election.

Business Agent. A full-time staff member of a local union often has the title "business agent" (often called a "B.A."). The term is most common in the building trades where business agents work daily with construction contractors trying to line up work for the union members. Elsewhere, the business agent is the full-time administrator of the day-to-day affairs of the local. Often the business agent is elected, but even when not elected, if the B.A. is the only full-time staff in the local, he or she can have more power than the elected officers.

Certification Election. An election usually conducted by the National Labor Relations Board or a state board, in which employees vote for or against union representation. Often several unions compete against each other in the election. "No representation" is automatically listed as an option on the ballot. Voting is secret.

Check-Off. A procedure in which an employer is authorized by a union member to deduct union dues from the member's salary and forward them directly to the union. This is often considered a "union security" provision because it guarantees that the union will have a steady income. In bygone days, dues were collected in the workplace by union representatives, or paid in person at the union hall.

Closed Shop. A union security provision of a contract that requires the employer to hire and retain only union members. This provision is generally prohibited under national and state legislation and should not be confused with Union Shop, which requires non-union employees to join the union.

Collective Bargaining. A process, usually regulated by law, in which a group of employees and their employer negotiate issues of wages, hours, working conditions and other conditions of the employer-employee relationship, for the purpose of reaching a mutually acceptable agreement, and the execution of a written contract incorporating that agreement.

Cost of Living Clause/Escalator Clause. A section of a contract providing that workers will receive an automatic raise in pay when the Consumer Price Index of the Labor Department goes up. The raise is based on a formula of so many tenths of a cent for each point's rise of the index.

District Council. Several local unions of the same international in a given geographic area may form a district council as a way of sharing staff and reducing overhead costs. The council coordinates bargaining and provides services to the members. Council leadership is elected by members of the locals.

ESOP (Employee Stock Ownership Plan). A plan whereby a block of company stock is transferred to employees. In some ESOPs, unions or employee organizations buy a controlling interest in a company and become the management. Other ESOPs are established by the existing management to protect themselves from corporate raiders, to secure tax benefits, or to avoid commitments to pensioners. The number of employees in ESOPs is growing very rapidly.

Fact Finder(s). An individual or group appointed to receive facts in an employment dispute and make recommendations for settlement. Fact finders are usually chosen by the parties to the dispute; they may be appointed by a court, or by a mayor or governor in the case of a public employee dispute.

Federal Mediation and Conciliation Service. A service provided by the government to help deadlocked negotiators reach a settlement. This agency is less concerned with the merits of the issues that are brought before it, and more concerned with avoiding or ending strikes.

Give-Backs. Contract gains that are given back to management by the union, usually upon the threat of layoffs or plant closings.

Grievance. A formal complaint by an employee which charges that management has violated some aspect of the union contract.

Grievance Procedure. A formal plan, specified in a union contract, which provides for the adjustment of grievances through discussion at progressively higher levels of authority in management and the union, usually culminating in arbitration. Such plans may also be found in companies and public agencies where there is no organization to represent employees. Arbitration is rarely a feature of these non-union plans.

International Representative. A staff member of an international union, often an organizer. International Reps. report directly to someone in the union's national headquarters, unlike business agents and other staff on local payrolls.

International Union. A national union is called international because it represents workers in Canada and/or Puerto Rico. It is the parent body of local unions and an affiliate of the AFL-CIO (although a very few unions are independent). The jurisdiction of an international union is usually industrial or craft in character, although in the last decade the lines have blurred. Today, many unions will organize any type of employee if the opportunity arises.

Joint Board. A structure very much like a District Council wherein the executive boards of several local unions of the same international will amalgamate themselves into a joint board for a certain geographic area or a trade (e.g., the Cloakmakers joint board of the International Ladies Garment Workers Union, or the Midwestern joint board of the Amalgamated Clothing and Textile Workers Union).

Local Representative. The staff member of a local union. People with this title perform a wide range of duties usually related to servicing contracts. Unlike a Business Agent, this is rarely an elected title. In unions where officers are often staff, there is a major distinction of power and standing between people elected to paid positions and those merely hired.

Mediation (Conciliation). An attempt by a third party to help in negotiations or the settlement of a labor dispute through suggestions, advice, or other ways of stimulating an agreement, short of dictating its provisions.

National Labor Relations Board (NLRB). An agency of the U.S. Government that enforces the Wagner and Taft-Hartley Acts, and conducts most private certification elections.

Negotiating Committee. A committee composed of members of a union that meets with company negotiators to negotiate a contract. Often the committee is a large body which has the responsibility of deciding the union's bargaining position. A smaller group of leaders of the committee may form the negotiating team, which participates in the actual meetings with management.

Occupational Health and Safety Administration (OSHA). The federal agency responsible for setting and maintaining health standards in the workplace, particularly related to toxic chemicals, noise, and air quality, as well as machine safety. OSHA has been rendered highly ineffective by reductions in the number of its inspectors. As a result, many unions are now establishing health and safety committees.

Ratification Election. When a negotiating committee reaches a tentative agreement, it must then by law, and usually the union's constitution, submit the agreement to the whole membership for a vote.

Regions. Like joint boards or district councils, regions are another form of intermediate organization between a local union and the international union. Joint boards and councils are usually composed of small locals and their service members. Regions more often have administrative and legislative functions, and are bodies through which the services of the international are delivered to the locals. Regions have staff and their officers are usually elected.

"Right to Work Laws." These are union busting laws, which have nothing to do with the right to work. National labor law allows state legislatures to outlaw the union shop. This prevents unions in those states, mainly in the South and West, from negotiating contracts requiring that all employees join the union. The union is nonetheless required to provide full services to all employees, members or not. The National Right to Work Committee is an employer organization that campaigns for the passage of such laws.

Shop Steward (Representative or Delegate). A first-line elected officer of a local union who works full time on the job rather than for the union. Workers with complaints or grievances go first to the steward. In many locals there is a chief steward and often a council of all the stewards. Contracts may require that stewards be given a certain amount of time off in which to conduct union business. In some union contracts, stewards get additional seniority or "super-seniority" to prevent them from being victimized by the employer. Usually, the only way to activate individual union members for political action is to go through the steward structure.

State Labor Federation (State Fed, State Labor Council). A body of the AFL-CIO organized on the state level. State Feds exist in all 50 states, and are composed of local unions and local labor councils. They function mainly as labor's political and legislative arm. Their officers are elected at a convention.

Taft-Hartley Act. A major piece of legislation regulating collective bargaining today. Passed in 1947 over the veto of President Truman, the Act was referred to by the legendary John L. Lewis of the United Mine Workers of America as, "the first ugly, savage thrust of Fascism in America." The act repealed many of the rights given to labor by the Wagner Act and the Norris-Laguardia Act. Among many other things, it re-instituted injunctions against

strikes and allowed for court-ordered "cooling-off" periods and bans on mass picketing. It permitted employers to sue unions for "unfair labor practices," abolished the closed shop, prohibited secondary boycotts, encouraged the passage of "right to work" laws, prohibited unions from making political campaign contributions, and required all union officers on every level to swear a non-communist affidavit.

Trusteeship (Receivership). In extreme circumstances, usually associated with corruption, a local union can lose its right to govern its own affairs, and a trustee will be designated by the international to supervise the local. Trustees are sometimes designated by a court of law. On rare occasions, trusteeship has been used against dissident members who are trying to reform the international leadership.

Unfair Labor Practice. A charge filed with a court or regulatory agency stating that an action by either an employer or an employee organization violates provisions of a national or state labor law.

Union Local. A branch of an international or national union. Locals are the one part of the labor structure which members actually join, and which represent them vis-à-vis their employers. Union members are local members first, and are members of national unions and of the AFL-CIO by virtue of being local members. A local's jurisdiction or "turf" may be one plant, office or shop. It may be one company. It may be geographic, covering a city or part of a state. On rare occasions, locals are nationally chartered (e.g., Local 925 of the Service Employees Union, and in its early history, Local 1199 of the Retail Drug Union, now the Hospital Workers Union).

Union Security. Protection of a union's status by provisions in a contract (e.g., sole representation, union shop, agency shop, maintenance-of-membership, check-off, etc.).

Union Shop. A contract provision that requires all employees to join the union within a specific period of time and to maintain union membership as a condition of employment.

Wagner Act (National Labor Relations Act). The main legislation regulating collective bargaining. In 1933, a year in which over 900,000 workers struck for union recognition,

Congress passed the National Industrial Recovery Act (NIRA) of which section 7 (a) guaranteed, for the first time in American history, that workers have the right to organize unions. After 1,500,000 workers struck for recognition in 1934 and 1,150,000 struck the next year, the Supreme Court invalidated the NIRA in May of 1935. In July, 1935, the Wagner Act was passed, again giving workers the right to organize and bargain collectively. The Act established the National Labor Relations Board to administer private sector bargaining and hold representation elections.

The Midwest Academy thanks Jim H. Williams for his help with this glossary.

Farmworkers build community support for their issues.

Union members participate in a statewide coalition lobby day.

19

The essence of direct action organizing is to find the other side's weakest point and to focus all of your strength on it. Tactical investigation is a major method for locating weak points. Although exposing tactical weaknesses doesn't in itself change the balance of power, it does open an avenue of

This chapter is a collective endeavor of the authors, Steve Askin, and the Industrial Union Department (IUD) of the AFL-CIO.

It was rewritten and updated in 1995 by Steve Askin, a research analyst at the Service Employees International Union. Askin worked as an investigative journalist in the United States and abroad for more than 15 years. Askin's work on this project was supported by the Industrial Union Department of the AFL-CIO.

The chapter includes, with permission, materials drawn from publications of the IUD and material written by Barry Greever and Barbara Samson for earlier editions of the manual.

It is based on the 1972 pamphlet "Tactical Investigations for People Struggles" by Barry Greever, which appeared in previous editions of the Midwest Academy Manual. The dean of tactical investigation, Greever has inspired a whole generation of organizers, researchers, and investigators.

It also includes material rewritten for the 1991 Manual with extensive help of Barbara Samson who has done research and investigative work for New Jersey Citizen Action, the Communication Workers of America in New Jersey, and others.

Tips for Investigations

Guide to Information Sources

Sources for Investigating Individuals

Other Specialized Research Topics

Tactical Investigations

attack as part of a larger strategy to change power relations. If a particular weakness were large enough to change the relationship of power, it would be a strategic weakness, not a tactical weakness. But a number of tactical weaknesses can add up to a strategic weakness.

Tactical weaknesses take many forms. An opponent who breaks the law or flouts regulation incurs a tactical weakness that can be exploited. Having a conflict of interest or lying in public does the same thing, as does acting inconsistently with an expected role. An elected official who takes a vacation trip paid for by a corporation has acted inconsistently with an expected roll, even without further evidence of wrongdoing. These are the things that tactical investigators look for. We will stress over and over that nothing automatically happens when an investigator uncovers a tactical weakness. It is only an avenue. Organization is required to utilize it.

Not Research, But Political/ Economic Intelligence

Research: A careful systematic study and investigation in some field of knowledge...
—Webster's Dictionary

Intelligence: Intelligence deals with all the things which should be known in advance of initiating a course of action...
—Brittanica

Many organizers, particularly those who are college graduates, call the process of locating information "research." But the word "research" often implies knowledge divorced from action. In the academic world, one is expected to approach a research project with an open mind, free of preconceived ideas or values.

"Intelligence," on the other hand, is about finding the strengths and weaknesses of an opponent. The distinction cannot be overemphasized: research requires one mindset, and intelligence another.

The following definition of intelligence, taken from a military training manual, makes the distinction clearer.

> [Intelligence is:] The product resulting from the collection, evaluation, analysis, integration and interpretation of all available information [which] is immediately or potentially significant to planning.

Intelligence, therefore, is oriented toward action. It has little to do with knowledge for the sake of knowledge. It involves gathering pieces of information, large and small, working with them until a pattern emerges, and then using that information tactically against an opponent. It would be self-defeating to do research for a citizen organization with the view that you are simply studying some field of knowledge. If you are working for a tenant organization, you must have the attitude that you are investigating the landlord, not studying him. If you are working in an election campaign, you are investigating the contributions of an opponent and looking for illegal campaign practices. Some examples will illustrate this point.

In Louisville, Kentucky, the aldermen appointed a "Mayor's Advisory Committee" to study a new housing code that had been proposed by a tenant organization. Tactical investigation revealed the following:

- Nine of the twelve Advisory Committee members owned property.
- Five of the nine were landlords.
- The value of the property being rented out by landlords on the committee was nearly half a million dollars, high by local standards.
- One committee member owned rental property jointly with the alderman who appointed him to the committee.

This information was used to alert the community, and to discredit the committee when it proposed a housing code biased against tenants. There was obviously a major conflict of interest here.

In New Jersey, landlords claimed that rent control increased property taxes for non-renting homeowners. Tactical investigation challenged this by comparing the rate of property tax increases in communities with and without rent control. The information was sent to legislators. It was used to get press, and was presented in testimony before city councils considering rent control. It showed that the landlord's organization could not be relied on to present accurate information to public bodies.

When insurance companies tried to justify rate hikes by claiming that they were losing money on their policies, citizen investigators revealed how much profit they were getting from investing the premiums. This changed the whole nature of the debate. Elected officials had to be more cautious about supporting the insurance industry that had deceived them.

A state government claimed that it was saving money by contracting out work, but union investigators demonstrated that contracting out was actually more expensive. This information was used in union contract negotiations when the state argued that union employees should take pay cuts to bring costs down to the private-sector level.

In Massachusetts, an organization was working to get a toxic dump site cleaned up. The group traced ownership of the land to a local bank, but couldn't force the bank to act. Further investigation showed that a nearby YMCA had substantial deposits in the bank. The organization pressured the "Y" to pressure the bank, and the cleanup soon began. It was not the expected role of the "Y" to be supporting a polluter. In this situation, the "Y" and other bank customers become secondary targets.

It should be clear from these examples that tactical investigation is essential to many successful campaigns. It is not a luxury, and organizations must budget money for it. Citizen organizations should hire a full-time investigator, or train other staff members in investigative skills. (Where such a position exists, it is usually called "researcher" or "policy analyst." Although the names imply a somewhat different conception of the job, people with those titles should think of themselves as investigators.)

The organization with the best information takes the leadership and media spotlight in issue and electoral campaigns or coalitions. Groups that must rely on others for investigative work and traditional issue research will often be somewhat marginally powerful, no matter how strong they are in other ways. Information gives you control over the issue, access to the press, and the ability to direct the debate. We have often seen large coalitions of citizen organizations, unions and other groups that revolve around a small public interest research organization in which a single investigator/researcher provides the information and thus has great power.

Tips for Investigations

A military manual made a comment that is strikingly applicable to investigative research by citizen organizations.

The collection of information is made difficult by the fact that the enemy makes every practicable effort to defeat collection attempts.

Accordingly, strengths, dispositions, and movements are concealed. Censorship and communications security measures are enforced; false information is disseminated and tactical measures designated to deceive are adopted.

This section will help you to overcome such difficulties.

Start with a Plan as Part of an Organizing Strategy

You don't have to be an expert. Investigations aren't the same as giving legal advice or prescribing medicine, so don't be afraid to jump in and get started. But first, have a plan.

The importance of the plan is that it tells you specifically what to look for. Without it, many investigators, particularly beginners, will try to substitute quantity for quality.

The investigation plan is determined by the overall strategy of the campaign. Often an organization will say, "lets do some investigating/research and see what comes up, then we can develop a strategy." This is an invitation to an open-ended investigative project that produces mush. The strategy comes first. Being told to look for some environmental official on whom to put pressure is an unfocused assignment. Being told to find information that will discredit the state environmental commissioner is more specific. In fact, you pretty much know what will do it. The person:

- Lied
- Failed to enforce the law
- Had a major conflict of interest
- Misspent money
- Issued inaccurate reports.

Finding any of this information is still a big job, but at least you know where to start. The organization must also understand that finding such evidence will not be sufficient in itself. What is critical is how the information is used and orchestrated, and what kind of campaign is mobilized around it.

The plan should include the following:

- What are you trying to accomplish? That is, what real-world result will occur through finding the information you are looking for? Investigation can be an endless process unless it is focused by having a clear, expected result. The result is not the same thing as the information you are looking for. It is what the information will be used to achieve.

- What information are you looking for?
- Where can you find it?
- What is the time line for each phase of the investigation?

Keep in Mind the Two Cardinal Principles of Investigation

Rule # 1. You Can Always Get the Information You Need. This is a necessary frame of mind. It is true. If you don't believe it, get a different job. Lack of tenacity plagues starting investigators. After one or two unsuccessful attempts to locate information, they quit, concluding that the information can't be found. This is precisely what government agencies, corporations and individuals with power want you to think. In reality, there are very few situations in which the needed information can't be found—one way or another.

Corollary # 1. Someone Already Did It. We live in the most over-studied society in the world. There are few things that you will ever want to know that someone hasn't found out already. The first step in any investigative assignment is to figure out who has already done it.

Corollary # 2. Someone Will. Look for a college professor who will assign the problem to students. Check with friendly journalists (although you risk losing control of the information). Talk with people at policy institutes, large service agencies, and even foundations. Someone wants to do this. Larger city libraries even have reference librarians who look things up for you. Regional offices of the Labor Department's Bureau of Labor Statistics and the Census Bureau will look up facts from their standard reports and give you information over the phone.

Rule # 2. It's Your Right! This too is a required attitude and frame of mind. It is also true (most of the time). It is easy for the inexperienced investigator to be cowed by public agencies and corporations. You are morally entitled to 100 percent and legally entitled to 95 percent of the information you are seeking. People who refuse to give it to you can be legitimately and publicly asked, "What are you trying to hide?"

Look for Patterns in Bits and Pieces of Information

An investigation rarely produces the big scoop or the spectacular story. Usually you find bits of information that must be assembled into a pattern before they are useful.

Suppose you find, by checking through the motor vehicle bureau, that your state representative buys a very expensive new car each year. This information doesn't tell you much by itself. But, add the fact that his personal financial disclosure statement, filed with the secretary of state, says that he has no outside business interests, no large amount of wealth, and no spouse. Throw in that he has campaigned on being a full-time legislator. Now add his statement that legislators need a pay raise and he is thinking of leaving politics because he can't live on his salary. A strong suspicion of an undisclosed source of income starts to emerge from all of this. If documented, it exposes a tactical weakness for the elected official because it is a crime to lie in a disclosure statement. A direction for the next tactical move is now established. Some embarrassing questions can be put to the representative in a public forum. There is also a direction for further investigation.

Learn to Use Computers

There are outstanding exceptions, but most organizers are still techno-peasants. Look at what a computer can do. One investigator made a database of all the contributions she could find from major corporations in her state to the Republican Party. She included contributions from various partners, officers, and directors of the companies as well as their families. Not only did she list money given to individual campaign committees, but to county committees, the state committee, the Governor's ball, etc. etc. The computer added up all the various contributions, produced a grand total from each company, and ranked the companies by amount contributed.

Next, the investigator made a separate data base of all the companies that got non-bid state contracts. That is, contracts that were given without competitive bidding. Then she cross checked the two data bases. Guess who got the non-bid state contracts?

The study resulted in two months of legislative hearings, and think of the value to the state employees' union. It was fighting the practice of contracting out state work to private companies, a practice the governor claimed would take the politics out of service delivery, and make the work more efficient.

Could she have done the same thing with a pack of index cards instead of a computer? Yes. But then, why not use a quill pen, or better yet, a wax tablet and a sharp stick? It all depends on how you want to spend your time.

Make Bureaucracy Work for You

Dealing with public officials can be both frustrating and rewarding. Usually they see their role as protecting themselves and those higher up. They, like community organizers, have long understood that in government and politics, information is power.

On the other hand, in many regulatory agencies there are staff who sincerely care about the issues at hand and are frustrated by the inaction of their superiors. These are the most valuable people to find. They can act as both guides and sources. Often, you find them by asking for meetings with department staff to have them explain regulations. There are a far larger number of staff people who have no particular private opinions and simply work to make a living. They will respond to you on the basis of things that have nothing at all to do with the issue.

In government, sometimes the most difficult people to deal with are often the lowest-level clerks who have been there for twenty years. Often, their job is to fend off people like you, and they are good at it. But these people can also be very helpful, and they can get you in. The best strategy here is to be polite and friendly. Over time, develop relationships that are helpful. Acting arrogantly or making threats will do you no good at all, neither will insisting on your legal rights. The issue of rights will be decided higher up, and much later.

It is often easier and faster for a college student to get information for a term paper than it is for a citizen organization to get the same information. The student doesn't put the bureaucracy on guard. However, the student won't be able to develop the ongoing relationships with agency staff that come with being direct about the organization you are representing and what you are trying to do. Each time you talk to someone, ask who else in the department knows about the subject and then contact that person. Eventually you will develop a road map of the internal structure of the department and learn who is helpful.

Figure out when is the best time to go. Don't show up first thing in the morning when the staff are still hanging up their coats. Don't come at lunch time when the office may be covered by only one person. Don't come late in the day when the staff are getting ready to close up. Ask the clerks if some days are busier than others. This is all part of being polite, making small talk and developing a relationship, as is remembering people's names.

Use Freedom of Information Laws

Freedom of information, open government, or sunshine laws exist federally and in many states and localities. Find out the specific laws in your area. In some states, every public agency is required to have someone who acts as the freedom of information officer.

A major difficulty in getting government information, even that which is covered by a Freedom of Information Act, is that you have to know specifically what you want. In other words, to find it, you must already know it exists. You can't just say, "Give me everything you have on toxics." There is no card catalogue such as in a library. That is why you need a guide, either a staff member, an elected official, and perhaps even a college professor or friendly clerk. As a matter of policy, some agencies routinely ignore all freedom of information requests until the threat of legal action prods them into action.

Often information released to the public will lead to more that has not been released. An official might say in a newspaper interview, "A study done by my department shows that there is no problem of toxic dumping in this community." Don't take at face value what the person says is in the study. Go and ask for it. The data often can be interpreted differently. Sometimes published material will footnote other sources such as, "Unpublished study by Department of Transportation, 1989." Again, this gives you a specific item to request. Many agencies issue annual reports similar to corporate annual reports in order to justify their budgets. Boards and committees have official minutes that are usually public.

Play Off One Set of Records Against Another

Companies, particularly utilities, whose rates are based in part on the value of their plant, often like to show the utility commission that their property is worth a great deal. To the tax collector, however, they maintain that it is worth less. Some companies keep multiple sets of books for different purposes. Often the documents they file with different agencies will have conflicting data.

Organize for Information

When other methods fail to produce the information you want, you can begin a long process of demanding it under freedom of information acts, but often it is faster and better to engage in direct action to get the information. Involve the press and take dramatic steps. If you have a friendly reporter, first try having that person ask for the information. You might get it that way, and if not, you may have gained an ally. Asking an elected official to request the information also works, and putting pressure on the official to make the request builds the organization.

Often agencies charge stiff fees, such as a "look-up fee," an "expedition fee" and usually a xerox fee. A xerox fee, for example, can be a dollar a page or higher to copy a one-hundred page study. Your organization can go public with the story that exorbitant fees are being used to defeat public access to information, and demand that fees be waived. Don't forget to say, "What are they trying to hide?" In general, organizing for information allows you to seize the moral high ground. It usually results in a victory for you and a mess for the other side.

Obviously, these methods are of much less

use against private corporations, over which you have very little power. Instead, pressure government regulatory agencies to request the corporate information for you. In investigation, as in organizing, a key principle is: **Look for the point of regulation.**

Keep Careful Records

Being able to document the source of information can be as important as the information itself. It can also save hours later, when you have to answer questions. Keep records and dates of everything you do and of every conversation. Make sure that all documents have the date of issue and the date when you got them. When xeroxing books and documents, first xerox the title page. Keep the names of people, even clerks, who give you documents and information. This can be useful later if, for example, someone failed to give you the most recent version of a report, and then their agency criticizes you for having old data.

Record investigative paths that led nowhere, as well as those that were helpful. In later years, you or someone else may have to go over the same ground, and having a complete record of your methodology will save weeks of work.

Issues to Consider in Organizing Your Research

Timing

It is never too early to start compiling information on individuals and organizations you need to understand. When community groups monitor the local real estate market, they may be able to intervene strategically before a notorious slumlord buys into the neighborhood. When trade unionists monitor changes in a company's leadership or ownership, they equip themselves to take effective action, advancing organizing and bargaining goals when the new management is most vulnerable to pressure. Major investors read the business press *every day* to find out what's happening to the companies whose shares they own. Activists must do the same.

It is also never too late to start. If you know where to look *and how to look*, you may be able to pull together the key financial and business facts on an individual or company with a few days of library research or a few hours at a computer keyboard. While you can't reclaim missed opportunities for strategic action, you can quickly bring your information up to date.

Using Information Technology: The Old and the New

There are literally thousands of print and computerized information sources that can help you understand companies, non-profit organizations, and government agencies. Though some types of organizations are harder to investigate than others, there is rarely a shortage of detailed information waiting to be found, if you know where to look. In most cases, your biggest problem will be information overload, not lack of data.

Space will not allow us to list every data source useful to your organization, so we will intersperse this chapter with references to other, more detailed guides which provide addresses and phone numbers for government disclosure offices or give you further advice on specific types of research. **There are three books so important that they should occupy a prominent spot on every activist researcher's shelf:**

Dennis King, *Get the Facts on Anyone,* Prentice Hall, New York, 1992. ($15, paperback). The best simple guide to techniques for investigating people; also has strong sections on court and property records.

Matthew Lesko, *Lesko's Info-Power II,* Visible Ink Press, Detroit, 1994. ($29.95, paperback). A massive, well-indexed, 1500+ page guide to public information sources.

Steve Weinberg, *The Reporter's Handbook: an investigator's guide to documents and techniques,* St. Martin's Press, New York. The best broad guide to techniques for investigating businesses and non-profit organizations. The third edition published in late 1995 is available from Investigative Reporters and Editors, 26A Walter Williams Hall, UMC School of Journalism, Columbia, MO 65211.

As information sources proliferate, finding the *right* publication or document becomes ever more complicated. Before the electronic information age, researchers knew that they had to walk into a large public or university library, find the business reference books, and dig in. Or go to the right government or private agency—the Securities and Exchange Commission for reports from publicly traded corporations, the Occupational Safety and Health Administration for reports on workplace injuries, the Foundation Center for information on donors to a non-profit employer, and so forth—and ask for the appropriate public documents.

Electronic databases are both the most valuable resource and the greatest source of confusion for researchers today. The "information superhighway" offers the fastest route to most of the information you need: an hour of "online" computer research may save you days of library work or help you find dozens of valuable sources otherwise not available in your local community. However, it's easy to get lost on the information superhighway. Without a road map, you'll never find the information you need. Moreover, if you make a wrong turn, tolls become very steep: the same database search might cost $10 if you do it the right way or $100 if you do it the wrong way.

Dozens of service providers offer thousands of computerized information sources. This chapter will give you enough information to get started using low-cost services; it will help you determine when to use more expensive and specialized databases.

The costs of electronic research vary widely and are changing rapidly. Though costs are generally declining, you can still spend hundreds of dollars in a matter of minutes on some online services.

In almost all cases it makes sense to start with the lowest-cost service you can understand, use it thoroughly, and then move on to higher-priced services when you must.

The accompanying box (and listings throughout this chapter) divide online services into three basic categories: free, lower cost, and higher cost. Within each category, we use boldface type to mark the services most useful to activist researchers.

General Computer Information Services Useful to Activists: A Search Hierarchy

	User-friendly	In-between	User-hostile
Free or almost free ☞	CD-ROM reference guides and other public services available at your local library **World Wide Web on the Internet**	**Most government services**	FTP and other non-graphic **Internet** activities
Lower cost ¢¢¢ (5-50¢/min)	**CompuServe** (Most news and many business sections)	**Some government services**	
Middle cost $/¢ ($1-$3/item or 50¢-$1/min)	**DataTimes CompuServe** (Some specialized sections)		
Higher cost $$$ ($2-$5/min, or $3-$50 per item, or more)	**CompuServe** (IQUEST and some other news and business sections) **Dow Jones** (with windows interface)	**Dow Jones** (without windows interface) **Lexis/Nexis NewsNet**	Dialog

A pointing hand (☞) directs you toward sources (print and electronic) which are free or very inexpensive. Use these first whenever you can. They include such traditional information resources as your local public library, the complex network of loosely linked electronic systems known as the "Internet," and a number of government-provided databases.

The ¢¢¢ symbol marks consumer services that your organization can use without too much fear of breaking the budget. This price class includes the mass market services which you or your fellow activists may already use on home computers, online services like CompuServe, America Online, or Prodigy. Within this category, CompuServe offers the widest range of information resources. CompuServe is currently the only mass market electronic information service worth subscribing to for activist research purposes. (If a member of your organization already uses another mass market service, such as America Online or Prodigy, you can usually get some research value out of it.)

The $$$ symbol identifies high-priced, business-oriented premium services. These services contain the most useful information, but accessing them can cost you 10-20 times the fee you'll pay for information obtained on the mass market services. And much (though not all) of the information they offer can also be found on CompuServe, if you know where to look.

Occasionally we will use a mixed symbol, $/¢ to mark moderately expensive services which offer good value for the price. Most notable among these is DataTimes. Some sections of CompuServe—such as the Disclosure database, which compiles mountains of Securities and Exchange Commission data into a standardized, relatively easy-to-use format—also fall into this category.

New and inexperienced users should confine their research to the lowest-cost services. Even within these services, however, you can run up high bills if you're not careful where you explore. Some CompuServe databases can be accessed for less than $3/hour; others can cost more than that per minute.

Unless you have an in-house expert, it may be more cost-effective to hire a professional researcher or "information broker" to gather information from higher-cost services and databases. Alternatively, in many communities, the local library will provide this service at cost or with a modest surcharge. Most lawyers use Lexis/Nexis, so you may also be able to arrange for searches through your organization's legal counsel.

Each major service offers hundreds of individual databases. On the Internet—which is not a single service but a web of independent information providers—there are thousands. The systems with the widest range of databases useful to activist researchers are shown in **boldface.**

Prices and available databases change constantly, so don't assume that this guide is complete or up to date. For the most part, prices drop with time, and new, less-expensive services are gradually becoming more available. We've included price information to give you an idea of the relative cost of various information sources; actual charges will change over time.

You will constantly face tradeoffs between time and money. For example, let's say that your target is a mid-size industrial company operating a hazardous, waste-burning cement kiln in your community. You want to find every significant mention of the company over the past three years in two different daily newspapers and the weekly business paper. You expect that this will mean looking at the titles of 200 articles which mentioned the company and making copies of the 25 most important ones. You'd also like to find a list of stories about the company in national business publications. You can:

☞ Spend a day or more in the library searching through microfilmed back issues of the local papers and the various indexes of business periodicals.
    Probable cost: $5-$10 for xeroxing.
    The tradeoffs: Cost is very low, but unless a comprehensive index exists for your local paper, you will waste lots of time and miss many key articles.

¢¢¢ Spend 30-60 minutes on three separate CompuServe searches, using CompuServe's Knowledge Index (cost 40¢/min) and its Business Database Plus ($1.50/article) which, taken together, cover about 30 local newspapers and hundreds of local and national business magazines.
    Probable cost: $25-$75.
    The tradeoffs: Knowledge Index is available only evenings and weekends, lets you look at only one paper at a time, and provides limited options for fine-tuning your information search. On the other hand, it's inexpensive and easy to use compared with other services, and it will find every reference to your company, even if it's buried toward the bottom of the article.

$$$ Carefully plan your search in advance and go online using a premium service like Dialog or Dow Jones News Retrieval to examine multiple

publications in a single operation which will take 10-30 minutes.

Probable cost: several hundred dollars.

The tradeoffs: Expensive, but covers many more newspapers than CompuServe, lets you examine as many or as few publications as you want in a single search, lets you refine your search very precisely to focus on only those aspects of the company you need to research: particular product lines, divisions, or personalities. Because these services cover many more newspapers and magazines than you'll find on CompuServe, they sometimes offer the only route to the data you need.

Guide to Information Sources

News and Information Sources Covering All Types of Organizations

Every activist group should identify and subscribe to a few of the trade and business publications that most often run stories about its areas of interest. **Do this now! Don't wait until you face a crisis.** Alternatively, you can use a computer information service like CompuServe to regularly compile your own "dossier" of news about the company from many different sources.

The sources you need to read—in print or online—depend on the organizations and topics you are monitoring.

For multinationals or major publicly traded U.S. companies, national business publications will be the best source of "big picture" information on issues affecting the company as a whole. Because it is a daily newspaper, *The Wall Street Journal* contains more information than any other general business publication. General business magazines like *Business Week, Forbes,* or *Fortune* contain fewer corporate details and cover fewer companies, but provide in-depth articles which give more analysis and explanation of trends affecting companies and industries. They are most likely useful if you

want to understand the national and global competitive situation for major industries.

Every industry, no matter how small, has its own specialized trade journals or newsletters. There are thousands of them. Reading one or two of these publications regularly will foster familiarity with the major issues and trends affecting the target company. It will help you identify vulnerabilities and develop strategies long before the campaign begins.

The following selected titles will give you an idea of the diversity of the business press:

A note on terminology: "public" and "private" companies

Corporate researchers need to understand the difference between "public" (or publicly traded) and "private" (or closely held) corporations.

"Public" does not mean that the company exists to benefit the public as a whole. Rather, it means that shares in the business are traded in a market (one of the Stock Exchanges or the "over-the-counter" market) where any member of the public can buy or sell them. The Securities and Exchange Commission requires the public corporations to make financial statements and other information available to the general public. In general, you know that a company is "publicly traded" if you find it listed in the stock tables of any daily newspaper that covers the major stock exchanges and the "over-the-counter" stock market.

A "private" corporation is generally owned by one or a small group of individuals. It does not offer shares to the general public, and is thus exempt from many disclosure requirements.

However, some industries — including broadcasting, health care and insurance — have their own special disclosure requirements which make it possible to obtain detailed financial data on "private" as well as "public" corporations in these industries.

Online Services of Potential Use to Activists

Service	Comments
¢¢¢ **CompuServe,** 1-800-848-8199.	The best *low-cost* service for corporate and most other activist research, though premium services often provide quicker results. If concerned about keeping costs down, start your research here before turning to the premium services. Prices vary widely from section-to-section. If cost is a factor, read the pricing information the first time you enter any CompuServe database. Its most useful areas include: — Knowledge Index (the low-cost, "after hours" version of Dialog.) — The AFL-CIO's private area, Labornet. — Executive News Service, which includes the lowest cost electronic "clipping service." — The Disclosure database, providing an extensive summary of company's SEC documents for about $40 per company. — Through its IQUEST service, provides a "Gateway" to many sections of Dialog and other high-priced services.
$/¢ **DataTimes,** 1-800-642-2525.	The most easily used premium online service, with an easy to use "natural language" search system and simple techniques for simultaneously searching *all* data sources. Offers most (but not all) of the news sources available on Dow Jones at a lower price. Lacks some crucial financial data sources which can be found on Dialog or Dow Jones.
$$$ **Dialog/Knight-Ridder Information Services,** 1-800-334-2564.	Features a formerly state-of-the-art, now somewhat outmoded DOS-based "search engine" that lets experienced users refine their searches very precisely, but makes searching extremely difficult for inexperienced users. Especially useful in investigating high-tech and research-intensive industries, including aerospace, defense, and pharmaceuticals, and for research on foreign companies. Also strong on tools for researching small privately held companies and has very strong collection of non-US business databases.
$$$ **Dow Jones News Retrieval,** 1-800-522-3567.	Lack of monthly fee and wide range of business databases makes this the cost-effective premium service for many users. Offers highly comprehensive electronic "clipping service." Has the widest range of sources for tracking publicly traded firms; probably not as useful as Dialog or Nexis for investigating individual executives or small, privately held companies.
☞ **Fed World,** 703-487-4608 (for information) Dial 783-321-3339 with your modem to log-on directly. Or go to http://fedworld.gov on the World-Wide Web.	This free computer "bulletin board" run by the *National Technical Information Service,* offers Gateways to more than 100 other U.S. government information systems, including a wide and growing range of business and economic database services. You can also connect to Fed World through the Internet. It is one of simplest and cheapest places to start when looking for federal government information online. Since Fed World's range of services is constantly growing, you should always check here before paying to access government data through a high-priced commercial service. If you're looking for federal government information, and don't know where to turn, Fed World is the best place to start.
☞, ¢¢¢, $$$ **Government database services**	The *Federal Data Base Finder* (published by Information USA) will tell you how to locate 4,000 federal database services; *Lesko's Info-Power II* (from the same company) contains some (though less extensive) listings at both federal and state levels. Fees (if any) vary widely, number of available services is constantly growing, the service you need may be hard to locate.
☞ **Internet.** Many providers. No central information source.	Lots of valuable information available for free or almost free, if you have the time and energy to figure out how to find it in this electronic maze. In general, the Internet is the first, best place to start looking for information produced by government agencies, both federal and state, but less useful than commercial services for privately produced information and data on private corporations.
$$$ **NewsNet,** 1-800-952-0122.	Provides online access to hundreds of specialized newsletters and many major wire services. Worth considering for use by union locals that need to track one of the industries in which this service is strongest, such as: aerospace, communications, energy, electronics, health care.
$$$ **Lexis/Nexis,** 1-800-227-4908.	Contains enormous information resources and easier to use than most premium services, but is probably the most expensive service. Access to public records at state and local level makes this service uniquely valuable for investigating smaller companies and individual executives. Also the best electronic route to many federal court and agency databases. *Access to corporate financial data weak compared with other premium services.* If you need access occasionally, find out if your organization's lawyer has a Lexis account you can use.
¢¢¢ **Peacenet,** 1-415-442-0106.	Low-cost, "alternative" electronic information system, providing news sources not found elsewhere, activist discussion areas, and access to the Internet. Especially useful for groups active on environmental, human rights, and international development issues. Weaker than major commercial systems on access to non-Internet research databases.

An important note: The above discussion of online information is already out of date! New services are appearing all the time, and old services are constantly changing their offerings.

American Printer, Bankers Monthly, Beverage World, Boating Industry, Defense Electronics, Engineering & Mining Journal, Electronic Chemicals News, Energy Daily, Food Manufacture, Footwear News, Grocery Marketing, Modern Healthcare, National Petroleum News, Nursing Homes, Oil and Gas Journal, Pets Supplies Marketing, Pharmaceutical Business News, Playthings, Pulp & Paper International, Rig Market Forecast, Semiconductor Industry & Business Survey, Telephone News, US Oil Week, Women's Wear Daily. There are, moreover, hundreds of specialized publications covering specialized areas of government and non-profit activity.

For all "target" organizations except the very smallest, the major wire services are also a great source of current information. Until recently, you had to own a newspaper to read the wires. Today, anyone can use "electronic clipping services" to collect the wire service stories that cover your company. For background on your company, back issues of your local newspaper can also be very useful.

☞ Almost all daily newspapers maintain detailed clipping files on local companies; a sympathetic reporter might let you take a look at the file. Or check with the newspaper's librarian: some papers will let members of the public access their clipping files, though they often charge a fee. Many public or university libraries also maintain good clipping files on local issues.

¢¢ Back issues of all the trade periodicals listed above, and hundreds more, are available in CompuServe's Business Database Plus. Cost: 25¢/min to review titles; $1.50/article to obtain full text copies. CompuServe's Executive News Service is the most cost-effective electronic clipping service. If you have a CompuServe account with the "executive option," just type GO ENS to get to this area. Online instructions will help you set up a "clipping folder" and automatically save every story about your company in the news sources you choose. Available sources include: *Associated Press, Dow Jones, PR Newswire, Reuters, United Press International, The Washington*

Post, and *Over The Counter NewsAlert.* Cost: 25¢ /min.

$$$ If you can't find the right industry journals and newsletters on CompuServe, you can turn to one of the premium online services (Dialog, Dow Jones, NewsNet, or Nexis). Dialog's PTS Newsletter and PTS Promt databases are especially convenient for simultaneously searching hundreds of business and trade newsletters. Dow Jones and NewsNet will also let you set up much broader electronic clipping files than CompuServe. Though per minute charges are steep, if you need to follow just one company, this may prove more economical than subscriptions to the magazines. Warning: You should expect to pay 5-10 times CompuServe's modest fee.

General Reference Works Covering All Types of Businesses

We live in an age of mergers, acquisitions, and diversification, of corporate concentration and global integration. To understand a business or a non-profit organization you need not only to follow the news but also to map the often unreported changes in corporate structures and external relationships.

The reference books listed in this section will help you map your company's internal and external power relationships. Almost all are available from one or several of the online database services. Hard copy versions of most will also be found in the reference or business section of a medium-size public library or university library. The references listed in this section cover both publicly traded companies (approximately 11,000 mostly larger firms which sell their shares to the public and must satisfy special reporting requirements) and smaller "private" firms.

Funk and Scott's Index of Corporations and Industries (commonly referred to as F&S). One of the best guides for current information of companies and industries. Updated monthly, it indexes most periodicals, newspapers, etc. Funk and Scott also publishes a quarterly *Index of Corporate Change*, which covers recent mergers and acquisitions.

$$$ Computer-searchable for 1980-present on Dialog as PTS F&S Index. Cost: $1.90/min.

Standard and Poor's Register of Corporations, Directors and Executives. Volume I lists approximately 37,000 public and private companies and the titles of over 400,000 corporate officials. Company information includes financial data, SIC number, products and services, and number of employees. Volume II lists 75,000 biographies of directors and executives. This guide, unlike others, often lists home addresses.

¢¢¢ Volume 2 is computer-searchable outside business hours on CompuServe's Knowledge Index. Cost: 40¢/min. $$$ Both volumes (and other S&P materials) are available on Dialog. Cost: $1.40/min plus per item surcharges.

Credit profiles are the business equivalent of your credit bureau report. Unlike personal reports—which are confidential information—credit bureaus can and do sell reports on businesses. They will help you find out the magnitude of a company's trade debts, the speed with which it pays its bills, and what classes of payments (if any) it may be delaying. They can provide a valuable early warning if you think the company is headed into financial troubles.

$$$ **Dun & Bradstreet** credit profiles, available via NewsNet, cost $45-$67.50 per company, plus a per minute connect charge of $1-$2.50/min. $$$ **TRW** business profiles on CompuServe cost $43 for the first company and $9 each for up to four additional reports ordered at the same time. NewsNet charges $41 (plus its steep per minute charge) for up to five companies requested together and offers a TRW Health Care Premium Profile for $45.

Dun and Bradstreet directories are the first place to turn for data on millions of small and medium-size companies. The company's print publications include *D&B's Million Dollar Directory* for basic officer, ownership, line of business, and sales data on 161,000 companies with more than $25 million/year in sales; 250+ employees or a net worth over $500,000. The

D&B's Middle Market Directory covers smaller companies. *D&B's Healthcare Reference Book* covers hospitals, nursing homes, and other health care institutions. *The Reference Book of Corporate Management* covers presidents, directors, vice presidents, and officers of public and private U.S. companies. Arranged by company, information includes titles, occupational history, education. outside corporate affiliations, date of birth, and marital status.

D&B — Dun's Market Identifiers offers some, though less-detailed personnel and financial information, on more than 7.5 million U.S. businesses; *D&B — Dun's Electronic Business Directory* covers 8.9 million U.S. businesses and professional people. Another electronic version, *Dun's Financial Records Plus,* provides in-depth information on about 750,000 firms.

☞ For a free copy of the *Dun's Online Code Guide,* which will help you interpret the information found in D&B publications, call (800) 223-1026.

$$$ D&B directories are available online through CompuServe, Dialog, Dow Jones and other electronic information providers in varying formats. Dialog and Dow Jones offer the most comprehensive versions. Dialog charges about $1.60-$2/min plus surcharges of several dollars per company. Dow Jones may offer better value for inexperienced users because its charges, though also high, are based purely on the amount of information examined, not the time spent finding it.

$$$ CompuServe (typically $7.50 or more per search and $7.50 per full company listing) offers easy access for occasional users but will actually prove more costly than the premium venders if you use D&B directories regularly.

Directory of Corporate Affiliations (Who Owns Whom) A valuable annual guide to 4,000 parent companies and 46,000 divisions, subsidiaries and affiliates of publicly traded corporations with considerable assets. Some private companies are included.

The Thomas Register of American Manufacturers and **Thomas Register Catalog File** offer, for some companies, more detailed data than most of the S&P reference works. But they cover a more limited range of several hundred thousand companies.

$$$ Thomas Register Online is available through Dialog at a cost of $1.80/min and $1.50/report; CompuServe charges $5/search and $5/report. (CompuServe is likely to be more economical for occasional users; Dialog offers better value for frequent users.)

Government Files Covering All Types of Businesses

The federal government collects vast amounts of data on publicly traded companies and has very detailed files on smaller firms in some types of employers, ranging from broadcasters to banks to non-profit organizations.

But to access the broadest repositories of public information—covering millions of businesses of all types and sizes—you must turn to records maintained at the local level, primarily by state and local agencies. These agencies are usually the best source of information on operational details of small companies and, in many cases, individual plants within larger firms. Many states have laws that open almost all their data for public inspection.

Since every state has its own data collection and disclosure systems, we can't tell you exactly what you'll need to do to get the right information in your state. Fortunately, many data systems are similar from state to state, and some states now pool industry information on a regional basis. In addition, a growing volume of state and local information is available electronically, making it easy for you to access remote goverment files without visiting the state where they are located. For "one-stop shopping," when you need to look electronically at several states at once, nothing beats Lexis/Nexis, but charges will be very high. However, since state and local paper files—and even electronic databases—are accessible free or very inexpensively in many cases, activists

working on a tight budget should view Lexis/Nexis as a last resort. In most communities, you'll find government officials at the working level to be accessible and quite helpful. Developing a good relationship with certain key officials can be an enormous asset in your research.

The first step in using state and local information is finding the officials who have the data you need.

- Most states have designated a specific office as the single point of contact for leading you to business and financial information. For a list of these offices, turn to *The Reporter's Handbook*.

- Use the *State Executive Directory* (published by Caroll Publishing Company, Washington, DC) or obtain the appropriate state, county, or municipal government directory, which should list the various departments and personnel.

- Call the state capital library (virtually all states have one) for help in finding the right document or official.

State and Local Business Records

You probably won't need any directory if you're looking for the three most basic types of business records: corporate registrations, UCC filings, and real estate records. In most states, these records are organized as follows:

Corporation and Partnership Records. Usually available from the Corporation Division in the office of the Secretary of State. The Articles of Incorporation detail the place of business, date of incorporation, nature of business, names and addresses of directors, officers and incorporators, names and addresses of agents, and capitalization. Other documents include the amendments to the Articles of Incorporation, notices of consolidation and mergers, and change of names. Most states require some kind of annual report to be filed, and these often contain some financial information.

Uniform Commercial Code (UCC) filings are also usually found in the Secretary of State's office. Records stored here will tell you if the company has borrowed against assets other than real estate. (Information on mortgages will be found in a separate set of offices, described below.) UCC filings normally give the name and address of the debtor and creditor, a description of the property used as collateral, and the maturity date of the loan. UCCs are an indispensable source of information on creditor relationships. If you don't know the name of a partnership, look in the index of "Fictitious Business Names" at the Corporations Registry or Recorder of Deeds.

Real property records in almost all states are maintained at the city or county level. They are essential for the corporate investigator. Real property records may show you that company-owned property is being undertaxed—a great campaigning issue for generating sympathy among local homeowners. They may reveal conflicts of interest involving corporate officers or board members involved in "sweetheart" real estate transactions with the company. However, they are easily misunderstood. To avoid embarrassing yourself and your organization, make sure you *fully* understand the documents before using them in your campaign.

- **Ownership information** will usually be found in Recorder or Registrar of Deeds' Office, which usually falls under the City or County Clerk. Whatever this office may be called, it is the place to locate real estate transaction records (mortgages and deeds) and records of liens (including tax liens) against property. These records will also let you identify mortgage lenders and, in many cases, building or renovation contractors. You will usually find these records indexed by name of buyer and seller, borrower and lender, etc., in a series of "Grantee/Grantor" volumes. In some jurisdictions, the indexes may be wholly or partly computerized. Records in this office will also sometimes reveal the terms of purchase of a privately held company or, for a public company, the terms of industrial revenue bonds designed to create a "healthy business climate" for the company.
- **Property tax records,** usually found in the Assessor's office, will give you information about the assessed value and tax payments on a property. Finding the right record is

normally a three-step process: First, you find the addresses of properties owned by the target company or individual; second, you look up the "lot and square" designations for those properties; third, you look up the assessment record for each lot/square designation. Note that assessed value is less than market value in some jurisdictions, so find out about local practices before charging that company (or company officials') property has been "underassessed."

- **Building departments or zoning boards** maintain files regarding issuance of zoning variances, building permits and the like. Their files may reveal that a company has built new facilities, made alterations without proper permission, or has committed other zoning or licensing violations.

Where available, electronic databases can be an enormous timesaver when searching any of these records, providing in minutes information that would take days or weeks to find by hand. Databases can help you identify *every* company listing a particular director or *every* property the company owns within the state (or states) whose records you are searching. In many cases, however, the database provides a directory listing only; you will still need to contact the appropriate state or county office to get the full documents.

☞ Many jurisdictions have computerized their property tax records. In some cases, you may be able to do a free computer search for all properties held by a particular owner. (Computerization of other property records, though not as advanced, is increasingly common.)

In some communities, current assessment data (and occasionally other property records) can also be found at major public libraries.

Locating the right records can be difficult. For a more detailed overview of property records research, including such specialized topics as federal real estate transactions, interstate land sales, and local zoning/planning regulations, turn to *The Reporter's Handbook*.

¢/$ State Secretaries of State and UCC offices charge widely varying fees for copies of corporate records in their files. *Lesko's Info-Power II* contains a complete directory of state corporate records and UCC offices, including information on walk-in, telephone and—for at least 16 states—online electronic access to some or all of the information. Fees for access to documents vary widely.

$$$ Lexis/Nexis provides recent property assessment and sales data for more than 30 states; corporation, partnership, or professional licensing records from at least 19 states; bankruptcy and other civil court filings from larger states including California, Illinois, New York, and Texas. Their Lexdoc service will let you order full texts of many documents by modem.

Court Records

Court records cover criminal and civil cases filed by and against individuals, groups, companies, and government bodies. Cases that may provide useful information include bankruptcies, complaints about a company from customers or consumers, claims by one company against another, government prosecution of an individual or company for illegal acts or practices, and divorces.

Some court records are available for public inspection, others may be temporarily or permanently "sealed." Because jurisdictions differ between courts, examining legal records can be tedious and time-consuming. Often, however, they can yield a wealth of information, and for private companies, can be one of the most comprehensive sources of data.

In the state and federal courts, records are kept and accessed through the court clerk's office. The researcher should examine the judgment book in the court clerk's office. This book lists cases by plaintiff and defendant. The researcher should look for information on the corporation or individual as both a plaintiff and as a defendant. The judgment book should yield a docket number for the cases that will lead to the actual records themselves.

☞ *Get the Facts on Anyone* contains the best available simple overview of the various types of available court records and techniques for accessing them.

☞ In a large and growing number of jurisdictions, plaintiff and defendant indexes are computerized. To save time, make sure you check for such an index before slogging through the judgment books.

¢¢ PACER, an online service coordinated by the administration office of the federal courts, offers direct online access to dockets, opinion texts, and court calendars from most district and appeals courts. In some situations (e.g., if you are looking for information on bankruptcy filings), terms of access and information availability vary, depending on the court you are interested in. Some files are accessible free of charge; others cost up to $1/min. Call (800) 676-6856 for information.

$$$ Lexis (and a competing service, Westlaw) gives you electronic access to state and federal appeals, district court decisions, and to some lower-level cases. These services will lead you to important or precedent-setting cases-—major suits over environmental or labor law violations, for example-—but won't help you track down most of the mundane monetary and personal disputes that are settled in the lower courts.

State and Local Economic Development Offices

Many states, counties, and cities have procedures by which companies can seek tax abatements, industrial revenue bonds (IRBs), or other financial benefits. In most cases, companies must submit detailed applications to obtain such benefits. In some jurisdictions, the application forms (which can be a gold mine of financial data) are available for public inspection.

☞ *Lesko's Info-Power II* contains a lengthy listing (pp. 729-753 in the 1994 edition) of state and local business development agencies. Check with the appropriate agency to find out what files on your target company are publicly accessible.

General References Covering Publicly Traded Companies

As we've already seen, commercial directories and databases contain a wealth of information on millions of companies of all sizes.

You can find even more information if your target is one of the 11,000 "public" companies which annually pour a wealth of data into the files of the U.S. Securities and Exchange Commission.

Ultimately you will want to look at the full text of the SEC documents. However, if you're new to corporate research—or if you need to see how your company is doing in comparison to others—it will be easier to start with some of the business reference books and databases which compile management and financial summaries based on SEC documents, news reports, and other sources. These publications include:

Standard and Poor's Publications and Databases

Standard and Poor's Corporate Descriptions gives history, basic financial data, capital structure information, lines of business, subsidiaries, lists of officers and directors, and much additional information on about 11,000 publicly traded companies. Related S&P services provide current news and short financial/management information summaries on these companies.

☞ The printed edition is widely available in libraries.

¢¢¢ The lowest-cost electronic version of these publications will be found in CompuServe's Knowledge Index section at a cost of 40¢/min. (Available evenings and weekends only.)

$$$ Available all hours on Dialog and NewsNet, with additional search options and a much higher price. An abbreviated version available on Dow Jones and CompuServe, S&P Online, provides limited information on 4700 companies.

Moody's Industrial Manual and Other Publications

An annual financial and historical report on selected publicly traded industrial corporations that includes a 20-year record of sales, profits, assets, dividends, equity, and other financial essentials. The directory lists banking agents for each bond or stock issue and also includes information about the company's record of acquisitions and mergers. Moody's also publishes a *Public Utilities Manual*, a *Transportation Manual*, and a *Bank and Finance Manual* that give the same information for companies in those industries.

$$$ Available on Dialog, with weekly updates. On Dialog, Moody's also provides a 10-year backfile of news summaries for all U.S. publicly traded firms and selected foreign companies. Cost: $1-$1.60/min plus substantial per company or per article surcharges.

Securities and Exchange Commission Documents From Publicly Traded Companies

All SEC filings are available to the public and, as the accompanying box shows, there are many different ways to obtain them.

What You'll Find in the SEC Files

For a full explanation of Securities and Exchange Commission filings and their contents, request a copy of "A User's Guide to the Facilities of the Public Reference Room," available from the U.S. Securities and Exchange Commission, Office of Filings, Information & Consumer Services, Washington, DC 20549. The following brief descriptions will stress the elements most useful to activists.

Annual Report to Shareholder. This is the principal document companies use to communicate directly with shareholders. It offers the company's view of itself, as presented by incumbent management. It generally begins with a letter to shareholders designed to present management in the best possible light. Annual reports normally offer some current history and general descriptions of current activities, along with audited balance sheet, income statement, and cash flow statement.

The letter to shareholders may prove especially useful in constructing contract demands, since it usually emphasizes the firm's financial successes. The audited financial statements (and especially the footnotes which follow) will provide a useful, but not complete, picture of the company's financial performance.

Learn to read between the lines: A description of a new plant, product line, or subsidiary may suggest fertile ground for organizing or show you how the company is diversifying away from products or services produced at unionized facilities. **Companies distribute annual reports and proxy statements to all shareholders, so buying a share of stock is an easy way to make sure that you receive these important documents as soon as they are released. Virtually all public companies have an investor relations department that will send the annual report, upon request, to anyone who requests one, shareholder or not.**

Proxy Statement or Notice of Annual Meeting. The proxy statement is the official notice mailed to every shareholder on matters to be brought before a company's annual meeting. It contains a wealth of information available nowhere else. It is especially helpful in preparing profiles of officers and directors, because it contains information on their fees, salaries, benefits and stock options, stock holdings in the company, principal outside business connections, and any business dealings between them and the company. It will also discuss any proposed merger, consolidation, or acquisition that requires shareholder approval. In this era of corporate consolidations, companies increasingly create plans (known on Wall Street as "shark repellant" or "poison pills") designed to discourage hostile takeovers. The appearance of such proposals—which may include staggered terms for directors, authority to issue extra stock, or other provisions giving directors broad discretion to restructure the company—may indicate that management fears a takeover bid. Like the annual report, this document is distributed to all shareholders.

Form 10-K, the most comprehensive SEC-required document, is filed by all public companies with more than 500 shareholders and $3 million in assets. Because the SEC precisely specifies the information that must be included and the form of presentation, companies find it hard to hide or obscure unfavorable information. This form will provide information on:

- State of incorporation.
- Address and telephone number for the principal executive offices.
- Title, number of shares, and exchange where traded for each class of stock.
- Aggregate market value of voting stock held by non-affiliates of the company.
- Details on principal products and services produced, the markets where they are sold, and the methods of distribution.
- Details on significant income-producing assets including plants, mines, patents, trademarks, licenses, and franchises.
- Details on conditions and activities which "materially" affect current or potential future income, including the competitive environment, research activities, and pending legal proceedings.
- Segment data: if the company has multiple subsidiaries or lines of business, three years of total sales and net income data for each segment that provides more than 10 percent of total sales or pre-tax income.
- Ownership data: the identity of any investor owning 10 percent or more of any class of securities, and the amount owned.
- Details on all securities held by officers and directors.
- Stock market data, including dividend payments and high- and low-stock prices for the past two years, plus a discussion of future dividend projections.
- Selected financial data including five years of figures on:
  — net sales
  — operating revenue
  — income or loss from continuing operations
  — total assets
  — long-term debt and other obligations
  — cash dividends per common share of stock.
- Management's discussion and analysis of financial condition and results of operation including:
  — liquidity
  — capital resources
  — results of operations
  — favorable and unfavorable trends
  — significant sources of future uncertainty

— explanation of any "material" changes in financial performance as a whole
— some data (though rarely as much as you will want) on subsidiary operations
— a discussion of the effects of inflation and changing prices.

- Financial statements and supplementary data including two years of audited balance sheets and three years of audited income and cash flow statements.

- Personal data on directors and executive officers including name, office, term of office, and a very brief biography.

- Pay, bonus, and benefits data for directors and the highest-paid officers.

- Exhibits, financial statements, schedules and reports from Form 8-K (see below) including complete audited financial information and a list of exhibits filed. Also, information on any unscheduled material events or corporate changes that occurred during the year (see discussion of Form 8-K below). [Researchers often fail to use this part of the 10-K, which can run to hundreds or thousands of pages, to the fullest advantage. You should examine it carefully for data on the company, its subsidiaries, assets, loan agreements, and banking relationships.]

Form 10-Q. A quarterly update of the 10-K, less reliable because it is *unaudited*. Important nonetheless, because it will report new lawsuits and any material changes in operations including long-term contracts, new financing, and mergers or acquisitions.

Form 8-K. This report must be filed within 15 days after any significant change in ownership or financing. It will contain the financial statements of any business bought or sold by the company and will report changes in control of the company, acquisition or disposition of significant assets, bankruptcy or receivership, a change in auditors, resignation of directors, and other "material" events. **Because 8-Ks provide the first notice of any major change in operations, they should be watched closely throughout your campaign since they contain highly significant information that may dramatically affect strategic choices.** The

corporate investigator should be especially careful to watch for these reports.

$$$ Since the timing of 8-Ks cannot be predicted in advance, you may find it useful during a campaign to subscribe through a company known as Disclosure (see box.) They will automatically be mailed to you upon receipt at a cost of $37 per report, with electronic delivery also available for a higher fee. (Disclosure also provides similar subscription services covering other SEC documents.)

Form 3, 4 and 5 document shareholdings by directors, officers, and owner of more than 10 percent of any class of equity securities. Form 3 is the initial filing; Form 4 reports changes in holdings, and Form 5 offers an annual summary.

Form 13-F is a quarterly report on the shareholdings of institutional investment managers including banks, insurance companies, investment advisers, investment companies, foundations, and pension funds that manage more than $100 million in equity securities. When used in conjunction with the *Money Market Directory* (see Sources of Information on Pension Funds), these documents can tell which shareholders/managers also manage funds for unions, public pension funds, church groups and other groups of investors who might be open to your groups' appeals for support.

Forms 13-D, 13E-3, 13-G, 14-D1 and 14-D9 document various aspects of attempted takeover of a company including share purchases by investors seeking a controlling interest, management responses to takeover attempts, and moves by any publicly traded company to "go private."

Form 20-F, filed by approximately 500 foreign companies that raise capital in the United States, provides a more limited version of the information U.S.-based public companies disclose in their 10-K forms.

Official Summary of Security Transactions and Holdings is a monthly SEC compilation of "insider" stock transactions covering all public companies. Reviewing it over time will help you discover who are the most active buyers and sellers of substantial blocks of shares.

Registration Statements for Stock Offerings (Forms S1-S3, S6-S18, N1 and N2) must be filed by a company before it may offer shares to the public. They contain much useful data including:

- Detailed information about the share issue including marketing agreements, distribution methods, issuance agreements, company relationships with any "experts" named in the registration, unregistered or "special" sales of shares, and the use to which stock sale proceeds will be put.
- Information about the company's subsidiaries, franchises, and concessions.
- Financial statements and related exhibits.

Registration of new securities may indicate that the company plans an expansion which will require large sums of money.

Registration Statements for Stock Trading (Forms 8-A, 8-B and 10) are required when a company has 500 or more shareholders and $5 million or more in assets *or* intends to have its shares trade on a national exchange. These forms offer an initial disclosure of financial and business information and establish the public file into which some of the other forms discussed above (such as the 8-K, 10-K and 10-Q) will ultimately be deposited.

Obtaining Financial Data on Non-Profit Organizations

How to Obtain Form 990 and Related Documents

Every tax-exempt organization must annually file **Form 990,** a public disclosure tax return, with the Internal Revenue Service. Schedule A, attached to the Form 990, contains useful details on compensation for executives, leading contractors and highly-paid employees.

There are three places to get these valuable documents:

How to Get SEC-Required Documents on Publicly Traded Companies	
Full text of documents filed with the SEC	☞ If you know how to use the World-Wide Web on the Internet, you can obtain most current corporate SEC filings (starting with 1994) by accessing a free government database known as EDGAR (Electronic Data Gathering and Retrieval). To get to: http://www.sec.gov/edgarhp.htm.
	¢¢¢ You can visit any of the SEC's four public reference rooms and examine any SEC filing for free or obtain copies for about 25¢/page. The reference rooms are located in: • Chicago: Everett McKinley Dirksen, Building 219, So. Dearborn Street, Chicago, IL 60604, (312) 353-7390. • Los Angeles: 5757 Wilshire Boulevard, Suite 500 East, Los Angeles, CA 90036, (213) 965-3998. • New York: 26 Federal Plaza, Room 100, New York, NY 10007, (212) 264-1615. • Washington: 450 5th Street, NW, Room 1024, Washington, DC 20549, (202) 272-7450. In addition, if you buy a share of the company's stock, they will automatically send you the annual report, proxy statement, and notice of annual meeting. Upon request, shareholders can also receive the company's 10-K form and other SEC's filings.
	$$$ Disclosure, Inc., the private contracter which operates SEC reference rooms, will (for a fee) gather the documents for you. Typical prices: $27 for the Annual Report to Shareholders, $35 for a 10-K form, $22 for a proxy statement. They will also sell you an annual "subscription" to all or part of a company's set of filings and can provide you a free list of covered companies. For more information, contact Disclosure Inc., 5161 River Road, Bethesda, MD 20861, (800) 638-8241. Disclosure is fast, reliable, and easy to use, but you may end up paying hundreds of dollars for documents available for free on the Internet.

SEC extracts	$/¢ The Disclosure SEC Database, available on CompuServe, Dialog, Dow Jones and Nexis, offers a standardized summary of the major SEC filings, including data extracted from the proxy statement, annual report, registration statements and 10-K, 20-F, 10-Q and 8-K forms.
	  CompuServe offers the lowest and most predictable cost: $42 for the full report on any company, with options that let you buy individual sections for less. Other online services use complex pricing schemes that can raise the cost per company to upwards of $150.
	  These extracts can be more useful than the full documents when you need basic information fast, or you want it in a standardized format that lets you easily compare several different companies. To assist in your analysis, ask Disclosure to send you a copy of their free publication: *A Guide to Database Elements.*

- from the IRS
- from state authorities
- from the organization itself

A) **The IRS.** Unfortunately, the first source, the IRS, is virtually useless. They are supposed to provide copies of all Form 990s upon request but typically take months or years to respond.

B) **The states.** State disclosure offices usually respond *much* more quickly, but their files do not cover all charities. In most cases, state filing requirements are based on public fundraising within the state—not physical location of the charity. (See *Annual Survey of State Laws Regulating Charitable Solicitations,* updated each year by the American Association of Fund-Raising Counsel, phone (212) 354-5799, for a state-by-state description of current disclosure requirements.) Thus, some groups file nowhere, while others file in many states. Some states require that charities note the availability of public filings in their fundraising mailings.

In some state capitals, among them Albany (NY) and Sacramento (CA), you can make an appointment to review charity registration files on premises. In some cases, these files will contain revealing correspondence between regulators and the charity, as well as other documents that may prove far more valuable than the 990s themselves.

Whenever you request charitable disclosures from a state, you should specify that you need "the last three years of (insert name of state report) and the federal Form 990 including Schedule A for _____ (*insert full name and address of target organization*) and all of its affiliates."

C) **The filing organization.** The only *sure* way to obtain Form 990s (along with some important related documents which may not be available from state disclosure offices) is to go directly to the main office of your target institution. Federal law requires that all non-profits permit public inspection during business hours. Groups cannot legally require an advance appointment. However, since many institutions profess ignorance regarding their legal obligations in this area, you should carry a memo explaining the law.

The organization does not have to make copies for you, but they must let you take detailed notes or make copies with your own portable copier or scanner. (If you plan to take notes by hand, bring several blank forms so you can quickly copy the numbers into the appropriate spaces. You can obtain copies of all forms from the IRS.)

D) **A brief note on the 990PF.** Grant-giving private foundations (ranging from Ford and Rockefeller to thousands of smaller organizations) must file annual 990-PF forms that list the beneficiaries of their largesse. Microfiche copies of virtually *all* 990-PFs are available for public inspection at libraries maintained in many cities around the United States by The Foundation Center. (Call the Washington, DC, Foundation Center (202) 331-1400 for information on the location nearest you.) Even more useful, The Foundation Center has also compiled a number of print publications and databases giving information by *grant recipient*. These will let you find out, for example, which major donors have contributed to a particular hospital or university. You can find their publications at many libraries; their databases are available on Dialog and other online services.

How to Read Form 990 and Related Documents

Useful items to look at in the federal charitable disclosures include the following:
(1) **Form 990**
Part I:
Line 1, **"Total Contributions, gifts, grants, etc."** tells you how much money an organization receives as charitable donations and government grants. This information can help you locate government agencies and private funders that may have influence over the organization.

Line 2, "Program Service Revenue." Total revenue from all sources. Examining changes in this figure (and the detailed breakdowns) over a three-year period will help you understand funding trends. Additional detail will be found in Part VII.

Line 18, "Excess (or deficit) for the year." Equivalent to "net profit" in the private sector. A high-profit rate can be used to document the organization's wealth and, in extreme cases, to challenge its non-profit status.

Line 21, "Net Assets or Fund Balances at End of Year." Equivalent to "retained earnings" in the private sector. Rapid growth in the fund balance may suggest that the institution is more interested in accumulating wealth than using its resources to serve the community.

Part II:

Line 43, "Other Expenses." This will sometimes give you evidence of spending inappropriate to a charity.

Part III: Statement of Program Service Accomplishments.

This section will give you valuable information on spending for specific segments of the employer's activity.

Part V: List of Officers, Directors, Key Employees.

This is often the most valuable portion of a Form 990, because it contains details on officers' salaries and benefits. In some cases, it will show that the director and other officers are grossly overpaid and that they are receiving much larger annual percentage increases than they pay their workers. To find out if executive pay is out of line with other organizations, check its figures against compensation surveys published annually in *The Chronicle of Philanthropy, Modern Healthcare* or other trade publications covering non-profits.

Part VI: Other Information

Answers to questions in this section may provide evidence of conflicts of interest or other irregularities. Conversely, if the statements made by the organization here contradict what you know about their operations, you may have grounds for questioning their tax exemption. Note especially Line 78 (and the related, more detailed disclosures in Part IX).

Part IX: Information Regarding Taxable Subsidiaries.

The information found here regarding for-profit affiliates can have important implications at the state level, because some states are more restrictive than the federal government on some tax exemption-related issues. In particular, use of the non-profit institution's buildings by a for-profit subsidiary could trigger a partial loss of real estate tax exemption. It some cases, it may be useful to contact the appropriate county, city, or town authorities to find out if real estate taxes are being paid and to protest any improper failure to pay.

(2) Form 990, Schedule A

This critically important document gives you pay and benefits data for the five highest-paid non-officer employees (usually the senior administrators) and the five highest-paid professional service providers. It also provides a wealth of information on lobbying expenditures (if any) and transactions with non-charitable organizations. Organizations often try to omit this form from their disclosures to state agencies and individual requestors. Make sure that this schedule is included with any Form 990s provided to you.

(3) Form 1023

This is the original application to the IRS for tax exemption. It is available from the institution or the IRS but may not be available from state authorities. Make sure you specifically request "all schedules and supporting documents or papers filed by the organization when it applied for exemption." Form 1023 includes detailed descriptions of the organization's charitable objectives, its links with other organizations, and various areas of potential conflict of interest.

Schedule C of Form 1023 provides additional information on non-profit hospitals. It describes the hospital's policies on treatment of the indigent, financing of charity care, and provision of subsidized office space to physicians. If claims made in this section are inaccurate (e.g., that the hospital is failing to adhere to its stated charity care policies or has spent more than the indicated amount on subsidies for doctors), this may provide a basis for challenging the tax exemption.

Schedule F provides similar information on nursing homes.

As with Part VI of Form 990, discrepancies between statements to the IRS and the actual practices of the exempt organization could provide a basis for challenging its exempt status.

(4) **IRS Form 990T.**

This form reports taxable "unrelated business income" (which *is* taxable) from activities not related to the institution's "charitable purpose." Analysis of taxable activities can be crucial to understanding a non-profit organization.

(Note: This is the one Form 990-related document which the organization may legally withhold; however, organizations unfamiliar with the rules have been known to release this document to requestors, when confronted with a request for access to "Form 990 and all related forms and schedules."

Obtaining Data on Financial Institutions

The banking industry has changed dramatically in recent years. Bank mergers have become an increasingly significant phenomenon. Many banks are now owned by holding companies. Brokerage firms, mutual funds, and other financial service companies are increasingly competing for business that traditionally belonged to banks.

Most larger banks and bank-holding companies are publicly traded and thus must file the standard Securities and Exchange

Commission disclosure documents. However, banks and other financial institutions must also comply with a number of even more detailed disclosure requirements.

Banks face much closer financial scrutiny than most other business entities and have some special legal obligations, most notably under the Community Reinvestment Act, to serve the public interest. In addition, banks are often more susceptible than other businesses to public pressure because they are more concerned than most with their image in the community.

Basic Reference Books on the Banking Industry

*   *Moody's Bank and Finance Manual* is an excellent quick reference on specific banks and for general banking information. It will be found in most major public libraries.
*   *Rand McNally Bank Directory* and *Thomson Bank Directory* give the name, financial statements, officers, directors, and branch locations for over 45,000 banks and subsidiaries in the United States and elsewhere.

Banking Records: Comptroller of the Currency

An arm of the U.S. Treasury Department, the Office of the Comptroller of the Currency (OCC), is one of four federal agencies that regulate the banking industry. It collects information on:

*   Nationally chartered banks (banks with "national" in the title).
*   District of Columbia banks.
*   Foreign banks with U.S. branch offices.
*   Bank-holding companies.
*   Corporations created to hold investments in foreign banks.

Most of the information provided to OCC by national banks is available to the public. The financial data in a bank's *Report of Condition* and *Report of Income* is available on request. *Bank Annual Reports* and *Registration of Securities Statements* are also publicly available, though some sections may be withheld as "proprietary information" at the request of the reporting institution. In addition, certain sections of a branch bank application are always confidential. All requests for OCC information must be made in writing to:

Communications Section
Comptroller of the Currency
490 L'Enfant Plaza East, SW
Washington, DC 20219

Banking Records: The Federal Reserve System (FRS)

The FRS performs two functions:

- It acts as the nation's central bank and executor of U.S. monetary policy.
- It assists in the regulation of commercial banks.

For the purposes of this manual, we are primarily interested in the regulatory function. Specifically, FRS regulates:

- State banks which are members of the Federal Reserve System.
- Bank-holding companies.
- International operating subsidiaries of U.S. banks (known as Edge Act corporations).

Information can be obtained from the FRS through two offices.

- The Banking Supervision and Regulation Division maintains the securities registrations and annual reports of publicly held banks. Requests for these documents can be made either in writing or by visiting the offices.
- The Freedom of Information Office provides general assistance in locating individual bank filings or in obtaining more general data gathered by the FRS.
Both offices can be contacted at:

Federal Reserve System
20th and C Streets, NW
Washington, DC 20551
(202) 452-3684

Reports to the FRS are generally open to the public, though like other bank regulators, FRS lets banks keep some forms partly confidential. The reporting forms are also similar to those provided by the OCC and the FDIC, but form numbers often differ.

Records Maintained Under Community Reinvestment Act (CRA)

By law, every bank must maintain a CRA file that is open to public inspection. CRA data includes detailed information on bank lending to low-income and minority borrowers. When a bank discriminates against the poor or minority group members, CRA records can provide a very powerful source of evidence.

Federal Deposit Insurance Corporation (FDIC)

The FDIC was set up in 1933 in response to Depression-induced bank failures. It insures the customers of member banks for up to $100,000 and regulates the activities of state-chartered banks that are not members of the Federal Reserve System (see below). In fulfilling its responsibilities, the FDIC conducts periodic examinations of member banks and requires them to provide periodic reports of condition and income. Like the OCC, much of the information gathered by the FDIC is available to the public. Reports of Condition and Reports of Income are available in their entirety. Under the public disclosure rules of the agency, individual member banks may request confidentiality for information that they consider proprietary. However, such requests are infrequently made and even less frequently granted. As with the comptroller, *requests for information must be made in writing*.

Much of the information gathered by the FDIC is similar to the OCC, but form numbers are slightly different. FDIC information overlaps with that available from the Federal Reserve but is often easier to obtain.

Requests for further details on the forms available from FDIC, and requests for copies of those forms should be addressed to:

Federal Deposit Insurance Corporation
Data Request Section
550 17th Street, NW
Washington, DC 20429

Federal Home Loan Bank Board (FHLBB)

This agency is responsible for regulating savings and loan associations and other home mortgage lenders. Its subsidiary, the Federal Savings and Loan Insurance Corporation (FSLIC), insures and monitors the activities of federally chartered savings and loan associations, which must become members of the Federal Home Loan Bank System.

State savings and loan associations are chartered by their respective state agencies but also have the option of joining the Federal Home Loan Bank System.

S&Ls that issue stock must supply proxy information to the FHLBB. Like other bank regulatory agencies, the FHLBB requires that savings and loans file semi-annual reports on member institutions' income and condition. In addition to basic financial data like that provided in reports filed with the OCC and the FDIC, these reports also show consultant and legal fees, advertising expenses, and reimbursements.

FHLBB is less experienced than other financial institution regulators in handling requests for information. To request access to FHLBB filings contact:

Federal Home Loan Bank Board
Public Affairs Office
1700 G Street, NW
Washington, DC 20552

Home Mortgage Disclosure Act (HMDA)

Also available from the bank, this form details the number of mortgage and home improvement loans, their amounts, and the geographic locations in which they were made. Together with the CRA statements, these documents can be used to determine whether a bank has illegally discriminated against certain residents of a particular community on the basis of race, income, or neighborhood (a practice often known as "redlining"). Evidence of redlining can be used to challenge bank applications for new branch licenses.

State Banking Commissions

State-chartered banks are regulated by state banking commissions. Laws vary from state to state, but most commissions collect detailed reports on bank income and condition. State banking commissions may also collect information on consumer complaints and stock transactions. They are almost always located in the state capital. For a listing of state banking commissions and a summary of their data

disclosure policies, see pp. 447-450 of *Lesko's Info-Power II*.

Finding Information on Government Contractors

Few business activities produce a more detailed public record than sales of goods or services to the government.

At the federal level, the *Commerce Business Daily* publishes listings of all U.S. government contracts and subcontracts, civilian and military, worth more than $25,000. Whether the contract is at the federal, state, or local level, a transaction with the government will result in creation of the following documents, most or all of which are available to the public.

- Lists of government contracts, dollar values, and products provided
- Bid specifications, detailing the goods or services to be provided and the exact conditions of delivery
- The actual bids and the government agencies evaluations of same (Bid documents may contain details on company operations and plant capacity, designed to show that the company is capable of producing the required product.)
- Government audits of the contracting company (At the federal level, the General Accounting Office has broad authority to audit activities of any government agency and its contractors. Call (202) 512-6000 to find out if your target company's government business activities have ever been examined. In addition, virtually all federal agencies have an Inspector General whose audit reports—or summaries thereof—are usually available to the public.)

☞ *Lesko's Info-Power II* (pp. 841-842) offers a list of state procurement offices. Contact the office in any state with which your company has contracts for details on public access to contract documents.

¢¢¢ The last 90 days of *Commerce Business Daily* contract announcements can be searched electronically on CompuServe. (Type GO CBD.) Cost: $1/search plus $2/full listing.

$$$ Nexis and Dialog offer *Commerce Business Daily* online for 1982 to the present. You can also arrange for Dialog to send you an electronic "alert" each time a particular company is mentioned in CBD. DMS/FI Contract Awards, also on Dialog, is a structured database of government prime contract awards over $25,000, with emphasis on military procurement. Similar in scope to CBD, but may provide additional information—or a more useful data presentation format—for some contracts and contractors.

Researching Foreign Investment and International Trade

Increasingly, activists find themselves in disputes involving foreign companies and multinationals which have "globalized" their operations so thoroughly that they are literally stateless.

Profiling such companies poses special problems, since U.S. reference sources may have only limited information on the foreign parent, subsidiary or affiliate companies. Yet understanding their operations around the world is crucial, because it may help your organization build broader coalitions, find overseas points of vulnerability, or even challenge their legal right to conduct certain operations.

Annual Reports

Global Research Company (1605 So. Big Bend Blvd, St. Louis, MO 63117, phone (314) 647-0081; fax (314) 647-4001) maintains an extensive library of foreign corporate annual reports and other documents and will search for overseas reports and documents not in their files. Price: $40-$60 for annual reports in their files; for an additional fee, they will search and obtain reports not in their files.

Directories

Directory of Foreign Firm Operations in the United States. Published by the World Trade Academy Press in New York, this is a useful reference source. This multivolume set can be found in larger public or university libraries.

D&B — Dun's European Market Identifiers and *International Market Identifiers*. A series of electronic directories offering basic information (company name, address, phone, sales, number of employees, executive names) for at least 2.4 million European, Asian, African, Canadian, and Latin American companies.

$$$ Available on Dialog and CompuServe. Regular users of this service should note that the Dialog version is less expensive and offers a wider range of search options.

Government Experts and Information Sources

The Department of Commerce maintains a vast information gathering and dissemination network that includes district offices in the United States, country and product experts in Washington, and business specialists stationed abroad. For many of these experts, giving out information is an important part of their official responsibilities. U.S. businesses use this network constantly to get up-to-date information on prospects for buying, selling, or investing abroad; foreign firms tap into the network to get data on U.S. markets and investment potential. But these experts work for all Americans—not just the corporations—and most of them are more than willing to share their knowledge with your organization. Although some of the information they receive is "classified" or "proprietary," most of it is available to the public. You can call these experts for advice on determining where a U.S. company sells its products abroad; what are the size, structure, and other investments of your foreign-owned employer, and much more. If you know in what other countries your employer operates, you can contact the U.S. "Overseas Commercial Counselor" in that country for information.

The broadest business expert network is maintained by the U.S. Department of Commerce. But the government also maintains a staff of specialized trade experts in areas including mining (U.S. Bureau of Mines), agricultural trade (U.S. Department of Agriculture), and oil and gas (U.S. Department of Energy). Most states also maintain international trade offices which can be useful in helping you track overseas investments by companies headquartered in the state or foreign investors operating in the state.

☞ Phone the expert and ask for the information you need! They are used to talking with information seekers and may answer your questions on the phone or direct you to a useful reference publication. You'll find a detailed list of international trade experts in *Lesko's Info-Power II* (pp. 843-860, 1994 edition). Or phone the public affairs office of the Commerce Department's International Trade Administration at (202) 482-0543.

☞ For electronic access to online computer databases maintained by the Commerce Department, U.S. Bureau of Mines, and other trade-related agencies, connect to Fed World. Phone (703) 487-4650 for information or (703) 321-8020 when dialing directly with your modem.

☞ More than 1400 university and public libraries across the country serve as federal depository libraries. You can visit any one of them to examine a wide range of trade-related (and other) U.S. government publications. (Even if the nearest university restricts public use of its general collection, they are required to provide free access to depository materials.)

Other Information Sources

The International Labor Rights Education and Research Fund (110 Maryland Avenue NE, Washington, DC, 20002, phone (202) 544-7198), works closely with the labor movement and has produced many publications on labor rights violations around the world. Its publications and expert staff members may be able to help you identify and analyze labor rights violations by foreign affiliates of your target company. They can also explain how the labor rights provisions in some international trade laws and treaties may sometimes be used to challenge imports of products produced abroad under unfair labor conditions.

¢¢¢ Peacenet carries a wide range of international news services, with special emphasis on the developing world. It maintains online news and discussion areas specifically focusing on international labor rights. Some (but not all) of these news sources are organized as electronically searchable databases that you can use to find information on the overseas activities of your target company.

Sources for Investigating Individuals

Courthouse Records

The county courthouse is a good place to start an investigation of individuals. In rural areas there may be a single building that contains all of the records mentioned here. In larger cities they will be spread throughout a number of offices.

Courthouse records can help you answer such questions as:

- Does the person own land? What is it worth? Is it mortgaged, and to whom?
- Is there other property or assets?
- Is the person delinquent in taxes?
- How much has been made from past property sales?
- Has the person been arrested, sued anyone, or been sued?

Grantor and Grantee Indexes. These are records of the sale and purchase of real estate. In every transaction there is a grantor, that is, a seller who grants the deed, and a grantee, the buyer who gets the deed. The bank lending the money for the mortgage may also be listed as the grantee because it receives the property as collateral. These two indexes are usually kept separately and are alphabetical by year. Be sure to look at both of them.

The indexes will refer you to the location of other documents that are registered separately. These include:

- **Deeds.** Include a description of property, date of sale, property boundaries, and usually the price.
- **Mortgages.** Include the names of borrower and lender, amount and terms.
- **Liens.** Usually the result of a court order saying that the property will be forfeited by a certain date for non-payment of a debt.
- **Trusts.** The property is managed by trustees who send the proceeds to someone else.

Tax Assessor's Records. These list the assessed value of every piece of property. You then figure out the taxes based on the tax rate for the type of property it is. Unpaid taxes are also listed, as is the address to which the tax bill is sent.

The assessed value is not the actual amount for which the property can be sold; generally, the assessed value is much lower. Often, assessments were made years ago, so check the date. The valuation of land and buildings will be made separately.

How such records are kept differs widely. Sometimes there is an alphabetical listing, sometimes you must locate the property on a map to find the assessor's number, and sometimes both systems are available.

As computerization proceeds, some localities have developed a real estate data index, an alphabetical listing of property owners. In other places, you must work from books and file cards. Various properties owned by the same individual will usually be listed separately and you must look them up separately.

While at the assessor's office, also check tax abatement roles and tax exemption roles. These records may give a hint that someone has received an unfair advantage, or is misusing a charitable or religious exemption (e.g., The Holey Garment Tailor Shop.) An example of how a community organization used the tax assessor's records is given below.

The Columbus Education Association wanted to increase the city's education budget. Volunteers were trained to search the assessor's records, looking for recent sales of commercial property. Having obtained the old valuation and the new selling price, the association challenged the assessments that were artificially low, demanding more accurate assessments and thus raising taxes on these commercial buildings. Without this, it might have taken years before the assessor routinely got around to reassessing the properties.

This is clearly an example of more traditional research. The same method was applied in a tactical way in Chicago when the tax assessor himself was made the target of the campaign. Researchers found a few big examples of under-assessed commercial property, and then demanded that the assessor conduct a thorough re-examination of his records. (The targets, chosen for their inability

to move out of the community, included a bank and a racetrack.)

Court Records. You can find out if people have been sued, or sued someone else, been arrested, or have had legal judgments entered against them by examining court records.

Every state has a different system. In general, you go to the clerk of each court. The clerk will have a list of all people initiating an action and another list of people against whom actions were entered. These records are usually organized by year, and only include events within the jurisdiction of that particular court. Note docket numbers.

Taking the docket number from the index, you can ask the clerk to locate the docket that outlines the case and its disposition. From the docket you can find the court papers and transcripts. Don't overlook bankruptcy, probate and divorce proceedings as a way of uncovering a person's assets.

For example, when a pro-landlord faction attempted to take over a tenant organization, an investigation of the faction's candidate for the board revealed that he was a disbarred lawyer who had gone to jail for cheating a client. When leaflets with this information were put under doors, he withdrew from the election. The investigator did not just start an open-ended search of court records. Someone remembered the story and the investigator documented it.

We need to add to this story, that the event raised a serious ethical question and split the organization. Many people felt that it was improper to distribute such information under doors in a person's own home, and they felt badly for his family. Consider this carefully. *Other Records of Personal Property.* These records differ widely from state to state. In some places, lists of automobiles are kept; in others, financial assets are also listed.

Voting Records. There can be a surprising amount of information here. In New York City, for example, a registration record available to the public will show a person's address, apartment number, home phone, employer at date of registration, age, previous address, citizenship status, mailing address if different from home address, date of registration, and party enrollment, as well as the person's signature. The reason for cancellation of registration is also noted (e.g., criminal conviction). There is also a list of all the elections in which the person voted.

Apart from using the above to augment other investigations, candidates have used this information to show that opponents actually lived outside the district, previously belonged to another party, or hadn't bothered to vote in major races.

Directories

There are directories for virtually everything. "Who's Who" type directories have become a big business. The books are produced to be sold not only to libraries, but also to all of the people listed. Reference librarians are often happy to advise and help you find material in these books.

Kline's Guide to American Directories. This is a very useful list of about 5,000 other directories. It tells you what to look for in the library. You will never actually consult most of these directories, which include such obscure listings as companies that pre-shrink textiles.

City Directories. These are published for many medium-sized cities. Polks and Coles are two of many companies which publish them. They list addresses, phone numbers, businesses, spouses and other household members.

Who's Who. Biographical information volunteered by the person listed is found in this famous book. The information usually includes spouses and family members, occupation, married names of children and their spouses, education, club membership, military service, honors, and religious affiliation. The major publisher is Marquis (much of the Marquis series is available on the Dialog data base), but there are many others. Among the many volumes are:

- *Who's Who in America*
- *Who's Who in The East (West, South Southwest, Midwest)*
- *Who's Who of American Judges*
- *Who's Who in World Jewry*

- *Who's Who of American Women*
- *Who's Who in Commerce*
- *Who's Who in Banking*
- *Who's Who in American Politics*
- *Who's Who in Insurance*
- *Who's Who in American College and University Administration.*

Lawyers: Martindale and Hubbell Law Directory. This directory is organized by state and county, and lists lawyers by name and by firm. It also sometimes lists representative clients of the firm. (Before the laws were liberalized in some states, this was the only form of advertising lawyers had.)

This directory can be useful for tracking down previous connections of judges, although back issues rarely remain on library shelves. It also helps identify conflicts of interest of lawyers running for office or appointed to public bodies. In most states the majority of the legislators are lawyers, and it is often helpful to know what firm a person comes from and who the other partners are.

Social Registers and Blue Books. These contain information on rich people.

National Data Book of Foundations, Foundation Directory, Foundation Reports. The *Data Book* lists all 27,000 U.S. foundations. The *Directory* is a listing of nearly 7,000 of the largest U.S. foundations, describing the purpose and financial situation of each. It also contains an index of their directors. In addition, many foundations produce annual reports telling to whom grants were given.

A non-profit organization, The Foundation Center operates 123 cooperative collections of foundation material which are located in the U.S., Canada, Mexico, and some other parts of the world. The collections include copies of Internal Revenue Service form 990 PF (see below). In addition, they contain information on area foundations. Some have a complete collection of materials on all foundations. For the collection nearest you, call 1-(800)-424-9836, or write

The Foundation Center
79 5th Ave.
New York, NY 10003

Citizen organizations usually use the Foundation Directory to write grant applications, but the index of directors is also good for tactical investigations. It sometimes leads to discovering conflicts of interest. Foundations with large assets but small grant outlays, for example, may be giving a hint that corporate money is being hidden from the tax collector, especially if they are family controlled. When opponents release a harmful study to the press, the article may indicate that it was paid for by a particular foundation grant. You will want to know who is behind that foundation. Foundation reports are helpful when you suspect that a corporation or industry group is financing a "public interest" organization that lobbies against you. All of this is helpful in locating secondary targets.

IRS form 990 PF. All non-profits must file annually. Lists officers, trustees, grants, and assets.

J.R. Taft publications: Foundation Reporter, Trustees of Wealth, and Corporate Reporter provide additional information on foundations.

Other Directories. There are many, many directories that have information on federal office holders, their staffs, and other elected officials. See *Kline's Guide,* for example.

Newspaper Morgues

All papers maintain indexed files of all their articles. They are under no obligation to allow you to use them, however. Relations with a friendly reporter can help a great deal if the newspaper isn't forthcoming. This is one way to get information on small local companies and individuals who are neither rich nor famous.

For example, a nationwide strike had received the support of the leaders of many major religious denominations. A committee aiding the strikers was arranging phone calls from the religious leaders to company board members of the same denomination. When they were unable to find a religious affiliation listed for one board member, they checked his name through his hometown newspaper and came up with a news story on his father's funeral. From that report, they were able to trace the family's religious background.

Small Town Libraries

Most of these libraries keep "vertical files" of newspaper clippings on local people, businesses, and issues that affect the community.

Other Specialized Research Topics

At both state and federal levels, a wide range of regulatory agencies monitor company performance and maintain files on companies that violate laws and guidelines. Space does not permit us to list all these agencies in detail.

Consumer Protection

A number of state and federal agencies maintain records about companies or products that have engendered consumer complaints. When available, they can be very useful in building public support against the target company by helping you document patterns of consumer abuse.

☞ For a list of State Consumer Protection agencies and details on data availability, see *Lesko's Info-Power II,* pp. 102-104.

Environmental Protection

Environmental impact studies are often required before companies may build or expand manufacturing facilities. These studies will contain information about water supply and quality, air quality, type of discharges, records of complaints, violations, and enforcement actions. They can often be used to generate opposition from community groups and citizens to a proposed facility. Court and regulatory findings regarding environmental violations can also provide organizing leverage. Environmental monitoring agencies gather vast amounts of potentially useful information. This brief list will merely scratch the surface.

☞ The U.S. Nuclear Regulatory Commission's NUDOC's system offers *free* online access to inspection reports, violation notices, and other records covering organizations that use radioactive material, including 110 nuclear power plants and 23,000 hospitals, universities, and other NRC licensees. It also contains a wide range of Congressional materials, hearing transcripts, and scientific data. For an access password, contact: Office of Information and Resource Management, U.S. Nuclear Regulatory Commission, MNBB 6219, Washington, DC 20555.

☞ The U.S. Department of Energy's TRANSET database provides access to shipment and accident records, from 1991 to the present, for nuclear waste and other radioactive materials. For free access contact: Division 6321, Sandia National Laboratories, Box 5800, Albuquerque, NM 87185.

¢¢¢ Peacenet and its sister system Econet offer more than a dozen news services and discussion "conferences" on environmental issues, with a strong emphasis on monitoring and reporting corporate abuses.

¢¢¢ Toxnet, a set of nine databases which comprise the Toxicology Data Network, is available through Medlars (see Occupational Safety and Health, below). Within Toxnet, you will find such valuable research tools as the Toxic Release Inventory—a record of toxic chemical releases since 1987—organized by company, location, and year. (Important note: This service is not available through the CompuServe/Paperchase gateway to Medlars.)

Occupational Safety and Health

Several services now offer electronic access to the past five years of Occupational Safety and Health Administration violation records.

¢¢¢ Medlars, the National Library of Medicine's system of more than 30 medical databases, offers public access with no membership fee or monthly minimum and an average usage charge of about 30¢/min. This system lets you search abstracts of articles on health-related topics— including occupational safety and health issues—and

offers you an opportunity to order copies of the full text of the articles. Call (800) 638-8480 for full information and sign-up instructions.

CompuServe subscribers can access a portion of the Medlars system (for a slightly higher fee) by typing GO PAPERCHASE. The CompuServe route will be more convenient for occasional users.

$$$ Dialog, Lexis/Nexis and Westlaw all offer some access to OSHA files.

Conclusion

Tactical investigation provides the ammunition for direct action organizing. The concept of tactical weakness and the skill in finding it need to be learned by all organizers and leaders in citizen organizations. Often an organization will have one person who does the investigative work. This is a lost opportunity because many can actually participate in it and in doing so, build leadership.

In fact, investigative work isn't limited to people with formal education. In a Chicago public housing project, tenants gathered up paint chips from their apartments, labeled them in little plastic bags, and took them to a meeting of the Chicago Housing Authority. There they demanded that the chips be tested for lead paint. This was a tactical investigation in every sense of the word. Evidence was collected, and a public agency was forced to analyze it. It was also a fine tactic that resulted in the apartments being painted for the first time in many years.

The integration of tactical investigation and direct action has proven to be a particularly powerful combination for building citizen power.

PART III
Support for Organization

20

Grassroots fundraising is raising money from and by your constituency. If approached like an organizing campaign, grassroots fundraising meets the Midwest Academy's three principles of organizing: win real victories, give people a sense of their own power, and change the relations of power.

Grassroots fundraising wins real victories on two levels. First, you can successfully raise money with your constituency, particularly if you set specific and realistic fundraising goals. Second, you will also win real victories because the money raised from grassroots fundraising can be used for whatever your group chooses (the use of money obtained from foundation funds is usually restricted in some way).

Grassroots fundraising gives people a sense of their own power. Leaders are developed and encouraged when they raise funds to support their own organization. Members and leaders feel a great deal more power when they raise $10,000 through an event than when one person writes a grant proposal and a foundation contributes $10,000. While the latter way raises money, it does not give leaders a sense of their own power.

Grassroots fundraising also changes the relations of power. If your group develops its own internal funding base via grassroots fundraising, you are seen as a much more powerful community player. Having a solid source of funds changes the relations of power between you and those in powerful positions,

Funding Sources

The Fundamentals of Grassroots Fundraising

Grassroots Fundraising Ideas

Grassroots Fundraising

because you will be more difficult to get rid of or "buy off."

Funding Sources

There are many ways to raise funds for your organization, including proposal writing, large-donor solicitation, direct mail appeals, canvassing, government and foundation grants, and grassroots fundraising. Most organizations find that they need a diversified funding base to sustain them over a period of time. As the following discussion shows, it is risky to depend too heavily on any one type of fundraising, except internally generated funds and grassroots fundraising.

Government or Foundation Fundraising

In the early 1980s, Richard Viguerie, the New Right direct mail guru, claimed that the number-one priority of the New Right was to defund the "Left." First, the Reagan Administration and then the Newt Congress slashed budgets for programs that provided funds for community organizations such as VISTA, Community Action Programs, legal services, and social service outreach programs. Some groups that depended primarily upon these funds had to close their doors. Others were severely crippled. The days in which groups could depend upon government funds are long past.

Although foundation grants have undergirded much of the important work of community organizations and state and national coalitions, it is important that these groups not become solely dependent upon just a few foundation sources. Some foundations are faddish in their giving, funding hunger this year and peace the next. It's great if your issue happens to be "in," but remember, it will be "out" soon. The other enormously frustrating aspect of foundation giving is that the foundations like "new" projects. They prefer to give "seed" money or fund a new project. Few foundations want to provide ongoing general support. So, even if you have a great program going, you have to figure out how to describe it in a "new" fashion, or you have to shift funds to new (possibly less significant) programs. Too many groups find themselves funder-driven, chasing foundation dollars by changing programs. Although a diversified funding plan will surely include seeking foundation grants, groups should also avoid total dependence on foundation funds.

Grassroots Fundraising

Grassroots fundraising not only makes theoretical sense, it also makes statistical, economic sense. According to the American Association of Fund-Raising Counsel, in 1993, 81 percent of U.S. contributions to charity came from individuals, 7 percent from bequests, and only 7 percent from foundations and 5 percent from corporations. Thus, 88 percent came from people, either living or deceased. Not only does most money come from individuals, but 85 percent of all money given comes from people with incomes of $50,000 or less. So groups can build a grassroots funding base from low- and moderate-income families.

Ideally, your organization should seek as much money as possible directly from its membership, in dues and contributions, and from grassroots fundraising events. Realistically, most organizations find that they must develop additional outside sources, such as foundations, to make ends meet. For assistance and information on a variety of fundraising approaches, visit one of the reference collections or cooperating collections of The Foundation Center, headquartered at 79 Fifth Avenue, New York, NY 10003. These collections are located in over 100 cities, with at least one in each state. To check on locations and current information, call (800) 424-9836.

The Fundamentals of Grassroots Fundraising

Set a Goal

Sometimes when groups talk about grassroots fundraising, they think about small garage sales or bakes sales. Grassroots fundraising certainly includes these, but they do not necessarily have to raise small amounts of money. In fact, if your organization's goal is to raise money, you should figure out how to work with your leaders to raise $20,000 instead of $2,000, especially if it will take comparable amounts of effort. Time, of both staff and volunteers, is a valuable resource and must be used wisely in grassroots fundraising.

Make a Fundraising Calendar

One of the benefits of grassroots fundraising is that you can control the timing on when you raise the funds. For many groups, the end of the summer is a tight financial time. If you know this, you can plan your grassroots fundraisers accordingly. You can also schedule special fundraising events at times of the year that are less hectic programmatically, although you may find that you raise the most money around the same time as your peak programmatic times.

Make a calendar of the coming year. Fill in regularly scheduled events, timing on grants and special appeals, holidays, heavy programmatic periods, and other relevant information. You can also plan fundraising events for times when your constituency has the most money. For example, the end-of-the-year events are difficult for most poor and working class people because they are buying Christmas or Hanuka gifts. On the other hand, upper management types may have just received their year-end bonuses and be flush with cash. Then decide when you need money the most and when would be the best times for your organization to hold grassroots fundraising events. By planning well in advance, you can recruit a solid core of people to serve on your fundraising committee(s).

Observe the Following Guidelines

Raise More Money Than You Spend! Just because another group made money on a certain project, don't assume that your group can. Carefully analyze why and how another group made money. One of the biggest traps is assuming that groups can sell inexpensive items, such as candy, and make money. Groups that make big money selling such things almost always have large numbers of willing sellers, usually children, whose parents buy much of the merchandise. Unless you have dozens of sellers, you may have trouble.

Lots of groups have lost money on concerts in which they had to pay for a hall and the performer. The performer was good, but not good enough to draw the numbers needed to make money. Many groups have had lots of T-shirts left over because someone overestimated the market, or the artistic design was not quite that appealing, or the quality of the shirt was poor. Selling cookbooks has not always served groups well, usually because the market was smaller and the sellers fewer than anticipated. On the other hand, many groups have made money from concerts, T-shirts and cookbooks. The key is careful analysis of both money and time.

Don't Try Risky Ventures Requiring Big Investments. Stick to projects that seem like sure things and that call for small investments, especially the first time. Once a project proves its ability to raise funds, you may be willing to invest more.

Raise Money for Your Issue Program. It is much easier to raise money to support a campaign to eliminate a food tax or to increase security in a building, than to raise money to pay back debt or the electricity bill. By raising money around your program, you also publicize the issue and potentially recruit new volunteers.

Have Fun. Lots of projects will raise money. Let people use their own creativity. If the fundraising committee has fun planning and implementing their event, they are likely to get involved again and to draw others to work with them.

Build on Past Successful Events. Don't skip from project to project. Once you identify a fundraising project that works, repeat it annually. Not only do you learn how to host the project more efficiently, but your group becomes identified with that annual event, making it easier to promote.

Remember, it seems that it takes groups several years to learn how to tap their true market. Most groups find that their fundraising income increases dramatically for a few years and then tends to level off. Typically, a small organization that raises $5,000 the first year can raise $10,000 the second year and about $20,000 the third year. After that, the amount of money tends not to increase much. Thus, it doesn't make sense to start over each year with new projects. Develop those that seem to have potential.

In order to facilitate increasing funds from year to year, it is important to keep careful records of all expenses, contacts, vendors and so forth. Immediately after the event, the planning committee should evaluate it and write down suggestions for the following year. These notes should be kept for use by the next year's committee.

Stay In Line with Your Image. A health organization can't be selling junk food, nor can a clean air group sell cigarettes. Grassroots fundraising is part of your overall program and thus must meet the same high standards as your program.

Maintain High Ethical Standards. It is essential that your organization remain both rigorously honest in all of its fundraising and accountable to its constituents. If not, the group's image could be tarnished and its overall political effectiveness diminished. It is better to raise money steadily and develop a solid reputation than to lurch forward, leaving ethical questions in people's minds.

Build Leaders. Grassroots fundraising should not only raise money, it should also develop leaders. Joan Flanagan, author of *The Grass Roots Fundraising Book* (see the bibliography for more information), and one of the best trainers on grassroots fundraising, suggests selecting co-chairs for your fundraising committee. Have each co-chair recruit four or five people for his/her group. Keep careful, measurable records on each person's contribution, such as who sells the most tickets or recruits the most participants. The co-chair whose group raises the most money should be given greater responsibilities, perhaps added to the board of directors, or given another important leadership role. The person who does the best among either group should be asked to be the co-chair for next year. Thus, you build in succession from year to year and assure that the best fundraisers are in leadership roles.

Budget Money to Raise Money. It is quite difficult to raise money without beginning with some. Budget some money. It not only is more realistic, but it also conveys to a committee how much you value and respect their work if you entrust them with funds.

Devote Organizational Time to Fundraising. All too often, groups treat fundraising like the ugly duckling, assuming no one will want to do it (at least no one in their right mind). Fundraising is discussed almost last on the agenda, after we've discussed all the "important" matters, again conveying that it is not valued as much as other contributions. Grassroots fundraising requires excellent leadership skills. Give fundraising and those who lead the efforts their due respect.

Follow the Religious Groups

Without question, the religious groups do the best grassroots fundraising. They follow many of the guidelines described above. Religious groups have learned how to:

Ask Frequently. Most religious groups ask at least 52 times per year, and no one gets upset. Figure out ways to structure regular giving from your membership or constituency. Make sure that people are asked to contribute every time you have a public meeting. Most people can, and will, give regularly if asked.

Ask Volunteers. Religious groups understand clearly that their most active members will be their most active givers. Everyone knows that if you get new people active in the church or synagogue, they will give more money. Unfortunately, too many organizers want to separate volunteers from givers. Don't accept anyone saying, "We can't ask our volunteers. They already give so much time." Volunteers who give time will also give money. The more volunteers you have, the more sources of regular givers you have as well.

Instill the Expectation of Giving. Everyone who joins a religious group expects to contribute to it: The value of giving is instilled with membership. From the very beginning, try to instill this value in your members. Don't shy away from discussing funds. Talk about it openly and ask the members to support the organization openly and regularly.

Organize Fundraising Committees. Most congregations have a committee that plans how it will raise the congregation's budget. The clergy are involved, but do not take primary responsibility for meeting the budget, the committee does. Sometimes there is more than one committee; one for the overall budget—one for bingo, one for the thrift store, and so forth.

Ask Personally and Publicly. Many congregations have a committee of people that meets with each member of the congregation and discusses what that person will "pledge" to the congregation for the next year. Members are encouraged to tithe (set aside a tenth of their income) for the work of the congregation. Your group may not feel it can ask for a tithe, but consider asking for 1 percent or X dollars per week. Consider setting up a committee to visit all your members and ask them personally to contribute for the next year. Volunteer committees can do this in organizations with

small memberships. Larger statewide organizations, like the Citizen Action organizations, use professional canvassers to personally ask the public for support.

Not only should members be asked personally to provide support, they should also be recognized publicly. In some congregations, people are asked to bring their contributions to the front of the congregation. This "public" request is effectively used by politicians as well. In congregational building campaigns, one frequently sees thermometers measuring the congregation's progress toward reaching the fundraising goals. Similarly, we need to make our needs visibly known to the community.

Grassroots Fundraising Ideas

Ask at Every Opportunity. This is the easiest idea. Ask for money at every meeting.

Raffles. As long as your raffle prizes are donated or very cheap, it is hard to lose money on a raffle. Consider holding a raffle in conjunction with other events, banquets or programs as an extra money maker. (Please note that most states and some cities have laws about raffles.)

Food Tastings. Many community groups organize food tasting events in conjunction with neighborhood restaurants. People pay to try small samples of food. It's fun for community people and good promotion for the restaurants. This is particularly successful if your community has different ethnic food restaurants. The food tasting events can be run in several ways. Some groups charge a space fee to the restaurants that sell their samples. Other groups sell tickets and divide the proceeds with the restaurants. Either way, it's hard to lose money. A side benefit is that you develop good relationships with area restaurants.

You might also consider a special kind of food tasting, such as desserts or wines. In Seattle Washington, State Representative Betty Sue Morris (18th District) held "The Chocolate Challenge" for two years in a row, and more are planned for coming years. Friends were asked to donate their favorite chocolate dessert and the chocolate tasting affair was held at the home of another friend. Fancy chocolate truffles and champagne were purchased to supplement the donated chocolates. Guests were asked to donate $50 to the campaign. The invitations, designed like a candy bar, were printed on brown paper with silver lettering and wrapped in foil. The affair, both easy and fun, grossed about $3,000 and netted about $2,400. Such events should be scheduled later in the evening, around 8:00 p.m., in order to attract the "after dinner crowd."

Songs. Consider asking a community or congregational choir to volunteer to sing songs to people for Valentine's Day. Songs can be sold for $15.00 each. In addition to the singers, you need a few good coordinators to publicize the "last-minute Valentine gift" and to organize who will call whom. Choir members will need to rehearse "My Funny Valentine" and other classics.

Phone-a-Thons. Phone-a-thons to your membership base are an excellent way to raise funds. Expenses are low when volunteers call from donated phones. Many organizations have found that regular solicitation of their memberships by phone is their best source of membership-related fundraising.

Benefit Concerts and Performances. If the performers and the hall are donated, benefit performances are usually good fundraisers. If your benefit performance meets the guidelines suggested above (primarily, it doesn't require lots of upfront money), you should not have difficulties. Be sure to use some of the program time to promote your organization and provide visible leadership roles. To minimize your risks and maximize your profits, get a copy of *Note by Note: A Guide to Concert Production,* listed in the bibliography.

Dinners. Many organizations hold fundraising dinners because they are enjoyable as well as good sources of funds. In order to make a significant amount of money, you have to charge a good deal more than the actual cost of the dinner, unless the food and cooking are donated. Most organizations try to sell whole tables (eight or ten seats) to allied organizations, corporations, unions, or neighborhood businesses. These groups do not always fill their

tables and thus you can use their seats to give discounted seats to members who might have trouble affording the dinner. In addition to selling tables, most groups use a raffle or ad book to boost the overall income of the event.

Ads/Ad Books. Individuals, organizations, and businesses like to see their names in print. Because of this, you can sell ads or charge individuals money to be listed in a booklet that will be distributed to people.

Connecticut Citizen Action Group (CCAG) has produced ad books for years and raised up to $20,000, although certainly not the first year or two. Leaders in local chapters across the state sold the ads. The ad book has included one-page descriptions of each chapter or region, one-page descriptions on each CCAG issue campaign, and the ads. The ads have been placed in three categories: 1) local businesses patronized by CCAG staff and leaders placed ads ranging from $50 to $1,000; 2) organizational allies, such as unions, and politicians placed ads in the same price range; and 3) CCAG leaders and former staff placed their names on specially designated pages for fees of $10 to $25 per person. Approximately 2,000 books were usually printed and distributed at all major CCAG events. Printing of the books cost the organization approximately $3,000. Connecticut Citizen Action Group discovered that more politicians placed ads if the ad book was produced right before election time.

Flowers. Consider selling flowers around holidays, such as lilies around Easter, poinsettias around Christmas, or nice potted plants for Mother's Day. Many local affiliates of Women's Action for Nuclear Disarmament (WAND) organize extremely successful "Mums for Mom" fundraising programs. The Buffalo affiliate began selling live flowers and now sells silk flowers. They always include a peace message with the flowers and information about their organization. They net approximately $5,000 per sales campaign. They began selling in malls, but switched to colleges and churches once the malls began charging fees. For information about flower sales for Mother's Day, order the *Mother's Day for Peace Action Kit* listed in the bibliography.

Rummage Sales. It's hard to lose money on a rummage sale because there are usually no overhead costs, unless you set up an ongoing thrift store. A key factor in most rummage sales is the weather. If it's a nice day and you can display items outside, you will make more money than inside. Be sure, however, to analyze the use of your staff and volunteer time. If the rummage sale requires lots of time and earns small amounts of money, it may not be worth it.

Baby Contests. The Baltimore NAACP chapter raises large amounts of money on an annual baby contest, called the "Human Dolls on Parade for Freedom" (children are actually eligible up to five years old). Recently, the organization grossed $60,000 and cleared approximately $50,000. Not bad for a baby contest! Most babies are sponsored by a church or organization. A few babies are entered as "independents." Votes are sold at $.25 per vote or $5.00 per book of votes. The baby who gets the most votes wins a fancy cup with an inscription, a $500 savings bond, and his or her picture on a billboard (the billboard is donated by a local company). The baby winner's church gets a special plaque. All "serious candidates" (those who bring in over $200 worth of votes) get their pictures published, with their parents, in *The Baltimore Afro-American*. The space is donated by the paper, but the NAACP covers the cost of the photographs. This Freedom Baby contest is an annual event and the church plaque has become prestigious for a congregation to receive.

Bingo. Depending on your area, bingo may be a potential source of funds for your group. Some groups run their own bingo games, while others band together to run them. After you have reviewed the potential market, check your state laws. Bingo is tightly monitored by the state government. The Midwest Academy ran a bingo for years that helped underwrite the cost of low-income participants at training sessions. In order to make it work effectively, you must find a dedicated core of volunteers who love bingo.

Conclusion

The above list of suggestions is not meant to be a comprehensive list. There are many other ways to raise funds from your constituency that will be fun, effective, and build leadership. Following the guidelines, choose a project that people want to develop, and try it. If it works, keep doing it!

Grassroots fundraising will probably not be the only source of support for your organization, but it needs to be a significant percentage, especially for community-based organizations. Grassroots fundraising demonstrates leadership commitment to the organization and invests its members in the future of the organization. People care about what happens to organizations that they give to, and for which they work to raise funds.

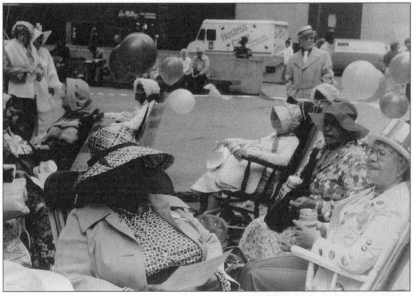

Metro Seniors in Action members raise money with a Rock-a-Thon in the Daley Plaza, Chicago.

21

Organizers need to be strong in three areas. The first is basic people skills. Most organizers are fairly good with people, although they may need to develop their ability to identify and appeal to people's self-interest. The second area is strategy and the ability to develop strong organizing plans. The bulk of this manual is designed to help organizers think and work strategically. The third area is basic administration. To do this, good organizers can't lose track of details. They have to call people back when they say they will. They have to remember to thank people. They have to find papers from six months ago. Basically, organizers have to get control of their work.

To do this, good organizers must develop administrative systems that work for them. This chapter is devoted to administrative systems for organizers. If you have a system that works, keep it; but if not, consider trying some of these suggestions.

Keeping Track of Tasks

One of the most frustrating aspects of an organizer's work is the need to keep track of millions of detailed tasks as well as the "big picture" strategy and plan. The following systems should help.

Campaign Timeline
For most organizing work, we need a general timeline so that we make sure major

Controlling Your Work: Administrative Systems

tasks get done. Small routine items should not go on this, but major projects should. This way, you can assess when you can add other work and when you cannot. This timeline also helps an organizer work with others in terms of what work can be added and what dropped. Computers are ideal for this job.

Calendars

Your calendar is different from the timeline. The timeline includes general categories of things that need to be done within a week such as "get out a mailing" or "do promotional work." The calendar notes particular meetings, or people you are supposed to call back, on a certain day. Any calendar will do, but one with space for expense information is especially useful.

Weekly "To Do" List

The weekly "to do" list is compiled by consulting the above two items. Go through your calendar and mark down the specific meetings or calls that need to be made. Review your campaign timeline and build in the major projects for the week. Place undone tasks from last week on this week's "to do" list. Then, add all the routine meetings and responsibilities that require time. If there is too much, figure out with your supervisor what should be cut or postponed. Behind the "to do" list, keep lists of the various items you want to talk about with people. This way, you're not constantly interrupting people, nor do you forget to tell them things.

Make sure that when you accomplish a task on your "to do" list, that you cross it out to get that feeling of accomplishment. Some organizers have been known to add things that weren't originally on their to-do list, but which they had done, in order to have the satisfaction of crossing them out.

Computer Programs

There are many new programs available for organizing time and projects. If you have a computer on your desk, these programs are wonderful. If not, you'd better stick to manual systems. (See Chapter 22 for more information on how computers can improve your organizing and administrative work.)

Clothesline and Clips

Steve Max has been known to use a clothesline strung across the desk with clothes pins attached. Notes with items to be done are clipped to the clothesline and removed once they are completed. Post-its may be the nineties' equivalent.

Giant Timeline

If you are working on one specific organizing campaign in which you have worked with a group to develop a timeline (generally on large sheets of newsprint), consider hanging the timeline on your wall. It will literally help keep the big picture in front of you!

Sample Timeline

This is a timeline for a community organizer working on a large community event to be held in the first week of February. The organizer is holding organizing/recruitment meetings with block clubs and large building committees in the community.

Week of Jan. 1
> Arrange for agenda planning committee
> Write summary for board meeting
> Call people for turnout/recruitment committee
> Staff meeting — Wednesday
> Set dates for organizing meetings and committees for next four weeks

Week of Jan. 8
> Hold agenda planning committee meeting
> Hold turnout/recruitment meeting
> Draft revised brochure
> Board meeting — Thursday
> Hold two organizing meetings

Week of Jan. 15
> Do follow-up to meetings
> Do prep work for next round of meetings
> Staff meeting — Wednesday
> Hold three organizing meetings

Week of Jan. 22
> Hold next agenda planning committee meeting
> Hold next turnout recruitment meeting
> Send press release for event
> Recruit volunteers to bring refreshments
> Set dates for next week for organizing meetings

Week of Jan. 29
> Hold final turnout/recruitment and agenda meetings
> Make press follow-up calls
> Review presentations with leaders
> Staff meeting — Wednesday
> Prepare materials for board meeting
> Hold two organizing meetings

Week of Feb. 5
> Do last-minute details for event
> *Hold event*
> Draft structure for block captains
> Board meeting — Thursday

Week of Feb. 12
> Do follow-up to event, including thank yous to leaders
> Staff meeting — Wednesday
> Call all senior clubs and congregations in area

Week of Feb. 19
> Attend training workshop — Thursday & Friday
> Meet with at least 3 senior clubs and 5 pastors of congregations
> Send thank-you notes after visits

Week of Feb. 26
> Staff meeting — Wednesday
> Write funding report
> Set up organizing meetings for month of March

Keeping Track of Paper

Most people need some sort of filing system. If you can find paper quickly, then your system is probably working. If you can't, then you need to find a new system or *use* the system you established. The purpose of any filing system is to *retrieve* items, not to file them. There are three types of file systems used by organizers.

Tickler Files

Tickler files are usually monthly, but they can be arranged weekly. They are files for upcoming time periods. Papers are placed in the appropriate file based on when they need to be acted upon or pursued. If you use a good combination of the calendar, timeline and "to do" lists, you probably don't need a tickler file system.

Issue/Project Files

Organizers develop dozens of files on particular issues and projects. It is usually easier to find items if you can divide your files into basic categories. For example, if you have a four-drawer file cabinet, you might put everything related to a specific organizing campaign in one drawer, organizational/office items in another (budgets, personnel policies, and internal memos), organizations in a third drawer, and background on general issues in the last drawer. Within each drawer, most file items should be in alphabetical order. If you hold lots of meetings or training sessions, you might want a series of files in chronological order. By making groupings of files, you can get to the right file drawer quickly.

Daily Files

Some organizers keep a file called a "daily" file. Actually, the file name is confusing. It is not one day's work, but rather, material is placed in it daily for a month or two. A copy of every letter sent and records of phone calls are kept in it in chronological order, with the most recent items going in the front of the file. For important items, a double filing system is used in which one copy is filed in the issue file and the other in the daily file. When the file is in use, it is kept in the front of a stand-up file on the desk so there is easy access to it. When the file becomes full in a month or so, it is moved to a less prominent spot.

A daily file is excellent if you talk with lots of different people or need to access information quickly. If you have forgotten whom you talked with last week about a certain issue, flip back a week through your daily file and find the record of the call or letter.

Managing Your Files

One of the biggest problems with organizers is not their filing system itself, but not using the filing system. Even with the best of systems, one has to file. Identify the time of day in which you are least productive and use it to file. Learn to file at least weekly, if not as you go along.

Before you change jobs, clean your files. Throw most things away, except financial information and the basic summaries and outlines of what happened. In general, people don't use other people's files. They should,

perhaps, but they don't. Most organizations accumulate mounds of unused, unread paper. A new staff member is much more likely to read and use twenty files from a previous staff person than two hundred. If there are two hundred files turned over, the new person probably won't go through any of the files. Of course, you must keep all legal files, such as financial records and board minutes.

If you can't bear to part with documents and you think they might have some historic value, send them to the Historical Society. When the Midwest Academy moved into new office space with less storage room, dozens of boxes of documents were sent to the Historical Society. The Society will sort and store the information.

Keeping Track of People, Calls, and Meetings

Because organizers deal with so many people over the course of a year, they just can't remember everything they would like. Thus, it is important to develop systems to keep track of people, things you say to them, and meetings you have with them. Devise your systems assuming that you will forget everything. The following systems are popular.

Leadership Records

Organizers must keep track of the key leaders and people with whom they work. These records are organized based upon how you organize. If you work by state legislative districts, the records are organized by district. If you work by buildings in a community, then the records are organized by buildings. These records always have the person's name, address and phone numbers. They frequently include such information as the best times to reach the person, interest or skill areas, spouse and children's names, committee participation, date of last conversation, and significant contacts. In the past, organizers kept these records in card files. Currently, most of this information is kept in computer databases.

Call Sheets

If you spend a lot of time on the phone, make a "record of phone call" form to jot down the date you talked, the essential points in the conversation, and the items to which you agreed. You may think you can remember each phone call, but you probably cannot if you make or receive lots of calls. Kim Bobo uses goldenrod-colored call sheets, so that the call forms stand out from other paper. The categories needed on your phone sheets will vary, but should probably include information similar to the call sheet pictured at the end of this chapter.

Please note the follow-up section. This is critical for organizers because it is so easy to forget to do things we promised over the phone. The call sheet should not be filed until each item on the follow-up section is dated, indicating when the follow-up task was completed.

These call sheets allow you to have consistent records of conversations and to avoid little scraps of paper scattered all over the desk with illegible notes hastily jotted down. The call sheets should be kept close to your phone so they're easy to reach.

For new organizers, these call sheets are a good tool for reviewing work and problems. The new staff member and his or her supervisor can discuss the calls using the information on the call sheets. They can also make it easier to delegate follow-up tasks.

Calling Logbook

Some organizers keep a log of all calls in one notebook. The date is put at the top of the page or at the beginning of the day's calls. The person's name, number and a brief summary of the call are listed for each call.

Computerized Records of Calls

Some organizers keep a word-processing file or database on each person talked with regularly. This is appropriate only if you have a computer at your desk. Headphones help as well.

Meeting records

Especially in organizing situations where someone else may have to organize based on your work, it is useful to have good records of meetings with people. A simple form can be developed that can be used for meetings with one person or with a group of people. Make sure to keep the form simple or it will become a burden and no one will complete it.

Postcards/Thank You Notes

It is very important to communicate with people, especially to thank them. Steve Max keeps a pile of postcards in his desk and drops people little thoughts as they come to him such as "You did a good job leading that meeting last week." Kim Bobo keeps a pile of thank you notes in her desk and a list of thank yous to send on a separate column on her "to do" list. Jackie Kendall carries cards with her on trips to write in her spare time. You may also want to keep extra get well and birthday cards.

Keeping Track of Time

This manual does not need to devote much space to time management because there are dozens of excellent books on the subject. A few basic guidelines are in order, however.

Know Your Energy Cycle

Some kinds of work are easier to do during certain parts of the day. For example, some people write best at the beginning of the day. Consequently, they should do all writing at the beginning of the day and save calls until the afternoon.

Batch Work

Even though there is a satisfaction in completing one task before moving on to the next, frequently, doing so is inefficient because it involves lots of moving around. It is silly to make a call, go to the typewriter and type a letter, gather materials, xerox, package and stamp a letter, file the xerox, and then start over again—call, type, gather, xerox, stamp, file. It's much more efficient to place ten calls, then type ten letters, and so forth. If you have good records of your calls and know what follow-up is needed, it is easy to batch work.

Don't Let the Phones Dictate Your Life

As organizers, it is important that we spend a lot of time on the phone. However, you also need time to think, write, and plan without phone interruptions. Don't take calls all the time—unplug your phone if necessary. If you are meeting with someone, don't take phone calls. It is disrespectful to the person and makes the meetings last twice as long. Answering machines are wonderful for our work.

Remember the "Deal with Paper Once" Rule

Even though it is not always possible to deal with paper only once, keeping the rule in your head can save you lots of time. Many items can be immediately tossed, a note scribbled on the top, or a thank you note sent quickly. Avoid reading and rereading documents. If you find yourself constantly shuffling paper from one pile to another, file or toss it.

Advocate for Labor-Saving Equipment and Systems

Most non-profit organizations are short on money, and thus it is hard to budget money for equipment that seems costly in the short run, even though it clearly makes sense in terms of long-term labor savings. Nonetheless, groups must budget for labor-saving devices because their most valuable asset is staff and volunteer time. Labor-saving devices include good photocopy machines that collate, electric staplers, fax machines, folding machines, and postage machines that seal envelopes. Calculate the amount of staff and volunteer time that could be saved by investing in additional equipment and begin advocating within your organization for adequate support to enhance your productivity. . . but don't be a nudge when money is tight.

Keep Track of Your Time

Most organizations have a timesheet that must be completed on a regular basis. Even if you do not fill out timesheets, keep careful records of your time in order to calculate vacation time and to answer questions that might arise about your hours (either too few or too many).

Organizers tend to work many nights and weekends, and thus it is important to keep track of your time to assure that you don't burn yourself out. Working too many hours over an extended period of time is as bad as working too few. The easiest way to keep records on your hours is just to write the total number of hours on your calendar for each day.

If you feel that your time is out of control, but you're not sure what the problems are, keep track of how you spend your time in fifteen-minute blocks over a two-week time period. Put down honestly everything you did during the day. At the end of the two weeks, analyze the timesheets and assess ways to work more efficiently.

If you want a better record of your work to meet funding requirements or for legal reasons, consider developing a timesheet that reflects the various parts of your job. You can complete the regular timesheet for accounting purposes, but keep a more detailed record for your own use.

Asking for Supervision

Although an entire chapter of this manual is devoted to supervision, a few comments are appropriate here as well, particularly for the person needing more supervision. No matter how good your administrative systems are and how efficiently you approach tasks, your work must meet the goals of the organization. The best person to consult about your work meeting the organization's goals is your supervisor.

Too many organizers receive inadequate supervision. They know it, but they do nothing about it. Think of one of your jobs as being to organize your supervisor so that he or she gives you the supervision you need. Don't wait for your supervisor to give you the kind of supervision you want. Go to him or her and explain precisely what you would like done. Don't demand hours, but suggest, for example: "Let's meet once a week for one hour. I will review my updated campaign timeline and my last week's 'to do' sheet and my current 'to do' sheet." Suggesting specific kinds of supervision is helpful to your supervisor. Most supervisors want to be good at their jobs, but they don't know how, especially given all the demands on their time.

Do your best to come to an agreement with your supervisor upon goals and objectives that are realistic and achievable. Use the administrative tools suggested above to monitor the progress of your work.

Surviving for the Long Haul

The struggle for social justice in our country is not a short-term one. Organizers are needed for the long haul. Thus, you must develop work habits and lifestyles that can be maintained over a long period of time. Chapter 25 suggests a number of ways to survive and not "burn out," but one part of surviving for the long haul is to develop strong administrative systems.

These systems can be used as tools to increase the professionalism of your work and provide structures that strengthen your ability to cope with work responsibilities. Poor organizing work habits will limit your productivity and your personal job satisfaction.

By developing better systems for controlling your time and work habits, you will be better equipped to plan realistically. This, in turn, will allow you to use resources (especially time) well, and also to win on issues without killing yourself in the process. Seeing success in your work will sustain you for future work.

Administrative systems are certainly not an end in themselves. Rather, they are a means to work more effectively and efficiently. Organizers need strong administrative systems that will complement their interpersonal skills and their skills in thinking and working strategically.

Record of Call

Name: _____   Phone: _____

Organization: _____   Date: _____

Summary of conversation:

Follow-up needed:

The Midwest Academy, 225 West Ohio, Suite 250, Chicago, Illinois 60610

Record of Meeting

Group/Organization: _____   Date: _____

Location: _____   Number Present: _____.

Contact Person: (Give name, address,
telephone number, and brief description)

Other Key People: (Describe as above)

Major Outcomes of the Meeting:

Follow-up needed:

Attach copies of sign-in sheet, promotional materials, follow-up letters, and other relevant information.

22

E very social change organization should use computers to make its work more effective. Computers are tools that can make our lives more organized and efficient. Although most social change organizations have computers available, they are frequently underutilized.

Below are some of the most common uses of computers in social change groups, followed by the most common computer problems, and some suggestions for what to do.

Common Organizational Uses of Computers

Word Processing

Word processing is the most widely used computer function among social change organizations. Most organizers have mastered a basic word processing program, although many need to learn to use the program's more sophisticated functions, such as mail merge which customizes individual addresses on letters and memos. Combined with an inexpensive ink-jet printer, most word processing will now produce high quality leaflets and brochures avoiding the need for an additional publishing program.

Financial Record-Keeping

Financial record-keeping is usually done by computer. Even small organizations can keep their financial records on computer and can generate checks and bills by computer.

Common Organizational Uses of Computers

Common Problems and How to Solve Them

Help Is Available

Using Computers for Organizing

Membership/Donor Records

Membership/donor records are kept in data management programs. Although many organizers don't know how to use these programs (and should), at least someone in the organization usually knows how to generate membership labels. Fortunately, new organizers won't get the opportunity to type and xerox pressure-sensitive labels!

The door-to-door and phone canvass operations around the country have pioneered in the usage of data management programs for organizing. Both door and phone canvassers receive printed cards of members describing when, where, and why they last contributed to the organization. It is almost inconceivable to be able to run a successful canvass operation without the use of computers.

Desktop Publishing

Desktop publishing is enabling many organizations to produce their own newsletters, flyers, and brochures. Although most desktop publishing programs require a fair amount of time to learn, even small organizations can produce professional-looking materials, faster and cheaper (once you've learned the system) than using outside typesetters.

Research Information

Information is available on every conceivable subject via the "information highway." Social justice organizations use them for a broad range of research. Databanks are useful for discovering patterns or

inconsistencies. They can provide background data for reports issued for media coverage. They can allow easy access to information that used to require hours of library research. Chapter 19 provides extensive detail on how to use computers for tactical investigations.

Electronic Mail

Increasingly, organizers are learning to communicate via electronic mail. It is inexpensive and fast. It is great for editing documents back and forth between staff and is also a real communication asset for organizations that have staff located in various locations. Although only 7 percent of the population were online in 1995, the numbers are expected to increase dramatically in the coming years.

Bulletin Boards

Bulletin boards allow organizations to provide information about issues and upcoming events to their membership and to the broader public. Bulletin boards are a good way to post information that one might have posted on the wall or mailed to people in the past. Most national organizations have bulletin boards, but many state and local organizations are using them as well.

The U.S. Guatemala Labor Education Project, an organization that seeks justice for workers in Guatemala, conducted a campaign to get Starbucks Coffee Company to develop a code of conduct for how it treats its coffee workers who pick coffee that ends up at

Starbucks. Concerned individuals and groups were asked to distribute flyers in front of Starbucks' stores, describing the working conditions for Guatemalan coffee workers. A message was posted on a bulletin board inquiring about Starbucks' stores at college campuses and if students were interested in helping with the campaign. Dozens of students responded and helped play critical roles in leafletting at campus stores.

Newsgroups

There are over 7000 newsgroups that allow people to collect and read articles about a specific topic and reply to them, if desired. This is particularly useful to groups that need to keep up on a particular topic or country. Because people self-select in reading the newsgroups, this computer resource provides a great opportunity to reach out to potential constituencies.

World Wide Web (WWW)

The World Wide Web (WWW) is the fastest, easiest, and most rapidly growing sector of the Internet. Locations on the WWW (called websites) are addressed by long, e-mail-like addresses called URLs (Uniform Resource Locator). The URL connects interested parties to a homepage—a sort of "front door" to your website that serves both to attract attention and inform those dropping by of what your website has to offer. However, without literally having an online "phone book" of URLs, it can be quite difficult to find a specific organization, as you must have the exact address. For example, if you wanted to see Virginia Citizen Action's homepage, you might run across it on the web; but to go there directly, you'd have to type its full URL:

http://www.crosslink.net/~edr/vcitaction.html.

Once there, you will find a homepage which offers a variety of choices. You can join the organization online. You can click "pesticides" and get background information on the pesticide campaign. If you want to send a message to a member of the Virginia congressional delegation, you can point and click and send off an e-mail message immediately. For additional information you will be directed to other organizations.

Your website can serve as a reference library for your organization. Instead of sending long files via e-mail, you can send short e-mail messages to others indicating that there is much longer background information available via your website.

As organizations explore the use of the WWW, they are finding that using the WWW for research has been great; however, setting up a homepage, while exciting and useful, has uncovered several problems:

1. Homepages are only useful if they are updated regularly. Otherwise, people will check in and check out. After a few times they will no longer check in.
2. Just because you have a homepage doesn't mean people know you are there. Include your URL on letterheads, publications, and all other printed materials. There are also several commercial indexes on the web where you can post your URL. Virginia Citizen Action could post its URL under environmental, citizen organizations, energy, public interest, etc.
3. Even those who are able to use e-mail and online services may not be able to reach you because they don't have the necessary hardware to use the WWW.
4. Most existing computers communicate too slowly to truly fulfill the WWW's promise of instant access to global information.

Although the potential use for organizers is unlimited and incredibly exciting, the technology is just in the beginning stages.

Neighborhood Mapping

Computers are wonderful for tracking crime trends in your neighborhood. A number of community organizations are working with coalitions to develop or implement neighborhood-mapping systems that track crime in particular areas and produce fancy maps showing what crimes occur where. These maps help communities organize around "hot spots" and focus their organizing efforts.

Graphics

Many groups now print charts and graphs for testimony and media events. Remember that the same computer programs can also make slides and transparencies for community presentations. The most sophisticated new computers ($2500 & up) will capture pictures from the TV screen and turn them into graphic images.

Fax Boards can automate the distribution of press releases to select local, state, and national lists, and can schedule releases to go out overnight so as not to tie up the phone.

Common Problems and How to Solve Them

Problem One: There Are No Computers

Only the smallest of organizations are without computers.

What to Do

Set up a committee to assess the organization's needs and to make recommendations to the organizational decision makers. In relatively new community organizations, you may want to set up a board committee to look into computers. In other organizations, most likely the staff would do the research and planning. The committee will probably follow a process like this:

Step One:	Identify software needs
Step Two:	Investigate software programs
Step Three:	Identify hardware needs
Step Four:	Comparative shop on costs
Step Five:	Develop a training plan
Step Six:	Make recommendation on purchases and training plans
Step Seven:	Implement incrementally.

Problem Two: There Aren't Enough Computers

This is one of the more common problems for social change organizations. Most staff probably need their own computers on their desk or one easily accessible. Organizing staff who travel out of town a great deal need a laptop.

What to Do

Consider making a five-year plan to purchase more computers. Attempt to estimate how much more efficient staff would be with additional computers. Compare that with staff salary costs. If it clearly makes financial sense to invest in more computers in order to improve staff productivity, begin advocating for additional computer purchases to be included in next year's budget.

There are some foundations and corporations that understand the need for computers and are willing to donate funds for the actual equipment. Consider writing a proposal for the equipment you need. Do not, however, accept donations of antiquated computer equipment or obsolete software. Some donations aren't worth the trouble. It will be extremely time-consuming to teach staff to use ancient equipment and programs. They will only have to learn all over again how to use more up-to-date equipment and programs. However, equipment that is only one "generation" behind can be quite useful.

Problem Three: Computers Are Underutilized

The biggest computer problem in social change organizations is that the majority of staff use the computer only for the most basic word processing functions. For example, the staff of one statewide organization faxes documents back and forth for editing, typing into the computer the changes each time, despite the fact that the office computers are all equipped with e-mail. Many organizers don't know their organization's database well enough to ask for particular sort selections that might help in organizing.

Computers can help staff be more efficient, but only if staff know how to use the computers' capabilities.

What to Do

Work with staff to develop training programs that they think would help them. Some people need hands-on help. Others need a class to attend. Still others need a manual to read. Set computer-literacy goals with staff that can be evaluated along with the achievement of other goals.

At one community organization the staff were literate but not fluent on computers, because there were always too many demands on their time during the workday. The board voted to offer all staff the opportunity to purchase computers for their own use at home with interest-free loans. Many of the staff took advantage of this offer and have since become proficient computer users.

Problem Four: Computers Are Too Old or Can't Communicate

Many social change organizations have a mishmash of computers and software, much of which are dreadfully out of date. This will always be somewhat of a problem, because computer equipment becomes dated soon after it is purchased. But the problem tends to be exacerbated by the fact that few organizations have comprehensive computer plans. Consequently, some members of the staff purchase and select their own software and hardware, resulting in a hodgepodge of equipment that cannot communicate well.

What to Do

Develop an office/organization-wide computer plan that will enable staff to communicate well with one another. Budget for replacing the oldest computers (or the ones that can't communicate with others) first. Then plan on replacing or adding computers each year.

Problem Five: Pirated Software

Too many community organizations try to save money by not purchasing software programs. It is not only illegal to copy software without purchasing it but unwise in the long run. It is extremely helpful to have the proper manuals that come with purchasing software programs. Many programs also have toll-free service numbers that can assist staff in using the software. The software companies also inform registered users of program upgrades when available and of bugs that have been discovered.

What to Do

Budget to replace bootleg copies of programs with legally purchased ones. Staff need the manuals and backup support that come with purchased software.

Problem Six: Tailored Software

In a well-intentioned effort to make the software more accessible to less experienced staff, the most proficient at the computer will make adjustments in software and tailor it to the needs of the organization. This leaves the organization dependent on the tailor. If no one else really understands what was done, the organization becomes hostage to this individual and at a total loss when the person leaves.

What to Do

Avoid custom software unless others in the organization learn the system very well. Most organizations should use common software programs that can be learned by anyone taking a class or reading a manual.

Problem Seven: The Staff Computer Expert

Many organizations have one computer expert who fixes all computer problems and can perform computer functions better than others who are familiar only with basic word processing. "Hackers" can be useful, but their expertise may present additional problems: staff is discouraged from utilizing their computers sufficiently, and hackers often let their other duties slide because they are dealing with the "computer problem."

What to Do

Ask the computer expert to train other staff in how to use the computer more efficiently rather than doing things for people. If the dependency cycle continues, ask the expert to keep track of how his/her time is used, in order to clarify which staff need additional encouragement in computers and to be sure that the expert has time to get the rest of his/her work done.

HELP IS AVAILABLE!!

There are non-profit technology resource centers that work with other non-profit organizations to improve staff and volunteers' abilities to use computers. Check with other organizations, the local United Way agencies, community foundations, or the library to find one nearest you.

Victory—More interesting than a computer.

Nebraska Governor, Ben Nelson (center), signs into law a bill supported by Citizen Action and the Sustainable Energy For Economic Development (SEED) Campaign, boosting renewable energy and repealing the state's previous blanket endorsement of nuclear power.

Left to Right
Duane Hovorka - NE Wildlife Federation, Bob Harris - NE Energy Office, State Senator Don Preister - the bill's author, Gov. Nelson, Walt Bleich - NE Citizen Action Director, Pete Castellano & Dorothy Lamphier - Sen. Preister's staff.

Photo by Christine Earl

23

In reading this chapter, you may note that there are many similarities between being a good supervisor and being a good leader. The similarity is not a coincidence: Being a good supervisor *is* being a good leader. And like leadership development, there are no easy steps for developing supervisors. Supervisors work with people, and people are seldom as predictable as we would like.

What Makes a Good Supervisor

Do Unto Others

One of the best ways to judge whether or not you are a good supervisor is to picture the kind of supervisor you would like to have and then consider whether or not you match that picture. Generally speaking, if we treat people as we would like to be treated, we will be well on the way to being good supervisors.

As with leadership, it's helpful to differentiate between skills and qualities. The qualities all good supervisors need include honesty, self-assurance, enthusiasm/positive attitude, commitment to the organization, and a willingness to work hard. Although sometimes these attitudes can be developed, they are not "learned" in quite the same ways skills are. The qualities reflect who you are as a person.

All supervisors must also develop strong skills in setting priorities, planning work, making wise decisions, delegating responsibility, providing constructive and supportive feedback, using time efficiently, and

What Makes a Good Supervisor

Principles of Supervision

Supervision

training staff. If you supervise organizers, you must learn to teach organizing skills to your staff as well.

In addition, most supervisory jobs require other special skills, such as public speaking or budgeting. As a supervisor you must evaluate your job, assess what skills are essential, and develop your weaker skills. Build to your strengths. Hire people around you who are stronger in your weaker areas, so that you can both learn from them and have a stronger team.

Balance Personnel and Program Supervision

A good supervisor provides both solid personnel and program supervision. Good personnel supervision is helping each person to become the best worker possible, and to develop his or her skills. It is also helping the staff work together as a whole. Good program supervision is building the organization-raising money, winning on issues, and developing the volunteer leadership of the organization.

These two types of supervision must always be balanced. You can't have good programs for long unless you are developing your personnel in ways that build your organization, too-helping them grow, learn new skills, and feel good about themselves. On the other hand, a supervisor's goal is not to win popularity contests by making staff feel good about themselves. While you should always get along with all staff and seek their respect, your main goal is to build the organization. Frequently you may have to ask staff to do jobs they don't like because non-profits never have enough staff.

Balancing program and personnel leadership is difficult.

A common complaint heard in any organization of people is poor "communication." On the face of things, it would appear that more personnel leadership is needed to correct this problem, and it may be that the supervisor needs to meet briefly with each staff member on a weekly basis. On the other hand, such complaints may be an indication that staff do not have a clear enough sense of program direction. If a supervisor ignores the program by failing to push the department or organization forward to win on issues, raise money, and develop leaders, then staff will not feel good about their work and direction, and this will become a personnel problem as well. Most of the time, a staff meeting narrowly focused on the strategy for a specific campaign is worth three meetings on how to communicate better.

Principles of Supervision

Establish Fair Personnel Procedures

Every organization should have a written personnel policy and an evaluation process that everyone knows about. The personnel policy should clarify all benefits including holidays, vacations, disability, sick days, and compensatory time. It should cover basic expectations in terms of dress, hours, and office procedures. It should explain the basic process for evaluations, probations, firing and grievances.

If you find your organization lacks a personnel policy, urge that a process be established to draft one immediately. The board will then need to approve the policy. Sometimes a personnel committee of the board will draft the policy, which must be updated regularly as new policy issues arise.

Make sure people have job descriptions that accurately reflect the work they are expected to do. If people do not have realistic job descriptions, you are in a poor position to question someone's work. (See the bibliography for references on writing personnel policies and job descriptions.)

Avoid Surprises

Regular Feedback. Talk with staff regularly about their strengths and growth areas. Nothing on an evaluation should be a surprise.

Evaluations. It's important for staff to receive regular evaluations. New organizing staff should receive a formal evaluation after their first three to six months. An annual evaluation is fine for everyone else. Do not do evaluations only when there is a problem. This kind of random behavior makes people dread evaluations. Be sure to clarify desired improvement goals in people's evaluations.

Probation. There should be no surprise firings. They are unjust, demoralizing to other staff, and make the organization vulnerable to lawsuits. If someone's work is not adequate, identify the criteria for improvement and support. Put the concerns in writing, give a copy to the person, and put one in the person's personnel file. If the matter is quite serious, place the person on probation. Again, make sure you have a written record. Then if the improvements are not made, the person can be fired.

Job Changes. Major office changes, work reassignments, or job changes should not be a surprise. If changes need to be made, prepare people as much as possible and then talk individually with everyone about the upcoming changes and how each person will be affected.

Make Any Decision Rather than Wallow in Indecision

It is hard to make decisions, particularly when people care deeply about issues. Once

input has been given and the options have been discussed, a decision must be made. Unless new information can be secured that is likely to affect the outcome of a decision, go ahead and make the decision even if it's not perfect. Obviously you want to make good decisions; but, at a certain point, any decision is better than none.

Make the Hard Decisions

Ask yourself if you are making the decision your replacement would make. New directors are sometimes able to view programs and work performances more objectively than those who have been around for a while, and thus it's useful to challenge yourself to view things as your replacement would.

Do not dump the difficult decisions on to others unless it is their area of responsibility and they want to make the decision. Be willing to make the difficult decisions, but do so humbly. Be willing to admit, up front, that it's a hard decision and you could be wrong, but your judgment is such and such, and the job calls for you to make this decision. Later, if you find you were wrong, admit it.

Involve People in Important Decisions and Recommendations that Directly Affect Them

Organizations run better if there is participatory decision-making. This is not consensus decision-making; it is involving people in the important decisions (or important staff recommendations to the board) and the decisions that directly affect them.

The decisions or recommendations to the board that everyone should be involved in (even if they don't want to be) include overall budget priorities, and organizational or departmental goals. In addition, people want to be a part of decisions that directly affect them, such as moving their desks (although they don't care if you move someone else's desk and it doesn't affect them). Sometimes it is difficult to figure out what recommendations or decisions people want to be involved in and what ones they don't. We can't have the luxury of involving everyone in every decision or every recommendation. That would be a waste of time. If you are unclear about what decisions people want to be a part of, ask them.

Some groups prefer consensus decision-making. According to *Building United*

Judgement: A Handbook for Consensus Decision-Making, there are some "prerequisite" group conditions that are important for successfully using consensus decision-making. Members of the group should have a unity of purpose, equal access to power, willingness to change attitudes, and be eager to learn skills. In addition, the group should be independent of external hierarchical structures and have plenty of time for making decisions. Because many social change groups cannot meet these conditions, they are unable to use consensus decision-making.

Clarify and "Routinize" Decision-Making

In general, when you are having a department or organizational meeting, it is helpful to clarify who is making the decision on a subject being discussed. Is the group going to decide? Are you going to decide? It is not good for you to approach a meeting thinking that if the group decides what you want, they make the decision, and if they don't, you make the decision. People will catch on quickly and feel taken advantage of. It's better to be upfront about seeking input and saying that you will make the decision if that's the case.

In addition, because many decisions arise on a regular basis, they should be "routinized." Everyone should understand who makes these regular decisions so that discussions do not need to take place about who makes most decisions. Clear, routine meetings that allow for input on a regular basis are useful for "routinizing" the participatory part of decision-making.

Try to Keep your Ego Out of Supervision. "Pride Goeth Before Destruction and a Haughty Spirit Before a Fall"

Because most people are insecure, their insecurities creep into their relationships with staff. All supervisors should struggle against letting their own egos enter into supervisory relationships. There are a number of things you can do in this respect:

- Encourage recognition of your staff from outside the organization or department. Don't take all the credit yourself.

- If there are any perks (special trips, speaking, training, dinners), share them.

- If you've made a decision that everyone hates (and it's not really an important one), don't stick to it out of pride. Apologize and change.

- Build in feedback opportunities for your staff. Take criticism seriously and try to grow from it. Share personal growth goals with staff and ask for their help.

- Avoid saying "I" when it should be "we," or "my" when it should be "ours."

Approach Supervision in a Positive, Problem-Solving Mode

The tone with which you approach personnel and program problems will be noted by the staff, and they will act accordingly. Don't ignore problems, but always approach them in a problem-solving fashion, as opposed to a griping, complaining way. Every time someone complains about a problem, help them think through how it can be addressed. Also, always assume the best about staff, particularly in terms of their desire to do a good job.

Make Sure You Are Clear

Because things are clear in our own minds, we assume what we say is clear to others. Unfortunately, this is not always the case. If staff do not seem to grasp what you want done, try putting your thoughts on paper. Also, set aside specific times to review programs and priorities so that directions are not given "on the run."

Understand Employees' Self-Interest

You will be a better supervisor if you understand what those you supervise want out of their jobs. Do they want to learn certain skills? Do they want a steady job? Do they want items to add to their resume? As in all organizing, we will work better with people if we understand their self-interest and find ways to meet or enhance it.

Expect High Quality, Not Perfection

Not everything we do needs to be perfect. We don't have time for perfection. When you hear a staff person bragging about being a perfectionist, try to indicate that perfection in all matters is not a goal. Perfectionists tend to drive themselves and others crazy. We need high quality work on the important matters, but on unimportant matters, it is better to just get the work done.

Strive To Be the Best Supervisor, Not Necessarily the Best Friend

One of the hardest things to learn as a supervisor is that sometimes you have to make decisions or suggest things that make people mad at you. You cannot always be a best friend to people. However, if you do a good job, you will be on good terms with almost all the staff you supervise. Face it, as long as you hold the final say over someone's job, you will never be "one of the gang."

Maintain Confidentiality on Personnel Matters

Reprimanding or putting someone on probation must be done with the utmost confidentiality. It is totally improper to discuss confidential personnel matters with other staff who do not need to know by virtue of their jobs. Only those who must know (personnel director and/or your supervisor) should be told. If people complain to you about a person's work and it seems legitimate, thank them and tell them you'll take care of the situation. Do not give details on how you will do it.

Lock personnel files that have evaluations, references, and/or letters requiring work improvements. Staff should not be tempted by unlocked records.

Strive To Be Too Supportive

You won't be. It is almost impossible to be too supportive if your praise is sincere. We all like positive feedback. Don't worry about giving too much. Always take the extra time to write positive comments on people's written work and to personally and publicly thank and praise them.

Offer Specific, Immediate Feedback

If you have a "feeling" about someone, but can't back it up with specific examples, you have a problem. Criticism should be focused on specific work-related problems and not feelings. While attitudes can affect people's work and thus be discussed if necessary, your random feelings about someone are inappropriate unless they are directly work-related.

The majority of people's work deserves immediate and specific feedback, both complimentary and constructive. Tell people what you like and what would strengthen their work performance. Don't ignore small problems if there are specific improvements that could be made. There are several important exceptions, however. When people are under a great deal of strain, such as making an important public presentation or conducting a large conference, they do not need to hear negative comments. Save them until later. Also, if you are mad at someone, you should wait to discuss a problem until you are not upset and can present your concerns calmly.

Develop Replacements Within Your Staff

Give the stronger staff members the opportunity to learn parts of your job that they are interested in and able to do. It is especially important that people develop supervisory skills. Because these are best learned by doing, it is important to allow some of your stronger people to train and supervise staff. This can be a gradual process, if appropriate.

Using the old "information is power" approach to keep things to yourself does not make you a good supervisor. Exercising power in a controlling fashion does not gain you respect or build the organization. The mark of a good supervisor is that when she or he leaves, things go on smoothly. Making yourself irreplaceable is a sign of insecurity, not leadership.

Supervise Directly Only Five or Six People

You can supervise more people, but only for a short period of time. If you have many more people, you will need to develop other supervisors within your staff.

Stress Achievement More Than Efforts

Effort counts for something, but not as much as achievement. We're here to build our organizations and we need to reward (for example, by publicly recognizing achievers or giving them additional responsibilities) people who help build the organization, and not just those who try hard and/or get along with everyone. For-profits say, "We're paying you for results, not for working hard." The same should apply to non-profits.

The key to rewarding achievement over effort is setting clear goals and evaluating them honestly. If the department or a staff member put lots of work into something and it failed miserably, either they did the work wrong, or it shouldn't have been done. Be sympathetic and understanding, but don't praise someone simply for working hard. And don't be a workaholic yourself.

Delegate, Don't Abdicate

You cannot make all the decisions and be directly responsible for everything in your department or agency. Even if you could, you wouldn't want to because it wouldn't develop staff.

How you delegate work responsibilities depends on the maturity and skills of the staff involved. The approach to delegation is a judgment call that you must make. Simply delegating, without taking into account the staff you are delegating to, is not good supervision. It is abdicating responsibility. As in developing a strategy, there can be many ways to approach a problem and many will be equally good. Be willing to have someone approach a problem somewhat differently than you if it still accomplishes the same goal.

Paul Hersey and Ken Blanchard have developed some useful theories on "situational leadership" in supervising staff. They suggest that different levels of task and relationship supervision are needed, based on people's skill and maturity. Below are categories they suggest. (For further details, see *Management of Organizational Behavior: Utilizing Human Resources,* listed in the bibliography.)

For skilled, mature staff: You should indicate the project you want accomplished and the general parameters, such as timeframe and budget. Ask if they have questions. Then tell them that you trust their ability to do the job and urge them to go ahead. Sometimes people may hesitate, but if you really think they are capable, then it is important to encourage them to take the responsibility. If people feel confident about doing the job and you give too much direction, they will be insulted.

For skilled, but not mature staff: If you know staff can do the job, but they tend to be lazy or inefficient with their use of time or money, you need to be much more directive about the parameters: "I want to see your first draft by next Monday."

For mature, but not skilled staff: Spend a fair amount of time outlining the job. Talk through the basic approaches with the staff member. Set a general timeline for the work with which the person feels comfortable. Urge the person to talk with you at any time about problems and approaches.

For immature and unskilled staff: In general, if you have staff who are both immature and unskilled, you should get rid of them, unless your organization's purpose is to train them. However, if you feel you must work with someone who is both immature and unskilled, you will need to spend a lot of time providing both strong instructions and extensive training.

Solicit and Use Ideas

Especially on important matters, it is good to solicit ideas from staff. More heads thinking on difficult program matters can come up with better approaches. Do not approach personnel matters this way because they need to be kept confidential. When an idea is good, use it and give credit to its originator.

Manage Your Time

Time management is critical for all supervisors. There is never enough time to do everything you want or are expected to do. Thus, you need to take control of your time and set priorities. Review the guidelines in Chapter 21 on administrative systems and check out some books from your public library on time management. There are many good books available on this subject. Be sure to:

- *Establish Administrative Systems that Work for You.* These include good file systems and daily "to do" lists.
- *Assure Certain Periods of Uninterrupted Work Time.* This can be done in numerous ways: set aside quiet hours in which no one can interrupt you and you don't take calls; arrive at work before everyone else does, or stay later; work at home one morning a week, or whatever works for you. Every supervisor needs uninterrupted time to think, plan, and write.
- *Keep Lists of Things to Talk about With People.* Don't interrupt your staff regularly

and they won't interrupt you. Keep a running list of things you want to talk about with people so that your meeting time is used efficiently and you remember all the important items people need to know. Staff are not very understanding about supervisors "forgetting" to tell them key pieces of information.

- *If Your Time Seems Out of Control, Keep Track of It in 15-Minute Blocks for Two Weeks.* Then assess your timesheets. Many professionals use the time management tool annually. This is also a good way to get control of what a staff person is doing if you are unclear about it. It's easier to request this of your staff if you have done it too.

- *Drop or Scale Back Work.* We can't do everything. As a supervisor, you have to help people in this area, including yourself.

- *Get Advice from Staff.* When you are feeling most stressed, it is useful to talk through problems with your staff. Get their advice and assistance in dealing with the craziness.

Build To Your Strengths

Each of us has strengths and weaknesses that we bring to our jobs. Identify the program strengths you bring to your particular position. Find helpful ways to offer those strengths to your staff. Strive to become solid in your weaker areas, and to get assistance from others in your department/organization who are stronger in your weaker areas.

Ask your supervisor, or the board president or chair of the personnel committee if you are the executive director, to give you an annual review in order to get objective input on your goals, accomplishments, strengths, and weaknesses. Urge the person conducting the review to get feedback from your staff on specific ways you could improve your supervision.

Plan, Revise, and Evaluate

Every supervisor needs to help staff plan their overall goals and work for the year. Quarterly or so, the plans need to be revised based upon new information and factors. At the end of the year, organizational work goals need to be evaluated. All supervisors need to provide program leadership in these three areas.

Many supervisors find it helpful to set joint organizational goals with their staff and then to make an overall organizational timeline for the year, so that everyone has a good sense of the big picture. Then, the supervisor should work with each individual staff member to make sure that his or her work fits in with the overall goals and that his or her timeline is realistic and includes the known organizational priorities. You may also want all those you supervise to share their plans with one another to build in mutual sharing and support.

Share Vision

As supervisors in social justice organizations, we are also called upon to share a vision of a more just society with those whom we supervise. We can help people see how their work contributes to the broader goals of the organization and the vision of a just world. Supervisors can play a part in transforming people and raising them to new levels of social consciousness. In doing so, both the person and the organization will grow. In addition to following all the above guidelines, we must convey enthusiasm and commitment toward the mission of the organization.

Conclusion

There are no magic means for becoming a good supervisor. It requires perseverance and hard work, especially with diverse personnel and when there are too few resources to accomplish all we hope to achieve. And yet, supervising staff can be enormously rewarding. You help people grow, you strengthen the organization, and you see concrete results. Your influence on staff not only affects their current performance, but can also influence the overall direction of their careers. Nothing can be more rewarding than knowing you strengthened the ranks of committed people working for social justice.

24

Operating a non-profit organization is serious business: there are legal and financial matters to which you must attend. This chapter is not meant to substitute for getting sound legal and financial advice. Rather, it is meant to suggest a number of areas to investigate and about which you may need to seek professional advice. Over the long haul, you will also want your organization to develop the internal capacity to handle routine legal and financial matters.

It is best to approach these complicated matters with a positive frame of mind. Think of your budget as an internal management tool and your financial records as painting pictures of your programs. If your accounting procedures are handled properly, then outside reports to funders, the Internal Revenue Service, and other government agencies should be relatively straightforward.

Basic Standards

The basic standards described below are recommended goals for each non-profit organization. Use them in developing your organization's internal capacity to handle financial and legal matters.

This chapter has been adapted from Sections 1 and 2 of the *Citizen Action Financial Manager Handbook*, written by Stuart Greenberg and Rochelle Davis. Ms. Davis, Jean Allison, and Paul Lawrence also updated sections with recent changes. The information in this chapter was current as of 1990.

Financial and Legal Matters

Personnel

Adequate Staffing. Even the smallest non-profit organizations must ensure that their staff are equipped to handle their legal and financial matters. Sometimes this is done by a volunteer treasurer on the board. This person should be familiar with legal and financial matters. As an organization grows, it should hire a competent financial manager and sufficient staff to handle reporting requirements.

Some new organizations use outside experts or technical assistants to administer financial and legal matters. Make sure that they share the information, so that your staff and leaders will understand what needs to be done in the future.

Independent Accountant. All but the smallest organizations should acquire consulting assistance from a professional accountant. This is usually done in connection with an audit.

Financial Committee. Every organization should have a financial committee. In some organizations, it is a joint board/staff committee; in others, these committees are separate. The committee(s) is responsible for monitoring the organization's financial position and performance, and proposing budgets and revisions to the board of directors.

Personnel Policy. Every organization needs clear and fair written personnel policies, which are distributed to all staff and board members. The personnel policy should cover procedures for hiring, firing, and setting salaries, as well as such matters as benefits, holidays, office hours, dress codes, reimbursements for expenses, and special staff expectations. Many policies also outline affirmative action plans. If adhered to rigorously, the policy will ensure that employees are treated fairly and will protect the organization from being sued.

Whoever interviews candidates for potential positions should be aware of the personnel policies and understand the kinds of questions not to ask. Questions asked in an interview, such as "What does your husband do?" or "How old are you?", could subject the organization to a discrimination suit.

Budgeting and Reporting Capability

Annual Budget. Seek to have a detailed projection of income and expenses approved at least two months prior to the start of the year, first by the finance committee and then by the board of directors. Minor budget revisions can be made at the beginning of the year to account for year-end actual figures. Larger organizations find it helpful to move toward a two-year budget.

Financial Statements. Every month the executive director should review timely and accurate balance sheet and operating statements, with budget variances and year-to-date totals. You will also need financial statements for each board meeting and financial committee meeting, unless they meet more than monthly.

Cash Flow Projections. Seldom does the same amount of money come in every week or every month. Nor are expenses the same weekly or monthly. Thus, an organization needs to develop a cash flow projection in order to anticipate when there will and won't be cash on hand. Each year, you should develop a monthly cash flow projection, which you then adjust based on actual receipts and disbursements. Some organizations need to do weekly cash flow projections as well, particularly in tight financial months.

Annual Audit and Internal Control

Annual Audit. Foundations or government agencies may require your organization to have an audit. Check their guidelines carefully. Even if not required, an annual audit can catch errors and discrepancies, and is highly recommended. If your budget is over $250,000, your board is likely to insist on an annual audit by a certified public accountant within six months of the close of the fiscal year. Because many foundations ask to see copies of your annual audit, an audit will support your fundraising efforts as well as ensure that your financial records are sound.

Internal Control. Every organization should develop a comprehensive system of internal controls to safeguard the organization's assets, ensure the accuracy of accounting records, and control disbursements. A good system of internal controls requires segregation of duties. You know you have internal controls if errors or irregularities would be discovered by employees during the regular course of business, not just by auditors. Your organization should have:

- A good budgeting system that allows you to compare budgeted amounts with actual amounts
- Controls over petty cash
- Reconciliation on a monthly basis
- At least two people counting cash
- Segregated duties.

Government Compliance

Payroll Tax Compliance. Every organization must provide for timely deposits of all federal, state and local taxes, and filing of tax reports. Federal tax deposits must be made within three days after your pay date unless the organization has a very small or very large payroll. State tax deposit regulations vary by state. Consult your accountant for rules that apply. The penalties for late deposits are enormous. Board members and key staff are personally liable for the withheld portion of federal payroll taxes.

Government Reporting Compliance. In addition to paying taxes, non-profit organizations must file the IRS Form 990 Annual Report and comply with state charitable solicitation registration and reporting requirements.

Workers' Compensation. Every organization with employees must pay workers' compensation insurance in a timely fashion. Some states have compulsory programs. Most states require that you purchase insurance through agents.

Disclosure Laws. Affected staff should understand and comply with the relevant items of the disclosure laws. Each office must have the last three years of its organization's IRS Form 990 on site for public inspection. A 501(c)(4) organization must disclose in writing, at the time of solicitation, that contributions to it are not tax-deductible. A 501(c)(3) organization that sponsors a fundraising event must notify contributors if the event contribution is not fully deductible. For example, if an organization sponsors a fundraising dinner and the actual cost of the dinner is $25, but the ticket price is $100, the contributor must be told that only $75 of the $100 ticket "contribution" is actually tax-deductible.

Because contributors to 501(c)(3) organizations are required to maintain official receipts of contributions claimed for tax deductions (and cancelled checks are not adequate), 501(c)(3) organizations need to supply adequate receipts of contributions to contributors. Many states also have extensive disclosure laws. See the State Solicitation section on page 236.

The *Lobbying Disclosure Act of 1995,* which went into effect January 1, 1996, establishes a new set of registration and reporting requirements for federal lobbying activity. One confusing aspect of the requirements is the definition of lobbying, which is significantly broader than the Internal Revenue Service definition of lobbying. Under the *Disclosure Act,* a 501(c)(3) organization must register and file semi-annual reports on its lobbying activities if one of its employees is a lobbyist (makes two lobbying contacts and devotes 20 percent of his or her time in lobbying activities) and the organization incurs, or expects to incur, $20,000 or more on lobbying expenditures in a six-month period (January–June, July–December). The threshold is $5,000 if an outside lobbyist is hired.

The *Lobbying Disclosure Act* definition of lobbying for 501(c)(3) organizations is different from the Internal Revenue Service's (IRS) definition in several ways:

1. The *Lobbying Disclosure Act* only applies to federal lobbying. It does not include lobbying state and local legislative bodies. The IRS is concerned about all efforts to influence legislative bodies.

2. The *Lobbying Disclosure Act* excludes grassroots lobbying activities at the federal level. The Internal Revenue Service is very restrictive concerning grassroots lobbying.

3. The *Lobbying Disclosure Act* applies to most self-defense lobbying, which is generally excluded from the IRS definition.

4. The *Lobbying Disclosure Act* covers efforts to influence decisions of the federal executive branch through contacts with members of Congress or their staffs or with senior executive branch officials. These activities are not considered lobbying under the IRS definition.

The 501(c)(3) organizations that must register are required to file a registration statement followed by semi-annual reports to the Secretary of the Senate and the Clerk of the House.

The *Lobbying Disclosure Act* also bans 501(c)(4) organizations that lobby from receiving any federal funds, including awards, grants, contracts or loans. For more information about the *Lobbying Disclosure Act*, contact Independent Sector, 1828 L Street, NW, Washington, DC 20036, (202) 223-8100.

Compliance with the Internal Revenue Service and Federal Election Commission. In order to maintain an organization's tax status, it must comply with the relevant Internal Revenue Service regulations. Organizations that are involved in federal electoral activity must comply with the Federal Election Commission regulations, and those involved in state electoral activity must comply with election laws.

Equal Employment Opportunity Compliance. Non-profit organizations that seek government contracts may need to comply with equal employment opportunity guidelines or may need to develop an affirmative action plan. Contracts will indicate if special reporting is necessary.

Contingency Planning

Contingency Plan. The financial committee should develop a contingency plan to respond to major over-spending and/or income shortfalls.

Contingency Fund. Work toward establishing a fund to cover budget shortfalls or cash flow difficulties. Fifteen percent of your annual budget is a recommended amount for standard cash-flow variations, although more or less may be needed given your organization's particular circumstances.

Generally Accepted Accounting Principles

The accounting profession has developed a body of accounting principles and procedures to provide uniformity in the preparation of financial statements. Uniformity is necessary so that statements can be properly interpreted and compared. This is especially important for non-profit organizations because of their accountability to the public for effective and prudent use of resources to achieve the organization's purposes.

The Financial Accounting Standards Board (FASB) and the American Institute of Certified Public Accountants (AICPA) prescribe accounting principles and reporting practices to be followed by certified public accountants (CPAs) when conducting audits. Collectively these are called "generally accepted accounting principles" (GAAP).

Adherence to GAAP is required of an organization only in preparation of financial statements that will be subject to an independent audit; departures from GAAP would be noted in a review or compilation. Otherwise, using GAAP is a matter of choice, depending upon their usefulness and practicality. For all but the smallest citizen organizations, however, using the following GAAP is desirable.

Accrual or Cash Basis

What Is It? Financial records can be kept either on an accrual basis or a cash basis. An accrual system of accounting shows the revenues and expenses in the accounting period in which the revenues were earned and expenses were incurred. A cash basis system, in contrast, records revenues when they are received and expenses when they are paid.

Why Choose One Over the Other? An accrual system generally results in a fairer presentation of an organization's financial position and the results of its operations. Cash-basis accounting can result in an inaccurate and distorted picture if it leaves out bills owed, but not paid, or fees earned, but not received. On the other hand, if an organization pays its bills immediately and has limited sources of income, a cash basis system may be simpler and an adequate reflection of your financial picture.

Double-Entry Basis

What Is It? The double-entry basis is a method of accounting in which each financial transaction must be recorded on the books with a debit and a credit entry.

Why Use It? This is a self-balancing system that ensures the mathematical accuracy of the bookkeeping entries.

Functional Basis

What Is It? A functional method of accounting enables you to generate year-end financial reports that separate your organization's expenditures into three broad functional categories: Program Services, General Administrative, and Fundraising. Program services are those activities related directly to the purpose for which your organization was formed. Look at the IRS Form 990 when you set up your accounts in order to make your end-year reporting as simple as possible.

Why Do It? The organization's management, donor constituency, and some government agencies want to know how much of each dollar raised goes to your program and how much goes to support. Some contributors make decisions on the basis of this percentage. Sometimes a high percentage figure in one area is used as a trigger for state audits.

Consistency

What Is It? Consistency means using the same methods of accounting (e.g., valuation of assets, accrual methods) from one period to another. *Why Do It?* Consistency ensures that comparable transactions are treated in a similar manner from year to year. Otherwise, one cannot tell if changes in financial statements reflect actual changes in performance and position, or result from changes in accounting methods.

Materiality

What Is It? An item is "material" if its disclosure or the method of treating it would be likely to "make a difference" in the judgment and conduct of a reasonable person reading the financial statements.

Why Do It? Materiality provides a standard for making judgments about how to treat questionable items.

Full Disclosure

What Is It? Full disclosure requires disclosure in financial statements, and the notes to the statements, of all financial and other information needed for a fair presentation of the organization's position and performance.

Why Do It? Having full disclosure covers items for which there is no specific disclosure rule to ensure that the reader is not misled by the statements. Full disclosure requires footnotes for material items not apparent in the statements so the reader has information to evaluate them properly.

Incorporation

Why Incorporate?

The main reason to incorporate is to limit the liability of people who are part of the organization—officers, directors, members, employees, etc. Incorporation, with rare exception (e.g., liability to the Internal Revenue Service for withheld taxes), means that only the organization's assets are at risk for its obligations, be they routine debts or the result of a lawsuit against the organization, unless those in charge are negligent or corrupt. Board members and directors must recognize that they are morally, legally, and financially responsible for the organization. They cannot escape responsibility by remaining ignorant of their organization's business affairs.

Non-Profit/Not-for-Profit

The things that distinguish a non-profit (not-for-profit) corporation from a business corporation are its purpose and its actual performance. A business organization's purpose is to realize a net profit for its owners. The non-profit's purpose is described in its founding documents (articles of incorporation and bylaws). Its purpose is to meet some socially desirable need of the community and it is prohibited by law from operating for the benefit of individuals or businesses.

"Non-profit" does not mean that the organization has to operate at a loss or that it is prohibited from generating a surplus ("profit"). No one can own or get a cut of the surplus, if there is one, and no part of the assets or income can go to its directors or members, except as payment for services. Any "profit" is retained by the organization to further its tax-exempt purpose.

Articles of Incorporation

The Articles of Incorporation is the governing document filed with the secretary of state at the time of incorporation. The Articles state the organization's name, purposes, powers, limits, classes of membership, incorporators (initial directors), and principal office. This step precedes applying for a federal tax exempt status from the Internal Revenue Service.

Purposes. The purpose clause of the Articles should limit the group's activities to those allowable in the Internal Revenue Code section under which a tax exemption is sought. Get IRS Form 1023 and Publication 557 for the language the Internal Revenue Service requires in your Articles of Incorporation.

Limits. The powers clause states that activities will be limited according to the Code section under which tax exemption (if any) will be sought; no part of the income or assets will be distributed to officers, directors, members, or other individuals; and that if the organization is dissolved, the assets will be disposed of only for tax-exempt purposes.

Bylaws

The bylaws are the internal procedural rules of the organization and generally do not need to be filed with the secretary of state. The bylaws state how directors and officers are chosen and removed, what decisions they can make, how meetings are called, how voting is conducted, number for quorums, and so forth. Read some sample bylaws from other non-profits to assist you in developing yours.

In considering a tax-exemption application (or in an audit), the Internal Revenue Service (IRS) reviews the bylaws to make sure that they are consistent with the Articles and the law, and that they provide the organizational structure to carry out the purposes stated in the Articles.

Membership definitions are important for organizations that want to be able work on federal elections. The Federal Elections Commission regulations require certain membership criteria for an organization to be able to communicate its electoral positions to its members. (See the discussion of the Federal Elections Campaign Act below.)

Bylaws may not seem important until the organization faces political disagreements. At that point, it matters who is on the board, how you get on the board, and how votes are counted. Make sure from the beginning that organizational control is lodged appropriately.

Tax-Exempt Status

A non-profit organization whose purposes are recognized in Section 501 of the Tax Code may be granted tax-exempt status. This allows

---

all surpluses the group may generate to be free from income tax.

The various types of tax-exempt organizations recognized by the Code have advantages and disadvantages. For organizations seeking political clout, a common practice is to set up three related organizations, a charitable organization (C-3), a civic/social welfare organization (C-4), and a political one (political action committee).

Generally it is best to have a lawyer experienced with non-profit organizations review your application before submission. The actual preparation can be done by anyone familiar with the organization. The application is long and tedious, but not difficult. Submit completed IRS Form 1023 or 1024 along with the state Articles of Incorporation, your bylaws, and current and projected financial data.

"C-3" Charitable Organizations—IRS Code Section 501(c)(3)

The key aspects of these organizations include:

- Their purposes may be educational, charitable and/or scientific.
- Contributions to them are tax deductible (i.e., donors can reduce their taxable income by the amount of the contribution).
- Foundations will generally make grants only to 501(c)(3) organizations.
- They are prohibited from participation in elections.
- They are limited in the amount of resources that can be devoted to lobbying to influence legislation, especially "grassroots" lobbying.
- They pay no federal income tax, except on unrelated business income or on excess lobbying expenditures.
- They can receive lower bulk mail rates.
- They can only conduct non-partisan voter registration.

"C-4" Civic/Social Welfare Organizations—IRS Code Section 501(c)(4)

The key aspects of these organizations include:
- Their purpose is the promotion of the public welfare.

- Contributions made to them are *not* tax deductible.
- Foundations generally will not make grants to them.
- They may engage in electoral activity, as long as it is not their primary purpose, but are subject to serious Federal Election Campaign Act (FECA) restrictions (see the section below on compliance with federal election laws).
- They are not limited on lobbying.
- They pay no federal income tax, except on unrelated business income or political activity, although activity is taxed only if the organization has investment income.

Political Action Committee (PAC), Connected

The key aspects of these organizations include:
- They are established as a Separate Segregated Fund (SSF) of the 501(c)(4) organization. (Please note: a non-connected PAC, called an Independent Committee, may be established. It cannot be related to or controlled by an organization, but can solicit funds from any U.S. citizen.)
- They can communicate electoral positions to the general public.
- Funds from a 501(c)(4) organization can be used only to set up, administer, and solicit contributions for the SSF, but cannot be used for electoral campaigns.
- The SSF is prohibited from soliciting contributions from the general public. It may only solicit contributions from the members of the 501(c)(4) organization.

Relationships Among the Three Organizations
- All three organizations must maintain separate finances (e.g., bank accounts) and financial records.
- They may share staff and facilities, but neither the PAC nor the 501(c)(3) organization may subsidize any of the other entities.
- The 501(c)(3) organization may contract with the 501(c)(4) organization to carry out part of its program. This program must be consistent with the 501(c)(3) organization's tax status (e.g., a contract to conduct a non-lobbying organizing program).

- The 501(c)(4) organization can pay for setting up and running the PAC (e.g., rent, phone, staff and solicitation costs). The 501(c)(4) organization's funds cannot be used by the PAC for contributions to candidates or for communication of electoral positions to the general public.

501(c)(4) Organization/PAC Relations

A 501(c)(4) organization may pay for the set-up, administrative, and fundraising ("solicitation") costs of its connected PAC. It may pay these either directly in expenses such as staff salaries, postage, or printing, or by reimbursing the PAC for such expenditures. It may not, however, pay the PAC's expenditures for electoral communications, except for communications with the 501(c)(4) organization's own members. In order to avoid possible problems, it may be best for the 501(c)(4) organization itself to pay for the communications with its members.

In turn, the PAC may purchase the 501(c)(4) organization's services to carry out its electoral activities (including, if desirable, electoral communication with the 501(c)(4) organization's members). Please note, however, that the law as interpreted by the Federal Election Commission (FEC) is quite strict: it permits only two approaches.

First, by making *payment in advance,* the PAC may purchase the services of the 501(c)(4) organization's employees at the commercial value of those services (i.e., what comparable services would cost if purchased from independent political consultants).

Second, the PAC may *directly pay 501(c)(4) organization employees* for the portion of their salaries and benefits that represents the percentage of their time spent working for the PAC—e.g., serving as campaign staff for candidates (PAC contributions) or communicating with the general public without having coordinated with the candidate's campaign (PAC independent expenditures).

The financial implications of these two alternatives can be very different. In the first case, the PAC's money could be used up quickly by applying very high "market" rates. In order to use this approach, however, it is essential that all services be paid for *in advance*.

The second approach permits the PAC's money to go a good deal further, since the PAC will be paying much lower rates for the employee's services. In order to make this approach work, the 501(c)(4) organization cannot simply pay its employee and then bill the PAC. Rather, the 501(c)(4) organization can only pay the employee for that portion of the employee's paycheck that represents "C-4" work. The PAC must cut a *separate check to the employee* for the other portion. The Federal Election Commission (FEC) does permit the 501(c)(4) organization to pay the employee's full benefits and then bill the PAC for its share. The PAC should pay the 501(c)(4) organization quickly.

In the fall of 1995, the FEC issued new regulations allowing certain 501(c)(4) organizations to use general organizational funds to communicate political positions to the general public. Consult an attorney experienced in FEC matters to determine if your organization can take advantage of these regulations.

501(c)(3) Organization/501(c)(4) Organization Relations

The Internal Revenue Service regulations contain only a few specific requirements or prohibitions on the relationships between 501(c)(3) and 501(c)(4) organizations. However, because 501(c)(4) organizations are permitted to conduct unlimited lobbying activities and engage in certain kinds of electoral activities, excessive intimacy between a 501(c)(3) organization and a 501(c)(4) organization is a serious problem. Below are some guidelines to avoid potential difficulties with the Internal Revenue Service:

- Maintain separate letterhead, phone numbers, financial books, and bookkeeping records for both organizations.
- If the two organizations share office space, make sure that a legal agreement exists between the organizations and that the 501(c)(3) organization does not subsidize the 501(c)(4) organization.
- Have as little board and officer overlap as possible between the two organizations.
- Each organization's board must meet and minutes of such meetings must be kept.

- The 501(c)(3) organization should produce its own work and distribute it in its own name. Research and other work cannot just be given to the 501(c)(4) organization.

- The 501(c)(3) organization may hire the 501(c)(4) organization to conduct specific programs that are consistent with the 501(c)(3) organization's purpose and tax status. For example, the 501(c)(3) organization may hire the 501(c)(4) organization to carry out a non-lobbying organizing program, such as organizing health care conferences. The 501(c)(4) organization should charge the 501(c)(3) organization no more than cost for such programs.

- Partisan electoral communication can be made by the 501(c)(4) organization to its members and to the general public if it has established a separate segregated fund; however, communication to 501(c)(3) contributors may not be made unless provisions exist for making them members of the 501(c)(4) organization.

Special care should be taken to avoid hidden subsidies. Some areas to look at include:

- Loans from a 501(c)(3) organization to a 501(c)(4) organization must be at commercial rates with terms similar to those the 501(c)(4) organization could get from a bank.

- You must keep solid back-up materials on the rationale for the allocation of overhead costs. Remember to include capital expenditures.

- Rentals of lists between the organizations must be made at commercially reasonable rates (i.e., you can't just hand over your lists to the other organization unless you do so to every group that requests them).

Finalize agreements between a 501(c)(3) organization and a 501(c)(4) organization with contracts approved by the two boards of directors. The contracts must contain specific requirements for the 501(c)(4) organization to report to the 501(c)(3) organization, or vice versa. It is important that the contracts articulate financial arrangements in great detail and that the boards of directors understand the contracts.

501(c)(3) Organization Grant Applications to Private Foundations

As indicated above, private foundations generally will make grants only to 501(c)(3) organizations. A grant application by a 501(c)(3) organization can state that it is affiliated with a 501(c)(4) organization and that it intends to use some or all of the grant funds to support strictly charitable and educational activities of the 501(c)(4) organization. But the 501(c)(3) organization must make it clear that support for the C-4 is subject to the review and control of the 501(c)(3) organization's board of directors.

Two Kinds of 501(c)(3) Organizations: Private Foundation or Publicly Supported Organization

There are two kinds of 501(c)(3) organizations. The 501(c)(3) organizations that are "private foundations" are subject to many more Internal Revenue Service (IRS) restrictions than "publicly supported" organizations. Consequently, it is important to get the proper determination from the Internal Revenue Service. In order to make this determination, the Internal Revenue Service must review the organization's actual support over at least an eight-month period. If, at the time of application for tax-exempt status, the organization has not been in operation for eight months, the Internal Revenue Service (IRS) will issue a provisional judgment on your private foundation status during an "advance ruling period" of up to five years. After the expiration of the advance ruling period, the IRS will request a report on the organization's sources of support during that time to determine if it qualifies as a publicly supported organization and not a private foundation.

An organization is considered to be publicly supported if it normally receives a substantial portion of its support from the government or from contributions made by the general public. "Substantial" here means one third and "normally" means a four-year average. The "public support fraction" is calculated as follows:

$$\frac{\text{Public Support}}{\text{Total Support}} \times 100 = \text{Public Support Fraction}$$

There are complications in this test because certain revenues are not included in the public support or total support categories. For example, contributions from any one contributor (other than another publicly supported charity or a governmental unit) of greater than 2 percent of total support are excluded from public support, but included in total support. All this, as you can see, can get extremely confusing and you may need assistance from an accountant or lawyer familiar with non-profit organizations.

Nonpartisan Voter Registration by 501(c)(3) Organizations

Nonpartisan voter registration is within the purview of the 501(c)(3) tax-exempt status. "Nonpartisan" means that the voter registration efforts cannot in any way, directly or indirectly, advocate the election or defeat of a candidate for public office.

Lobbying Expenditures

The 501(c)(3) organizations cannot spend a "substantial part" of their budgets on lobbying. According to the Internal Revenue Service, lobbying is defined as attempting to influence legislation before Congress, a state legislature, city council, or other "legislative body," or a referendum, constitutional amendment, or ballot initiative. Efforts to influence executive, judicial, and administrative bodies (e.g., housing authorities, zoning boards, or sewer districts) are not considered lobbying. Nonpartisan analysis, study, or research is not lobbying. Please note that this definition is different from the one used by the *Lobbying Disclosure Act of 1995*. The definition of lobbying may change in the next few years, so be sure to check with an attorney familiar with the definitions.

Because the lobbying regulations are so unspecific (i.e., what does "substantial part" mean?), organizations can choose to be covered by the "lobbying election." The lobbying election provides specific limits on the amounts that can be spent on grassroots and direct lobbying. These levels are based upon an organization's "exempt purpose expenditures," which are specifically defined in the IRS Code of 1986. For organizations with exempt purpose expenditures of less than $500,000, they may spend up to 20 percent of those exempt purpose expenditures on *direct* lobbying communications, as long as not more than 5 percent of the exempt purpose expenditures are spent on *grassroots* lobbying communications. Organizations with larger budgets have lower percentage limitations. (See Schedule A of IRS Form 990.) A communication with a member or employee of a legislative body that reflects a view on specific legislation is direct lobbying. A communication to your organization's members or to the general public urging people to take action on specific legislation is grassroots lobbying (i.e., lobbying expenses to influence public opinion).

If your 501(c)(3) organization does no lobbying or does so little that you are confident that it could not be considered substantial, then you should choose not to report lobbying expenditures. But remember, if you do not choose the lobbying election and you are found to be spending a substantial part of your budget on lobbying (however the Internal Revenue Service may happen to define it), you will lose your IRS 501(c)(3) tax status.

If your 501(c)(3) does some lobbying as part of its regular program, it is best to "elect" to be subject to the expenditure test limits described. You will need to keep track of your direct and grassroots lobbying expenditures and report them on Schedule A of IRS Form 990. It is important to keep track of these expenditures; if the Internal Revenue Service discovers in an audit that you are over the expenditure limits, you will be subject to fines on excessive lobbying. If expenditure limits are violated over a four-year period, you will lose your 501(c)(3) tax status. You need to know if your expenditures are pushing the allowed limits.

Compliance with Federal Election Laws

As a tax-exempt organization, a 501(c)(4) organization is permitted to take electoral positions as long as such activity does not constitute its primary activity. However, as a corporation, the 501(c)(4) organization becomes subject to the same Federal Election Commission restrictions that any other corporation does. For the purposes of the Internal Revenue Service regulations, "primary" has been interpreted in this context to mean 50 percent or more of expenditures. Thus, expenditures of less than 50 percent for electoral activity (i.e., support of candidates for public office) are permitted.

Under the Federal Election Campaign Act (FECA), any corporation is prohibited from using general treasury funds to make contributions or expenditures in connection with federal elections, but this does not include communications to the organization's members. This Act only applies to federal elections. The laws governing state and local elections vary from state to state.

Under FECA, an incorporated 501(c)(4) membership organization can participate in federal elections in the following ways:

Communication with Members

A membership organization may communicate its preference for and opposition to candidates for federal office to its *bona fide* members (you must be careful in defining who is a member). For example, a member can be given a printed flyer indicating the organizations's support of or opposition to a candidate for an elective office. Such a flyer must not be given to anyone who is not a member. If the costs of partisan communications to members exceed $2,000 per election, a report must be filed with Federal Election Commission.

Under the Federal Election Commission (FEC) definition of membership, an organization's members include persons who have: (1) interest and rights in the organization, (2) some right to participate in the governance of the organization, and (3) an obligation to make regular donations of a set amount to the organization.

To comply with FEC requirements, your bylaws should contain a statement on classes of members, voting rights, and dues obligations. Members should be given written notice of membership rights (e.g., a membership card) and of the time and place of the next membership meeting. Membership rolls should be maintained. Members who are not current in their dues must be removed. An organization may not have an indefinite membership period.

Partisan Voter Registration and Get-Out-the-Vote Campaigns

A membership organization may conduct partisan registration and get-out-the vote drives, if they are aimed only at organization members. The organization may set up a phone bank for this purpose and may transport members to the polls, but assistance to members may not be withheld on a partisan basis.

Use of Facilities

An organization's employees and members may make "incidental use" of facilities (phones, typewriters, office space) for individual volunteer activities in connection with a federal election, but they may not use an organization's photocopier. For example, the office phone can be used for calls related to an individual's *volunteer* work on a campaign. "Incidental use" of facilities means that the use is so minimal that it does not interfere with the organization's usual activity (one hour a week or four hours a month is considered incidental). When the use of facilities is incidental, the individual is only required to reimburse the organization for any increased overhead or operating expenses relating to the activity. If incidental use is exceeded, a fee based on the used services' commercial value must be paid.

If someone other than an employee or member uses the organization's facilities for federal campaign purposes, commercially reasonable charges must be paid within a commercially reasonable time.

Any person (including employees and members) who uses equipment or supplies to produce material for a federal campaign must reimburse the organization for the usual and normal charges within a commercially reasonable time.

If the organization customarily makes its meeting rooms available to civic and community groups, it may also offer meeting rooms to political committees. The rooms must be made available on a nonpartisan basis and on the same terms given to other groups.

Use of the organization's vehicles by a campaign must be reimbursed at commercially reasonable rental charges within a commercially reasonable time.

Political Action Committee (PAC)

A Separate Segregated Fund (a political action committee affiliated with a 501(c)(4) organization) can make contributions to federal campaigns and can make expenditures to influence the general public in federal elections. The Separate Segregated Fund can only solicit voluntary contributions from the organization's members and employees. There is a federal PAC contribution limit of $1,000 per candidate per election, or $5,000 if it qualifies as a multi-candidate PAC.

All printed material distributed by the Separate Segregated Fund must contain one or the other of the following authorization notices, depending on whether or not the communication was authorized by the candidate:

> Paid for by (Your Organization's) Political Action Committee and Authorized by the Mary Smith for Senate Committee, or

> Paid for by (Your Organization's) Political Action Committee and Not Authorized by Any Candidate or Campaign.

State Solicitation Registration

Most states have charitable solicitation laws that require a non-profit organization to (1) register with a regulatory agency of the state (usually the attorney general's office) prior to soliciting contributions from the general public and to (2) file annual financial statements with a state agency. Some states may require a connected political action committee (a Separate Segregated Fund) to register.

If a professional fundraiser is used, there may also be annual registration and bonding requirements. The definition of a professional fundraiser varies from state to state. If the 501(c)(4) organization's membership program solicits tax-deductible contributions for the 501(c)(3) organization, both organizations may have to register.

Many states use the IRS Form 990 as their annual financial reporting form, sometimes with additional schedules required. Many states require audited financial statements.

Call your secretary of state's or state attorney general's office to learn your state's requirements and which state office regulates charitable solicitation. You may want to consult a lawyer on these requirements.

Liability Insurance and Bonding

In recent years, many non-profit boards have investigated the cost of board liability insurance. Most small non-profit organizations have found the cost of insurance prohibitive and the likelihood of suits small. Given our litigious society, the need for liability insurance may increase, although the costs are unlikely to decrease.

Some organizations have added "indemnification clauses" to their bylaws. These clauses indicate that as long as a board or staff member is acting in good faith, the organization will be responsible for any suits that might be filed against the individual for his or her work on behalf of the organization.

Many organizations bond their staff people who handle money with what is called an employee "dishonesty" bond. This is not expensive unless lots of people handle money.

Summary of Agency Reporting Requirements

Internal Revenue Service

All of the following Internal Revenue Service publications and forms can be ordered by calling 1-800-424-FORM.

- *Form SS-4* is for requesting a Federal Employer Identification Number (all organizations with staff must have an identification number).
- *Forms 1023 and 1024* are for applying for tax exemption for a 501(c)(3) organization and a 501(c)(4) organization, respectively. Publication 557 describes in detail who can and should apply. Publication 557 also includes a good section on how to write Articles of Incorporation that will suit the Internal Revenue Service.
- *W-4* is the Employee Withholding Allowance Form that needs to be completed

for new employees or when an employee's family circumstances change and the person's exemptions change. If any employee claims more than ten exemptions, the Internal Revenue Service must be notified.

- *I-9* is the Employment Eligibility Verification Form, required by the Immigration Reform Control Act of 1986. It must be completed within three working days by all new employees, and is kept in their personnel files.

- *Form 941* is the Quarterly Return of Withholding Tax Form for reporting on wages paid and federal income and social security taxes withheld. It must be sent within thirty days after each quarter ends (January 31, April 30, July 31, and October 31).

- *Form 940* is the Employer's Annual Federal Unemployment (FUTA) Tax Return. A 501(c)(3) organization does not have to file. A 501(c)(4) organization does. It is due thirty days after the end of the calendar year (i.e., January 30 for the previous year).

- *Form 940-EZ* is a simplified version of Form 940. It may be used by organizations that pay unemployment contributions in only one state in a timely manner and do not have taxable FUTA wages that are exempt from state unemployment tax.

- *Form 990* is the Return of Organization Exempt from Income Tax. This annual financial information form must be filed by most 501(c)(3) and 501(c)(4) organizations that have revenues of $25,000 or more. A 501(c)(3) organization must also file Schedule A of Form 990. It is due on the 15th day of the fourth month after the end of the fiscal year (April 15 for calendar year organizations).

- *Form 990-EZ* is slightly shorter than Form 990 and can be used in place of Form 990 by organizations with gross receipts of less than $100,000 and end-of-year total assets below $500,000.

- *Form 990-T* is needed to report unrelated business income of more than $1,000. Unrelated business income is income that is unrelated to the organization's tax-exempt purposes or that is competitive with taxable enterprises in the marketplace. Unrelated business income includes unrelated advertising in your organization's magazine, rental incomes from other groups (if you own a building), gifts shops, and bingo. Unrelated business income *is not* holding securities or conducting fundraising events. Holding one car wash is not unrelated business income, but setting up a regular car wash business is.

- *Form 2758* is used to extend the filing deadline for your Form 990, Schedule A and Form 990-T for up to two months. This form must be filed on or before the regular due date for Form 990.

- *Form 5768* is used by 501(c)(3) organizations for "electing" to expend a limited, but more than "insubstantial" amount of expenditures on lobbying.

- *W-2 Form* is the Wage and Tax Statement form that is sent to employees about their previous year's wages and tax withholdings. These must be mailed to the employee by January 31 and to the IRS by February 28.

- *W-3 Form* is the Transmittal of Income and Tax Statements Form that summarizes the W-2 forms sent to employees. The W-3 form must be mailed to the Internal Revenue Service by February 28.

- *Form 1099* is used to report consulting payments of $600 or more. It must be sent to the individual consultants by January 31. This form is comparable to the W-2 form for employees.

- *Form 1096* is the Annual Summary and Transmittal of 1099 forms. This is comparable to the W-3 form and must also be mailed to the Internal Revenue Service by February 28.

State Agencies

The following documents and forms may be required by your state. Which office you file which report with varies from state to state.

- Incorporation papers, Articles of Incorporation.
- State payroll tax forms.
- Workers' Compensation, payments and forms.
- Periodic corporate filings may be required; these are unrelated to the above items.

- Out-of-state corporation filings for organizations operating in a state other than the one in which they are incorporated.
- *FEC Form 3X* must also be filed by a political action committee in the state in which the candidate supported by the PAC was seeking office.
- For state and local elections, campaign finance reports by the 501(c)(4) organization or the political action committee.
- State lobby registration and annual report.
- Initial registration for solicitation in the state.
- Annual charitable solicitation financial report, usually similar to IRS Form 990.
- Professional fundraiser annual registration.

Federal Elections Commission

- *FEC Form 1* is for filing the initial registration. This form must be filed within ten days of establishing a Separate Segregated Fund PAC to participate in federal elections.
- *FEC Form 3X,* is for political action committees to report on receipts and disbursements. In election years, pre- and post-election reports, as well as quarterly reports, are due. In non-election years, semi-annual reports are due.

Running Non-Profit Organizations Is Serious Business

It is hard work to manage a non-profit organization efficiently and to stay abreast of all the necessary legal and financial matters. Take your responsibilities seriously. Make sure that adequate board and staff time and training are devoted to the financial and legal matters of the organization. You cannot claim ignorance and expect sympathy from the Internal Revenue Service or government agencies, let alone your membership and financial supporters.

The director of every organization must devote a significant amount of time to managing the operation. All other staff must provide good records and draft reports, or assist in other appropriate ways. Board members must not hesitate to ask questions to assure themselves that the legal and financial matters of the organization are in order.

Caution—this chapter is not meant to substitute for an attorney experienced in non-profit and election law. Opponents of a participatory democracy often seek changes in these regulations to prevent or hamper legitimate organizational activity.

25

Organizers aren't simply "discovered." Nor are they born with special "organizing genes." Rather, they're developed, cared for, and groomed, usually by other organizers.

The movement needs organizers who can hang in there for the long haul. Social change does not occur in a year or two. It is a lifetime occupation requiring lifetime commitments as well as lifetime support systems.

Organizing can be the most rewarding work we do. We are able to express our values through our daily work. We see people grow and develop, and gain a sense of their own power. We also see powerful organizations built, and real improvements made in the quality of life in society. We don't earn the highest salaries, but we are able to feel good about ourselves and our contributions to the world.

Organizing also brings frustrations. As organizers, we need to be clear about some of the issues related to sustaining and developing organizers for the long haul.

Addressing Insecurities

Most people do not find it natural to organize. We are taught to be polite and to accept things as they are. Organizers sometimes need to push the limits of what is socially acceptable in order to bring about change.

We are taught to respect authority. Organizers challenge authority when authority is unresponsive to people's needs.

Addressing Insecurities

Training and Supervision

Achieving Balance in Your Life

Vision

Working for the Long Haul

We are taught to value individualism. Organizers have to bring individuals together for group action and to build organizations.

We are brought up to think of traditional occupations. How do you even explain what an organizer is to your parents?

It is not surprising that organizing puts some very special pressures on organizers. These pressures, along with the many uncertainties of organizing, may increase an organizer's feelings of insecurity. Dealing with these pressures and feelings of insecurity is central to being a good organizer, and a happy one.

There are usually three ways organizers respond to insecurity, and we discuss these below.

Denial of Insecurity and Exerting Control

Some organizers deal with events that are seemingly out of their control by denying that they feel insecure, or by not being aware of what they feel at all. This approach allows an organizer to charge ahead and get a great deal accomplished. By providing clear direction, such an organizer generates staff confidence, and gives real leadership.

But not acknowledging uncertainty can be detrimental to the organization, staff, and organizer alike. The organization, for example, may give too much control to the organizer who has all the answers, and less to people learning leadership. This can forestall giving people a sense of their own power and team building, since people may be directed, but not trained, to direct. This style also holds the possible danger of the organizer becoming authoritarian and turning off people who are less clear, articulate, or self-confident. It rarely allows for building collegial relations as a group, and instead substitutes one-on-one relations that are easier to handle. In short, it undermines the group's solidarity and spirit.

To members or staff, the organizer may convey an impatience, especially with those who are less experienced or do not share this style. People who imply that they have all the answers and seek to maintain control belittle others' contributions. New ideas are rejected on first glance, and more important, people who may want to offer new ideas are intimidated, as are people whose ideas diverge from those of the organizer. Pushing opposition underground may make it go away for a while, but eventually confrontations erupt, challenging existing power and illegitimate authority. Often this style of behavior is combined with difficulty in giving praise or in admitting one's own mistakes. Others feel wary and critical in return.

For the organizer, this insecurity creates enormous pressures, both personal and organizational. Because such an organizer feels a need to provide the lead, he or she may force an inadequate division of labor. Others may not be "trusted" to produce or may withdraw from volunteering. At the personal, or "internal" level, the organizer may become overburdened and stretched too thin. Filled with frustrations and few places to vent them, he or she may burst out with misdirected anger and complaints.

An organizer who is aware of this dynamic

can take action to accommodate it. One way is to establish routine group review meetings, where the basic directions are discussed and problems shared. Someone who sets a positive group tone should chair these sessions. An organizer can also deal with his or her insecurity by finding another organizer to talk with regularly. This other organizer should be someone the person trusts, and with whom anger, frustrations, and fears can be shared. This person can assist the organizer in working out plans for addressing problems and learning how to rely more on others.

Problems related to control questions do not stem solely from insecurity. They can also be the result of overconfidence, a chaotic organizational structure, or staff conflicts. Whatever the cause, organizations must combat one person exerting too much control.

Submission and Falling Victim

A second reaction to the demands and uncertainties of organizing is to become overwhelmed by them and respond to them with a kind of fear. The organizer may engage in very hard work, and may work long hours to compensate for feeling inadequate, but his or her priorities may be off. The person focuses on details, not on the organization's long-term goals.

In one way, this fear of acting may provide a temporary basis for effective organizing because such fear may make the organizer particularly sensitive to the needs of others, responding generously and kindly to problems, but adapting the organizing to meet people's individual needs. This kind of organizer may be very good at building others' confidence because of his or her "people" focus. But like the "controlling" organizer, this person can create problems organization-wide.

When an organizer's insecurity expresses itself by submission and falling victim to problems, he or she avoids making decisions, especially difficult ones such as firing someone, cutting the budget, or deciding on a risky course of action. But the life of a social change organization is bold, direct, and timely action. It is the kiss of death for an organizer to avoid decisions. Postponing decision-making in order to avoid making the "wrong" decision makes the organization stumble for lack of strong

leadership and allows outside forces to control situations.

For other staff, such indecisiveness leads to group insecurity. While relations between people may be fine under such an organizer, there may not be enough going on to challenge the staff to develop new skills and a broader vision. Not achieving enough, members and staff may drift off to more rewarding pursuits. An organization is designed to build collective power, and in doing so, to build individual power. Without models of self confidence, the potential for gaining that power is undermined.

The organizer will simply end up feeling bad or worse as a result of his or her indecisiveness, taking issues personally and looking for personal, rather than organizational, solutions. The organizer's worst fears and anxieties will be heightened, creating a vicious cycle of self-criticism, less effective action, and more self-criticism. The organizer may feel the victim of circumstances and blame others, but fail to correct the problems, real or perceived (e.g., "I did not get good supervision," or "My leaders are not committed enough").

Instead of bemoaning a situation and falling victim to problems, an organizer must look for solutions, and then take responsibility and action. As with the previous problem, one of the best ways for an organizer to address this form of insecurity is to find another organizer who sees the big picture and can help re-instill a sense of vision in both the organizer and the organization.

This organizer also needs a clear plan of action for each campaign and a clear division of labor so work is approached efficiently. Clear processes and deadlines for reaching decisions will help ensure that the organizer does not feel forced to make decisions in isolation.

Recognition and Building Partnership

The healthier way to approach dealing with feelings of insecurity is to acknowledge to yourself what you are feeling and to turn what might otherwise be a weakness into a strength.

Once you are in touch with your own feelings, you know what you know and what you don't. You know that building a team and an organization are primary goals. You understand the importance of developing others' confidence. You recognize that how you are feeling often mirrors the reality others are feeling. You trust people and you place your trust in a group process, thus freeing yourself from having to know every answer. You will have a new power if you use this insight to build a team that works together to solve problems.

Developing means for addressing our insecurities is important in learning to work more effectively with people and in enabling us to build powerful organizations that win real victories. Don't underestimate the importance of self-confidence in developing styles of behavior that are healthy and sustaining for the long term.

Training and Supervision

Making sure you receive adequate training and direction has been discussed in several other places in this manual, but it cannot be overemphasized. Ultimately, people can only develop a positive sense of their own abilities if they succeed in work situations. Who wouldn't wonder about themselves if everything they worked on failed? Amorphous jobs don't help one develop self-confidence. The only way most organizers can be successful is with good training and direction. You can't always control how you are feeling in a situation, but you can control what you do. Make sure that you seek out and insist upon the training and direction you need. "Organize your supervisor" is a good motto. Find ways to get the supervision you need.

Both new and experienced organizers should consciously seek to know organizers working in other fields and groups, by joining formal networks or associating with informal ones. It helps to share war stories, learn from one another, and find out about the best organizing resources and support structures in your area.

Formal training opportunities, such as with the Midwest Academy, should be sought. If you are totally new to organizing, try to work for a few months before coming to a training session so you have more questions to ask. If a group of people in your organization need organizing training, it may be more beneficial and less expensive to arrange for a special on-site training session. Again, there are trainers around who can help you design a training program for your organization.

Achieving Balance in Your Life

Social change doesn't occur overnight. Thus, we can't continually work in a frenzy expecting the revolution to come tomorrow. It won't. If we burn ourselves out today, we won't be around for tomorrow's struggles.

Time

Organizing is never a nine-to-five job. It often is 50 to 60 hours a week, but it shouldn't routinely be nine-to-nine, seven days a week. Yes, there are times when you will have to put in extremely long hours, but there need to be times when you work at a steadier, leisurely pace and regroup. If you find yourself blowing up at people, getting irritated over the least little problem, or not enjoying your work, you need to review your work habits. If you are working excessive hours, you will become less effective in the time you do work and will begin thinking of yourself as a martyr (and everyone will avoid you). The social change movement of the nineties does not need more martyrs. It needs effective, well-balanced organizers who are building power by involving people in winning real victories.

Friends and Families

In the past, too many organizers neglected their friends and families, only to regret it when they lost them. We all need personal support networks, families and close friends, who can share our joys and sorrows. Developing close relationships requires time. We can't ignore friends and families for long periods and then expect them to "be there" when we are ready or need them. Strong relationships provide organizers with a base of support for sustaining themselves for the long haul and assistance in developing self confidence.

Interestingly enough, a large percentage of people who have been organizing for long periods of time, ten years or more, tend to have stable relationships. Although it's certainly not the case that if one has a good relationship, one becomes a good organizer, it does seem to be a factor in helping people survive for the long haul.

If we have children, we have to and want to spend time with them. Having children can help organizers relax and get away from their work-playing basketball with the kids or reading stories. It can also be stressful trying to juggle work schedules and child care responsibilities. Not all non-profits have policies geared toward family life and you may need to consider proposing new policies.

Relaxing

As well as developing close relationships, organizers need to develop means for relaxing. Sometimes relaxing and developing relationships are the same thing. Many organizers find it important to exercise on a regular basis, particularly to release stress. Others find it helpful to practice hobbies, such as playing musical instruments, singing, or reading novels. The key is to find things to do that take your mind off your organizing work.

Vacations are important. If you are always "too busy" to take a vacation, something's wrong. Vacations help sustain you for the long haul and can be even more effective in the short haul. Organizers return from vacations with new ideas and renewed vigor and enthusiasm for their work. Even if you can't afford to "go" somewhere, you can find something totally different to do for several weeks. Take vacations!

If your organization does not have a sabbatical policy, consider trying to implement one. After a staff person has worked at an organization for seven to ten years, it is helpful for them to develop new skills and seek a fresh perspective. Sabbatical policies also encourage staff to stay with the organization for longer periods of time.

Vision

Organizing for the long haul demands a sense of vision, a sense of where we are going. If we only see the short-term tasks before us, it is easy to become frustrated and discouraged. Everyone needs a sense of the vision. If organizers see only their work assignments, it's easy to become discouraged or overwhelmed. We must be constantly reminded of our short-term and our long-term goals. We must review how our work contributes toward meeting both sets of goals. We must remember

our past successes by sharing our past victories with newcomers; otherwise, human nature leads us to forget the past victories and dwell on our failures. Lest we become pollyannaish, we must carefully analyze and learn from both our successes and mistakes, in light of how we are moved toward the greater vision. And finally, we must celebrate changes, successes, and movements in the direction of a more just and fair society. Saul Alinsky used to say you can tell the calibre of an organization by the quality of their celebrations.

Organizers who work for the long haul are not concerned solely about winning just this immediate issue, involving just those specific people, or building just that particular organization. Meeting the three principles of direct action organizing in any given context is important, but not enough. Organizers need a broader sense of vision that allows them to place their work in a more historical context, to understand that they are parts of the broader movement for social justice in our society.

Vision, like self-confidence, isn't achieved by taking a pill or reading a book. A sense of vision grows out of a set of values, experiences, individual reflections, and organizational wisdom and direction. Organizers must see their work in the broader context of efforts to make our society more just and compassionate to all, to involve large numbers of low- and moderate-income people in the process of democracy, and to build accountable democratic institutions that can work for the good of humankind. If we see how our work supports and contributes to the larger vision, our work will seem more meaningful and can be more directed.

The book of Proverbs says, "Where there is no vision, the people perish." Hopefully we won't perish immediately without it, but we will be better equipped to sustain and encourage ourselves and others if we take time to reflect on where we've been and where we are going. If you master all the details of this manual, but have no vision, it will be hard to sustain yourself and continue motivating others.

One concrete suggestion for getting a sense of vision is to attend the Midwest Academy's biennial annual retreat, usually held one weekend in July. Although not a "retreat" in the usual sense of the word (woods, quiet time, peaceful setting), it is an excellent time to reflect on your work, share ideas with others, and get a sense of vision from key leaders of the progressive social change movement. Hundreds of progressive change activists, thinkers, trainers, and commentators meet there each year to share visions and jointly plan directions for the coming year's work. It gives you a chance to see how your work fits into the big picture. You are welcome to attend the Academy's annual retreat (use the tear-off card in the back to request additional information).

The 1990s began as a decade of change. Transformations occurred across Europe, Central America, Southern Africa, and parts of Asia. What happens in the U.S. matters, not just for ourselves and our communities, but for people around the world.

Care for yourself, learn to appreciate your abilities, and develop a vision that provides focus and meaning for your work. We've chosen this work, not as a job, but as a commitment to a better world. We can change history. Justice can govern if we take the future into our own hands.

Fun tactics, and winning on issues, help keep people involved for the long haul.

26

Every era calls for a different intermediate strategy for social change in the context of our long-term vision. Short-term strategy for particular issue campaigns is much easier to conceive, though victory itself may be difficult. Intermediate strategy, that is, how to change the big picture now, is the most difficult level at which to operate and the one to which the Midwest Academy has always urged its students to give particular attention. The first edition of this book was written at the end of the Reagan-Bush era. The economic problems that caused Bush's defeat had already surfaced, Democrats controlled Congress, and although Bill Clinton had not yet emerged as a candidate, the end of the conservative period seemed close at hand. Indeed, Clinton was soon to be given an opportunity to implement his platform of economic and social change, as well as for universal health care.

Today progressives face new challenges. The middle class and the poor are paying the price of the recent 1994 Republican victory in Congress. In this period it has become extraordinarily difficult to successfully address the five main problems on which communities most often call for action—jobs, education, housing, crime, and social services. The cost in human terms was most graphically stated by an organizer in Chicago public housing who told a recent session of the Midwest Academy, "My job is to try to save the 8-year-olds, so we don't lose them the way we lost the 10-year-olds." Whatever the limitations of the Democratic Party (and there are many), whatever the

Toward a Program for the Year 2000

shortcomings of a largely electoral strategy, progressives must prevent Right-wing control of Congress. Halting the assault on the poor is literally a matter of saving lives.

A large part of the middle class has become politically confused and often supports the representatives of the rich. While the Right uses a language that appeals to both the healthy values and unhealthy prejudices of the middle class, it pursues policies that transfer the income of working people to the rich while blaming the poor.

Feeling that they have already done more than their share, taxpayers are digging in and refusing to part with another penny, even for services necessary to the middle class. Unable to raise wages, people try to lower taxes through political activity. Unless something happens to change these circumstances, many justice issues will be lost, and many people lost with them. This concluding chapter focuses on the reasons that budget cutting and budget balancing resonate so strongly with the middle class and why the Right's program of pure meanness is gaining strength, though it goes so directly against the grain of the American character. The chapter also suggests some unconventional ways to change the game and break the standoff.

Toward an Intermediate Strategy

The first of three key parts of an intermediate strategy is to raise to visibility, through issue campaigns and education, the real underlying causes of the problems for which the Right wing offers false and divisive solutions, and to put real solutions on the agenda.

The swing voters, who are often middle class, represent one key to the present political situation. People in this category, typically in the mid-60 percent of the income range, do not identify with the poor and decidedly are not part of the rich. In terms of their own consciousness and political behavior, they tend to act as a separate group although there are many divisions among them. Their susceptibility to Right-wing appeals has swung the political balance to the Republicans and has intimidated many liberal Democrats. But, they are also open to a progressive populist point of view. Only by posing an alternative to the Right's program that makes sense to these voters can the country's drift toward disaster be halted.

The second key to the situation is to expand and deepen organization among the base of people who are traditionally more progressive, low-income people and people of color; liberal churches, community, citizen, and consumer organizations; senior and women's organizations, unions, environmentalists, civil rights organizations and many others. The three problems to be overcome here are an increasing sectoral narrowness as each group pursues its own interests and issues, a growing sense of despair causing people to drop out of organizing activity, and a disgust with the system that results in lower voter participation.

The third key is to realign issues around

broadly cut common themes that address the real causes of social problems and ones that bring swing voters and traditional progressives into alliance with each other, and then to put that alliance to work in the electoral arena.

The '90s: Falling Living Standards for Working People

The real causes of social problems lie not in the national debt or the unbalanced budget but in the fact that the mid-1990s have seen the living standard continue to drop for all social groups except the richest 20 percent of the population. Says *Business Week*:

"U.S. companies continue to drive down costs as if the economy were in a tailspin. Many are tearing up pay systems and job structures, replacing them with new ones that slice wage rates, slash raises, and subcontract work to lower-paying suppliers. These trends have been dragging down the economy throughout the recovery."[1]

A *New York Times* headline, "Male Educated and Falling Behind," told a surprising story: College-educated men in their late 40s and 50s—normally the prime earning years—are suffering a steep decline in wages, finally getting caught in the downward mobility that has hit other sectors of male workers.[2]

Hourly earnings have continued to fall, and family income was lower in 1993 than in 1973. Between 1989 and 1991 poverty rose by 4.2 million people, more than half of whom were white.[3]

For what is really the first time in post-war America, middle-class people feel squeezed and anxious about the life chances of their own children. They attack spending for the poor in an effort to ease their own unfair tax burden. Although poverty and unemployment continue to fall disproportionately upon minorities, the increasing downward mobility of the entire middle class is necessary to understanding recent political trends including the rise of rightist paramilitary groups.

Business Week summed up the problem and pointed toward the solution when it said,

"Experts of all political stripes have worried about the widening inequality between high- and low-skilled workers in recent years. And the gap continues to swell because blue-collar types are

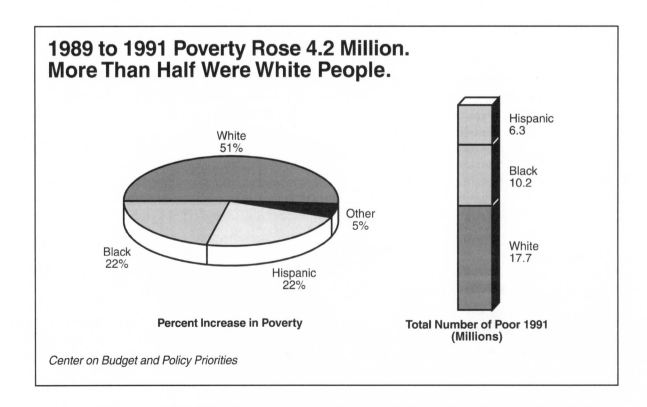

1989 to 1991 Poverty Rose 4.2 Million. More Than Half Were White People.

White 51%

Other 5%

Black 22%

Hispanic 22%

Percent Increase in Poverty

Hispanic 6.3

Black 10.2

White 17.7

Total Number of Poor 1991 (Millions)

Center on Budget and Policy Priorities

slipping faster than professionals. In the past few years, however, all but the most elite employees have landed in the same leaky boat. If they all come to stress their common fate more than their differences, it could spell trouble for corporations and politicians alike."[4]

Missing: 44 Million Decent Jobs

The fundamental economic problem is that 44 million adequate jobs are missing from the economy. This means that roughly one-third of the work force, plus a substantial number of people who could be working, either cannot find a job at all or cannot find a job that pays an amount sufficient to sustain traditional family life.[5] Family breakup, hopelessness, and addiction often follow. Children, seniors, and those in ill health are particularly vulnerable to harm.

The Federal Reserve Board, an agency of the nation's central bankers, has adopted a policy of slowing economic growth. The Fed believes that the unemployment rate should be at least 6 percent in order to prevent inflation. As of June 1995, unemployment was under 5.5 percent, but each increase of one-tenth of 1 percent (0.1) in the unemployment rate equals an additional 240,000 people out of work. On an average family basis, this means nearly half a million lives are disrupted.

The Federal Reserve has raised interest rates 14 times in recent years in order to slow economic growth and prevent the number of unemployed from dropping.[6] The reason for this seemingly counterproductive policy is that low unemployment increases the bargaining power of working people, enabling them to win higher wages. Though many economists disagree, the Fed believes that rising wages contribute to inflation, and inflation undercuts the value of investments in bonds and in fixed interest loans made by banks.

The Fed policy protects wealthy investors and banks at the expense of working people and the unemployed.[7] Perhaps the members of the Federal Reserve Board can't fully realize the very explicit message that their policy sends to millions of poor and working people: Your lives don't matter, and we will never allow you to have decent jobs and earn a real living.

Meanwhile, the Rich Get Richer

At the other end of the spectrum, the concentration of wealth is increasing. Between 1977 and 1992, virtually all the growth in after-tax family income went to the richest 20 percent of the people. Of them, the richest 1 percent increased their income by 136 percent.

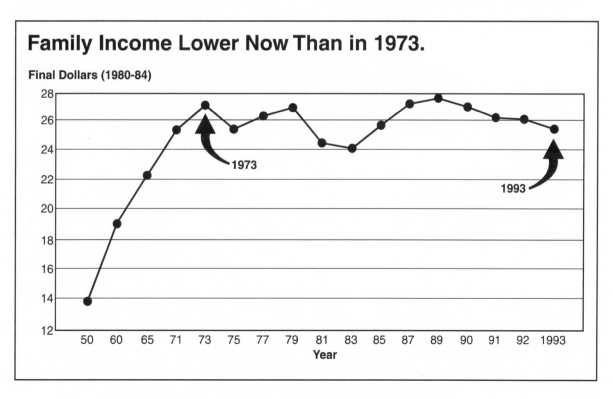

Family Income Lower Now Than in 1973.

Final Dollars (1980-84)

Year

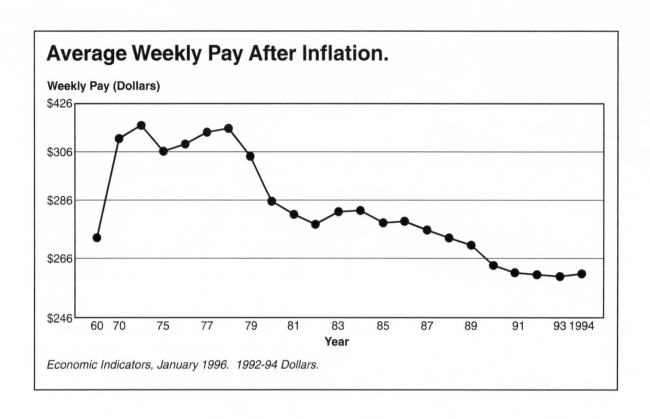

Average Weekly Pay After Inflation.

Weekly Pay (Dollars)

Economic Indicators, January 1996. 1992-94 Dollars.

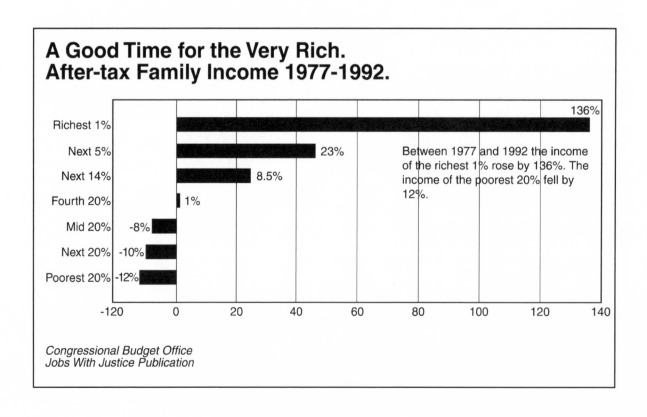

A Good Time for the Very Rich.
After-tax Family Income 1977-1992.

Between 1977 and 1992 the income of the richest 1% rose by 136%. The income of the poorest 20% fell by 12%.

Congressional Budget Office
Jobs With Justice Publication

People in the bottom three-fifths of the population lost income. The tax burden has been increasingly shifted to the middle class, while 1,555 U.S. corporations with assets of more than $250 million each pay *no* federal taxes. Corporate profits for the 900 companies tracked by *Business Week* rose by 40 percent in 1994.[8]

Government in Crisis

The social conditions resulting from the lack of adequate jobs in the economy place a growing burden on the education system, the health care system, the welfare system, and the criminal justice system. The costs of these services rise dramatically while the quality declines, creating the basis for the false Right-wing claim that government costs more and delivers less because of its size. Government at all levels is in financial crisis. To make matters worse, elected representatives are more often openly for sale to the highest bidder. Corruption becomes rampant at every level of government. Officials enact contradictory and senseless policies. One agency sends welfare mothers to work, a second cuts day care, while a third reduces the number of jobs.

With income inequality increasing, and class differences intensifying, racial and ethnic groups battle each other to escape from the jobs gap. Rising chaos, poverty, and crime suggest that the fabric of American life is coming apart in ways that are reminiscent of the rise of European fascism. The tendency to blame basic structural economic problems on minorities, welfare moms, and immigrants is another parallel to the Hitler period, as is the development of paramilitary groups stockpiling weapons under the protection of Right-wing office holders.[9]

The Republican/corporate Right has taken advantage of the situation to launch a wholesale attack on basic democratic institutions. Elections are perverted by corporate campaign contributions. The budget and power of democratically elected government is reduced, while its functions are taken over by corporations and unelected agencies. The ability of government to pass protective regulations is stripped away in the name of promoting economic growth. Corporations, attempting to escape from legal responsibility for defective products, are bankrolling legislation to limit access to the courts and trial by jury. They deceptively call it "Common Sense Legal Reform." Under the pretext of fighting crime, basic civil liberties are curtailed. Unelected international bodies take over essential roles in managing trade. The most politically damaging aspect is the people's loss of confidence in the belief that through government they can improve their lives, which makes control of government seem not worth fighting for.

A major step toward restoring confidence is getting the big money out of politics through public campaign financing which can take away campaign contributions as the principal weapon of corporations and the Right. Progressives should focus on democracy as the issue here, while exposing special interest contributions and conducting public attacks on those who sell their votes. Special interest groups should be forced to resort to illegal bribery instead of legal campaign contributions, the consequences of which might even result in some interesting arrests.

Enter the Voices of Reaction

Enter the voices of reaction—Gingrich, Gramm, Limbaugh, Pat Robertson, and Ralph Reed. Their economic program serves the corporate rich and is combined with a radical religious and political agenda. They mask it as a populist revolt against an elite liberalism that has failed the middle class economically and morally. Behind their populist-sounding message lies a social meanness and repressive fundamentalism that point toward an authoritarian end to democracy. Nonetheless, parts of it resonate with middle-class people who have lost patience with politics as usual.

Whatever hope there is for continuing democracy and achieving social justice in this country depends, in the short run, on regaining jobs and raising incomes. If economic hardship moves the middle class from anxiety to desperation, then reactionary ideas about how society ought to be governed will gain enough credibility to be tested. Perhaps the most telling indictment of the Right wing is that in order to increase its social base among the middle class, it must ensure that neither the government nor the economy can function adequately. Lacking a coherent explanation for the economic problems that does not offend their wealthy contributors, the Right (and some of the Democrats) has shifted the debate from the economy to social and racial issues.

Where Will the Jobs Come From? Two Views

Where will the needed jobs come from? There are basically two different but related approaches to the question, both of which require action. The first view says that enough legislative power can wring a sufficient number of adequate jobs out of the existing industrial system. The second view says that, for both employment and environmental reasons, the way in which industry itself is conceived must change.

In the first view, Americans need to organize for a set of policies that will revitalize the economy, raise incomes, and create more jobs. Realizing any of this program would be a major breakthrough. These policies include:

- Low interest rates that promote corporate borrowing for expansion.
- Public investment in people, infrastructure, and new technology, paid for by getting rid of corporate subsidies and tax breaks for the rich.
- Labor law reform to promote union organization that will increase wages, benefits, occupational safety, and job security.
- Universal health care, pension portability, and higher minimum wages to boost economic security.
- Trade restrictions on countries that don't uphold labor and environmental standards comparable with the United States.
- Tax laws that favor investment in long-term job creation and penalize speculation. Industrial policy.
- The 35-hour work week to employ more people.[10]

These policies make sense, but in addition the economy needs solutions that don't depend on changes in trade or imports. Indeed, every industrial country, including those that export most heavily to America, appear to be having the same problems—not enough good jobs. Nor should solutions require giving business more money to invest in industry because the amounts spent on speculation such as corporate takeovers, as well as on U.S. investment abroad, show that there is no shortage of capital.

The second view suggests that the real problem is the production of more goods than the world can consume, given existing income levels, *resulting in a shortage of profitable opportunities to invest in industrial expansion.* This is one of the keys to understanding the problem.

What is really happening in industry today is something similar to what happened in agriculture fifty years ago. Farmers became so productive that fewer and fewer of them were needed. Farm employment fell rapidly, but food production went up and up. Today, because of rising productivity, fewer people are needed to work up aluminum into engine blocks, while more people are needed to work up beef patties into hamburgers—fewer good jobs, more bad jobs.[11] This is not to say that low wages and falling income are due entirely to the changing job structure. Corporations are, of course, also driving down wages in industries that used to be considered "good" jobs.

Environmental Limits of the Old Technology

Increasing the number of jobs in industry requires increasing people's ability to buy the things that will be produced. But raising all Americans to a middle-class living standard (were it politically possible) comes smack up against the environmental limits of industrial and agricultural pollution, increasing waste in the environment, and using up non-renewable resources. Given the present nature of industrial production, bringing the underdeveloped world up to the American living standard (which must surely be attempted) would cause an environmental crisis. The problem is not merely political and economic, it is environmental as well.

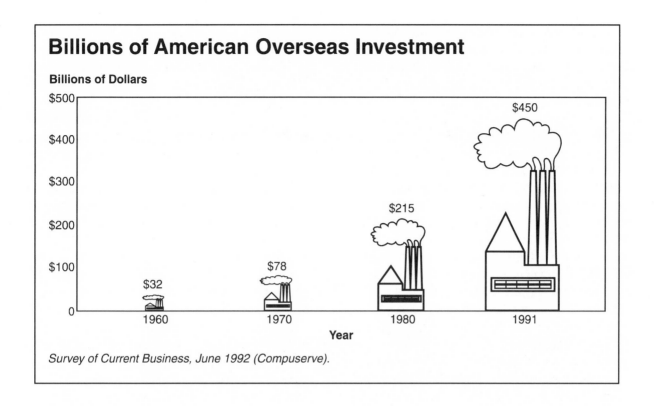

Billions of American Overseas Investment

Billions of Dollars

$32 (1960)
$78 (1970)
$215 (1980)
$450 (1991)

Survey of Current Business, June 1992 (Compuserve).

The Environmental Solution Is Also the Economic Solution

An environmental approach to technology is also the best way to increase jobs, but it means looking at the problem in a whole new way. Fortunately, the environmental solution is also a major step toward the economic solution. It calls for taking advantage of fast-developing methods of producing energy, running industry and agriculture, and providing transportation that are both *renewable* and *sustainable*. Renewable means it doesn't get used up—making electricity from wind power, for example. Sustainable means that it can be done for a long time without polluting anything: sustainable farming uses natural pest control and fertilizers instead of petroleum-based chemicals.

Under the old system, industry is encouraged to use technology to reduce jobs: fewer jobs = higher profits. That the technology might also be environmentally disastrous long went unchallenged, and the Right is now insisting that it continue to be ignored. The priorities should be reversed, and industry and business encouraged to use the least polluting technology, *especially* when it means creating more jobs. Changes in the tax structure can help to accomplish this. Currently, the tax system rewards waste and penalizes labor, whereas it should reward labor and penalize waste.

Consider, for example, the printer who uses a highly volatile, cancer-causing solvent to clean the ink out of presses. There are cheaper, less dangerous solvents, but they work more slowly. The printer is encouraged to use the dangerous solvent to save time. But remove the tax from labor and place it on the solvents as a sales tax in proportion to how dangerous they are, and there is now a tax incentive to use a safer product. The tax rates can be set so there is no overall change in the printer's tax bill after switching to the safer solvent. Neither would there be a change in the amount of taxes collected by government; the tax would simply be shifted away from something good, jobs, and on to something bad, pollution. There is no reason why, for example, Social Security couldn't be paid for with pollution taxes as well as with payroll taxes.

In some cases there are no additional costs for adopting technology that helps the environment and creates jobs. Electricity from wind generators is now as cheap as power from coal plants and cheaper than nuclear power. Servicing wind turbines is labor-intensive and creates more jobs without harm to the environment. In other cases, determining the expense of environmentally sound technology is more complicated and requires first having to figure out the real costs of the old polluting methods.

The Real Costs of Production

To understand the meaning of the real costs of old methods, take for example the small town in Massachusetts where the resident's fee to use the town dump rose from twenty-five dollars a year to eighty dollars. The dump had literally filled up, and the increased fee was used to haul the trash to a distant site. When the rates went up, people thought about all the things they had thrown in that dump over the years—jars, bottles, cans, newspapers, beach chairs, refrigerators, and endless cardboard boxes. Those things could have been recycled, but it was so much cheaper not to. That is, until the day the dump filled up. At the same time, manufacturers were allowed to make all those non-refundable jars, cans, and bottles with no thought as to who would pay the cost of disposing of them. Now that the bill has come due, it is clear that while those companies got a good deal, it is society as a whole that has paid. Had the bottle company been required to pay for disposal in the first place, it would have started recycling long ago, because recycling is much less expensive than trucking empties overland and finding a place to bury them.

If this had happened in only one town it would be insignificant, but dumps are filling up everywhere—garbage dumps, toxic-waste dumps, nuclear-waste dumps. Rivers and lakes are polluted, the air is increasingly contaminated, drinking water quality is degrading, our bodies are permeated with toxic chemicals, and everyone is paying the price. The costs of waste disposal are industrial production expenses that are just as valid as those of raw materials and labor. When these expenses are added into the costs of doing business, then using methods that reduce pollution becomes good economic sense. In the long run, companies save money and lives while creating jobs. This is particularly true in the energy industry. According to Amory Lovins of the Rocky Mountain Institute, energy efficiency, that is, insulating buildings and making products to save electricity, creates two-to-five times as many jobs as would building a new power plant to generate the power wasted, and energy efficiency doesn't pollute.[12]

Rethinking Technology

People the world over are rethinking technology. German ideas include an "intelligent product system." Products like cars, refrigerators, or TVs would always remain the responsibility of the company that made them. When worn out, they would be returned to the company for recycling or rebuilding. Instead of thinking only of the value of the product as it goes out the door, the manufacturer would have to consider its value when it comes back in. This plan favors companies that design components in ways that last the longest and can be most efficiently rearranged, changed, and reused. Designing products so that they can be disassembled and remanufactured will require *more labor*, a cost that can be paid for by using less raw materials, less energy, and by creating less waste.[13]

These are just a few examples of new ways to think about industrial jobs and the environment. In the Midwest, farmers are now talking about the new technology that converts crops to a gas which fuels electric power plants. Between this "bio-power" and wind turbines, electricity can become a major agricultural product. When native perennial grasses are grown for fuel, pesticide and fertilizer use is greatly reduced, as is soil erosion from annual plowing. The result is a stronger rural economy and a safer environment.

What makes this new view of industry more than just another good idea is that the technology actually exists now in many areas, more is being developed all the time, and costs are coming down. New businesses such as wind developers and co-generators are starting to look for political allies. Meanwhile, the "fossil brotherhood" of old industries based on coal and petroleum is using every commercial and regulatory trick to put the newcomers out of business. A behind-the-scenes battle is raging between the forces of the new technology and those companies that are trying to protect their investment in the old and dangerous ways.

The Political Implications

Politically, the Right wing has allied itself with the old industrial forces, which puts it on the side of lower employment and higher pollution. This opens a division between the Right and many people who might otherwise be conservative, but who want both economic growth and environmental protection. A recent campaign in the Midwest highlighted these divisions. Citizen organizations advanced a plan to put money back into the rural economy by developing wind and bio-power. Some conservatives then took a negative position, saying that utility companies shouldn't consider the economic development impact of their operations, and that it was better to keep burning coal than to do something new. This surprised many farmers who thought that those conservatives were on their side. Significantly, other conservatives did see the logic of the organization's argument and supported it. Hope therefore exists that by cutting across traditional ideological lines, coalitions can be built on this issue, uniting all who would be midwives to the new technology, to economic development, and to environmental preservation. On the opposing side stand those who, for ideological or financial reasons, cling to the old methods. They are by no means all Right wingers; many Democrats, and people who would otherwise be liberal, also fail to realize that it is a great advantage to being on the side of what is new and emerging in history.

The Midwest farm belt is a long way from the nation's cities, but the cities have corresponding issues of transportation, weatherization, and utility rates, all of which can save people money and create jobs in ways that are also environmentally sound. These are often seen as being of lower priority in urban areas, but their urgency was highlighted by the heat wave in the summer of 1995 that, in the course of a single weekend, took over 460 lives in Chicago alone. Many of those lives would have been saved had the Chicago building code required houses to be refitted according to modern energy efficiency principles. Although the heat wave was a freak occurrence, houses that become excessively hot in summer also tend to become excessively cold in winter, due to the same construction flaws. In summer, a lack of insulation allows the sun's heat to enter a top-floor apartment through a black tar roof. In winter, it allows the building's heat to leave through the same roof. The death toll indicates not only a life-threatening summer situation but widespread winter discomfort as well. It also shows that homeowners' landlords and housing authorities are wasting large sums on fuel and electricity. Energy efficiency pays for itself, and in rentals, city-sponsored energy efficiency loans could be given with the requirement that the landlord share the savings with tenants.

The restructuring of the utility industry on the state and national level is an area where rural, suburban, and urban cooperation can prevent utilities from giving price cuts to industry and shifting the cost to residential consumers, as is now happening in many states. There are other related utility issues, but the point is that a new political alignment, based on a new conception of technology, is now possible. It can create new alliances, mobilize new social forces, and break some of the old deadlocks.

Strategy Summary

Looking toward the year 2000, the times call for four strategic tasks to be carried out simultaneously by progressive organizations. Every organization ought to decide which it is best equipped to do.

1. Through issue campaigns and media work, it must be made clear to all working people, and to swing voters in particular, that conservatives are their enemies, not their friends. For example, a Michigan organization staged a media event in front of an auto parts plant owned by a conservative Republican member of Congress. The event, held a month before the plant was scheduled to close, announced that on that very day the Congressman was in Canada opening a new plant. The true story behind the nation's economic problems must be told.

2. Organizations of traditionally progressive social groups must be strengthened by promoting issues that bring them together rather than dividing them.

3. Progressives must take the initiatives on job creation both through traditional measures and by linking jobs with preservation and restoration of the environment. They must combat falling wages through union organization and legislation.

4. Move all of these efforts into the electoral arena and elect people loyal to progressive organizations.

This is a strategy, not a program. It therefore isn't intended to deal with such problems as housing, education, discrimination or taxes. It is a way of changing the balance of political power so that problems that seem impossible today can at last be successfully addressed. It isn't the only strategy, nor necessarily the best, but it is a start toward a plan to change the big picture.

This is not the first time in history that progress and democracy have been severely threatened, while ignorance, reaction, and bigotry seem to have the upper hand, but Americans have always risen to the occasion and returned to the most basic principles: that government is instituted to ensure the rights of life, liberty, and the pursuit of happiness, deriving its just powers from the consent of the governed. As long as our efforts are based on this wisdom, justice will prevail.

July 25, 1995

The Midwest Academy is grateful to Ira Arlook, Executive Director of Citizen Action, for portions of this section.

NOTES

1. *Business Week*, 17 July 1995, p. 55. Noting that wages are falling while productivity is rising, this publication says: "The unnerving question that is starting to creep into the discussion: Are we simply in the midst of an especially long and wrenching transition, or have structural changes in the economy severed the link between productivity improvements and income growth?"

2. *The New York Times*, 11 Feb. 1994.

3. By contrast, worker productivity has risen. Citing figures through 1994, Larry Mishel of the Economic Policy Institute states, "We are also witnessing a celebration of America's renewed competitiveness. As manufacturing productivity soars, U.S. exports regain their world prominence, manufacturing products close the quality gap with foreign goods, and unit labor costs continuously fall relative to those of other advanced countries. Alan Greenspan, Chair of the Federal Reserve Board, has pronounced that we have never been as 'competitive.' Ditto for the National Association of Manufacturers."

4. *Business Week*, ibid, p. 62. The magazine warns, "...it would be folly for the U.S. to give back gains in economic efficiency that have been achieved through the past decade of corporate restructuring. But sooner or later, the promise of this economic strategy has to be fulfilled for the majority of Americans. The sight of bulging corporate coffers co-existing with continuous stagnation in America's living standards could become politically untenable."

5.

Unemployed (actively seeking work)	8,700,000
Unemployed (discouraged)	6,300,000
Part-time (looking for full-time jobs)	6,300,000
Poverty Wage Earners	23,047,000
Total	44,347,000
Civilian Work Force	128,040,000
Shortfall	34%

Corporate Power and the American Dream, The Labor Institute, Rutgers Education Center, 853 Broadway, Room 2014, New York, NY 10003, (212) 674-3322, 7 March 1995.

6. "The Fed is betting that the economy will grow below its potential, creating slack labor markets. That will chill any wage pressures.... So far, though, the economy has eluded the weedy creep of rising prices. The slow pace of wages has clearly helped to plow under inflation. And for the rest of 1995, Greenspan and his cohorts stand ready with spades and pesticides, intent on keeping inflation out of the well-manicured economic outlook." *Business Week*, 8 May 1995, p. 30.

"'The danger zone for unemployment seems...to be lower than I had been previously estimating,' says Robert Gordon, a professor of economics at Northwestern University. As recently as last month, Professor Gordon advised the Federal Reserve Board that the inflation trigger was an unemployment rate that was probably 6%, and possibly as high as 6.5%. 'I'm the guy who sold 6% to the world,' he says. Today, he thinks that the trigger point is probably closer to 5.5%—and could be as low as 5%." *The Wall Street Journal*, 24 Jan. 1995.

7. According to Wallace C. Peterson, author of *The Silent Depression*, the richest 1% of the population own 78% of all bonds. The next richest 9% of the population own another 14% of all bonds. The remaining 90% of the people own the rest of the bonds.

8. *Business Week*, 6 March 1995. "Whoo-ee. It was one for the record books," p. 98.

9. Anyone recalling the police shootings and arrests that eliminated the lightly armed Black Panther Party of the 1960s can only wonder how it is that the so-called militias have been able to stockpile heavy weapons without it coming to the attention of local authorities.

10. This list is largely drawn from an article by Jeff Faux of the Economy Policy Institute in the Spring 1995 issue of *American Prospect* magazine.

11. Union organization and raising the minimum wage address this problem, but there

are at least theoretical limits. Applying labor to aluminum to make an engine block adds a great deal of value to the metal, value in which labor can share if it has the power. Much less value is added to beef by making hamburgers out of it, so there is less to share. Higher wages can come out of profits, but if profits fall below the average level, owners will pull their capital out and go elsewhere.

12. Lovins includes the area of passive solar energy in his calculations. Passive solar means siting and constructing buildings to maximize the sun's energy for heating, cooling, and light, thereby reducing the need for other fuels and electricity.

13. *The Ecology of Commerce.* Paul Hawkins.

PART IV
Resources

Selected

Print Materials

Introduction to Organizing

Saul D. Alinsky, *Rules for Radicals and Reveille for Radicals*, Random House, Inc. (New York, NY), 1989, $7.96 and $9.00, respectively. The classic organizing handbooks.

Robert N. Bellah et al., *Habits of the Heart: Individualism and Commitment in American Life*, Perennial Library (New York, NY), 1986, $13.00. A thought-provoking text read by many organizers. Helpful distinctions between private and public life.

Harry C. Boyte, *Commonwealth: A Return to Citizen Action*, The Free Press (New York, NY), 1989, $27.95. Boyte's newest book presents a good introduction to and understanding of the organizing work of the Industrial Areas Foundation.

Gary Delgado, *Beyond the Politics of Place: New Directions in Community Organizing in the 1990s*, Applied Research Center (440 Grand Ave, Suite 401, Oakland, CA 94610), $10. A short, insightful book.

Gary Delgado, *Organizing in the Movement: The Roots and Growth of ACORN*, Temple University Press (Philadelphia, PA), 1987, $18.95. Helpful insights into ACORN's organizing approach.

Print Materials

Training Videos

Sources for Progressive Audio-Visuals

Citizen Action State Organizations

Songs

Resources

Ed Hedemann, ed., *War Resisters League Organizer's Manual*, War Resisters League (339 Lafayette St, New York, NY 10012), 1981, $10.00. An excellent compilation of organizing tips. The chapters on designing leaflets and organizing street fairs are particularly good supplements to this manual.

Sanford D. Horwitt, *Let Them Call Me Rebel: Saul Alinsky—His Life and Legacy*, Random House, Inc. (New York, NY), 1992, $15.00. A new detailed history (548 pages) of Alinsky's life.

Si Kahn, *Organizing: A Guide for Grassroots Leaders*, National Association of Social Workers, (750 First St, NE, Suite 700, Washington DC 20002-4241), 1991, $29.95. A solid introduction to organizing.

John P. Kretzmann & John L. McKnight, *Building Communities From the Inside Out*, Center for Urban Affairs & Policy Research, Northwestern University (2040 Sheridan Rd., Evanston, IL 60208, (708) 491-3518, Fax (708) 491-9916).

Lee Staples, *Roots to Power: A Manual for Grassroots Organizing*, Praeger Press (New York, NY), 1984, $19.95. Based on ACORN's model of neighborhood organizing. Instructive for all organizers. Good chapters on the role of organizers, group maintenance, and dealing with details.

Building Coalitions

Cherie R. Brown, *The Art of Coalition Building: A Guide for Community Leaders*, The American Jewish Committee (165 East 56th St, New York, NY 10022, (212) 751-4000), 1990, $3.50. An excellent guide to coalition-building, including a good chapter on building unity across ethnic, religious, and class divisions.

The National Assembly of National Voluntary Health and Social Welfare Organizations, *The Community Collaboration Manual*. National Collaboration for Youth (1319 F St, NW, Suite 601, Washington DC 20004, (202) 347-2080), 1993. A helpful manual for social service agencies interested in working together to solve common problems.

Recruiting Volunteers

Bruce Ballenger and Adela Awner, *Membership Recruiting Manual*, Northern Rockies Action Group (9 Placer St, Helena, MT 59601), 1981, $10.00. One of the best manuals on the subject.

Michael J. Brown, *How to Recruit People to Your Organization*. Order from Michael J. Brown (54-C Trowbridge St, Cambridge, MA 02138 (617) 492-3071), $10.00 plus $2.00 shipping. A 40-page practical manual to help organizations increase and strengthen the commitment of members.

The Sperry and Hutchinson Company, *Membership Handbook: A Guide for Membership Chairmen*, The Sperry and Hutchinson Company (330 Madison Ave, New York, NY 10017), 1981, free. Not necessarily the "best," but the price is right.

Marlene Wilson, *The Effective Management of Volunteer Programs*, Volunteer Management Associates (320 South Cedar Brook Rd, Boulder, CO 80302), 1976, $8.95 plus $2.25 shipping and handling.

Marlene Wilson, *How to Mobilize Church Volunteers*, Augsburg Publishing House (Minneapolis, MN), 1983, $11.99. A superb book on mobilizing volunteers. Most of the author's suggestions are applicable in non-church settings.

Planning and Facilitating Meetings

Brian Auvine et al., *A Manual for Group Facilitators*, The Center for Conflict Resolution (Madison, WI), 1985. One of the best books available on group facilitating. Available for $11.70 (includes shipping) from New Society Publishers, P.O. Box 582,Santa Cruz, CA 95061-0582, (800) 333-9093).

Michel Avery et al., *Building United Judgment: A Handbook for Consensus Decision Making*, The Center for Conflict Resolution, (Madison, WI), 1985. A great manual on making consensus decision making function smoothly. Available for $11.70 (includes shipping) from New Society Publishers (see address above).

Robert C. Biagi, *Working Together: A Manual for Helping Groups Work More Effectively*, Center for Organizational and Community Development (225 Furcolo Hall, University of Massachusetts, Amherst, MA 01003), 1978, $7.00 plus $2.25 postage and handling. A helpful resource for community organizations and citizen boards.

Bradford Leland Powers, *Making Meetings Work: A Guide for Leaders and Group Members*, Pfeiffer & Co., (8517 Production Ave, San Diego, CA 92121), 1976, $19.95.

Helpful guidebook for internal organizational meetings.

George M. Prince, *The Practice of Creativity: A Manual for Dynamic Group Problem Solving*, 1972. Out of print, but worth looking for in libraries. Excellent suggestions on extracting creativity from a group.

Media Relations

American Federation of Teachers, *An Activist's Guide to the Media*. American Federation of Teachers (555 New Jersey Avenue, NW, Washington, DC 20001-2079), $.25 per copy or $20.00 per 100. A simple, incredibly information-packed brochure on using the media.

Virginia Bortin, *Publicity for Volunteers: A Handbook*, Walker and Company (New York, NY), 1981, $10.95. One of the best books available on the mechanics of using the media. Lots of helpful examples.

Robbie Gordon, *We Interrupt This Program: A Citizen's Guide to Using the Media for Social Change*, Center for Organizational and Community Development (225 Furcolo Hall, University of Massachusetts, Amherst, MA 01003), 1978, $10.00 plus $2.25 postage and handling.

Jason Salzman, *Let the World Know: Make Your Cause News*, Rocky Mountain Media Watch (P.O. Box 18858, Denver, CO 80218), 1995.

Designing and Leading a Workshop

Duane Dale, Dave Magnani, and Robin Miller, *Beyond Experts: A Guide for Trainers*, Center for Organizational and Community Development (225 Furcolo Hall, University of Massachusetts, Amherst, MA 01003), 1979, $7.00 plus $2.25 postage and handling.

Bill Draves, *How to Teach Adults*, The Learning Resources Network (1554 Hayes Drive, Manhattan, Ks 66502 or call (800) 678-LERN), 1984, $7.95, plus $1.00 shipping. An excellent introduction to working with adults.

Organizing for Social Change

Bill Draves, *How to Teach Adults in One Hour*, The Learning Resources Network (1554 Hayes Dr., Manhattan, KS 66502, (800) 678-LERN), $7.95, plus $1.00 shipping. Another useful book, especially if you conduct short sessions.

Jane Vella, *Learning to Listen, Learning to Teach*, Jossey-Bass Publishers (San Francisco, CA), 1994, $26.95. A great introduction to adult education techniques.

Jane Vella, *Learning to Teach: Training of Trainers*, Save the Children Federation (P.O. Box 950, Westport, CT 06881), 1989. Designed initially for training trainers to work overseas, but the techniques are appropriate anywhere.

Working with Community Boards

Board Member Manual, Aspen Publishers, Inc. (7201 McKinney Circle, Frederick, MD 21701, (800) 368-8437), $29.00. This manual helps boards improve long-range planning, run more effective committees, strengthen fundraising, and develop a sense of a team. Aspen Publishers have produced two training videos for board members. The videos can only be purchased if one purchases a manual.

John Paul Dalsimer, *Understanding Nonprofit Financial Statements: A Primer for Board Members*, National Center for Nonprofit Boards (2000 L Street, NW, Suite 510-P, Washington, DC 20036-4907, (202) 452-6262), $10.00. Especially helpful for board members who are new to financial responsibilities or to nonprofit accounting. Critical for community board members of large social service agencies or community development corporations.

Joan Flanagan, *The Successful Volunteer Organization: Getting Started and Getting Results in Nonprofit, Charities, Grassroots and Community Groups*, Contemporary Books, Inc. (Dept. N, 180 N. Michigan Ave, Chicago, IL 60601), 1984, $14.95. One of the best overviews of what it takes to develop a successful volunteer organization.

Nancy Haycock, *Dare to Chair: The Art of Chairing a Nonprofit Board of Directors*,

Community Resource Exchange (17 Murray St, New York, NY 10007), $10.00 plus $3.00 postage and handling.

National Center for Nonprofit Boards, *The Nonprofit Board's Guide to Finding, Hiring, and Evaluating the Chief Executive*, National Center for Nonprofit Boards (2000 L Street, NW, Suite 510-P, Washington, DC 20036-4907, (202) 452-6262), $28.00. This package of three publications helps boards recruit, support, and evaluate the chief executive.

Charles N. Waldo, *A Working Guide for Directors of Not-for-Profit Organizations*, Greenwood Press, Inc. (Westport, CT), 1986, $45.00. A very helpful guide. Geared toward larger non-profits, but useful for others.

Working with Religious Groups

Mary Baudouin, *Building Legislative Networks: Acting for Justice in the Public Arena: A Workbook*, U.S. Catholic Conference, Department of Social Development and World Peace (3211 Fourth St, NE, Washington, DC 20017, (202) 541-3195). A practical handbook for developing legislative networks within Catholic dioceses. Appropriate for other denominations as well.

Kenneth B. Bedell, ed., *Yearbook of American and Canadian Churches*, Abingdon Press (Nashville, TN), published annually. An invaluable resource book for groups working with state and national religious bodies. Lists the bishops and comparable religious leaders and their addresses for each denomination.

Kimberley A. Bobo, *Lives Matter: A Handbook for Christian Organizing*, 1986. Out of print. A solid organizing guidebook for helping churches get more involved in social justice issues. Lots of how-to examples. Can also be ordered from the Midwest Academy or Bread for the World.

Harry Fagan, *Empowerment: Skills for Parish Social Action*, Paulist Press (Ramsey, NJ), 1979, $4.95. A handbook for assessing and planning parish social action.

Samuel Freeman, *Upon This Rock: The Miracles of a Black Church*, Harper Collins (New York, NY), 1993. An inspirational book about organizing with churches.

C. Eric Lincoln, *Race, Religion, and the Continuing American Dilemma*, Hill and Wang (New York, NY), 1984, $9.95. The leading scholar on Black religion, Lincoln examines the ways race and religion have shaped American society. Helpful background for organizing with the religious community.

Gregory F. Pierce, *Activism That Makes Sense: Congregations and Community Organization*, ACTA Publishers (4848 North Clark St, Chicago, IL 60640, (800) 397-2282), 1984, $8.95. A good introduction to church-based community organizing.

Rabbi David Saperstein, ed., *Social Action Manual: A Practical Guide for Organizing & Programming Social Action in the Synagogue*, Union of American Hebrew Congregations, (New York, NY), 1983. One of the best resources for organizing in synagogues.

Ronald J. Sider, *Cry Justice: The Bible Speaks on Hunger and Poverty*, 1980. Out of print. A handy collection of Biblical passages on poverty and justice. Great for someone looking for passages for a sermon or worship theme.

Tactical Investigations

Larry Makinson, *Follow the Money Handbook*, Center for Responsive Politics (Washington, DC), 1994, $10.00. Explains how to trace campaign contributions from special interest groups. Includes a helpful discussion of reforming campaign financing.

Shel Trapp, *Who, Me a Researcher? Yes You!* National Training and Information Center, (810 N. Milwaukee Avenue, Chicago, IL 60622, (312) 243-3035), $3.50. A great guide to grassroots community research.

U.S. General Services Administration and U.S. Department of Justice, *Your Right to Federal Records: Questions and Answers on the Freedom of Information Act and the Privacy Act*

(Washington, DC), 1981, $.50. This 32-page booklet describes how to use the Freedom of Information Act and Privacy Act to obtain records from the federal government. Order from R. Woods, Consumer Information Center-N, P.O. Box 100, Pueblo, CO 81002. Make $.50 check payable to Superintendent of Documents.

Grassroots Fundraising

Joan Flanagan, *The Grass Roots Fundraising Book*, Contemporary Books, Inc. (Dept. N, 180 N. Michigan Ave, Chicago, IL 60601), 1992, $14.95. The most popular how-to book on grassroots fundraising.

Joan Flanagan, *Successful Fundraising: A Complete Handbook for Volunteers and Professionals*, Contemporary Books (180 N. Michigan Ave, Chicago, IL 60601), 1991, $17.95. Practical guides on raising big money.

The Grantsmanship Center, *The Whole Nonprofit Catalog*, (P.O. Box 6210, Los Angeles, CA 90014). Available free because it advertises the Center's training courses. Frequently includes excellent fundraising articles.

Kim Klein, *Fundraising for Social Change*, Chardon Press (P.O. Box 11607, Berkeley, CA 94712), 1985, $25.00 plus $2.00 for postage and handling. Excellent chapters on direct mail, telephone solicitation, and major donor campaigns.

Mellon Bank, *Discover Total Resources: A Guide for Nonprofits*, Community Affairs Division, Mellon Bank Corporation (One Mellon Bank Center, Pittsburgh, PA 15258), free. Available in quantity to groups.

ResourceWomen, *Religious Funding Resource Guide*. Available from ResourceWomen (4529 South Dakota Avenue, NE, Washington, DC 20017, (202) 832-8071), $75.00. The guide includes application forms and grant lists from 37 religious funding sources.

Joanie Shoemaker, ed., *Redwood Cultural Work, Community Music, and Friends, Note by*

Note: A Guide to Concert Production, Redwood Cultural Work (P.O. Box 10408, Oakland, CA 94608), 1989, $15.95 plus $2.00 shipping and handling. The definitive book on planning and producing a benefit concert.

Women's Action for Nuclear Disarmament (WAND), *Mother's Day for Peace Action Kit*, WAND (691 Massachusetts Ave, Arlington, MA 02174). Call the WAND headquarters at (617) 643-6740 for price information. Includes a good section on sponsoring fundraising activities around Mother's Day.

Administrative Systems

Patricia Wyzbinski, "An Overview of Office Management Procedures," The Grantsmanship Center (1031 South Grand Ave, Los Angeles, CA 90015), 1981. This short article covers office procedural manuals, supply systems, petty cash fund, filing, forms, and telephones.

Supervision

David Bradbury, *Managing for Excellence: The Guide to Developing High Performance in Contemporary Organizations*, Weley Publishing (New York, NY), 1984, $12.95. A recent "classic" management book.

Andre Delbecq et al., *Group Techniques for Program Planning: A Guide to Nominal Group and Delphi Processes*, Scott Forsman (Glenview, IL), 1986, $18.00. A helpful book, despite the confusing title.

Mortimer R. Feinberg, *Effective Psychology for Managers*, Prentice Hall, Inc. (Englewood Cliffs, NJ), 1986. The chapter on "How to Manage Creative People" makes the entire book worth buying.

Paul Hersey and Kenneth H. Blanchard, *Management of Organizational Behavior: Utilizing Human Resources*, Prentice Hall, Inc. (Englewood Cliffs, NJ), 1988, $28.00. Explains in great detail the need to use different kinds of management and supervisory styles with different personnel.

Ann Jardin and Margaret Hening, *The Managerial Woman*, Anchor Press, (Garden City, NJ), 1983. Out of print. A little heavy on climbing the corporate ladder, but good chapters on typical women's supervisory problems.

Jerry Jensen, "Employee Evaluation: It's a Dirty Job, but Somebody's Got to Do It," The Grantsmanship Center (1031 South Grand Ave, Los Angeles, CA 90015), 1980. A short, helpful article. Includes a sample personnel evaluation form.

Jerry Jensen, "Letting Go: The Difficult Art of Firing," The Grantsmanship Center (1031 South Grand Ave, Los Angeles, CA 90015), 1981. A short, helpful article on firing employees.

Jerry Jensen, "Personnel Policies for Your Agency: Get Them in Writing Now," The Grantsmanship Center (1031 South Grand Ave, Los Angeles, CA 90015), 1979. Eleven pages covering the basics on personnel policies. Includes a sample policy for you to review.

Gracie Lyons, *Constructive Criticism: A Handbook*, Wingbow Press (Berkeley, CA), 1988, $6.95. A good book, especially for those who find it hard to give criticism well.

Financial and Legal Matters

American Institute of Certified Public Accountants, *Audit and Accounting Guide for Certain Non-Profit Organizations*, American Institute of Certified Public Accountants (1211 Avenue of the Americas, New York, NY 10036-8775, (212) 575-6590), $14.50 plus $3.95 for shipping. A standard guide for most organizations.

Perkins Coie, *Non-profit Organizations, Public Policy, and the Political Process: A Guide to the Internal Revenue Code and Federal Election Campaign Act*, Citizens Vote, Inc. (New York, NY), Dec, 1987. An excellent book explaining the details on relationships between 501(c)(3) organizations, 501(c)(4) organizations, and separate segregated funds (PACS).

CPAs for the Public Interest, *The Audit Process: A Guide for Not-for-Profit Organizations*, CPAs for the Public Interest (222 South Riverside Plaza, Chicago, IL 60606), 1989, $8.50. Covers the audit process from the initial decision of whether or not to have an audit to planning for next year's audit.

John P. Dalsimer, CPA, *Self-Help Accounting for the Volunteer Treasurer*, Energize Books (Philadelphia, PA), 1989, $18.75. Simple guide for volunteer treasurers.

Maryland Bar Association, ed., *Starting a Nonprofit Organization: A Practical Guide to Organizing, Incorporating and Obtaining Tax Exempt Status*, The Community Law Center and The Maryland Association of Nonprofit Organizations (190 W. Ostend St, Baltimore, MD 21230, (800) 273-6367), 1992. A very practical short book.

Arnold J. Olenick and Philip R. Olenick, *Making the Non-profit Organization Work: A Financial, Legal and Tax Guide for Administrators*, Institute for Business Planning, Inc., Prentice Hall (Englewood Cliffs, NJ), 1983, $49.95. One of the most helpful resources for a non-profit. Unfortunately, it is out of print so check your local library.

Michael B. Trister, *An Advocate's Guide to Lobbying & Political Activity for Nonprofits*, Children's Defense Fund (Washington, DC), 1991. A great simple booklet on what you can and cannot do.

United Way of America, *Accounting and Financial Reporting: A Guide for United Ways and Not-for-Profit Human-Service Organizations*, United Way of America (701 North Fairfax St, Alexandria, VA 22310-2045), Mar 1989. An excellent introduction to accounting for non-profits. Order for $35.00 plus $2.50 for shipping and handling.

Organizing for the Long Haul

Mary Field Belenky, ed., *Women's Ways of Knowing: The Development of Self, Voice, and Mind*, Basic Books (New York, NY), 1988,

$15.00. A helpful book on the question of women's self-confidence and self-esteem.

William L. Bryan, "Preventing Burnout in the Public Interest Community," The Grantsmanship Center (1031 So. Grand Ave, Los Angeles, CA 90015), 1980. An excellent article addressing the causes and solutions to burnout.

Carol Gilligan, *In a Different Voice: Psychological Theory and Women's Development*, Harvard University Press (Cambridge, MA), 1993, $9.95. A challenging book that explores men, women, and the differences between them.

Jean B. Miller, *Toward a New Psychology of Women*, Beacon Press (Boston, MA), 1986, $10.95. An affirmative psychological analysis of women's approach to the world.

Brian O'Connell, *Finding Values that Work: The Search for Fulfillment*, Walker and Company (New York, NY), 1978. A down-to-earth approach to working and sustaining one's self in non-profit work.

Anne Wilson Schaef and Diane Fassel, *The Addictive Organization: Why We Overwork, Cover Up, Pick up the Pieces, Please the Boss, and Perpetuate Sick Organizations*, Harper and Row (San Francisco, CA), 1990, $11.00. Helps explain addictive behavior in non-profit organizations and steps that can be taken toward recovery. Fascinating reading for people who work in non-profit organizations.

Recent U.S. Social Change History

Taylor Branch, *Parting the Waters: America in the King Years 1954-1963*, A Touchstone Book (New York, NY), 1989, $16.00. A superb history, filled with the details about which organizers are interested.

Sara Evans, *Personal Politics: The Roots of Women's Liberation in the Civil Rights Movement and the New Left*, Random House (New York, NY), 1980, $8.76. An insightful look at women's development during their involvement in the civil rights movement and the new left.

Philip S. Foner, *Organized Labor and the Black Worker: 1619-1981*, International Publishers (New York, NY), 1982, $6.50. One of the best books available on the relationship between organized labor and African-Americans.

David M. Gordon, Richard Edwards, and Michael Reich, *Segmented Work, Divided Workers: The Historical Transformation of Labor in the United States*, 1982. Out of print. A tightly written historical analysis of changes in the labor process and the structure of the labor market.

James Miller, *Democracy Is in the Streets: From Port Huron to the Siege of Chicago*, Harvard University Press (Cambridge, MA), 1994, $14.95. An intellectual history of the student movement of the 1960s, from which came the leadership of many of today's organizations.

Juan Williams, *Eyes on the Prize: America's Civil Rights Years 1954-1965*, (New York, NY), 1988, $11.95. Another excellent history on the civil rights period.

Howard Zinn, *People's History of the U.S. and People's History of the U.S. - 20th Century*, Harper and Row (New York, NY), 1980, $13.00. Zinn adds more on people's struggles for justice than is normally covered in traditional history books.

Introduction to Economics

John Kenneth Galbraith and Nicole Salinger, *Almost Everyone's Guide to Economics*, 1978. Out of print. A clear, easy to read introduction to (liberal) economics.

Bob Hulteen and Jim Wallis, eds., *Who Is My Neighbor? Economics as if Values Matter*, Sojourners (2401 15th St, NW, Washington, DC 20009, (800) 714-7474), 1994. A study guide that helps groups understand the current economic choices, dream of a different world, and make plans to change the world. Good for religious or peace/social action groups.

Robert Lekachman and Borin Van Loon, *Capitalism for Beginners*, Pantheon Books (New York, NY), 1981. Highly readable, and illustrated with cartoons. Explains the theories of Adam Smith, Karl Marx, John Maynard Keynes, Milton Friedman, and others.

Walter Russell Mead, *Mortal Splendor: The American Empire in Transition*, Houghton Mifflin Company (Boston, MA), 1988, $9.70. A provocative look at America's decline since the mid-1960s. Views the United States in an international perspective.

Michael Wolff, *Where We Stand*, Bantam Books, (New York, NY), 1992. A chart book of international comparisons. Good for article and speech writing when you want to know if the United States is behind or ahead of the rest of the world.

Jobs and the Industrial Base

Barry Bluestone and Irving Bluestone, *Negotiating the Future: A Labor Perspective on American Business*, Basic Books (New York, NY), 1994, $13.00. A good overview of the relationship between U.S. business and jobs in the economy.

Sam Bowles, David Gordon, and Thomas Weisskopf, *After the Economic Wastelands: A Democratic Economics for the Year 2000*, ME Sharpe Publishers (Armenk, NY), 1991, $19.95. A democratic alternative to economic decline.

Harry Braverman, *Labor and Monopoly Capitalism: The Degradation of Work in the Twentieth Century*, Monthly Review Press (New York, NY), 1976. $10.00. A classic theoretical work on the changing nature of work and the people who do it. Draws parallels between the de-skilling of craft work, and the present day de-skilling of white collar and managerial work.

Michael Brower, *Cool Energy*, MIT Press (Cambridge, MA), 1992. Authoritative discussion of renewable energy sources. Includes policy recommendations and further reading sources.

Stephen Cohen and John Zysman, *Manufacturing Matters: The Myth of Post-Industrial Economy*, Basic Books (New York, NY), 1988, $9.95. Explores the myth of post-industrial economy and why a service economy can't succeed without an industrial base.

David Dembo and Ward Morehouse, *The Underbelly of the U.S. Economy*, Council on International and Public Affairs (777 United Nations Plaza, New York, NY 10017, (212) 972-9878), 1994. A most useful pamphlet on jobs, wages, and the pauperization of work. Calculates the true jobless rate, as distinct from the government unemployment rate. Updates previous editions of this valuable research.

Public Health Institute and The Labor Institute, *Jobs and the Environment*, Public Health Institute and The Labor Institute (853 Broadway, #2014, New York, NY 10003), 1994. A workbook and discussion guide mainly for union members but good for more general audiences. Covers why environmentalism is not the cause of unemployment, basic and workplace environmental issues.

Power and Politics

Donald Barlett and James Steele, *America - What Went Wrong*, Andrews and McMeel, (Kansas City, MO), 1992. A description of how corporate influence in Washington has undermined the middle class.

Harry Boyte, Heather Booth, and Steve Max, *Citizen Action and the New American Populism*, Temple University Press (Philadelphia, PA), 1986, $24.95. Analyzes the rise of grassroots progressive activity during the 1980s and its right-wing counterpart.

Citizens for Tax Justice, *The Hidden Entitlements*, Citizens for Tax Justice (1311 L St, Washington, DC, (202) 626-3780). Explains how the tax structure is set up to give billions to the rich and corporations.

G. William Domhoff, *The Power Elite & the State: How Policy Is Made in America*, Arline de Gruyter, 1990, $24.95. Domhoff leads the way on documenting the relationship between monied interests and politics.

William Greider, *Who Will Tell the People: The Betrayal of the American Democracy*, Touchstone Books, 1993, $13.00. A widely read book on how politicians are "bought."

Michael Harrington, *Socialism Past and Future*, NAL-Dutton (New York, NY), 1990, $9.95. Harrington's last book analyzes past strengths and weaknesses of the socialist movement and argues that socialism is still the best hope for a decent livable world.

The Labor Institute, *Corporate Power and the American Dream*, The Labor Institute (853 Broadway, #2014, New York, NY 10003), 1995. A workbook and discussion guide on jobs, earnings, mergers, corporate welfare, and the economy. Written with a trade union audience in mind, but good for wider groups.

Ferdinand Lundberg, *The Rich & Super-Rich*, Carol Publishing Group, $14.95. An excellent introduction into the U.S. elite.

Kevin P. Phillips, *Boiling Point: Republicans, Democrats, and the Decline of Middle-Class Prosperity*, Harper Collins (New York, NY), 1994, $13.95. Describes the concentration of wealth and its political consequences, and why the middle class is squeezed.

Sam Pizzigati, *The Maximum Wage: A Common-Sense Prescription for Revitalizing America—by Taxing the Very Rich*, The Apex Press (New York, NY), 1992. A popular book on one approach to addressing the increasing concentration of wealth.

Martin Schram, *Speaking Freely: Former Members of Congress Talk About Money in Politics*, Center for Responsive Politics (Washington, DC), 1995, $12.00. Details the impact of money on decisions in Congress.

Malcolm X, *Autobiography of Malcolm X*, Ballantine Books (New York, New York), 1981, $5.99. A classic book that every American should read.

Publications and Mailing Lists

Center on Budget and Policy Priorities, 236 Massachusetts Ave, NE, Suite 305, Washington, DC 20002. Frequent mailings dealing with current government spending and tax and social welfare issues affecting low-income people. Basic subscription package is $25.00 per year. Comprehensive package of all reports for $40.00 per year.

Dollars & Sense, 1 Summer St, Somerville, MA 02143. An easy to read progressive monthly magazine on economics. $19.50 per year.

Economic Notes, 80 E. 11th St, New York, NY 10003. Monthly publication on labor-related economic issues. $30.00 per year.

Economy Policy Institute, 1730 Rhode Island Ave, NW, Suite 812, Washington, DC 20036. (202) 775-8810. Frequent studies and policy papers on work, jobs, trade, and many other issues. Individually priced. Write or call for publications list.

Focus, Joint Center for Political Studies, 1301 Pennsylvania Ave, NW, Suite 400, Washington, DC 20004, (202) 626-3500. A Black think tank on issues that affect African-Americans. Subscription: $15.00 per year. Call for additional publications list.

Grassroots Fundraising Journal, P.O. Box 11607, Berkeley, CA 94701. Best current nuts-and-bolts advice on grassroots fundraising for community organizations. $20 per year.

In These Times, ITT Customer Service, 1921 Debs Ave, Mt. Morris, IL 61054. A weekly newspaper of use to all organizers. Covers the news not covered in regular daily papers. Regular subscription: $34.95 per year. Student and senior rate: $24.95 per year.

International Labour Reports (ILR), P.O. Box 5036, Berkeley, CA 94705. Published out of England, ILR is the most comprehensive monthly news magazine on international labor issues from a progressive perspective. U.S. subscription: $28.00 per year.

Labor Notes, 7435 Michigan Ave, Detroit, MI 48217, (313) 842-6262. A monthly publication providing short stories on progressive labor struggles around the U.S. Subscription: $10.00 per year.

Labor Research Review, Midwest Center for Labor Research, 3411 W. Diversey Ave, Suite 14, Chicago, IL 60647. Over one hundred pages of articles on unions and the economy. Two issues published a year. Subscription: $13.00 per year.

New Perspectives Quarterly, Center for Study of Democratic Institutions, 11500 West Olympic Blvd., Suite 302, Los Angeles, CA 90064. Examines social and political thought on economics, religion, politics, and culture. Subscription: $30.00 per year.

The Nonprofit Times, P.O. Box 408, Hopewell, NJ 08525-0408. Monthly tabloid full of good ideas and case studies. Available free to full-time, non-profit directors.

Too Much: A Quarterly Commentary on Capping Excessive Income and Wealth, Share the Wealth, 37 Temple Place, Third Floor, Boston, MA 02111 (617) 423-2148. Subscription: $15.00 per year, or included as part of a $25 membership to Share the Wealth. Make checks payable to CIPA.

Unity, P.O. Box 29293, Oakland, CA 94604. A bilingual publication that describes organizing campaigns not usually covered in other publications. Subscription: $12.00 per year.

World Policy Journal, World Policy Institute, 777 United Nations Plaza, New York, NY 10017. Contains essays, interviews, and forum debates on current U.S. foreign policy, international economics, regional political developments, and domestic U.S. policy. Individuals: $20.00 per year. Institutions: $26.00 per year.

Training Videos

Board Member Manual and Videos, Aspen Publishers, Inc., 7201 McKinney Circle,

Frederick, MD 21701, (800) 368-8437, Manual: $29.00, Videos: $49.00 each. Aspen Publishers have produced two training videos for board members. The videos can only be purchased if one purchases a manual.

Chicago Video Project, *Accessing the Media*, ACTA Publications, 4848 N. Clark Street, Chicago, IL 60640, (800) 397-2282, $24.95. This 12-minute video trains groups how to focus their messages, pitch stories or events, follow up on press releases, and deal with journalists on-site to maximize the coverage received.

Chicago Video Project, *Running Good Meetings*, ACTA Publications, 4848 N. Clark Street, Chicago, IL 60640, (800) 397-2282, $24.95. Excellent 12-minute video that teaches the basic elements of running good meetings, including pre-planning, starting and ending on time, developing and sticking to agendas, and dealing with naysayers.

Joan Flanagan, *Fund-Raising Training Videotapes*. These three tapes sell for $30.00 each or $75.00 for all three. The topics are: Getting Started, Asking for Money, and Fund Raising Forever. Checks should be made payable to the Bowman Gray School of Medicine and sent to Partners in Caregiving Program, The Bowman Gray School of Medicine, Medical Center Blvd., Winston-Salem, NC 27157-1087, or call (910) 716-4941.

Kim Klein, *Grassroots Fundraising Videotapes*, Funding Exchange, 666 Broadway, #500, New York, NY 10012, $500. A six-video series. The six topics are: Planning for Fundraising, Role of the Board, Raising Money by Mail, Asking for Money and Prospect Identification, Major Gift Solicitation, and Special Events.

Sources for Progressive Audio-Visuals

Below are sources for films and videos on organizing and progressive issues. Call or write for their free catalogues.

Cambridge Documentary Films, Inc.
P.O. Box 385
Cambridge, MA 02138
(617) 354-3677

Canadian Labour Congress
2841 Riverside Drive
Ottawa, Ontario, Canada KIV 8X7
(613) 521-3400
The Educational Film and Video Project
5332 College Avenue, Suite 101
Oakland, CA 94618
(510) 655-9050

Films Incorporated
5547 N. Ravenswood Avenue
Chicago, IL 60640
(312) 878-2600
Outside of Illinois: (800) 323-4222

First Run/Icarus
153 Waverly Place, Sixth Floor
New York, NY 10014
(212) 243-0600

Fusion Video
100 Fusion Way
Country Club Hill, IL 60478
(708) 799-2350 or (800) 338-7710

Kartemquin Films
1901 W. Wellington
Chicago, IL 60657
(312) 472-4366

Media Network of New York
39 W. 14th Street, Suite 403
New York, NY 10011
(212) 929-2663

Media Process Group
770 N. Halsted, Suite 507
Chicago, IL 60622
(312) 850-1300

New Day Films
220 Hollywood Avenue
Hohokus, NJ 07423
(201) 652-6590

Third World Newsreel
Media Distribution Project
335 W. 38th Street, Fifth Floor
New York, NY 10018
(212) 947-9277

Videos for a Changing World
Turning Tide Productions
P.O. Box 864
Wendell, MA 01379
(800) 557-6414

In addition, audio-visual resources are available at public, university, and union libraries.

Citizen Action State Organizations

The Midwest Academy provides leadership and staff training for all the Citizen Action state organizations and local offices. These Citizen Action organizations are good resources for progressive issues in their states.

Alabama
Alabama Citizen Action
P.O. Box 4247
Montgomery, AL 36103
Phone: (334) 264-8969
Fax: (334) 264-9082
E-Mail: suuz14a@prodigy.com

Arizona
Arizona Citizen Action
2039 E. Broadway, #133
Tempe, AZ 85282
Phone: (602) 921-3090
Fax: (602) 829-1469
E-Mail: jdriscoll@igc.apc.org

Connecticut
Connecticut Citizen Action
Group
45 S. Main Street
West Hartford, CT 06107
Phone: (203) 561-6006
Fax: (203) 561-6018

Florida
Florida Consumer Action Network
4100 W. Kennedy Boulevard
Suite 128
Tampa, FL 33609
Phone: (813) 286-1226
Fax: (813) 286-1315

Georgia
Georgia Citizen Action
741 Piedmont Avenue NE
Suite #1B
Atlanta, GA 30308
Phone: (404) 875-4035
Fax: (404) 875-4341

Iowa
Iowa Citizen Action Network
3520 Beaver, Suite E
Des Moines, IA 50310-3290
Phone: (515) 277-5077
Fax: (515) 277-8003
E-Mail: hn2289@handsnet.org

Idaho
Idaho Citizens Network
904 W. Fort Street
Boise, ID 83702-5425
Phone: (208) 385-9146
Fax: (208) 336-0997

Illinois
Illinois Public Action
68 E. Wacker Place
Chicago, IL 60601
Phone: (312) 782-7900
Fax: (312) 782-0505

Indiana
CA Coalition of Indiana
3951 N. Meridian
Suite 300
Indianapolis, IN 46208
Phone: (317) 921-1120
Fax: (317) 921-1143

Kentucky
P.O. Box 6808
Louisville, KY 40206
Phone: (502) 899-7664
(Voice Mail Only)

Louisiana

Louisiana Citizen Action
7434 Picardy Avenue
2nd Floor, Suite D
Baton Rouge, LA 70809
Phone: (504) 769-8896
Fax: (504) 769-8899

Massachusetts

Citizen Action of Massachusetts
160 Second Street #208
Cambridge, MA 02142
Phone: (617) 491-8859
Fax: (617) 576-3544

Maryland

Citizen Action of Maryland
6900 Wisconsin Avenue #303
Bethesda, MD 20815
Phone: (301) 718-8755
Fax: (301) 718-9407
E-Mail: scraver@aol.com

Maine

Maine People's Alliance
65 W. Commercial Street
Portland, ME 04101
Phone: (207) 761-4400
Fax: (207) 761-1863

Michigan

Michigan Citizen Action
4990 Northwind Drive
Suite 210
East Lansing, MI 48823
Phone: (517) 333-3628
Fax: (517) 337-2833

Minnesota

Minnesota COACT
2233 University Avenue West
Suite 300
St. Paul, MN 55114
Phone: (612) 645-3733
Fax: (612) 645-4339

Missouri

Missouri Citizen Action
11340 Hammack Drive
Suite 405
Bridgeton, MO 63044
Phone: (314) 731-5312
Fax: (314) 731-2729
E-Mail: pkharvey@aol.com

Nebraska

Nebraska Citizen Action
The Terminal Building
941 O Street, Suite 600
Lincoln, NE 68508
Phone: (402) 477-8689
Fax: (402) 476-1645

New Hampshire

New Hampshire Citizen Action
10 Ferry Street, Box 319
Concord, NH 03301
Phone: (603) 225-2097
Fax: (603) 228-3360

New Jersey

New Jersey Citizen Action
400 Main Street
Hackensack, NJ 07601
Phone: (201) 488-2804
Fax: (201) 488-1253

New Mexico

New Mexico Citizen Action
620 Roma NW
Albuquerque, NM 87102
Phone: (505) 243-5929
Fax: (505) 246-9797

New York

Citizen Action of New York
94 Central Avenue
Albany, NY 12206
Phone: (518) 465-4600
Fax: (518) 465-2890
E-Mail: canyalb@aol.com=20

North Carolina

1003 W. Cabarrus Street
Raleigh, NC 27603
Phone: (919) 829-3855
Fax: (919) 829-3818

Ohio

Ohio Citizen Action
402 Terminal Tower
Cleveland, OH 44113
Phone: (216) 861-5200
Fax: (216) 694-6904

Oregon

Oregon Fair Share
702 NE Schuyler
Portland, OR 97212-3923
Phone: (503) 280-1762
Fax: (503) 280-1766

Pennsylvania

Pennsylvania Citizen Action
35 South 4th Street
Philadelphia, PA 19106
Phone: (215) 592-4474
Fax: (215) 592-4473

Tennessee

Tennessee Citizen Action
2012 21st Avenue South
Nashville, TN 37212
Phone: (615) 297-2494
Fax: (615) 297-8372
E-Mail: cbmcguire@aol.com

Texas

Texas Citizen Action
1714 Fortview, Suite 103
Austin, TX 78704
Phone: (512) 444-8588
Fax: (512) 444-3533
E-Mail: danlambe@versa.com

Virginia

Virginia Citizen Action
6 North 6th Street
Suite 403-F
Richmond, VA 23219
Phone: (804) 643-6713
Fax: (804) 643-6829
E-Mail: vcitaction@aol.com

Washington

Washington Citizen Action
Suite 240
100 S. King Street
Seattle, WA 98104-2885
Phone: (206) 389-0050
Fax: (206) 389-0049
E-Mail: davidlwest@aol.com

Wisconsin

Wisconsin Citizen Action
152 W. Wisconsin Avenue
Suite 308
Milwaukee, WI 53203
Phone: (414) 272-2562
Fax: (414) 274-3494

West Virginia

West Virginia CAG
1324 E. Virginia Street
Charleston, WV 25301
Phone: (304) 346-5891
Fax: (304) 346-8981

SOUTHERN REGIONAL OFFICE

Citizen Action
758 Lexington Avenue
Charlottesville, VA 22902
Phone: (804) 984-0928
Fax: (804) 984-0929
E-Mail: Mwether@aol.com

WASHINGTON, DC OFFICE

1730 Rhode Island Avenue, NW
Suite 403
Washington, DC 20036
Phone: (202) 775-1580
Fax: (202) 296-4054

SONGS

Lift Every Voice

Lift ev'ry voice and sing, til earth and heaven
    ring,
Ring with the harmonies of liberty;
Let our rejoicing rise, high as the list'ning skies,
Let it resound loud as the rolling sea.
Sing a song full of the faith that the dark past
    has taught us,
Sing a song full of the hope that the present has
    brought us;
Facing the rising sun of our new day begun,
Let us march on till victory is won.

Stony the road we trod, bitter the chast'ning rod,
Felt in the days when hope unborn had died;
Yet with a steady beat, have not our weary feet,
Come to the place for which our fathers sighed?
We have come over a way that with tears has
    been watered,
We have come, treading our path thro' the blood
    of the slaughtered,
Out of the gloomy past, till now we stand at last,
Where the white gleam of our bright star is cast.

God of our weary years, God of our silent tears,
Thou who hast brought us thus far on the way;
Thou who hast by Thy might led us into the
    light,
Keep us forever in the path, we pray,
Lest our feet stray from the places, our God,
    where we met Thee,
Lest our hearts, drunk with the wine of the
    world, we forget Thee;
Shadowed beneath Thy hand, may we forever
    stand,
True to our God, true to our native land.

Let us keep onward still, keep our resolve until,
We achieve brotherhood for all mankind;
Look to the rising sun, new work each day is
    begun,
Daily we strive til we true freedom find.
Save our hope that we so long and so dearly did
    cherish,
Lest our hearts weary with cruel disillusion
    should perish;
Stretch forth a loving hand, you who in power
    stand,

Lose not our faith, lose not our native land.

-James Weldon Johnson (v.4 Henrietta McKee)

It Could Have Been Me

Students in Ohio and down at Jackson State
Shot down by a vicious fire one early day in
    May
Some people cried out angry "You should have
    shot more of them down"
But you can't bury youth my friend, youth
    grows the whole world round

It could have been me but instead it was you
So I'll keep doing the work you were doing as if
    I were two
I'll be a student of life, a singer of songs,a
    farmer of food and a righter of wrongs
It could have been me but instead it was you
And it may be me dear sisters and brothers
    before we are thru
But if you can die* for freedom - freedom (3x)
If you can die for freedom, I can too
*(other v. substitute: sing, live, fight)

The junta took the fingers of Victor Jara's hands
They said to the gentle poet "Play your guitar
    now if you can"
Well, Victor started singing til they shot his
    body down
You can kill a man but not a song when it's
    sung the whole world `round

A woman in the jungle so many wars away
Studies late into the night, defends a village in
    the day
Altho' her life and struggle are miles away from
    me
She sings a song and I know the words and I'll
    sing them til she's free

One night in Oklahoma, Karen Silkwood died
Because she had some secrets big companies
    wanted to hide
Well they talk of nuclear safety, they talk of
    national pride

But we all know it's a death machine and that's
    why Karen died

Our sisters are in struggle, from Vietnam to
    Wounded Knee
From Mozambique to Puerto Rico and they look
    to you and me
To fight against the system that kills them off
    and takes their land
It's our fight too if we're gonna win, we've got
    to do it hand in hand

It's gonna be me and it's gonna be you
So we'll keep doing the work we've been doing
    until we are thru
We'll be students of life, singers of song,
    farmers of food and fighters so strong
It's gonna be me and it's gonna be you
But it will be us dear sisters and brothers before
    we are thru
`Cause if you can fight for freedom, freedom
    (3x)
If you can fight for freedom, we can too!

-Holly Near

1974 Hereford Music (ASCAP). New verses
1983. Used by permission.

Mountain Song

I have dreamed on this mountain
Since first I was my mother's daughter
And you can't just take my dreams
Away - not with me watching
You may drive a big machine
But I was born a great big woman
And you can't just take my dreams
Away - without me fighting

(bridge) This old mountain raised my many
    daughters
Some died young, some are still living
If you come here for to take our mountain
Well, we ain't come here to give it

I have dreamed on this mountain
Since first I was my mother's daughter
And you can't just take my dreams
Away - not with me watching

No, you can't just take my dreams
Away - without me fighting
No, you can't just take my dreams away

-Holly Near

1978 Hereford Music (ASCAP). Used by
permission.

No More Genocide

Why do we call them the enemy
This struggling nation that's won independence
    across the sea?
Why do we want these people to die?
Why do we say North and South, o why, o why,
    o why?

Well, that's just a lie! One of the many and
    we've had plenty
I don't want more of the same/no more genocide
    in my name!

Why are our history books so full of lies
When no word is spoken of why the Indian dies
    and dies?
Or that the Chicanos love the California land
Do our books all say it was discovered by one
    white man?

Why are the weapons of the war so young?
Why are there only rich ones around when it's
    done?
Why are so many of our soldiers black or
    brown?
Do we think it's because they're good at cutting
    other people down?

Why do we support a colony
When Puerto Rican people are crying out to be
    free?
We sterilize the women and rob the copper
    mines
Do we think that people will always be so blind?

Nazi forces grow again, ignorance gives them a
    place
The Klan is teaching children to hate the human
    race

Where once there was a playground, now an
MX missile plant
Do they think it's fun to see just how much we
can stand?

-Holly Near

Union Maid

There once was a union maid who never was
afraid
Of goons and ginks and company finks and the
deputy sheriffs who made the raids
She went to the union hall when a meeting it
was called
And when the company boys came `round she
always stood her ground

Chorus:
O you can't scare me, I'm sticking to the union
I'm sticking to the union, I'm sticking to the
union
O you can't scare me, I'm sticking to the union
I'm sticking to the union til the day I die

This union maid was wise to the tricks of
company spies
She never got fooled by a company stool, she'd
always organize the guys
She always got her way, when she struck for
higher pay
She'd show her card to the company guard and
this is what she'd say:

Chorus

You women who want to be free, take a little tip
from me
Break outa that mold we've all been sold, you
got a fighting his-to-ree
The fight for women's rights with workers must
unite
Like Mother Jones, move those bones to the
front of every fight!

Chorus

-w: Woody Guthrie (new v. anon.) m: trad.
("Redwing")

This Land Is Your Land

This land is your land, this land is my land
From California to the New York Island
From the redwood forest to the Gulf Stream
waters
This land was made for you and me

As I was walking that ribbon of highway
I saw above me that endless skyway
I saw below me that golden valley
This land was made for you and me

I've roamed and rambled and I followed my
footsteps
To the sparkling sands of her diamond deserts
And all around me, a voice was sounding: / This
land...

When the sun came shining and I was strolling
And the wheat fields waving and the dust clouds
rolling
As the fog was lifting, a voice was chanting/
This...

As I went walking, I saw a sign there
On the sign it said "No Trespassing"
But on the other side it didn't say nothing
That side was made for you and me!

In the shadow of the steeple I saw my people
By the relief office, I seen my people
As they stood there hungry I stood there asking
Is this land made for you and me?

Nobody living can ever stop me
As I go walking that freedom highway
Nobody living can make me turn back/ This...

-Woody Guthrie

If I Had a Hammer

If I had a hammer, I'd hammer in the morning
I'd hammer in the evening, all over this land
I'd hammer out danger, I'd hammer out a
    warning
I'd hammer out love between my brothers and
    my sisters
all over this land

2. If I had a bell, I'd ring it in the morning...
3. If I had a song, I'd sing it in the morning...
4. Well I got a hammer and I got a bell
    And I got a song to sing all over this land
    It's the hammer of justice, it's the bell of
    freedom
    It's a song about love between...

-Lee Hays and Pete Seeger

Amazing Grace

Amazing grace! How sweet the sound
That saved a wretch (soul) like me
I once was lost and now am found
Was blind but now I see

`Twas grace that taught my heart to fear
And grace my fears relieved
How precious did that grace appear
The hour I first believed

The Lord has promised good to me
His word my hope secures
He will my shield and portion be
As long as life endures

Thru many dangers, toils and snares
I have already come
`Tis grace that brought me safe thus far
And grace will lead me home

When we've been here 10,000 years
Bright shining as the sun

We've no less days to sing God's praise
Than when we first begun

Allelujah (3x) Praise God! (repeat)

Amazing grace has set me free
To touch, to taste, to feel
The wonders of accepting Love
Have made me whole and real

w: John Newton m: trad (v.5 by John P. Rees.
v.6 by New York YM Quakers)

Bread And Roses

As we go marching marching in the beauty of
    the day
A million darkened kitchens, a thousand mill
    lots gray
Are touched with all the radiance that a sudden
    sun discloses
For the people hear us singing: bread and roses,
    bread and roses!

As we go marching marching, we battle too for
    men
For they are women's children and we mother
    them again (for men can ne're be free `til
    our slavery's at an end)
Our lives shall not be sweated from birth until
    life closes
Hearts starve as well as bodies, give us bread
    but give us roses

As we go marching marching, unnumbered
    women dead
Go crying thru our singing their ancient call for
    bread
Small art and love and beauty their drudging
    spirits knew
Yes it is bread we fight for, but we fight for
    roses, too

As we go marching, marching, we bring the
    greater days
The rising of the women means the rising of the
    race
No more the drudge and idler, ten that toil
    where one reposes
But a sharing of life's glories - bread and roses,
    bread and roses!

w: James Oppenheim

O Freedom

O freedom, O freedom
O freedom over me!
And before I'd be a slave I'll be buried in my
    grave
And go home to my Lord and be free

No more killin's (3x) over me...
No more fear...
No more hunger...
There'll be joy...
There'll be singing...
There'll be peace...

trad. (adapted by SNCC)

Solidarity Forever

When the union's inspiration, thru the workers'
    blood shall run,
There can be no power greater anywhere
    beneath the sun.
Yet what force on Earth is weaker than the
    feeble strength of one,
But the union makes us strong.

Chorus: Solidarity forever! (3x)
              For the union makes us strong.

Is there aught we hold in common with the
    greedy parasite,
Who would lash us into serfdom and would
    crush us with his might?
Is there anything left to us but to organize and
    fight?
For the union makes us strong.

It is we who plowed the prairies, built the cities
    where they trade,
Dug the mines and built the workshops, endless
    miles of railroad laid.
Now we stand outcast and starving `mid the
    wonders we have made,
But the union makes us strong.

All the world that's owned by idle drones is
    ours and ours alone.
We have laid the wide foundations, built it
    skyward stone by stone.

It is ours not to slave in, but to master and to
    own,
While the union makes us strong.

They have taken untold millions that they never
    toiled to earn.
But without our brain and muscle not a single
    wheel can turn.
We can break their haughty power, gain our
    freedom when we learn
That the union makes us strong.

In our hands is placed a power greater than their
    hoarded gold,
Greater than the might of armies magnified a
    thousand-fold.
We can bring to birth a new world from the
    ashes of the old,
For the union makes us strong.

- w: Ralph Chaplin m: Battle Hymn of the
Republic

People Like You

Old fighter, you sure took it on the chin.
Where'd you ever get the strength to stand
Never giving up to giving in.
You know, I just want to shake your hand,
Because...

Chorus: People like you help people like me
              Go on, go on
              People like you help people like me
              Go on, go on

Old Battler, with a scar from every town,
Thought you were no better than the rest.
You wore your colors every way but down.
All you ever gave was your best.
But you know that...

Chorus

Old dreamer, with a world in every thought
Where'd you get the vision to keep on?
You sure gave back as good as what you got
I hope that when my time is almost gone
They'll say that...

Chorus

-Si Kahn

This Little Light Of Mine

This little light of mine, I'm gonna let it shine
    (3x)
Let it shine (3x)

Everywhere I go...etc.

Shine on people everywhere...etc.

`Til we all get organized..etc.

Equal rights for everyone...etc.

All around the neighborhood...etc.

All around the universe...etc.

This little light of Mine, I'm gonna let it shine
    (3x)
Let it shine (3x)

-trad.

Study War No More

Gonna lay down my sword and shield down by
    the riverside
Down by the riverside, down by the riverside,
Gonna lay down my sword and shield down by
    the riverside
And study war no more

Chorus: I ain't gonna study war no more (6x)

2. Gonna put on that long white robe, down by
    the riverside...etc.
3. Gonna put on that starry crown...
4. Gonna walk with the Prince of Peace...
5. Gonna shake hands around the world...
6. Gonna lay down those atoms bombs...

Gonna lay down my income tax/I ain't gonna
    pay for war no more
Gonna lay down my GE stock/and live off war
    no more
Gonna lay down my Honeywell job/and work
    for war no more
Gonna lay down those Congressional hawks/and
    vote for war no more

trad. (new v. anon.)

We Shall Not Be Moved

We shall not, we shall not be moved (2x)
Just like a tree that's standing by the water
We shall not be moved

1. The union is behind us, we shall not be
    moved (2x)
    Just like a tree...
2. We're fighting for our freedom...
3. We're fighting for our children...
4. We'll build a mighty union...
5. _____ is our leader...
6. Black and White together....
7. Young and old together...

No nos, no nos moveran (2x)
Como un arbol firme junto al rio
no nos moveran

1. Unidos en la lucha, no nos moveran...
2. Unidos en la huelga, no nos moveran...

-w: textile workers (Spanish v: from a
Salvadoran union organizer)

Will The Circle Be Unbroken

I was standing by my window on a cold and
    cloudy day
When I saw the hearse come rolling for to carry
    my mother away

Will the circle be unbroken by and by, Lord, by
    and by?
There's a better home a-waiting in the sky,
    Lord, in the sky

Lord I told that undertaker "Undertaker, please
  drive slow
For this body you're a hauling, Lord I hate to
  see her go"

I followed close behind her, tried to hold up and
  be brave
But I could not hide my sorrow when they laid
  her in the grave

-Charles H. Gabriel

Will the circle be unbroken, by and by Lord by
  and by?
There's a better way to live now, we can have it
  if we try

I was singing with my sister, I was singing with
  my friends
And we all can sing together, cause the circle
  never ends

I was born down in the valley where the sun
  refused to shine
But I'm climbing up to the highland gonna
  make that mountain mine!
-Cathy Winter, Betsy Rose and Marcia Taylor.

New words _1988 Authors. Used by permission.

We Shall Overcome

We shall overcome, we shall overcome
We shall overcome some day
Oh, deep in my heart I do believe
We shall overcome someday

1. We'll walk hand in hand...etc .
2. We shall live in peace...
3. Black and White together...
4. We are not afraid...
5. We will organize...
6. The union makes us strong...

-trad.

Joe Hill

I dreamed I saw Joe Hill last night
Alive as you and me
Says I, But Joe, you're ten years dead
I never died, says he
I never died, says he

In Salt Lake, Joe, by God says I
Him standing by my bed
They framed you on a murder charge
Says Joe, but I ain't dead
Says Joe, but I ain't dead

The copper bosses killed you, Joe
They shot you, Joe, says I
Takes more than guns to kill someone
Says Joe, I didn't die
Says Joe, I didn't die

And standing there as big as life
And smiling with his eyes
Says Joe, What they forgot to kill
Went on to organize
Went on to organize

From San Diego up to Maine
In every mine and mill
Where workers strike and organize
That's where you'll find Joe Hill
That's where you'll find Joe Hill

I dreamed I saw Joe Hill last night
Alive as you and me
Says I, But Joe, you're ten years dead
I never died, says he
I never died, says he

-1938, Earl Robinson and Alfred Hayes

E.R.A. SONG

What's gonna happen in 2004
When your grandchildren ask
What you did before
Before you get all old and grey
There's gonna be your judgement day

Were you there in the olden days, Grampa?
Were you there when they tried to say Grandma

Wasn't equal to you in every way
Tell us how you helped pass the E.R.A.

It'll sure sound funny when you tell those kids
Just what their grandpa really did
`Cause they just won't believe their own grandpa
Tried to keep down their own grandma

(*Chorus*)

What you gonna tell `em on Judgement Day,
That their grandpa voted no on the E.R.A.?
What you gonna tell those little kids?
How you gonna tell them what you did?

- 1980, Jackie Kendall

I Woke Up This Morning

(women)	I woke up this mornin with my mind
(men)	Where was your mind?
(women)	Centered on justice.
(women)	I woke up this mornin with my mind.
(men)	Where was your mind?
(women)	Centered on justice.
(women)	I woke up this mornin with my mind.
(men)	Where was your mind?
(women)	Centered on justice.

(men)	Say it on.
(women)	Say it on.
(men)	Say it on.
(women)	Say it on.
(all sing)	Justice will be won
	And when your mind's on the right
	We'll win the fight
	Our minds're on justice, forevermore.

w: slightly adapted by Kimberley Bobo
m: traditional

Workers and Health Care

There once was a working maid, who really was
      afraid. To tell her
boss her health care costs were not within her
      means to pay.

This maid is not alone; all workers long have
      known:
If health's a perk that comes with work
      employers must be shown . . .

Chorus: That the time has come, we're going
            for health care
            We're going for health care! We're
            going for health care!
            That the time has come, we're going
            for health care!
            We're going for health care! Health
            care for all!

There's many an employee, to raise a family,
Must toil all day at minimum pay to still wind
      up in poverty.
It's also all-too-rare, for them to get health care.
The boss, you see, gets off scot free and doesn't
      pay her share.

w: Jeff Kirsh; m: "Redwing" ("Union Maid")

Open the Doors! (To Health Care for All)

There's a crisis in this country that's affecting
      you and me.
The doors that lead to health care, don't open
      easily.
The costs are astronomical; no care if you are
      poor.
It's time we organize ourselves to open up the
      doors!

Chorus: Open the doors! Open the doors!
           Hear the people knocking loudly-
           heed their call.
           Open the doors! Open the doors!
           The time has come for health care
           for all!

Medicare has passed despite the fight of doctors
      and their friends
To give the seniors health care, on which they
      could depend.
But who knew the docs who fought it, would
      make a mint instead,
And leave the seniors' pocketbooks forever in
      the red.

Many women having babies do without
    pre-natal care.
We let that crime go forward, as if we're not
    aware,
That the children are our future, our real
    security;
Instead of building missiles we should make all
    health care free.

There are thirty seven million who are outside
    looking in.
They are workers, they are children; they're our
    neighbors and our kin.
They need universal health care, to keep them
    safe and sound;
We're mad about those health care doors and
    aim to knock `em down.

Oh, those doors are artificial and they ain't
    made out of steel.
They are put there by a system that's forgotten
    how to feel.
All the fear that people live with when an illness
    comes to call.
The system needs some changin' and its called
    health care for all!

-Jeff Kirsch

Midwest Academy Fight Song

Mine eyes have seen the power of our coalition
    board.
We are tramping on the targets who want all the
    wealth to hoard.
We have loosed a great constituency and
    brought new folks aboard,
Through concrete victories!

Chorus: Plan the strategy together.
             Work the strategy together.
             Win the strategy together.
             Organizing makes us strong!

On the newsprint at the meetings, we our goals
    articulate.
Coalition building strategies we must succinctly
    state.
We identify the forces to whom we can best
    relate,

Through concrete victories!

We identify the people who can give us what we
    need.
We develop all the actions that will make
    THEM pay us heed.
And give back to common people what
    THEY'VE stolen in THEIR greed!
Through concrete victories!

w: Peter Shuchter and other participants in the
spring, 1990 Midwest Academy training session
in Philadelphia

m: Battle Hymn of the Republic

Index

The **Midwest Academy,** a training institute for progressive organizers and activists, conducts six to eight week-long training sessions yearly. The Academy also provides ongoing consulting and training for a limited number of organizers and organizations. If your current staff is not able to provide this, we recommend that you contract with an experienced organizer for at least a year to provide ongoing support and training. A new organizer who comes to a Midwest Academy training session and has someone back home to provide ongoing help is much more likely to succeed than those who return to fend for themselves. Some foundations that support your organization may be willing to provide additional technical assistance funds for your organizing staff.

The Midwest Academy also leads on-site training and planning sessions for boards, staffs, and leaders of organizations across the country. Training and planning sessions are adapted to meet the specific needs of the contracting organizations.

Begun as a reunion for training session graduates, the biennial conference, sponsored with Citizen Action, attracts over a thousand progressive activists and organizers, including many progressive elected officials and national leaders.

Use the mail-in card to request more information about the Midwest Academy and its programs.

---✂-----

Please send me information about the following Midwest Academy programs and resources:

☐ Week-long intensive organizer training sessions
☐ Midwest Academy/Citizen Action Conference
☐ On-site training sessions
☐ Promotional flyers describing this manual
☐ Other organizing resources

Name: _____

Organization: _____

Address: _____

_____

Phone (daytime): _____

Mail to: **Midwest Academy,** 225 W. Ohio, Suite 250, Chicago, IL 60610
Phone: (312) 645-6010   Fax: (312) 645-6018

---✂-----

Please send me information about the following Midwest Academy programs and resources:

☐ Week-long intensive organizer training sessions
☐ Midwest Academy/Citizen Action Conference
☐ On-site training sessions
☐ Promotional flyers describing this manual
☐ Other organizing resources

Name: _____

Organization: _____

Address: _____

_____

Phone (daytime): _____

Mail to: **Midwest Academy,** 225 W. Ohio, Suite 250, Chicago, IL 60610
Phone: (312) 645-6010   Fax: (312) 645-6018

For additional copies of **ORGANIZING FOR SOCIAL CHANGE** *write:*
Seven Locks Press, P.O. Box 25689, Santa Ana, CA 92799

☐ Please sent me copies of **ORGANIZING FOR SOCIAL CHANGE** for $19.95 per copy plus a $4.00 shipping and handling charge for the first book and $1.00 for each additional book.

Name _____

Organization _____

Address _____

City _____ State _____ Zip _____

Qty.		**Total**	
_____	**Organizing for Social Change,** $19.95	$ _____	**FOR**
	Shipping & Handing: $4.00 for first book,	_____	**FASTEST SERVICE**
	$1.00 for each add'l	_____	**ON**
	TOTAL ENCLOSED	$ _____	**CHARGE ORDERS**

Payment Method: ☐ Check ☐ Visa ☐ MasterCard
Card # _____ Expires _____
Signature _____

CALL US TOLL FREE:

1-800-354-5348

- ✂ - - -

For additional copies of **ORGANIZING FOR SOCIAL CHANGE** *write:*
Seven Locks Press, P.O. Box 25689, Santa Ana, CA 92799

☐ Please sent me copies of **ORGANIZING FOR SOCIAL CHANGE** for $19.95 per copy plus a $4.00 shipping and handling charge for the first book and $1.00 for each additional book.

Name _____

Organization _____

Address _____

City _____ State _____ Zip _____

Qty.		**Total**	
_____	**Organizing for Social Change,** $19.95	$ _____	**FOR**
	Shipping & Handing: $4.00 for first book,	_____	**FASTEST SERVICE**
	$1.00 for each add'l	_____	**ON**
	TOTAL ENCLOSED	$ _____	**CHARGE ORDERS**

Payment Method: ☐ Check ☐ Visa ☐ MasterCard
Card # _____ Expires _____
Signature _____

CALL US TOLL FREE:

1-800-354-5348

- ✂ - - -

For additional copies of **ORGANIZING FOR SOCIAL CHANGE** *write:*
Seven Locks Press, P.O. Box 25689, Santa Ana, CA 92799

☐ Please sent me copies of **ORGANIZING FOR SOCIAL CHANGE** for $19.95 per copy plus a $4.00 shipping and handling charge for the first book and $1.00 for each additional book.

Name _____

Organization _____

Address _____

City _____ State _____ Zip _____

Qty.		**Total**	
_____	**Organizing for Social Change,** $19.95	$ _____	**FOR**
	Shipping & Handing: $4.00 for first book,	_____	**FASTEST SERVICE**
	$1.00 for each add'l	_____	**ON**
	TOTAL ENCLOSED	$ _____	**CHARGE ORDERS**

Payment Method: ☐ Check ☐ Visa ☐ MasterCard
Card # _____ Expires _____
Signature _____

CALL US TOLL FREE:

1-800-354-5348

SEVEN LOCKS PRESS CURRENT OFFERINGS

National Public Radio
The Cast of Characters
by Mary Collins   Cloth
Photographs by Jerome Liebling   0-929765-19-2
                                   $39.95

"..informative, charming, even compelling.. It tells the story of a special institution and special people.
—Doug Bennet, former NPR President

No Anchovies on the Moon
Three Score and Ten
Washington Pictures and Poems
by Paul Boswell
With an Introduction by   Cloth
James H. Billington   0-929765-33-8
The Librarian of Congress $29.95

A wonderful story 46 years in the making. A glorious achievement by a modest man.

The Secret Government
The Constitution in Crisis   Cloth
Bill Moyers   0-932020-61-5
                                   $16.95
                                   Paper
                                   0-932020-60-7
                                   $9.95

This acclaimed book, based on a PBS documentary, analyzes threats to constitutional government by those who have tried to take foreign policy into their own hands.

The Rhino Man
and Other Uncommon Environmentalists   Paper
Winthrop P. Carty and Elizabeth Lee   0-929765-10-9
                                        $12.95

Stories of a unique group of individuals who are working to save our planet from destruction.

Citistates
How Urban America Can
Prosper in a Competitive World   Cloth
Neal R. Peirce with   0-929765-16-8
Curtis W. Johnson & John Stuart Hall $24.95
                                   Paper
                                   0-929765-34-6
                                   $18.95

"Neal Peirce is the best writer on urban affairs in the country."
—Henry Cisneros, Secretary of Housing & Urban Development

QUALITY BACKLIST TITLES

Global Dumping Ground
The International Traffic in Hazardous Waste
Center for Investigative Reporting & Bill Moyers
Paper   0-932020-95-X $11.95

The Media & the Gulf War
The Press & Democracy in Wartime
Edited by Hedrick Smith
Cloth   0-932020-99-2 $24.95

Please Call or Write for Complete Catalogue

- -

METHOD OF PAYMENT

❏ Check enclosed
    (Payable to Seven Locks Press)
❏ Visa ❏ Master Card   Exp. Date _____

Account # _____
Signature _____

When you order with this form your order will be shipped Freight Free.

SEVEN LOCKS PRESS
P.O. Box 25689
Santa Ana, CA 92799

ORDER FORM

Send to:
NAME _____
ADDRESS _____
_____
_____
PHONE # _____

Title	Qty	Price	Total

Total _____
Phone   800-354-5348
        714-545-2526
Fax   714-545-1572